ENCOUNTER GROUPS:
BASIC
READINGS

ENCOUNTER GROUPS:
BASIC READINGS

Edited by

Gerard Egan

Loyola University of Chicago

Brooks/Cole Publishing Company
Belmont, California

A Division of Wadsworth Publishing Company, Inc.

L.C. Cat. Card No.: 72-159763
Printed in the United States of America
ISBN: 0-8185-0017-4

1 2 3 4 5 6 7 8 9 10—75 74 73 72 71

This book was edited by Phil Cordova and designed by Linda Marcetti. It was typeset at Design Service, Fullerton, California, and printed and bound at Hamilton Printing Company, Rensselaer, New York.

Acknowledgments

I would like to thank Dr. Wayne Matheson of the University of Alberta, Dr. Lawrence Solomon of United States International University, and Dr. Sumner B. Morris of the University of California at Davis for reading the manuscript and making many helpful suggestions. The deficiencies of the final product, however, are certainly my own. Thanks also to James Martin, Dennis Simon, and Robert Walsh for their assistance and especially for their patience.

Contents

Interactions: Communication Processes, Self-Disclosure, Expression of Feeling, Support, and Confrontation 175

Communication Processes 176

Self-Disclosure 200

Expression of Feeling 234

Support 264

Confrontation 288

Cautions, Research 299

Epilogue 341

Indexes   343

ENCOUNTER GROUPS:
BASIC READINGS

Introduction

For whom is this book meant? These articles are meant to be read by college students or by anyone with the equivalent in educational experience who either has participated or would like to participate in an encounter group. The articles have been chosen to help the participant get more deeply involved in the group interaction and to encourage him to reflect on groups in which he has already participated, but they might also be read with profit by anyone interested in the theory of encounter groups.

The articles are supplemental in two senses. First, they are meant to supplement the group experience rather than to take its place. Second, they are meant to supplement a text which presents an integrated theory of encounter groups. The specific text which they are meant to supplement is Egan's *Encounter: Group Processes for Interpersonal Growth* (hereafter abbreviated *E:GPFIG*).

In organizing the articles and comments in this book, I have made an attempt to follow the general pattern of *E:GPFIG*. The first several articles are designed to orient the reader to small, face-to-face groups in general and the encounter group in particular; subsequent articles deal with the major aspects of the encounter group which are presented in *E:GPFIG*. Introductions and comments by the editor accompany each article. Since there are great communalities from one encounter-group experience to another—no matter what group theory, structure, and methodology are used—it is assumed that this book of readings could supplement any text dealing with encounter groups.

Laboratory Training and
the Encounter Group

The subject of this book has many names. Popularly, it is called "sensitivity training." In the psychological literature it is called a basic encounter group or, simply, an encounter group, a basic human-relations laboratory, a laboratory in interpersonal relations, a T-group. The most generic term for these small-group experiences is "sensitivity training"; but less ambiguous and certainly less emotionally weighted are the terms "laboratory training" and "laboratory learning," which refer to the same kinds of experiences. Laboratory training is the genus of which the basic encounter group is a species.

First, a word about the genus. Laboratory training is a kind of "education" in which the participants have the opportunity to experiment with their behavior—that is, to try out different or unaccustomed modes of behavior in an attempt to find more effective ways of involving themselves with the people with whom they work or live. In laboratory-learning situations, the participants learn not principally through lectures and discussions (at least not in the traditional sense) but by engaging in certain kinds of behavior and then (or concomitantly) reflecting on these behaviors; thus, the principal subject of discussion and learning is the "here-and-now" behavior of the participants. For instance, laboratory training for a group of business managers might consist of a series of group decision-making exercises the purpose of which is to reveal to the participants their managerial styles. In the course of their training the participants would give one another feedback with respect to how constructively (or obstructively) they involve themselves in the exercises. Through this process they come to know more about the various dimensions of their managerial behavior—for example, their ability to cooperate, the quality of their communication, and, in general, their interpersonal assets and deficits as managers.

There are many species of laboratory learning—for instance, laboratories in basic human relations, in management, in higher education, in community relations, in consulting skills, in the management of conflict, in organizational development, and in black-white relations. Usually, the small face-to-face training group (T-group) is central to the laboratory-learning experience. In the T-group the participants emit various kinds of interpersonal behavior (the kinds of behavior are usually related to the goals of the particular lab) and receive feedback from one another with respect to this behavior. This brief description of laboratory behavior (for more complete presentations see Bradford, Gibb, and Benne, 1964 and Schein and Bennis, 1965) will be supplemented in the following pages, which deal with a specific kind of laboratory, the basic encounter group.

The Encounter Group

A number of writers suggest that it is impossible to give an adequate written explanation of encounter groups. Not unlike the holy man who declared that he would rather feel compunction than know how to define it, they claim that the only authentic way of knowing what an encounter group is like is to participate in one. I suppose that such a statement has something in its favor, but it does seem possible to let the prospective participant know, at least in a general way, what lies before him. In fact, I sometimes think that he should be told as clearly as possible what an encounter-group experience is like and then be left free to choose or not choose the experience.

I will explain my understanding of the nature of the encounter-group experience in terms of a "contract." My reason for doing so is this: I believe that a degree of structure in encounter groups makes them more effective, for then both the goals of the experience and the means of achieving them are clear. A "contract" is one way of providing such structure. I discuss encounter groups in terms of structure and "contracts" more extensively elsewhere (see *E:GPFIG*, Chapter 2, and Egan, 1970a). The following contract, then, is an attempt to answer the question: to what does the participant "contract" when he enters the average encounter group?

1. *Goals.* The overriding goal of the group is interpersonal growth, an admittedly vague term, but one which will take on clearer definition in terms of the present contract. Interpersonal growth involves your becoming more aware of your present interpersonal style and discovering more effective ways of being present to others. Personal growth, too, is a goal of the group, but it is assumed that personal-growth factors (for example, reduction of anxiety, enhanced feelings of self-worth, a keener sense of self-identity) ultimately subserve a more effective interpersonal life. Man is a relational being and the height of his growth lies in his relationships with others. A more immediate goal of this experience, then, is to experiment with "new" (for you) and perhaps more growthful ways of relating to others. You will be able to achieve these goals more readily if, together with your fellow participants, you can establish a community in which such experimentation will be encouraged and supported. This does not mean, however, that it will be a community devoid of conflict and confrontation.

Besides these general goals, you may well have more specific goals of your own. One of your tasks in the group is to let the other participants know what these goals are. It is also assumed that your personal goals are at least generally compatible with the overall goals of the group experience.

2. *Leadership.* The group will have a kind of leader, but do not expect him to be a leader in a traditional, authoritarian sense. Although he is skilled in group dynamics and has had experience with encounter groups, he will not force the group to move in directions in which it does not want to move. He might better

be termed a facilitator rather than a leader, for he is a resource person who is prepared to put his knowledge and experience at the service of the group. One way he might do this is by "modeling" (engaging in) the kinds of behavior spelled out in this contract. He might also comment from time to time on what he sees to be the tempo, mood, direction, style, or agenda (hidden or above-board) of the group. Ultimately, however, leadership is best seen as a set of *group* functions which must be fulfilled if the group is to achieve its goals. Therefore, all members of the group are to assume the responsibility for initiating the kinds of interaction outlined here. Diffusion of leadership is the ideal. Whoever is helping the group move ahead by responsible participation is, by that fact, participating in the leadership function of the group.

3. *Laboratory.* The experience you are about to enter is called a laboratory for a number of reasons. First of all, you will learn by *doing*; that is, you will learn to relate to others more effectively by actually relating. You will have an opportunity to see yourself in action, as it were, and to discuss the ways in which you relate to the other members of the group. Others will give you "feedback" with respect to your interpersonal behavior; that is, they will tell you how you "come on" in the group, how you affect them. The experience is also designed to allow you to experiment with new behavior. The word "new" does not refer to anything esoteric; "new" ways of relating to others imply ways that are not part of your present interpersonal style. For instance, if you tend to be silent in a group, experimenting with speaking up would constitute for you a new way of relating. Or if you tend to swallow your emotions in your dealings with others, trying to get your emotions more effectively "into community" would be for you another new way of relating. Then, as you act and react in the group, you will receive feedback from the other participants to help you come to a better understanding of your interpersonal abilities and limitations.

In order to engage in such "experimentation," it will be necessary for you to lower your ordinary defenses a bit. This is hardly the same as surrendering all your defenses or allowing others to strip you of them. This would be foolhardy and unproductive. However, you may find that you may be able to take a few more interpersonal risks in the safety and support of the encounter group than you can in your day-to-day life. To lower your defenses a bit and take reasonable risks might well increase your level of anxiety, but a moderate degree of anxiety can be a spur to productive activity. If you find yourself too comfortable in the group, it may be that you are doing little or nothing.

4. *The Core Interactions.* Certain interactions constitute the core of the encounter-group experience and therefore the heart of this contract. Each of these interactions, explained briefly below, is a way of contacting others, of involving yourself with others; therefore, each of them offers possibilities for growing with others.

(a) *Self-disclosure.* You are asked to be open about yourself. This means that you arc to try to talk about yourself in such a way that something of the inner person that is you is translated to the other participants. Self-disclosure is a kind of invitation: what you say about yourself should encourage others to "come in," to respond to and make contact with you, to involve themselves with you. It is up to you just how you will talk about yourself and what you will say. This may sound very abstract right now, but it will be easier to determine in the give-and-take of the group interaction. Most important is what may be called here-and-now honesty; that is, you are asked in a special way to reveal what is going on inside you with respect to the group interaction itself. For instance, if you are anxious, let others know that you are anxious rather than expending a great deal of energy in trying to conceal the fact. If you are bored by the interaction, then let others know as soon as possible. It is deadly to wait an hour and then tell others that you *have been* bored. This means that you have been sitting there in judgment on the interaction without saying anything. If you do not speak up, you are responsible for your own boredom.

There are various levels of self-disclosure: the more personal something is, the deeper it is. The general level of self-disclosure is ordinarily determined by what is happening in the group itself and depends on a number of factors—for instance, the level of trust in the group and the willingness of individuals to take responsible risks. However, individual group members, rather than the terms of the contract, determine the level at which the members will work. You will, undoubtedly, reveal yourself at a level at which you feel comfortable, or perhaps a little beyond; that is, the moderate anxiety you feel in revealing yourself to others will constitute a reasonable and a growthful risk for you.

Obviously, there are areas of self-disclosure other than what is going on inside individual participants during the group interaction. It is impossible to legislate what should be disclosed in any particular group; however, self-disclosure is not an end in itself. It is a way of contacting others, of involving yourself with others. You are not asked to reveal your past life or your darkest secrets—that is, not unless you want to, and then only if such revelation makes sense in the context of the group interaction. *You* are important, not your secrets. Wanton self-revelation may constitute a kind of psychological exhibitionism which is carried out principally for its dramatic impact. It is difficult to see how such behavior would be growthful. If you do talk about the past or about what you do and what happens to you outside the group, you must make what you say relevant to *these* people in *this* group; otherwise, you might well lose your audience. Extended talk about the "there-and-then" tends to weaken the feeling of immediacy in the group and makes it more difficult for the members to attend. Perhaps an example will help illustrate how such a difficulty might be avoided. Let us say a participant speaks of the problems he has communicating with his wife and family. He might make that relevant to the group in this way: "At home I find myself withdrawing from my wife and children more and more.

It seems that there is just nothing to say. And I also find myself doing the same thing here. I am content to sit and listen passively to you without responding." Such self-disclosure would tend to stimulate here-and-now interaction rather than merely a discussion of the member's family life.

Finally, if you allow others to extort information from you, you may be sorry afterward. You should reveal yourself because you want to move more effectively into community with others.

(b) *The expression of feeling.* You are encouraged to let emotion be part of the group experience. Many of us tend to truncate the emotional dimensions of our interpersonal lives: too often we swallow our feelings (for instance, our anger), only to let them filter out in rather unproductive ways (we become cold and uncooperative, make snide remarks, etc.); or we save up our feelings until they rush out and overwhelm others. There is an alternative to such behavior, however: during the give-and-take of group interaction, you can speak as frankly as possible about your emotion-laden contacts with your fellow participants. Perhaps being frank in the group about your feelings for yourself and others, coupled with a desire to work through your feelings without simply abdicating them, would constitute for you a new way of being present to others.

(c) *Listening.* It is amazing to discover how poorly we listen to others. In the encounter group you are asked to examine your ability to listen. Listening does not mean just hearing words and sentences and understanding their meaning; rather, it means something more active: reaching out for what another has to say. It means listening to persons rather than just ideas. Learning to pick up all the cues that others emit, both verbal and nonverbal, is part of listening. Often, when we communicate with one another, we embed surplus messages in our overt communications by the *way* we say things. Facial expressions, gestures, a shrug of the shoulders, bodily positions—all of these are sources of communication. Listening, then, also means becoming sensitive to the surplus-message aspects of communication.

(d) *Support.* It is difficult for people to "put themselves on the line"—that is, to engage in meaningful self-disclosure and to express feelings openly. When you and the other members of the group do make sincere attempts to fulfill the contract, then you need support. It is assumed that you are basically supportive—that is, that you have some kind of basic acceptance of others simply because they *are*; otherwise, you probably would not be participating in the group. It is also assumed here that support and approval are not synonymous. You can accept others without always approving of everything they do. It may be, for instance, that you reveal things about yourself which you yourself do not approve. Obviously, then, though you would hope that others would support you in your act of self-disclosure, you would hardly expect them to approve of things that you disapprove of in yourself.

Support has two phases. The antecedent phase consists in encouraging others to fulfill the contract. For instance, one of the best ways of encouraging others to fulfill the contract is to fulfill it yourself. The second phase refers to your support of those who do engage in contractual interaction. Others will reveal themselves; they will express their feelings. Support in this case means giving them some kind of recognition that they have acted in a way that is beneficial for the group. Support means being responsive to the behavior of others. For instance, if one of the members engages in self-disclosure, you may give him a good deal of support by revealing something about yourself that responds to his concern.

Although support is absolutely necessary for effective group operation, it is also perhaps one of the most difficult of the contractual provisions. When someone "invites you in" by being open about himself, you may feel gauche and find it difficult to respond to him. When someone speaks feelingly about himself or to you, it is too easy to ignore his feelings (for they may make you uncomfortable) and to try to deal with him on a purely intellectual level—for instance, by asking him a number of questions. However, if you are made uncomfortable by what another says, if you are unable to respond in what you think might be a meaningful way, do not pretend that you can. Perhaps a frank admission of your discomfort might be supportive in itself. Counterfeit support, expressed in such clichés as "I understand," and "I know how you feel," deadens group process. Do not try to show cliché sympathy to others merely because you think that you have to say something.

Learning to be present to one another in meaningful support is one of the most important tasks of the group experience, and one of the most difficult.

(e) *Confrontation.* One goal of the group is to establish a cooperative community, but one that can sustain both conflict and confrontation. Sometimes you will find it impossible to agree with what another person is saying or doing. If this is the case, tell him so as honestly as you can, and tell him why. This is confrontation. Growthful confrontation is, basically, an invitation to another to examine or reflect upon his behavior. For instance, perhaps one of the members of the group has remained quite passive and thus has not participated at all in the contractual behavior of the group. If you tell him this and ask him to examine his behavior, then you are confronting him.

The *way* you confront, however, is extremely important. The cardinal rule is that you should confront another because you are concerned about him and want to involve yourself with him, not because you have an impulse either to "tell him off" or to "write him off" or both. If you are merely punishing another by your confrontation, you might find some satisfaction in this (for instance, relief from your anger), but you are doing little to set up interpersonal contact between you and the other. Punishment, research shows, is not very effective when used as a motivational force—even when it is used cautiously. Undeniably, confrontation will always have some punitive side effects (none of us likes to be challenged for allegedly negative forms of behavior), but punishment cannot constitute the rationale of confrontation. Merely punitive confrontation inevitably elicits either defensiveness or counterattack, and neither of these puts people in growthful contact with one another.

(f) *Responding to confrontation.* If confrontation is responsible—that is, if it is really an invitation to self-examination in the community of the encounter group—the best response (but *not* the easiest) *is* self-examination and not the more instinctual responses of defense and counterattack. It is often far easier to respond to the punitive side effects of confrontation rather than to the substance of the confrontation itself. Try to listen to what the one confronting you is saying and not just to the feelings he is evoking in you. If what he says is true and if, in addition, he wants to involve himself with you, then it is to your advantage to listen to him, examine yourself, and respond to him. If what he says also evokes strong feelings in you, try to handle these openly in community also. Again, no one claims that this is easy, but it is frequently rewarding.

Self-disclosure, expression of feeling, active listening, giving authentic support, confrontation, and nondefensive response to confrontation—these interactions, expressed in straightforward, noncliché language when possible, are the cardinal forms of interpersonal behavior with which you are asked to experiment. It is hypothesized here that engaging freely and responsibly in such interactions constitutes interpersonal-growth behavior.

5. *Flight.* Engaging in the kinds of interaction described above is not always easy, and therefore we often find ways of running away from the process. We tend to run away for a number of reasons: we are anxious; we prefer not to know the truth about ourselves; and it is painful, perhaps, to be the object of another's concern. You are asked, then, to take a stance against all the different forms of flight from intimate group interaction: calling upon humor whenever things get too serious, speaking in generalities and abstractions, making speeches to the group in order to cut down on one-to-one contact, keeping one's feelings to oneself, spending a good deal of time analyzing and interpreting the behavior of others so that they might find "insight," saying "you" or "one" or "they" or "we" when you really mean "I," siphoning off issues that are a concern of the group by discussing them with individuals outside the group (in general not saying inside the group what you say about individual participants or the group itself outside the group), remaining passive and silent—there are many more. You must become sensitive to the ways you yourself flee group process and to the different ways in which the group as a whole tends to flee (for example, by tacitly deciding not to talk about certain subjects). Confronting modes of flight

in yourself and in the group is essential to the life of the group. One mode of flight is extremely destructive—cynicism about the worth of the experience even before one enters into it. The person who comes to the group believing that he will get nothing from it will ordinarily leave having fulfilled his own prophecy. It would probably be better if such a person were to decline an invitation to join in the first place. Try not to flee from your anxiety by employing self-defeating and group-defeating defenses. Rather, handle your anxiety by dealing with it in the group. Silence and withdrawal are types of flight. Perhaps in other kinds of groups the nonactive member profits from just being there, even though he adds little more than his presence. This cannot be the case in a group in which interpersonal contact is cardinal.

6. *Freedom.* You are obviously free to enter the group or not. Even if you do enter, this contract is meant not to constrain you but to help channel the energies of the group. It says, for instance, that self-disclosure is a value in this group, but it does not say what you must talk about, nor does it dictate the level of disclosure. This is something that you yourself must work out in the give-and-take of the group interaction. You must choose the kinds of interaction most meaningful to you. In the group do not simply be pressured into doing things you do not want to do. On the other hand, if you fail to exercise interpersonal initiative and agency, the group experience will probably have little meaning for you.

At present, few encounter groups use such explicit contracts. Nevertheless, if the above contract sounds inviting and challenging to the reader, then he might be ready to commit himself to the group experience itself. There are numerous formats for the encounter group—two-week residential laboratories conducted by professional organizations, courses in colleges, and weekend experiences conducted by church groups, to mention but a few. But, to stress a point made earlier, reading about encounter groups in any extended way without participating in one is a sterile pursuit indeed.

The articles that follow are drawn from a variety of sources. Some deal directly with encounter-group phenomena, and others explain group processes as such. Since a number of the articles come from the field of counseling and psychotherapy (and encounter groups are essentially experiences for "normals"), perhaps a word or two of explanation is in order.

Therapy or Training or Both

In my opinion, there is too much concern among professionals as well as laymen as to whether encounter groups are therapy or not. Since encounter groups are at least theoretically composed of people who are relatively well adjusted and are looking for an experience that will further help them to release and develop personal and interpersonal potentialities, then by definition they are not therapy groups. But such a statement is too simplistic; it rests upon a questionable assumption, that is, that people can be divided into two groups—those who need therapy (the disturbed, the problem-ridden, the maladjusted) and those who do not (the well-adjusted, the normal). If Maslow (1968) is right—if what we call "normal" is really, for the most part, a "psychopathology of the average"—is it better to be a person who is forced to wrestle with life (a maladjusted person) or one who lets life pass him by (the "average" person)? Some researchers have found, much to their concern, that some seemingly well-adjusted, normal people are "colorless" and that certain disturbed people are "dramatic and engaging" (Hendin, Gaylin, and Carr, 1965). On the other hand, in setting up an advanced encounter group whose participants were chosen because of their "functional excellence" in vocation, marriage, and friendship, Bugental and Tannenbaum (1965) found that even these carefully selected participants tended to deal with the negative and pathologic within themselves. Even more disturbing evidence comes from a series of studies reported by Carkhuff and Berenson (1967). These studies indicated that there is relatively little human nourishment in the average personal encounter and that even experienced counselors and therapists, on the average, interact with their clients in such a way as to stifle rather than promote growth. In the face of such evidence, who is ready to draw strong lines between the adjusted and the maladjusted, and what criteria is he to use?

In general, people with deeper and more persisting emotional problems are too afraid to enter the relatively high anxiety situation of the encounter group; sometimes, for a variety of reasons, others discourage them from participating. Some professionals claim that the maladjusted cannot cope with the free-wheeling interaction found in training groups, while others suggest that those with deep problems which they are not currently handling very well occupy too much of the concern of the group. They drain the group of its resources so that the other members do not get their fair share of "on-time" in the group.

Neither the problem of who should participate in encounter groups nor the question of whether such groups are therapy or not has yet been resolved, either theoretically or practically (see Yalom's article in Part One of these readings; it deals with the training-therapy issue). However, one point that has influenced the selection of articles for this book of readings seems to be getting clearer and clearer: psychotherapy as an interactional process is not as far removed from human living as many might think; that is, the kinds of interaction that make therapy a growthful and redeeming process are the kinds of interaction that nourish mature human living. If people are deprived of human nourishment, if for one reason or another they find themselves "out of community," then they need human nourishment in an intensive way. This we call therapy. What makes life go is what makes therapy go, not vice versa. Carkhuff and Berenson (1967) suggest that therapy become a way of life—that is, that the interactions associated with therapy become part of man's daily interpersonal living. Self-disclosure, acceptance, respect, genuineness, empathy, understanding, warmth, support, freedom to express feeling, responsible confrontation, a nondefensive posture toward those who challenge one's behavior, concreteness of communication, translation of self into noncliché language, a refusal to flee demanding and sometimes painful interactions—these are the behaviors that either constitute or lead to human growth. As such they belong in life, and because they belong in life they belong in therapy. *This* is the reason why articles dealing with therapy are included in this set of readings, not because sensitivity training and therapy are being equated.

Some of the articles deal with research findings, and others are theoretical in nature. Still others rely on observational and clinical data that have not been formalized in explicit empirical research. All the articles have been chosen to give the participant or the prospective participant a deeper feeling for the process to which he commits himself.

Bibliography: Introduction

Bradford, L. P., Gibb, J. R., & Benne, K. D. (Eds.) *T-Group theory and laboratory method.* New York: Wiley, 1964.

Bugental, J. F. T., & Tannenbaum, R. Sensitivity training and being motivation. In E. H. Schein & W. G. Bennis (Eds.), *Personal and organizational change through group methods: The laboratory approach.* New York: Wiley, 1965, pp. 107-113.

Carkhuff, R. R., & Berenson, B. G. *Beyond counseling and psychotherapy.* New York: Holt, Rinehart and Winston, 1967.

Egan, G. Contractual approaches to the modification of behavior in encounter groups. Paper presented at the 137th annual meeting of the American Association for the Advancement of Science, December 1970. (a)

Egan, G. *Encounter: Group processes for interpersonal growth.* Belmont, Calif.: Brooks/Cole, 1970. (b)

Hendin, H., Gaylin, W., & Carr, A. *Psychoanalysis and social work: The psychoanalytic study of the non-patient.* Garden City, N.Y.: Doubleday, 1965 (Anchor Books Edition published 1966).

Maslow, A. H. *Toward a psychology of being* (2nd edition). Princeton, N.J.: Van Nostrand, 1968.

Schein, E. H., & Bennis, W. G. (Eds.) *Personal and organizational change through group methods: The laboratory approach.* New York: Wiley, 1965.

Part One.
Groups: Orientations and Structures

This first set of articles explores the similarities among different kinds of small, face-to-face groups as well as those factors that set the basic encounter group apart from other groups. Theoretically, the more both the facilitator and the participants in an encounter group know about face-to-face groups in general, the more effective, other factors being equal, will be their participation. These "other factors," however, are extremely important. For instance, Plato (or his critics and misinterpreters) notwithstanding, knowledge in groups is not necessarily virtue. There are people with deep academic and research knowledge of small groups who, if they were to aspire to be group leaders, would inspire in me something akin to terror. There are others who, although they know next to nothing about the field of group dynamics in any formal sense, would, almost by instinct (or rather through academic, creative, and social intelligence), be effective group facilitators. Furthermore, participants who have read some text on group experiences are not necessarily the best participants; frequently, they stumble over their newly acquired conceptions of group process—knowledge, in this case, impeding virtue. Still, if given my choice, I would opt for the enlightened facilitator and the enlightened participant. I generally disapprove of the many forms of subtle control that man exercises over man in our society (London, 1970), and I see no reason why either the facilitator or the structure of the encounter experience itself should "control" the participant unnecessarily. Therefore, general knowledge of group dynamics and specific knowledge of the inner workings of the encounter group may have a liberating effect on both facilitator and participant.

The Process of the Basic
Encounter Group

Carl R. Rogers

Editor's Introduction: Our society is looked upon by many as too emotionally restrictive; and, because education in our society deals too exclusively with cognitive input, many people have found encounter groups rewarding. They have been free in such groups to explore the deeper emotional dimensions of their lives in the only way meaningful to them—experientially. The first article in this book, by Carl Rogers, a pioneering researcher in the field of counseling and psychotherapy, deals with what Rogers describes as the experience of the "basic encounter group." Rogers does more than merely map out the kinds of interactions characterizing such groups; rather, by using the actual words of the participants, he tries to convey the emotional impact of these interactions. His article is an honest one. It does not glorify group experiences but rather spells out the risks, the uncertainties, and the potential negative impact of encounter experiences.

Rogers, who has long been identified with the "nondirective" or "client-centered" approach in counseling and psychotherapy, is presently at the Center for Studies of the Person in La Jolla, California, where he works extensively with the encounter-group process.

I would like to share with you some of my thinking and puzzlement regarding a potent new cultural development—the intensive group experience.[1] It has, in my judgment, significant implications for our society. It has come very suddenly over our cultural horizon, since in anything like its present form it is less than two decades old.

I should like briefly to describe the many different forms and different labels under which the intensive group experience has become a part of our modern life. It has involved different kinds of individuals, and it has spawned various theories to account for its effects.

From *Challenges of Humanistic Psychology* by J. F. T. Bugental (Ed.). Copyright © 1967 by McGraw-Hill, Inc. Used by permission of McGraw-Hill Book Company and the author.

[1] In the preparation of this paper I am deeply indebted to two people, experienced in work with groups, for their help: Jacques Hochmann, M.D., psychiatrist of Lyon, France, who has been working at WBSI on a U.S.P.H.S. International Post-doctoral Fellowship, and Ann Dreyfuss, M.A., my research assistant. I am grateful for their ideas, for their patient analysis of recorded group sessions, and for the opportunity to interact with two original and inquiring minds.

As to labels, the intensive group experience has at times been called the *T-group* or *lab group,* "T" standing for training laboratory in group dynamics. It has been termed *sensitivity training* in human relationships. The experience has sometimes been called a *basic encounter group* or a *workshop*—a workshop in human relationships, in leadership, in counseling, in education, in research, in psychotherapy. In dealing with one particular type of person—the drug addict—it has been called a *synanon.*

The intensive group experience has functioned in various settings. It has operated in industries, in universities, in church groups, and in resort settings which provide a retreat from everyday life. It has functioned in various educational institutions and in penitentiaries.

An astonishing range of individuals have been involved in these intensive group experiences. There have been groups for presidents of large corporations. There have been groups for delinquent and predelinquent adolescents. There have been groups composed of college students and faculty members, of counselors and psychotherapists, of school dropouts, of married couples, of confirmed drug addicts, of criminals serving sentences, of nurses preparing for hospital service, and of educators, principals, and teachers.

The geographical spread attained by this rapidly expanding movement has reached in this country from Bethel, Maine (starting point of the National Training Laboratory movement), to Idyllwild, California. To my personal knowledge, such groups also exist in France, England, Holland, Japan, and Australia.

In their outward pattern these group experiences also show a great deal of diversity. There are T-groups and workshops which have extended over three to four weeks, meeting six to eight hours each day. There are some that have lasted only 2½ days, crowding twenty or more hours of group sessions into this time. A recent innovation is the "marathon" weekend, which begins on Friday afternoon and ends on Sunday evening, with only a few hours out for sleep and snacks.

As to the conceptual underpinnings of this whole movement, one may almost select the theoretical flavor he prefers. Lewinian and client-centered theories have been most prominent, but gestalt therapy and various brands of psychoanalysis have all played contributing parts. The experience within the group may focus on specific training in human relations skills. It may be closely similar to group therapy, with much exploration of past experience and the dynamics of personal development. It may focus on creative expression through painting or expressive movement. It may be focused primarily upon a basic encounter and relationship between individuals.

Simply to describe the diversity which exists in this field raises very properly the question of why these various developments should be considered to belong together. Are there any threads of commonality which pervade all these widely divergent activities? To me it seems that they do belong together and can all be classed as focusing on the intensive group experience. They all have certain

Groups: Orientations and Structures

similar external characteristics. The group in almost every case is small (from eight to eighteen members), is relatively unstructured, and chooses its own goals and personal directions. The group experience usually, though not always, includes some cognitive input, some content material which is presented to the group. In almost all instances the leader's responsibility is primarily the facilitation of the expression of both feelings and thoughts on the part of the group members. Both in the leader and in the group members there is some focus on the process and the dynamics of the immediate personal interaction. These are, I think, some of the identifying characteristics which are rather easily recognized.

There are also certain practical hypotheses which tend to be held in common by all these groups. My own summary of these would be as follows: In an intensive group, with much freedom and little structure, the individual will gradually feel safe enough to drop some of his defenses and facades; he will relate more directly on a feeling basis (come into a basic encounter) with other members of the group; he will come to understand himself and his relationship to others more accurately; he will change in his personal attitudes and behavior; and he will subsequently relate more effectively to others in his everyday life situation. There are other hypotheses related more to the group than to the individual. One is that in this situation of minimal structure, the group will move from confusions, fractionation, and discontinuity to a climate of greater trust and coherence. These are some of the characteristics and hypotheses which, in my judgment, bind together this enormous cluster of activities which I wish to talk about as constituting the intensive group experience.

As for myself, I have been gradually moving into this field for the last twenty years. In experimenting with what I call *student-centered teaching,* involving the free expression of personal feelings, I came to recognize not only the cognitive learnings but also some of the personal changes which occurred. In brief intensive training courses for counselors for the Veterans Administration in 1946, during the postwar period, I and my staff focused more directly on providing an intensive group experience because of its impact in producing significant learning. In 1950, I served as leader of an intensive, full-time, one-week workshop, a postdoctoral training seminar in psychotherapy for the American Psychological Association. The impact of those six days was so great that for more than a dozen years afterward, I kept hearing from members of the group about the meaning it had had for them. Since that time I have been involved in more than forty ventures of what I would like to term—using the label most congenial to me—*basic encounter groups.* Most of these have involved for many of the members experiences of great intensity and considerable personal change. With two individuals, however, in these many groups, the experience contributed, I believe, to a psychotic break. A few other individuals have found the experience more unhelpful than helpful. So I have come to have a profound respect for the constructive potency of such group experiences and also a real concern over the fact that sometimes and in some ways this experience may do damage to individuals.

The Group Process

It is a matter of great interest to me to try to understand what appear to be common elements in the group process as I have come dimly to sense these. I am using this opportunity to think about this problem, not because I feel I have any final theory to give, but because I would like to formulate, as clearly as I am able, the elements which I can perceive at the present time. In doing so I am drawing upon my own experience, upon the experiences of others with whom I have worked, upon the written material in this field, upon the written reactions of many individuals who have participated in such groups, and to some extent upon the recordings of such group sessions, which we are only beginning to tap and analyze. I am sure that (though I have tried to draw on the experience of others) any formulation I make at the present time is unduly influenced by my own experience in groups and thus is lacking in the generality I wish it might have.

As I consider the terribly complex interactions which arise during twenty, forty, sixty, or more hours of intensive sessions, I believe that I see some threads which weave in and out of the pattern. Some of these trends or tendencies are likely to appear early and some later in the group sessions, but there is no clear-cut sequence in which one ends and another begins. The interaction is best thought of, I believe, as a varied tapestry, differing from group to group, yet with certain kinds of trends evident in most of these intensive encounters and with certain patterns tending to precede and others to follow. Here are some of the process patterns which I see developing, briefly described in simple terms, illustrated from tape recordings and personal reports, and presented in roughly sequential order. I am not aiming at a high-level theory of group process but rather at a naturalistic observation out of which, I hope, true theory can be built.[2]

Milling Around. As the leader or facilitator makes clear at the outset that this is a group with unusual freedom, that it is not one for which he will take

[2] Jack and Lorraine Gibb have long been working on an analysis of trust development as the essential theory of group process. Others who have contributed significantly to the theory of group process are Chris Argyris, Kenneth Benne, Warren Bennis, Dorwin Cartwright, Matthew Miles, and Robert Blake. Samples of the thinking of all these and others may be found in three recent books: Bradford, Gibb, & Benne (1964); Bennis, Benne, & Chin (1961); and Bennis, Schein, Berlew, & Steele (1964). Thus, there are many promising leads for theory construction involving a considerable degree of abstraction. This chapter has a more elementary aim—a naturalistic descriptive account of the process.

Groups: Orientations and Structures

directional responsibility, there tends to develop a period of initial confusion, awkward silence, polite surface interaction, "cocktail-party talk," frustration, and great lack of continuity. The individuals come face-to-face with the fact that "there is no structure here except what we provide. We do not know our purposes; we do not even know one another, and we are committed to remain together over a considerable period of time." In this situation, confusion and frustration are natural. Particularly striking to the observer is the lack of continuity between personal expressions. Individual A will present some proposal or concern, clearly looking for a response from the group. Individual B has obviously been waiting for his turn and starts off on some completely different tangent as though he had never heard A. One member makes a simple suggestion such as, "I think we should introduce ourselves," and this may lead to several hours of highly involved discussion in which the underlying issues appear to be, "Who is the leader?" "Who is responsible for us?" "Who is a member of the group?" "What is the purpose of the group?"

Resistance to Personal Expression or Exploration. During the milling period, some individuals are likely to reveal some rather personal attitudes. This tends to foster a very ambivalent reaction among other members of the group. One member, writing of his experience, says:

There is a self which I present to the world and another one which I know more intimately. With others I try to appear able, knowing, unruffled, problem-free. To substantiate this image I will act in a way which at the time or later seems false or artificial or "not the real me." Or I will keep to myself thoughts which if expressed would reveal an imperfect me.

My inner self, by contrast with the image I present to the world, is characterized by many doubts. The worth I attach to this inner self is subject to much fluctuation and is very dependent on how others are reacting to me. At times this private self can feel worthless.

It is the public self which members tend to reveal to one another, and only gradually, fearfully, and ambivalently do they take steps to reveal something of their inner world.

Early in one intensive workshop, the members were asked to write anonymously a statement of some feeling or feelings which they had which they were not willing to tell in the group. One man wrote:

I don't relate easily to people. I have an almost impenetrable facade. Nothing gets in to hurt me, but nothing gets out. I have repressed so many emotions that I am close to emotional sterility. This situation doesn't make me happy, but I don't know what to do about it.

This individual is clearly living inside a private dungeon, but he does not even dare, except in this disguised fashion, to send out a call for help.

In a recent workshop when one man started to express the concern he felt about an impasse he was experiencing with his wife, another member stopped him, saying essentially:

Are you sure you want to go on with this, or are you being seduced by the group into going further than you want to go? How do you know the group can be trusted? How will you feel about it when you go home and tell your wife what you have revealed, or when you decide to keep it from her? It just isn't safe to go further.

It seemed quite clear that in his warning, this second member was also expressing his own fear of revealing *him*self and *his* lack of trust in the group.

Description of Past Feelings. In spite of ambivalence about the trustworthiness of the group and the risk of exposing oneself, expression of feelings does begin to assume a larger proportion of the discussion. The executive tells how frustrated he feels by certain situations in his industry, or the housewife relates problems she has experienced with her children. A tape-recorded exchange involving a Roman Catholic nun occurs early in a one-week workshop, when the discussion has turned to a rather intellectualized consideration of anger:

Bill: What happens when you get mad, Sister, or don't you?
Sister: Yes, I do—yes I do. And I find when I get mad, I, I almost get, well, the kind of person that antagonizes me is the person who seems so unfeeling toward people—now I take our dean as a person in point because she is a very aggressive woman and has certain ideas about what the various rules in a college should be; and this woman can just send me into high "G"; in an angry mood. *I mean this.* But then I find, I. . . .
Facil.:[3] But what, what do you do?
Sister: I find that when I'm in a situation like this, that I strike out in a very sharp, uh, *tone,* or else I just refuse to respond—"All right, this happens to be her way"—I don't think I've ever gone into a tantrum.
Joe: You just withdraw—no use to fight it.
Facil.: You say you use a sharp tone. To *her,* or to other people you're dealing with?
Sister: Oh, no. To *her.*

This is a typical example of a *description* of feelings which are obviously current in her in a sense but which she is placing in the past and which she describes as being outside the group in time and place. It is an example of feelings existing "there and then."

---

[3]The term "facilitator" will be used throughout this paper, although sometimes he is referred to as "leader" or "trainer."

Expression of Negative Feelings. Curiously enough, the first expression of genuinely significant "here-and-now" feeling is apt to come out in negative attitudes toward other group members or toward the group leader. In one group in which members introduced themselves at some length, one woman refused, saying that she preferred to be known for what she was in the group and not in terms of her status outside. Very shortly after this, one of the men in the group attacked her vigorously and angrily for this stand, accusing her of failing to cooperate, of keeping herself aloof from the group, and so forth. It was the first *personal current feeling* which had been brought into the open in the group.

Frequently the leader is attacked for his failure to give proper guidance to the group. One vivid example of this comes from a recorded account of an early session with a group of delinquents, where one member shouts at the leader (Gordon, 1955, p. 214):

You will be licked if you don't control us right at the start. You have to keep order here because you are older than us. That's what a teacher is supposed to do. If he doesn't do it we will cause a lot of trouble and won't get anything done. [Then, referring to two boys in the group who were scuffling, he continues.] Throw 'em out, throw 'em out! You've just *got* to make us behave!

An adult expresses his disgust at the people who talk too much, but points his irritation at the leader (Gordon, 1955, p. 210):

It is just that I don't understand why someone doesn't shut them up. I would have taken Gerald and shoved him out the window. I'm an authoritarian. I would have told him he was talking too much and he had to leave the room. I think the group discussion ought to be led by a person who simply will not recognize these people after they have interrupted about eight times.

Why are negatively toned expressions the first current feelings to be expressed? Some speculative answers might be the following: This is one of the best ways to test the freedom and trustworthiness of the group. "Is it really a place where I can be and express myself positively and negatively? Is this really a safe place, or will I be punished?" Another quite different reason is that deeply positive feelings are much more difficult and dangerous to express than negative ones. "If I say, 'I love you,' I am vulnerable and open to the most awful rejection. If I say, 'I hate you,' I am at best liable to attack, against which I can defend." Whatever the reasons, such negatively toned feelings tend to be the first here-and-now material to appear.

Expression and Exploration of Personally Meaningful Material. It may seem puzzling that following such negative experiences as the initial confusion, the resistance to personal expression, the focus on outside events, and the voicing of critical or angry feelings, the event most likely to occur next is for an individual to reveal himself to the group in a significant way. The reason for this no doubt is that the individual member has come to realize that this is in part *his group*. He can help to make of it what he wishes. He has also experienced the fact that negative feelings have been expressed and have usually been accepted or assimilated without any catastrophic results. He realizes there is freedom here, albeit a risky freedom. A climate of trust (Gibb, 1964, Ch. 10) is beginning to develop. So he begins to take the chance and the gamble of letting the group know some deeper facet of himself. One man tells of the trap in which he finds himself, feeling that communication between himself and his wife is hopeless. A priest tells of the anger which he has bottled up because of unreasonable treatment by one of his superiors. What should he have done? What might he do now? A scientist at the head of a large research department finds the courage to speak of his painful isolation, to tell the group that he has never had a single friend in his life. By the time he finishes telling of his situation, he is letting loose some of the tears of sorrow for himself which I am sure he has held in for many years. A psychiatrist tells of the guilt he feels because of the suicide of one of his patients. A woman of forty tells of her absolute inability to free herself from the grip of her controlling mother. A process which one workshop member has called a "journey to the center of self," often a very painful process, has begun.

Such exploration is not always an easy process, nor is the whole group always receptive to such self-revelation. In a group of institutionalized adolescents, all of whom had been in difficulty of one sort or another, one boy revealed an important fact about himself and immediately received both acceptance and sharp nonacceptance from members of the group:

George: This is the thing. I've got too many problems at home—uhm, I think some of you know why I'm here, what I was charged with.
Mary: I don't.
Facil.: Do you want to tell us?
George: Well, uh, it's sort of embarrassing.
Carol: Come on, it won't be so bad.
George: Well, I raped my sister. That's the only problem I have at home, and I've overcome that, I think. (*Rather long pause.*)
Freda: Oooh, that's *weird!*
Mary: People have problems, Freda, I mean ya know. . . .
Freda: Yeah, I know, but *yeOUW!!!*
Facil. (*to Freda*): You know about these problems, but they still are weird to you.
George: You see what I mean; it's embarrassing to talk about it.
Mary: Yeah, but it's O.K.
George: It *hurts* to talk about it, but I know I've got to so I won't be guilt-ridden for the rest of my life.

Clearly Freda is completely shutting him out psychologically, while Mary in particular is showing a deep acceptance.

The Expression of Immediate Interpersonal Feelings in the Group. Entering into the process sometimes earlier, sometimes later, is the explicit bringing into the open of the feelings experienced in the immediate moment by one member about another. These are sometimes positive and sometimes negative. Examples would be: "I feel threatened by your silence." "You remind me of my mother, with whom I had a tough time." "I took an instant dislike to you the first moment I saw you." "To me you're like a breath of fresh air in the group." "I like your warmth and your smile." "I dislike you more every time you speak up." Each of these attitudes can be, and usually is, explored in the increasing climate of trust.

The Development of a Healing Capacity in the Group. One of the most fascinating aspects of any intensive group experience is the manner in which a number of the group members show a natural and spontaneous capacity for dealing in a helpful, facilitative, and therapeutic fashion with the pain and suffering of others. As one rather extreme example of this, I think of a man in charge of maintenance in a large plant who was one of the low-status members of an industrial executive group. As he informed us, he had not been "contaminated by education." In the initial phases the group tended to look down on him. As members delved more deeply into themselves and began to express their own attitudes more fully, this man came forth as, without doubt, the most sensitive member of the group. He knew intuitively how to be understanding and acceptant. He was alert to things which had not yet been expressed but which were just below the surface. When the rest of us were paying attention to a member who was speaking, he would frequently spot another individual who was suffering silently and in need of help. He had a deeply perceptive and facilitating attitude. This kind of ability shows up so commonly in groups that it has led me to feel that the ability to be healing or therapeutic is far more common in human life than we might suppose. Often it needs only the permission granted by a freely flowing group experience to become evident.

In a characteristic instance, the leader and several group members were trying to be of help to Joe, who was telling of the almost complete lack of communication between himself and his wife. In varied ways members endeavored to give help. John kept putting before Joe the feelings Joe's wife was almost certainly experiencing. The facilitator kept challenging Joe's facade of "carefulness." Marie tried to help him discover what he was feeling at the moment. Fred showed him the choice he had of alternative behaviors. All this was clearly done in a spirit of caring, as is even more evident in the recording itself. No miracles were achieved, but toward the end Joe did come to the realization that the only thing that might help would be to express his real feelings to his wife.

Self-acceptance and the Beginning of Change. Many people feel that self-acceptance must stand in the way of change. Actually, in these group experiences, as in psychotherapy, it is the *beginning* of change. Some examples of the kind of attitudes expressed would be these: "I *am* a dominating person who likes to control others. I do want to mold these individuals into the proper shape." Another person says, "I really have a hurt and overburdened little boy inside of me who feels very sorry for himself. I *am* that little boy, in addition to being a competent and responsible manager."

I think of one governmental executive in a group in which I participated, a man with high responsibility and excellent technical training as an engineer. At the first meeting of the group he impressed me, and I think others, as being cold, aloof, somewhat bitter, resentful, and cynical. When he spoke of how he ran his office it appeared that he administered it "by the book," without any warmth or human feeling entering in. In one of the early sessions, when he spoke of his wife, a group member asked him, "Do you love your wife?" He paused for a long time, and the questioner said, "OK, that's answer enough." The executive said, "No. Wait a minute. The reason I didn't respond was that I was wondering if I ever loved anyone. I don't think I *ever* really *loved* anyone." It seemed quite dramatically clear to those of us in the group that he had come to accept himself as an unloving person.

A few days later he listened with great intensity as one member of the group expressed profound personal feelings of isolation, loneliness, and pain, revealing the extent to which he had been living behind a mask, a facade. The next morning the engineer said, "Last night I thought and thought about what Bill told us. I even wept quite a bit by myself. I can't remember how long it has been since I have cried, and I really *felt* something. I think perhaps what I felt was love."

It is not surprising that before the week was over, he had thought through new ways of handling his growing son, on whom he had been placing extremely rigorous demands. He had also begun genuinely to appreciate the love which his wife had extended to him and which he now felt he could in some measure reciprocate.

In another group one man kept a diary of his reactions. Here is his account of an experience in which he came really to accept his almost abject desire for love, a self-acceptance which marked the beginning of a very significant experience of change. He says (Hall, 1965):

During the break between the third and fourth sessions, I felt very droopy and tired. I had it in mind to take a nap, but instead I was almost compulsively going around to people starting a conversation. I had a begging kind of a feeling, like a very cowed little puppy hoping that he'll be patted but half afraid he'll be kicked. Finally, back in my room I lay down and began to know that I was sad.

Several times I found myself wishing my roommate would come in and talk to me. Or, whenever someone walked by the door, I would come to attention inside, the way a dog pricks up his ears; and I would feel an immediate wish for that person to come in and talk to me. I realized my raw wish to receive kindness.

Another recorded excerpt, from an adolescent group, shows a combination of self-acceptance and self-exploration. Art had been talking about his "shell," and here he is beginning to work with the problem of accepting himself, and also the facade he ordinarily exhibits:

Art: I'm so darn used to living with the shell; it doesn't even bother me. I don't even know the real me. I think I've uh, well, I've pushed the shell more away here. When I'm out of my shell—only twice—once just a few minutes ago—I'm really me, I guess. But then I just sort of pull in the [latch] cord after me when I'm in my shell, and that's almost all the time. And I leave the [false] front standing outside when I'm back in the shell.
Facil.: And nobody's back in there with you?
Art (crying): Nobody else is in there with me, just me. I just pull everything into the shell and roll the shell up and shove it in my pocket. I take the shell, and the real me, and put it in my pocket where it's safe. I guess that's really the way I do it—I go into my shell and turn off the real world. And here: that's what I want to do here in this group, ya know, come out of my shell and actually throw it away.
Lois: You're making progress already. At least you can talk about it.
Facil.: Yeah. The thing that's going to be hardest is to stay out of the shell.
Art (still crying): Well, yeah, if I can keep talking about it, I can come out and stay out, but I'm gonna have to, ya know, protect me. It hurts; it's actually hurting to talk about it.

Still another person reporting shortly after his workshop experience said, "I came away from the workshop feeling much more deeply that 'It is all right to be me with all my strengths and weaknesses.' My wife has told me that I appear to be more authentic, more real, more genuine."

This feeling of greater realness and authenticity is a very common experience. It would appear that the individual is learning to accept and to *be* himself, and this is laying the foundation for change. He is closer to his own feelings, and hence they are no longer so rigidly organized and are more open to change.

The Cracking of Facades. As the sessions continue, so many things tend to occur together that it is difficult to know which to describe first. It should again be stressed that these different threads and stages interweave and overlap. One of these threads is the increasing impatience with defenses. As time goes on, the group finds it unbearable that any member should live behind a mask or a front. The polite words, the intellectual understanding of one another and of relationships, the smooth coin of tact and cover-up—amply satisfactory for interactions outside—are just not good enough. The expression of self by some members of the group has made it very clear that a deeper and more basic encounter is *possible,* and the group appears to strive, intuitively and unconsciously, toward this goal. Gently at times, almost savagely at others, the group *demands* that the individual be himself, that his current feelings not be hidden, that he remove the mask of ordinary social intercourse. In one group there was a highly intelligent and quite academic man who had been rather perceptive in his understanding of others but who had not revealed himself at all. The attitude of the group was finally expressed sharply by one member when he said, "Come out from behind that lectern, Doc. Stop giving us speeches. Take off your dark glasses. We want to know *you.*"

In Synanon, the fascinating group so successfully involved in making persons out of drug addicts, this ripping away of facades is often very drastic. An excerpt from one of the "synanons," or group sessions, makes this clear (Casriel, 1963, p. 81):

Joe (*speaking to Gina*): I wonder when you're going to stop sounding so good in synanons. Every synanon that I'm in with you, someone asks you a question, and you've got a beautiful book written. All made out about what went down and how you were wrong and how you realized you were wrong and all that kind of bullshit. When are you going to stop doing that? How do you feel about Art?
Gina: I have nothing against Art.
Will: You're a nut. Art hasn't got any damn sense. He's been in there, yelling at you and Moe, and you've got everything so cool.
Gina: No, I feel he's very insecure in a lot of ways but that has nothing to do with me. . . .
Joe: You act like you're so goddamn understanding.
Gina: I was *told* to act as if I understand.
Joe: Well, you're in a synanon now. You're not supposed to be acting like you're such a goddamn healthy person. Are you so well?
Gina: No.
Joe: Well why the hell don't you quit acting as if you were.

If I am indicating that the group at times is quite violent in tearing down a facade or a defense, this would be accurate. On the other hand, it can also be sensitive and gentle. The man who was accused of hiding behind a lectern was deeply hurt by this attack, and over the lunch hour looked very troubled, as though he might break into tears at any moment. When the group reconvened, the members sensed this and treated him very gently, enabling him to tell us his own tragic personal story, which accounted for his aloofness and his intellectual and academic approach to life.

The Individual Receives Feedback. In the process of this freely expressive interaction, the individual rapidly acquires a great deal of data as to how he appears to others. The "hail-fellow-well-met" discovers that others resent his exaggerated friendliness. The executive who weighs his words carefully and speaks with heavy precision may find that others regard him as stuffy. A woman who shows a somewhat excessive desire to be of help to others is told in no uncertain terms that some group members do not want her for a mother. All this can be decidedly upsetting, but as long as these various bits of information are fed back in the context of caring which is developing in the group, they seem highly constructive.

Feedback can at times be very warm and positive, as the following recorded excerpt indicates:

Leo (*very softly and gently*): I've been struck with this ever since she talked about her waking in the night, that she has a very delicate sensitivity. (*Turning to Mary and speaking almost caressingly.*) And somehow I perceive—even looking at you or in your eyes—a very—almost like a gentle touch and from this gentle touch you can tell many—things—you sense in—this manner.
Fred: Leo, when you said that, that she has this kind of delicate sensitivity, I just felt, *Lord yes!* Look at her eyes.
Leo: M-hm.

A much more extended instance of negative and positive feedback, triggering a significant new experience of self-understanding and encounter with the group, is taken from the diary of the young man mentioned before. He had been telling the group that he had no feeling for them, and felt they had no feeling for him (Hall, 1965):

Then a girl lost patience with me and said she didn't feel she could give any more. She said I looked like a bottomless well, and she wondered how many times I had to be told that I *was* cared for. By this time I was feeling panicky, and I was saying to myself, "My God, can it be true that I can't be satisfied and that I'm somehow compelled to pester people for attention until I drive them away!"
At this point while I was really worried, a nun in the group spoke up. She said that I had not alienated her with some negative things I had said to her. She said she liked me, and she couldn't understand why I couldn't see that. She said she felt concerned for me and wanted to help me. With that, something began to really dawn on me, and I voiced it somewhat like the following. "You mean you are all sitting there, feeling for me what I say I want you to feel, and that somewhere down inside me I'm stopping it from touching me?" I relaxed appreciably and began really to wonder why I had shut their caring out so much. I couldn't find the answer, and one woman said: "It looks like you are trying to stay continuously as deep in your feelings as you were this afternoon. It would make sense to me for you to draw back and assimilate it. Maybe if you don't push so hard, you can rest awhile and then move back into your feelings more naturally."
Her making the last suggestion really took effect. I saw the sense in it, and almost immediately I settled back very relaxed with something of a feeling of a bright, warm day dawning inside me. In addition to taking the pressure off of myself, however, I was for the first time really warmed by the friendly feelings

which I felt they had for me. It is difficult to say why I felt liked only just then, but, as opposed to the earlier sessions, I really *believed* they cared for me. I never have fully understood why I stood their affection off for so long, but at that point I almost abruptly began to trust that they did care. The measure of the effectiveness of this change lies in what I said next. I said, "Well, that really takes care of me. I'm really ready to listen to someone else now." I *meant* that, too.

Confrontation. There are times when the term "feedback" is far too mild to describe the interactions which take place, when it is better said that one individual *confronts* another, directly "leveling" with him. Such confrontations can be positive, but frequently they are decidedly negative, as the following example will make abundantly clear. In one of the last sessions of a group, Alice had made some quite vulgar and contemptuous remarks to John, who was entering religious work. The next morning, Norma, who had been a very quiet person in the group, took the floor:

Norma (*loud sigh*): Well, I don't have *any* respect for you, Alice. *None*! (*Pause.*) There's about a hundred things going through my mind I want to say to you, and by God I hope I get through 'em all! First of all, if you wanted us to respect you, then why couldn't you respect *John's* feelings last night? Why have you been on him today? Hmm? Last night—couldn't you—couldn't you accept—*couldn't you* comprehend in any way at all that—that *he felt* his unworthiness in the service of God? Couldn't you accept this, or did you have to dig into it today to find something *else there?* And his respect for womanhood—he *loves* women—yes, he does, because he's a real person, but you—you're not a real woman—to me—and thank God, you're not my mother! ! ! ! I want to come over and beat the hell out of you! ! ! I want to slap you across the mouth so hard and—oh, and you're so, you're many years above me—and I respect age, and I respect people who are older than me, *but I don't respect you, Alice. At all!* And I was so *hurt* and *confused* because you were making someone else feel *hurt* and *confused.* . . .

It may relieve the reader to know that these two women came to accept each other, not completely, but much more understandingly, before the end of the session. But this *was* a confrontation!

The Helping Relationship outside the Group Sessions. No account of the group process would, in my experience, be adequate if it did not make mention of the many ways in which group members are of assistance to one another. Not infrequently, one member of a group will spend hours listening and talking to another member who is undergoing a painful new perception of himself. Sometimes it is merely the offering of help which is therapeutic. I think of one man who was going through a very depressed period after having told us of the many tragedies in his life. He seemed quite clearly, from his remarks, to be

Groups: Orientations and Structures

contemplating suicide. I jotted down my room number (we were staying at a hotel) and told him to put it in his pocket and to call me anytime of day or night if he felt that it would help. He never called, but six months after the workshop was over he wrote to me telling me how much that act had meant to him and that he still had the slip of paper to remind him of it.

Let me give an example of the healing effect of the attitudes of group members both outside and inside the group meetings. This is taken from a letter written by a workshop member to the group one month after the group sessions. He speaks of the difficulties and depressing circumstances he has encountered during that month and adds:

I have come to the conclusion that my experiences with you have profoundly affected me. I am truly grateful. This is different than personal therapy. None of you *had* to care about me. None of you had to seek me out and let me know of things you thought would help me. None of you had to let me know I was of help to you. Yet you did, and as a result it has far more meaning than anything I have so far experienced. When I feel the need to hold back and not live spontaneously, for whatever reasons, I remember that twelve persons, just like those before me now, said to let go and be congruent, to be myself, and, of all unbelievable things, they even loved me more for it. This has given me the *courage* to come out of myself many times since then. Often it seems my very doing of this helps the others to experience similar freedom.

The Basic Encounter. Running through some of the trends I have just been describing is the fact that individuals come into much closer and more direct contact with one another than is customary in ordinary life. This appears to be one of the most central, intense, and change-producing aspects of such a group experience. To illustrate what I mean, I would like to draw an example from a recent workshop group. A man tells, through his tears, of the very tragic loss of his child, a grief which he is experiencing *fully,* for the first time, not holding back his feelings in any way. Another says to him, also with tears in his eyes, "I've never felt so close to another human being. I've never before felt a real physical hurt in me from the pain of another. I feel *completely* with you." This is a basic encounter.

Such I-Thou relationships (to use Buber's term) occur with some frequency in these group sessions and nearly always bring a moistness to the eyes of the participants.

One member, trying to sort out his experiences immediately after a workshop, speaks of the "commitment to relationship" which often developed on the part of two individuals, not necessarily individuals who had liked each other initially. He goes on to say:

The incredible fact experienced over and over by members of the group was that when a negative feeling was fully expressed to another, the relationship grew and the negative feeling was replaced by a deep acceptance for the other. . . . Thus real change seemed to occur when feelings were experienced and expressed in the context of the relationship. "I can't *stand* the way you talk!" turned into a real understanding and affection for you the *way* you talk.

This statement seems to capture some of the more complex meanings of the term "basic encounter."

The Expression of Positive Feelings and Closeness. As indicated in the last section, an inevitable part of the group process seems to be that when feelings are expressed and can be accepted in a relationship, a great deal of closeness and positive feelings result. Thus as the sessions proceed, there is an increasing feeling of warmth and group spirit and trust built, not out of positive attitudes only, but out of a realness which includes both positive and negative feeling. One member tried to capture this in writing very shortly after the workshop by saying that if he were trying to sum it up, ". . . it would have to do with what I call confirmation—a kind of confirmation of myself, of the uniqueness and universal qualities of men, a confirmation that when we can be human together something positive can emerge."

A particularly poignant expression of these positive attitudes was shown in the group where Norma confronted Alice with her bitterly angry feelings. Joan, the facilitator, was deeply upset and began to weep. The positive and healing attitudes of the group, for their own *leader*, are an unusual example of the closeness and personal quality of the relationships.

Joan (*crying*): I somehow feel that it's so *damned* easy for me to—to put myself *inside* of another person and I just guess I can feel that—for John and Alice and for you, Norma.
Alice: And it's *you* that's hurt.
Joan: Maybe I am taking some of that hurt. I guess I am. (*crying.*)
Alice: That's a wonderful gift. I wish I had it.
Joan: You have a lot of it.
Peter: In a way you bear the—I guess in a special way, because you're the—facilitator, ah, you've probably borne, ah, an extra heavy burden for all of us—and the burden that you, perhaps, you bear the heaviest is—we ask you—we ask one another; we grope to try to accept one another as we are, and—for each of us in various ways I guess we reach things and we say, *please* accept me. . . .

Some may be very critical of a "leader" so involved and so sensitive that she weeps at the tensions in the group which she has taken into herself. For me, it is simply another evidence that when people are real with each other, they have an astonishing ability to heal a person with a real and understanding love, whether that person is "participant" or "leader."

Groups: Orientations and Structures

Behavior Changes in the Group. It would seem from observation that many changes in behavior occur in the group itself. Gestures change. The tone of voice changes, becoming sometimes stronger, sometimes softer, usually more spontaneous, less artificial, more feelingful. Individuals show an astonishing amount of thoughtfulness and helpfulness toward one another.

Our major concern, however, is with the behavior changes which occur following the group experience. It is this which constitutes the most significant question and on which we need much more study and research. One person gives a catalog of the changes which he sees in himself which may seem too "pat" but which is echoed in many other statements:

I am more open, spontaneous. I express myself more freely. I am more sympathetic, empathic, and tolerant. I am more confident. I am more religious in my own way. My relations with my family, friends, and coworkers are more honest, and I express my likes and dislikes and true feelings more openly. I admit ignorance more readily. I am more cheerful. I want to help others more.

Another says:

Since the workshop there has been a new relationship with my parents. It has been trying and hard. However, I have found a greater freedom in talking with them, especially my father. Steps have been made toward being closer to my mother than I have ever been in the last five years.

Another says:

It helped clarify my feelings about my work, gave me more enthusiasm for it, and made me more honest and cheerful with my co-workers and also more open when I was hostile. It made my relationship with my wife more open, deeper. We felt freer to talk about anything, and we felt confident that anything we talked about we could work through.

Sometimes the changes which are described are very subtle. "The primary change is the more positive view of my ability to allow myself to *hear,* and to become involved with someone else's 'silent scream.' "

At the risk of making the outcomes sound too good, I will add one more statement written shortly after a workshop by a mother. She says:

The immediate impact on my children was of interest to both me and my husband. I feel that having been so accepted and loved by a group of strangers was so supportive that when I returned home my love for the people closest to me was much more spontaneous. Also, the practice I had in accepting and loving others during the workshop was evident in my relationships with my close friends.

Disadvantages and Risks

Thus far one might think that every aspect of the group process was positive. As far as the evidence at hand indicates, it appears that it nearly always is a positive process for a majority of the participants. There are, nevertheless, failures which result. Let me try to describe briefly some of the negative aspects of the group process as they sometimes occur.

The most obvious deficiency of the intensive group experience is that frequently the behavior changes, if any, which occur, are not lasting. This is often recognized by the participants. One says, "I wish I had the ability to hold permanently the 'openness' I left the conference with." Another says, "I experienced a lot of acceptance, warmth, and love at the workshop. I find it hard to carry the ability to share this in the same way with people outside the workshop. I find it easier to slip back into my old unemotional role than to do the work necessary to open relationships."

Sometimes group members experience this phenomenon of "relapse" quite philosophically:

The group experience is not a way of life but a reference point. My images of our group, even though I am unsure of some of their meanings, give me a comforting and useful perspective on my normal routine. They are like a mountain which I have climbed and enjoyed and to which I hope occasionally to return.

Some Data on Outcomes. What is the extent of this "slippage"? In the past year, I have administered follow-up questionnaires to 481 individuals who have been in groups I have organized or conducted. The information has been obtained from two to twelve months following the group experience, but the greatest number were followed up after a three- to six-month period.[4] Of these individuals, two (i.e., less than one-half of 1 percent) felt it had changed their behavior in ways they did not like. Fourteen percent felt the experience had made no perceptible change in their behavior. Another fourteen percent felt that it had changed their behavior but that this change had disappeared or left only a small residual positive effect. Fifty-seven percent felt it had made a continuing positive difference in their behavior, a few feeling that it had made some negative changes along with the positive.

A second potential risk involved in the intensive group experience and one which is often mentioned in public discussion is the risk that the individual may become deeply involved in revealing himself and then be left with problems which are not worked through. There have been a number of reports of people

---

[4]The 481 respondents constituted 82 percent of those to whom the questionnaire had been sent.

who have felt, following an intensive group experience, that they must go to a therapist to work through the feelings which were opened up in the intensive experience of the workshop and which were left unresolved. It is obvious that, without knowing more about each individual situation, it is difficult to say whether this was a negative outcome or a partially or entirely positive one. There are also very occasional accounts, and I can testify to two in my own experience, where an individual has had a psychotic episode during or immediately following an intensive group experience. On the other side of the picture is the fact that individuals have also lived through what were clearly psychotic episodes, and lived through them very constructively, in the context of a basic encounter group. My own tentative clinical judgment would be that the more positively the group process has been proceeding, the less likely it is that any individual would be psychologically damaged through membership in the group. It is obvious, however, that this is a serious issue and that much more needs to be known.

Some of the tension which exists in workshop members as a result of this potential for damage was very well described by one member when he said, "I feel the workshop had some very precious moments for me when I felt very close indeed to particular persons. It had some frightening moments when its potency was very evident and I realized a particular person might be deeply hurt or greatly helped but I could not predict which."

Out of the 481 participants followed up by questionnaires, two felt that the overall impact of their intensive group experience was "mostly damaging." Six more said that it had been "more unhelpful than helpful." Twenty-one, or 4 percent, stated that it had been "mostly frustrating, annoying, or confusing." Three and one-half percent said that it had been neutral in its impact. Nineteen percent checked that it had been "more helpful than unhelpful," indicating some degree of ambivalence. But 30 percent saw it as "constructive in its results," and 45 percent checked it as a "deeply meaningful, positive experience."[5] Thus for three-fourths of the group, it was *very* helpful. These figures should help to set the problem in perspective. It is obviously a very serious matter if an intensive group experience is psychologically damaging to *anyone*. It seems clear, however, that such damage occurs only rarely, if we are to judge by the reaction of the participants.

Other Hazards of the Group Experience. There is another risk or deficiency in the basic encounter group. Until very recent years it has been unusual for a workshop to include both husband and wife. This can be a real problem if significant change has taken place in one spouse during or as a result of the workshop experience. One individual felt this risk clearly after attending a

---

[5] These figures add up to more than 100 percent since quite a number of the respondents checked more than one answer.

workshop. He said, "I think there is a great danger to a marriage when one spouse attends a group. It is too hard for the other spouse to compete with the group individually and collectively." One of the frequent aftereffects of the intensive group experience is that it brings out into the open for discussion marital tensions which have been kept under cover.

Another risk which has sometimes been a cause of real concern in mixed intensive workshops is that very positive, warm, and loving feelings can develop between members of the encounter group, as has been evident from some of the preceding examples. Inevitably some of these feelings have a sexual component, and this can be a matter of great concern to the participants and a profound threat to their spouses if these feelings are not worked through satisfactorily in the workshop. Also the close and loving feelings which develop may become a source of threat and marital difficulty when a wife, for example, has not been present, but projects many fears about the loss of her spouse—whether well founded or not—onto the workshop experience.

A man who had been in a mixed group of men and women executives wrote to me a year later and mentioned the strain in his marriage which resulted from his association with Marge, a member of his basic encounter group:

There was a problem about Marge. There had occurred a very warm feeling on my part for Marge, and great compassion, for I felt she was *very* lonely. I believe the warmth was sincerely reciprocal. At any rate she wrote me a long affectionate letter, which I let my wife read. I was *proud* that Marge could feel that way about *me*. [Because he had felt very worthless.] But my wife was alarmed, because she read a love affair into the words—at least a *potential* threat. I stopped writing to Marge, because I felt rather clandestine after that.

My wife has since participated in an "encounter group" herself, and she now understands. I have resumed writing to Marge.

Obviously, not all such episodes would have such a harmonious ending.

It is of interest in this connection that there has been increasing experimentation in recent years with "couples workshops" and with workshops for industrial executives and their spouses.

Still another negative potential growing out of these groups has become evident in recent years. Some individuals who have participated in previous encounter groups may exert a stultifying influence on new workshops which they attend. They sometimes exhibit what I think of as the "old pro" phenomenon. They feel they have learned the "rules of the game," and they subtly or openly try to impose these rules on newcomers. Thus, instead of promoting true expressiveness and spontaneity, they endeavor to substitute new rules for old—to make members feel guilty if they are not expressing feelings, are reluctant to voice criticism or hostility, are talking about situations outside the group relationship, or are fearful of revealing themselves. These old pros seem to be attempting to substitute a new tyranny in interpersonal relationships in the place of older, conventional restrictions. To me this is a perversion of the true group process. We need to ask ourselves how this travesty on spontaneity comes about.

Implications

I have tried to describe both the positive and the negative aspects of this burgeoning new cultural development. I would like now to touch on its implications for our society.

In the first place, it is a highly potent experience and hence clearly deserving of scientific study. As a phenomenon it has been both praised and criticized, but few people who have participated would doubt that *something* significant happens in these groups. People do not react in a neutral fashion toward the intensive group experience. They regard it as either strikingly worthwhile or deeply questionable. All would agree, however, that it is *potent.* This fact makes it of particular interest to the behavioral sciences since science is usually advanced by studying potent and dynamic phenomena. This is one of the reasons why I personally am devoting more and more of my time to this whole enterprise. I feel that we can learn much about the ways in which constructive personality change comes about as we study this group process more deeply.

In a different dimension, the intensive group experience appears to be one cultural attempt to meet the isolation of contemporary life. The person who has experienced an I-Thou relationship, who has entered into the basic encounter, is no longer an isolated individual. One workshop member stated this in a deeply expressive way:

Workshops seem to be at least a partial answer to the loneliness of modern man and his search for new meanings for his life. In short, workshops seem very quickly to allow the individual to become that person he wants to be. The first few steps are taken there, in uncertainty, in fear, and in anxiety. We may or may not continue the journey. It is a gutsy way to live. You trade many, many loose ends for one big knot in the middle of your stomach. It sure as hell isn't easy, but it is a *life* at least—not a hollow imitation of life. It has fear as well as hope, sorrow as well as joy, but I daily offer it to more people in the hope that they will join me. . . . Out from a no-man's land of *fog* into the more violent atmosphere of extremes of thunder, hail, rain, and sunshine. It is worth the trip.

Another implication which is partially expressed in the foregoing statement is that it is an avenue to fulfillment. In a day when more income, a larger car, and a better washing machine seem scarcely to be satisfying the deepest needs of man, individuals are turning to the psychological world, groping for a greater degree of authenticity and fulfillment. One workshop member expressed this extremely vividly:

[It] has revealed a completely new dimension of life and has opened an infinite number of possibilities for me in my relationship to myself and to everyone dear to me. I feel truly alive and so grateful and joyful and hopeful and healthy and giddy and sparkly. I feel as though my eyes and ears and heart and guts have been opened to see and hear and love and feel more deeply, more widely, more intensely—this glorious, mixed-up, fabulous existence of ours. My whole body and each of its systems seems freer and healthier. I want to feel hot and cold, tired and rested, soft and hard, energetic and lazy. With persons everywhere, but especially my family, I have found a new freedom to explore and communicate. I know the change in me automatically brings a change in them. A whole new exciting relationship has started for me with my husband and with each of my children—a freedom to speak and to hear them speak.

Though one may wish to discount the enthusiasm of this statement, it describes an enrichment of life for which many are seeking.

Rehumanizing Human Relationships. This whole development seems to have special significance in a culture which appears to be bent upon dehumanizing the individual and dehumanizing our human relationships. Here is an important force in the opposite direction, working toward making relationships more meaningful and more personal, in the family, in education, in government, in administrative agencies, in industry.

An intensive group experience has an even more general philosophical implication. It is one expression of the existential point of view which is making itself so pervasively evident in art and literature and modern life. The implicit goal of the group process seems to be to live life fully in the here and now of the relationship. The parallel with an existential point of view is clear cut. I believe this has been amply evident in the illustrative material.

There is one final issue which is raised by this whole phenomenon: What is our view of the optimal person? What is the goal of personality development? Different ages and different cultures have given different answers to this question. It seems evident from our review of the group process that in a climate of freedom, group members move toward becoming more spontaneous, flexible, closely related to their feelings, open to their experience, and closer and more expressively intimate in their interpersonal relationships. If we value this type of person and this type of behavior, then clearly the group process is a valuable process. If, on the other hand, we place a value on the individual who is effective in suppressing his feelings, who operates from a firm set of principles, who does not trust his own reactions and experience but relies on authority, and who remains aloof in his interpersonal relationships, then we would regard the group process, as I have tried to describe it, as a dangerous force. Clearly there is room for a difference of opinion on this value question, and not everyone in our culture would give the same answer.

Conclusion

I have tried to give a naturalistic, observational picture of one of the most significant modern social inventions, the so-called intensive group experience, or basic encounter group. I have tried to indicate some of the common elements of the process which occur in the climate of freedom that is present in such a group. I have pointed out some of the risks and shortcomings of the group experience. I have tried to indicate some of the reasons why it deserves serious consideration, not only from a personal point of view, but also from a scientific and philosophical point of view. I also hope I have made it clear that this is an area in which an enormous amount of deeply perceptive study and research is needed.

References

Bennis, W. G., Benne, K. D., & Chin, R. (Eds.) *The planning of change.* New York: Holt, Rinehart and Winston, 1961.

Bennis, W. G., Schein, E. H., Berlew, D. E., & Steele, F. I. (Eds.) *Interpersonal dynamics.* Homewood, Ill.: Dorsey, 1964.

Bradford, L., Gibb, J. R., & Benne, K. D. (Eds.) *T-group theory and laboratory method.* New York: Wiley, 1964.

Casriel, D. *So fair a house.* Englewood Cliffs, N.J.: Prentice-Hall, 1963.

Gibb, J. R. Climate for trust formation. In L. Bradford, J. R. Gibb, & K. D. Benne (Eds.), *T-group theory and laboratory method.* New York: Wiley, 1964.

Gordon, T. *Group-centered leadership.* Boston: Houghton Mifflin, 1955.

Hall, G. F. A participant's experience in a basic encounter group. (Mimeographed) Western Behavioral Sciences Institute, 1965.

Editor's Comment. In this article Rogers expresses a deep respect for the power of the intensive group experience. If the participants, for one reason or another, refuse to lower their defenses moderately and put aside the masks and facades used in day-to-day living, the experience can be shallow, frustrating, and fruitless. But, as Rogers suggests, nondefensive behavior is a function of the level of trust in the group. A group that fails to develop a climate of trust will either stagnate or move toward self-destruction.

Many of the sample interactions quoted by Rogers involve a good deal of talk about then-and-there problems rather than here-and-now problems. I find that the most productive groups are those in which the participants deal principally with their here-and-now relationships with one another. In such groups there is a great deal of "you-me" talk. The then-and-there is not avoided, but it is dealt with insofar as it has an impact on the here-and-now relationships of the group. Encounter groups in which there-and-then problems are dealt with continuously or exclusively really follow a counseling rather than an encounter model.

There are many different styles of encounter groups. Rogers describes certain factors common to most of these groups, but the reader should not therefore conclude that Rogers is describing the only approach to encounter experiences. Subsequent articles will suggest different styles. The encounter-group movement is, relatively speaking, in its infancy. As Rogers suggests, good research is needed; still, there is no need prematurely to curtail the wide exploration that is taking place in growth centers, universities, and a variety of other institutions. While some of the exploration seems irresponsible, it is perhaps the price that must be paid for the development of a process that has already had a constructive impact on thousands of participants and on many of our society's institutions.

Interface of the T-Group
and Therapy Group

Irvin D. Yalom

Editor's Introduction. One way to provide some kind of orientation for the encounter-group experience is to distinguish it from related experiences. Yalom describes the similarities and the differences between group therapy and encounter-group experiences. The principal difference, according to Yalom, concerns the composition of the groups. While the members of an encounter group may be afflicted in varying degrees with what Maslow (1968) calls the "psychopathology of the average," members of a therapy group have more deeply disrupted intra- and interpersonal relations and, because of these disruptions, they have a more survival-based orientation to learning. Yalom maintains that these factors result in interactional and procedural differences between the two groups, both in the early stages and in the later, "working-through" stages of the group experience. One note on semantics. Earlier in the chapter from which the following selection has been excerpted, Yalom makes a distinction between "encounter groups" and "T-groups." He says that "generally encounter groups have no institutional backing, are far more unstructured, are more often led by untrained leaders, may rely more on physical contact and nonverbal exercises, and generally emphasize an experience, or getting 'turned on,' rather than change per se" (p. 341). The phenomena he describes here certainly exist, but I object to their being designated by the rubric "encounter group." Other researchers (for instance, Rogers, in the previous article) use the term in a much more neutral way. It would be unfair to let the reader think that when he sees the term "encounter group," it represents the phenomena described by Yalom under that rubric. In this book the most common term used to designate the group experience under consideration is "encounter group."

Starting from their widely different points of origin, the recent course of the T-group and the therapy group have shown a convergence to the point where there is a considerable interface between the two fields. Indeed, so many similarities are present that many observers wonder whether there are any intrinsic differences between the two types of group work.

"Interface of the T-group and Therapy Group," pp. 357-371 of *The Theory and Practice of Group Psychotherapy* by Irvin D. Yalom, © 1970 by Basic Books, Inc., Publishers, New York. Used by permission of the publisher.

Development of the Individual's Positive Potential

The traditions from which each have derived have undergone considerable evolution, which has resulted in a major shift in group goals, theory, and technology. Human relations education, as we have shown, has changed its emphasis from the acquisition of specific theory and interpersonal skills to the present goals of total enhancement of the individual. Human relations education now means that the individual becomes educated about his relationship to others as well as to his various internal selves. In the field of psychotherapy there has been a gradual evolution from the model of personality development based on the transmutations of the individual's libidinal and aggressive energies to the current emphasis on ego psychology. Many theorists have posited the existence of an additional positively valenced drive which must perforce be allowed to unfold rather than be inhibited or sublimated: thus Hendrick's "instinct to master,"[36] Berlyne's "exploratory drive,"[37] Horney's "self-realization,"[38] White's "effectance motivation,"[39] Hartmann's "neutralized energy,"[40] Angyal's "self-determination,"[41] and Goldstein's, Rogers' and Maslow's "self-actualization."[42] The development of the individual entails more than the inhibition or sublimation of potentially destructive instinctual forces. He must, in addition, fulfill his creative potential, and the efforts of the therapist should be directed toward this goal. Horney[38] states that the task of the therapist should be to help remove obstructions; given favorable circumstances the individual will realize his own potential, "just as an acorn will develop into an oak." Similarly Rogers refers to the therapist as a facilitator. A closely related trend in psychotherapy, beginning perhaps with Fromm-Reichmann, Erickson, Lindemann, and Hamburg, has been the strategy of building on the patient's strengths. Psychotherapists have come to appreciate, for example, that individuals may encounter great discomfort at certain junctures in the life cycle, not because of poor ego strength but because there have been inadequate opportunities for the learning relevant to that life stage to occur; psychotherapy may be directed toward the facilitation of this learning. Hamburg, in particular, has explored adaptive methods of coping with severe life challenges and has suggested strategies of psychotherapy based on the facilitation of coping.[43]

This shift in therapy orientation has brought the group therapist and the T-group trainer closer together. The T-group has always espoused the goal of acquisition of competence. To the T-group leader the reinforcement of strengths is no less vital than the correction of deficiencies.

Outcome Goals

Hoped-for changes occurring in the individual as a result of his T-group experience closely parallel (despite differences in language) the changes that group therapists wish to see in their patients. For example, one T-group outcome study[44] investigated these fifteen variables: sending communication, receiving communication, relational facility, risk taking, increased interdependence, functional flexibility, self-control, awareness of behavior, sensitivity to group process, sensitivity to others, acceptance of others, tolerance of new information, confidence, comfort, insight into self and role.

Supra-individual Focus

One important difference between T-groups and therapy groups present in their early phases but now diminished was that the T-group often had supra-individual goals, whereas the therapy group concerned itself solely with the personal goals of each individual member. For example, the first T-group described earlier had the goal of facilitating the operation of the Connecticut Fair Employment Practices Act. Other T-groups frequently have the supra-individual goal of increasing the effectiveness of the contracting agency. Group therapy, on the other hand, had no goals other than the relief of suffering of each of its members.

Both disciplines have altered their original positions. T-groups often consist of strangers each of whom have highly personalized goals, while many of the supra-individual goals are split off from the T-group and assigned to other activities of the human relations laboratory. Psychotherapy, on the other hand, has gradually become more aware of the importance of supra-individual goals. Stanton and Schwartz[45] in 1954 first noted that in a large group, the psychiatric hospital, the improvement or deterioration of the individual patient was a function of the structural properties of the large group. For example, if the large group had evolved norms which prevented the resolution of intrastaff conflict, then patients were more likely to have psychotic exacerbations. Similar observations have been made in military, prison, and community settings. Gradually an important principle of psychotherapeutic intervention has evolved: a supra-individual focus—the cohesiveness and norms of the large group—can facilitate the attainment of each member's individual goals. In fact, often there is little choice; for example, the great majority of therapists would agree that the individual treatment of the underprivileged adolescent drug user without involvement of his social group is a futile endeavor. The small therapy group analogue of this principle was fully described in Chapter 3 in the discussion of cohesiveness as a curative factor in group psychotherapy.

Group Composition

T-group and therapy group composition have also grown more similar over the years. No longer do psychotherapists solely treat individuals with major mental health problems. An increasing number of fairly well-integrated individuals with minor problems in living are seeking psychotherapy. A number of factors are responsible: increased public acceptance and understanding of psychotherapy, curiosity-arousing mass media depictions of psychotherapy, and increased affluence and leisure time which have resulted in a shift upward on the hierarchy of needs. Conversely many patients have erroneously considered the short intensive T-group, especially the weekend marathon variety, as crash psychotherapy programs. Indeed, as Rogers observed,[46] a new clinical syndrome—the group addict—has arisen; these individuals spend every weekend in some T-group, searching them out up and down the West Coast. (I recently attended a marathon group in which three of the members had, the previous evening, just completed another marathon group!)

The Common Social Malady

Both T-groups and therapy groups highly value self-disclosure, and the content of what is disclosed is remarkably similar from group to group. Loneliness, confusion, and alienation haunt T-groups and therapy groups alike. The great majority of individuals, both patients and nonpatients, share a common malady, which is deeply imbedded in the character of modern Western society. In much of America the past two decades have witnessed an inexorable decomposition of social institutions which ordinarily provide for human intimacy; the extended family living arrangement, the lifelong marriage (one out of two California marriages ends in divorce), the small, stable work group and home community are often part of the nostalgic past. Organized religion has become irrelevant to many of the young, often little more than a "Sunday morning tedium,"[47] while the neighborhood merchant and the family doctor are rapidly disappearing.

Modern medical practice is a case in point. Spurred on by advances in medical technology, the doctor has become an efficient scientist. But at what a price! The president of the American Medical Association stated recently:

In the future, the family doctor will be almost as extinct as a dodo. When you're hurt, or sick, you'll go to the nearest hospital for emergency treatment, administered by physicians especially trained in these procedures.

You may not even see the doctor on your initial visits. Your case history will be taken by assistants—even, eventually, by computers. Trained aides may do some of the preliminary examination.

The kindly old gentleman with the bedside manner was wonderful in his day, but society can no longer afford him. The modern doctor is more efficient, more scientific and less subject to error.

Unfortunately, he is often more impersonal. But people are already beginning to accept this, as they are beginning to accept changes in all areas of personal service.

It's part of a normal trend in society. In all forms of human service, there is less concern for the individual. We are no longer served as well as we used to be in stores and restaurants. The relationship between people and those who provide them with services is deteriorating, and there is no chance of its return.[48]

In short the institutions which provide intimacy in our culture have atrophied and their replacements—the supermarket, dial-a-prayer, and the television set—are the accoutrements of the lonely crowd. Yet the human need for closeness persists and intimacy-sponsoring endeavors like the T-group have multiplied at a near astronomical rate in the past few years. As the future comes upon us, a periodic social immersion—a rehumanization station (God forbid)—may become a necessity if we are to survive the relentless dehumanizing march of a socially blind scientific technology.

Modern man is personally as well as socially alienated; he is separated from his own self and gropes for some sense of personal identity. The modeling process by which children establish their personal and sexual identity has been disrupted. The broken homes, the confused role of the mother-homemaker-career woman, the father whose occupation is invisible or incomprehensible to the child, the television teaching machine, the absent extended kinship, all contribute to the identity confusion. The current generation is the first in the history of the world which has nothing to learn from grandparents; in fact, the pace of change is such that children can scarcely learn from peers five years older. One can, in passing, only muse about the effects on the unused identificatory figures. What does it mean to the father who is unable to extend himself into the future through his son?*

Increased literacy, education, mass media, leisure time have made modern man, patient and nonpatient alike, more aware of a discrepancy between his values and his behavior. Many enlightened individuals who consider their chief life values to be humanitarian, esthetic, egalitarian, or intellectual find that, under self-scrutiny, they pay only lip service to these and instead base their

---

*Has the rapidity of change precluded the type of relationship that the Odysseus of Kazantzakis experienced with Telemacus?

He who has borne a son dies not; the father turned,
and his sea-battered vagrant heart swelled up with pride.
Good seemed to him his young son's neck, his chest and sides,
the swift articulation of his joints, his royal veins
that from tall temples down to lithesome ankles throbbed.
Like a horse-buyer, with swift glances he enclosed
with joy his son's well-planted and keen-bladed form.
"It's I who stand before my own discarded husk,
my lips unshaven, my heart still covered with soft down,
all my calamities still buds, my wars, carnations,
and my far journeys still faint flutterings on my brow."[49]

behavior on the values of aggrandizement: the "philistine triumvirate"[50] of material wealth, prestige, and power. The awareness of this discrepancy may result in a pervasive anxiety, self-abrogation, and sense of emptiness which often beget a harried attempt to avoid reflection by compulsive working and hobbying.

Another discrepancy is experienced between work and one's sense of creativity; the great majority of individuals rarely experience a sense of pride, completion, or effectiveness in their work. The gap between the worker and the finished product, originally a blight of the industrial revolution, continues to widen as the technological maelstrom whirls man into an anonymous automation. These developments result in a growing sense of personal inadequacy. Although the individual may obtain some sense of pride from the achievements of his megagroup, generally the individual's sense of personal worth is inversely proportional to the size and power of the megamachine, to use Mumford's term,[51] in which he is ensconced.

Although any of these concerns may be more important to one group member than another, each is likely to have some real meaning to all, be they labeled patient, student, delegate, trainer, or therapist. All these factors, then, indicate that there is an enormous overlap between T-groups and therapy groups. Both types of groups have similar goals, similar views of man, rely on similar change or curative factors, have similar ground rules (here-and-now, inter- and intrapersonal honesty, feedback, admitting weaknesses and uncertainty, establishing mutual trust, understanding and analyzing behavior) and similar shared concerns. Obviously groups with so many shared properties will and must go through comparable processes.

The groups are so similar that practically any T-group meeting may be mistaken for a therapy group meeting, and yet the total course of the two types of groups may be distinguished from one another. There are, I believe, some fundamental differences between the therapy and the T-group.

Therapy Groups and T-Groups—Differences

I must take a few explicatory points before discussing these differences. First we must note that many of these issues are generalizations and need to be qualified. The nature of the T-group or the therapy group depends upon the goals and techniques of the leader. Certain trainers and therapists, particularly those who straddle both fields, may lead their groups in such similar fashion that differences between the two are blurred, whereas others operate so differently that even the unpracticed observer can readily enumerate fundamental differences. In other words, the differences *within* both the T-group field and the therapy group field may be greater than the differences *between* the two fields. Secondly there are both extrinsic and intrinsic differences. Extrinsic or procedural differences are expendable and arise from the different customs, settings, and traditions of the two fields from which the two types of groups originated and are not valuable indicators in understanding underlying principles of the groups. Intrinsic differences, on the other hand, are core differences and arise from the vital differences in the goals and composition of the two types of groups. Even here, however, we must acknowledge the overlap; many trainers and group therapists will contest the distinctions which I shall make.

Extrinsic Differences

Setting. The T-group differs from the therapy group in size, duration, and physical setting. Generally it consists of twelve to sixteen members who may be total strangers or who may be associates at work. Often the T-group meets as part of a larger residential human relations laboratory lasting one to two weeks. The T-group, in this setting, usually meets in two- to three-hour sessions once or twice a day. The members usually spend the entire day with one another and the T-group atmosphere spills over into other activities. Often T-groups meet like therapy groups, in shorter sessions spaced over a longer period of time. Almost always, however, the T-group's life spans a shorter period of time.

Unlike the therapy group, the T-group's ethos is one of informality and pleasure. The physical surroundings are often resort-like, and more consideration is given to the pursuit of fun. Laughter is heard more often in the T-group. The leader may often tell jokes to explicate certain issues in the group. Many leaders of the newer encounter groups emphasize that it is important to them that the group members have a good time. Not only does the group have more fun during the meetings, but it devotes more attention to the role fun occupies in the lives of each of the members. To the reasonably well-integrated T-group member, the ability to play and to enjoy the leisure his affluence has brought him is an issue of considerable import. To the more survival-oriented psychiatric patient, fun occupies a less pressing, more distant position in his hierarchy of needs.

Role of the Leader. Generally there is a far greater gap between the leader and the members in a therapy group than in a T-group. This is a result both of the leader's behavior and the characteristics of the members. Although the T-group members may, as we have mentioned, overvalue the leader, generally they tend to see him more realistically than do psychiatric patients. T-group members, due in part to their greater self-esteem and also due to a greater opportunity to socialize between meetings with the leader, perceive the leader to be similar to themselves, except insofar as he has superior skill and knowledge in a specialized area. Whatever prestige he enjoys in the group the trainer earns as a result of his contributions. Eventually he begins to participate in a similar manner to the other members and in time assumes full membership in the group although his technical expertise continues to be appreciated and employed.

Part of the trainer's task is to transmit not only his knowledge but also his skills; he expects his group members to learn methods of diagnosing and resolving interpersonal problems. Often he explicitly behaves as a teacher; for example, he may, as an aside, explicate some point of theory and may introduce some group exercise, verbal or nonverbal, as an experiment for the group to study. It is not unusual for T-group members to seek further human relations education and subsequently to become trainers. (Occasionally this has had some unfortunate repercussions resulting in excesses since some members, without the necessary skills, and background, have considered one or two experiences as a group member sufficient training to launch them on new careers as group leaders.)

Group therapists are viewed far more unrealistically by their group members. (See Chapter 5.) In part the therapist's deliberately enigmatic and mystifying behavior generates this distortion. He has entirely different roles of conduct from the other members in the group; he is rarely transparent or self-disclosing and too often reveals only his professional front. It is a rare therapist who socializes or even drinks coffee with his group members. In part, however, the distortion resides within the patients and springs from their hope for an omniscient figure who will intercede in their behalf. They do not view the therapist merely as an individual similar to themselves aside from his specialized professional skills; for better or for worse they attribute to him the archetypal abilities and powers of the healer. Often the group members and the therapist conspire together then to define his role: the leader often chooses, for technical reasons, to be perceived unrealistically, and the group members, for survival reasons, do not allow his real personage to emerge. Although, as the group proceeds, the therapist's role may change so that he behaves more like a member, he never becomes a full group member: he almost never presents his personal problems in living to the group; his statements and actions continue to be perceived as powerful and sagacious regardless of their content. Furthermore, the therapist is not concerned with teaching his skills to the group members; it is a rare instance for a therapy group member to use his group experience to launch himself on a career as a group therapist.

Intrinsic Differences

Beyond the Common Social Malady. Most of the fundamental differences between T-groups and therapy groups derive from the difference in composition. Although overlapping may occur, the T-group is generally composed of well-functioning individuals who seek greater competence and growth, whereas the therapy group has a population of individuals who often cannot cope with

Groups: Orientations and Structures

minor everyday stress without discomfort; the latter seek relief from anxiety, depression, or from a sterile and ungratifying intra- and interpersonal existence. We have described a common social malady that to a greater or lesser degree affects all individuals. However, and this is a point often overlooked by clinically untrained T-group leaders, psychiatric patients have, in addition, a set of far deeper concerns. The common social malady is woven into the fabric of their personality but is not synonymous with their psychopathology.

To illustrate, consider the concept of self-alienation—one of the common results of the "culture game" described above. Horney's formulations, to use one of several available personality constructs, also postulates an alienation from the self as a core problem of many individuals. (She defines neurosis as a "disturbance in one's relationship to self and to others.")[38] However, whereas the "culture game" concept describes self-alienation as a commonplace phenomenon emanating from the facade-wearing ritual of the adult world, Horney describes self-alienation as a defensive maneuver occurring early in the individual's life as a response to basic anxiety stemming from severe disharmonies in the parent-child relationship. The child is faced with the problem of dealing with parents too wrapped up in their own neurotic conflicts to conceive of him and treat him as a separate individual with his own needs and potential. As a survival mechanism the child diverts his energies, which would ordinarily be devoted to the task of actualization of his real self, to the construction and realization of an idealized self—a self the individual feels he should and ought to become for the sake of survival. Horney then proceeds to delineate a complex development of the individual in terms of the relationship between his ideal self, his potential self, and his actual self (the person he perceives himself to be), but this need not concern us now. *The important point is that this split occurs early in life and profoundly influences all aspects of subsequent development.* The individual attempts, all his life, to shape himself in the form of the idealized (and unattainable) self, develops a far-reaching pride system based on idealized characteristics, blots out opposing trends in himself, experiences self-hatred when the discrepancy between the idealized and actual selves seems particularly great, and evolves a pervasive network of claims on the environment and restrictive demands on himself. In light of the far-reaching consequences of these developments on the neurotic person, it would seem that little benefit could accrue from a brief human relations training group, such as a twelve-hour (six two-hour meetings) course recently advertised in the newspaper,[52] which was entitled "The Courage to be Real" and which planned to ". . . deal with such problems as telling the difference between phoniness and reality in one's self and in others . . ."

To return to the central issue, the fact that patients and nonpatients alike share many common concerns should not obscure the point that patients have, in addition, a far deeper basis for their alienation and dysphoria.

Orientation to Learning. The basic task of the T-group—the acquisition of interpersonal competence—requires a degree of interpersonal skill which most psychiatric patients do not possess. T-group trainers ordinarily make certain assumptions about their group members: they must be able to send and receive communications about their own and other members' behavior with a minimum of distortion; they must, if they are to convey accurate information and be receptive about themselves, have a relatively high degree of self-awareness and self-acceptance. Furthermore, participants must desire interpersonal change. They must be well intentioned and constructive in their relationship to the other members and must believe in a fundamental constructive attitude on the part of the others if a cohesive, mutually trusting group is to form. The members must be willing, after receiving feedback, to question previous cherished beliefs about themselves (unfreezing) and be willing to experiment with new attitudes and behavior, which may replace older, less successful modes of behavior.

The participants must then transfer these modes of behavior beyond the group situation to interpersonal situations in their "back-home" life. Generalized adjunctive learning is also necessary; for example, Argyris[53] notes:

. . . if the individual learns to express his feelings of anger or love more openly, he may also have to develop new competence in dealing with individuals who are threatened with such openness. It is important, therefore, for the individual to learn how to express these feelings in such a way that he minimizes the probability that his behavior will cause someone else to become defensive, thereby creating a potentially threatening environment.

These intra- and interpersonal prerequisites which trainers take for granted in their group members are the very attributes sorely deficient in the typical psychiatric patient, who generally has lower levels of self-esteem and self-awareness. The stated group goals of increased interpersonal competence are often perceived as incompatible with their personal goals of relief from suffering. Their initial response to others is often based on distrust rather than trust and, most important of all, their ability to question their belief system and to risk new forms of behavior is severely impaired. In fact, the inability to learn from new experience is central to the basic problem of the neurotic. To illustrate with a classic example, consider Anna Freud's study of Patrick, who during the London blitz in 1943, was separated from his parents and developed an obsessive-compulsive neurosis. In the evacuation center he stood alone in a corner and chanted continuously, "Mother will come and put on my overcoat and my leggings, she will zip my zipper, she will put on my pixie hat," etc.[54] Consequently Patrick, unlike the other children, could not avail himself of the learning opportunities in the center. He remained isolated from the other adults and children and formed no other relationships which could have relieved his fear and permitted him to continue his growth and the development of his social skills. The frozen compulsive behavior did provide some solace for Patrick by preventing panic but so tied up his energy that he could not appraise the situation and take new, adaptive action.

Not only does the neurotic defense preclude reality testing and resolution of the core conflict, but it characteristically generalizes to include an ever-widening sphere of the individual's life space. Generalization may occur directly or indirectly. It may operate directly, as in traumatic or war neuroses in which the feared situation takes an increasingly broader definition. For example, a phobia once confined to a specific form of moving vehicle may generalize so as to apply to all forms of transportation. Indirectly the individual suffers since, as with little Patrick, the inhibition prevents him from exploring his physical and interpersonal environment and developing his potential. A vicious circle arises since maladaptive interpersonal techniques beget further stress and may preclude the formation of gratifying relationships.

The important point is that the individual with neurotic defenses is frozen into a closed position; he is not open for learning, he is generally searching not for growth but for safety. Argyris[53] puts it nicely when he differentiates a "survival orientation" from a "competence orientation." The more an individual is competence-oriented the more receptive and flexible he is. He becomes an "open system" and in the interpersonal area is able to use his experience to develop greater interpersonal competence. On the other hand, an individual may be more concerned with protecting himself in order to survive. Through the use of defense mechanisms he withdraws, distorts, or attacks the environment.

This, in turn, begins to make the individual more closed and less subject to influence. The more closed the individual becomes, the more his adaptive reactions will be controlled by his internal system. But since his internal system is composed of many defense mechanisms, the behavior will not tend to be functional or economical. The behavior may eventually become compulsive, repetitive, inwardly stimulated, and observably dysfunctional. The individual becomes more of a "closed" system.[53]

The survival-oriented individual does not give or accept accurate feedback; if left to his own devices he will generate those kinds of experiences which will strengthen his defensive position. He may, for example, be particularly attentive to feedback that confirms the rationality of his having to be closed. Similarly the feedback he gives to others may be highly colored by his survival orientation: he may be far more concerned with engendering in others certain attitudes toward himself than with giving accurate feedback.

Individuals are neither all open or all closed, they may be closed in specific areas and open in others; nor, as we have stated, are all therapy group members more closed than all T-group members. There is little data bearing on this point and one must be cautious about overgeneralization. Consider for a moment the vast scope and diversity of the group therapies; it is possible, for example, that the affluent members of an analytic group in Manhattan may be as integrated and congruent as the members of an average T-group. The label of "patient" is often a purely arbitrary one which is a consequence of the request for help, not of the need for help. (It is possible that once the therapist has labeled an individual as a patient he initiates a self-fulfilling prophecy: by expecting, and unwittingly reinforcing, patient-like behavior he elicits closed rather than open behavior.) Generally, however, the therapy group is composed of individuals with a survival rather than a competence orientation and who therefore cannot readily take advantage of the interpersonal learning opportunities of the group. Therapy group members cannot easily follow the simple T-group mandate to be open, honest, and trusting when they are experiencing profound feelings of suspicion, fear, distrust, anger, and self-hatred. A great deal of work must be done to overcome these maladaptive interpersonal stances so that patients can begin to participate constructively in the group. Jerome Frank came close to the heart of the matter when he said that "therapy groups are as much or more concerned with helping patients to unlearn old patterns as they are with helping them to learn new ones."[6] Accordingly in therapy groups the task of interpersonal competence acquisition goes hand in hand with (and sometimes straggles far behind) the task of removing maladaptive defenses.

Differences Early and Late. Thus there are two intrinsic differences between T-groups and therapy groups, both emanating from the composition and goals of the group. First, therapy group members are in a greatly different state of readiness to learn. Secondly, although they share many aspects of a common social malady with T-group members, they nevertheless have deep highly personalized splits within themselves explicable only on the basis of each one's developmental history. Each member must be helped to understand the form, the irrationality, and the maladaptive implications of his behavior. This type of exploration can only occur once a highly cohesive, mutually trusting group with highly therapeutic norms has been formed. In one sense this work begins at a point where many T-groups end. The improved interpersonal sensitivity and communication which may be the goal of the T-group is a means to an end for the intensive therapy group. Frank, while acknowledging he was overstating the point for purposes of explication, noted, "The therapy group reaches maximal usefulness at the point where the T-group ceases to be useful."[6]

The therapy group, then, differs from the T-group early and late. It differs early by beginning more painfully and laboriously. T-group members may begin a group with trepidation; they face an unknown situation in which they will be asked to expose themselves and to take risks. Nevertheless, they are generally backed up by a relatively high self-esteem level and a reservoir of professional and interpersonal success. Psychiatric patients, on the other hand, begin a

Groups: Orientations and Structures

therapy group with dread and suspicion. Self-disclosure is infinitely more threatening in the face of a belief in one's basic worthlessness and badness. The pace is slower; the group must deal with one vexing interpersonal problem after another. The T-group after all does not often have to face the problem of an angry paranoid patient, or a suicidal depressive one, or a denying patient who attributes all his difficulties in living to his spouse, or a fragile borderline schizophrenic individual, or the easily discouraged members who constantly threaten to leave the group. The therapist, unlike the trainer, must constantly modulate the amount of confrontation, self-disclosure, and tension the group can tolerate.

The therapy group differs later by having a different termination point for each member. Unlike the T-group which invariably ends as a unit and generally at a predetermined time, the therapy group continues for each member until his goals have been reached. In fact, as Frank points out, one reason that the therapy group is so threatening is that its task, "broad personal modification," has scarcely any limit and furthermore there is no restriction as to what can, and perhaps must, be discussed.[6] Often in a T-group it is enough for the group to recognize and to surmount a problem area; not so in the therapy group in which problem areas must be explored in depth for each of the members involved.

For example in a twelve-session T-group of mental health professionals which I recently led, the members (who were also my students) experienced great difficulty in their relationship to me. They felt frightened and inhibited by me, vied for my attention, addressed a preponderance of their comments to me, overvalued the wisdom of my remarks, and harbored unrealistic expectations of me. I responded to this issue by helping the group members recognize their behavior,* their distortions, and unrealistic expectations. I then helped them appreciate the effects of their unrealistic and dependent attitudes toward me on the course of the group and called their attention to the implications of this phenomenon on their future role as group therapists. Next we discussed some of the members' feelings toward the more dependent members of the group: for example, how it felt to have someone ostensibly talk to you but at the same time fix his gaze on the leader. Once these tasks were accomplished, I felt that it was important that the group move past this block and proceed to focus on other facets of the group experience, for it was abundantly clear that the group could spend all of its remaining sessions attempting to resolve fully its struggle with the issue of leadership and authority. One way in which the leader can facilitate this process is to be reality-oriented and transparent in his presentation of self. I shared with the group my feelings of uncertainty and anxiety and my response to being feared and overvaluated; I discussed the issue of my double

---

*During the height of this phase I scheduled a leaderless meeting in order to allow the group to sample the sense of liberation and disinhibition which occurred without me. This helped the group to be quite clear that it was my presence, rather than some other factor, which was oppressive.

role, that of teacher-evaluator and of T-group leader, and helped them distinguish the real from the irrational. For example, many members felt that they must conceal their feelings of inadequacy or confusion from me lest I "grade" them unfavorably and thus influence their future careers. I pointed out to them that not only was my administrative power overestimated but that, given my own still vivid and still present struggle with similar feelings, and my belief in the value of self-exploration and self-understanding, it was unthinkable for me to behave as a critical judge. I helped to focus the group's attention on other current but untouched group issues—for example, their feelings about three silent and seemingly uninvolved members, the hierarchy of dominance in the group, and the general issue of intermember competition and competence, always a specter looming large in T-groups of mental health workers.

In a therapy group the leader would approach the same issue in a different fashion with different objectives in mind. He would encourage the patients especially conflicted in this area to discuss in depth their feelings and fantasies toward him. Rather than consider ways in which to help the group move on, he would help plunge them into the issue so that each member might understand his overt behavior toward him, as well as his avoided behavior and the fantasied calamitous effects of such behavior. Although he would, by a degree of transparency, assist the members in their reality testing, he would attempt to modulate the timing of this behavior so as to allow the formation and full exploration of their feelings toward him. (See Chapter 5 for a detailed discussion of this issue.) The goal of clarifying other facets of group dynamics is, of course, irrelevant for the therapy group; the only reason for changing the focus of the group is that the current issue is no longer the most fertile one for the therapeutic work: either the group has pursued the areas as far as possible at that time or some other more immediate issue has arisen in the group.

To summarize, the basic intrinsic difference between T-groups and therapy groups arises from the differences in composition (and thereby the goals) of the groups. As a general rule psychiatric patients have different goals, more deeply disrupted intra- and interpersonal relations, and a different (closed, survival-based) orientation to learning. These factors result in a number of process and procedural differences both in the early stages and in the late working-through stages of the group.

References

1. "Sensitivity Training," *Congressional Record—House,* June 10, 1969, pp. H4666-H4679.

2. C. Rogers, "Interpersonal Relationships: Year 2000," *J. Appl. Behav. Sci.,* 4: 265-280, 1968.

3. *Int. J. Group Psychother.,* 17: 419-505, 1967.

4. L. Horwitz, "Transference in Training Groups and Therapy Groups," *Int. J. Group Psychother.*, *14*: 202-213, 1964.

5. S. Kaplan, "Therapy Groups and Training Groups: Similarities and Differences," *Int. J. Group Psychother.*, *17*: 473-504, 1967.

6. J. Frank, "Training and Therapy," in L. P. Bradford, J. R. Gibb, and K. D. Benne, (eds.), *T-Group Theory and Laboratory Method; Innovation in Education* (New York: John Wiley and Sons, 1964).

7. E. H. Schein and W. G. Bennis, *Personal and Organizational Change Through Group Methods: The Laboratory Approach* (New York: John Wiley and Sons, 1965), pp. 329-334.

8. H. Coffey, personal communication, 1967.

9. A. Bavelas, personal communication, 1967.

10. A. Marrow, "Events Leading to the Establishment of the National Training Laboratories," *J. Appl. Behav. Sci., 3*: 144-150, 1967.

11. L. P. Bradford, "Biography of an Institution," *J. Appl. Behav. Sci., 3*: 127-144, 1967.

12. K. Benne, "History of the T-Group in the Laboratory Setting," in Bradford, Gibb, and Benne, *op. cit.,* pp. 80-135.

13. K. Lewin, R. Lippit, and R. K. White, "Patterns of Aggressive Behavior in Experimentally Created Social Climates," *J. Soc. Psychol.,* 10: 271-299, 1939.

14. K. Lewin, "Forces Behind Food Habits and Methods of Change," *Bull. Nat. Res. Council., 108*: 35-65, 1943.

15. D. Stock, "A Survey of Research on T-Groups," in Bradford, Gibb, and Benne, *op. cit.,* pp. 395-441.

16. R. R. Blake and J. S. Mouton, "Reactions to Intergroup Competition Under Win-Lose Conditions," *Management Science, 7*: 420-435, 1961.

17. Schein and Bennis, *op. cit.,* p. 41.

18. *Ibid.,* p. 43.

19. A. Camus, cited in *ibid.,* p. 46.

20. J. Luft, *Group Processes: An Introduction to Group Dynamics* (Palo Alto, Calif.: National Press, 1966).

21. I. R. Wechsler, F. Messarik, and R. Tannenbaum, "The Self in Process: A Sensitivity Training Emphasis," in I. R. Wechsler and E. H. Schein (eds.), *Issues in Training* (Washington, D.C.: National Education Association, National Training Laboratories, 1962), pp. 33-46.

22. M. Rosenbaum and M. Berger (eds.), *Group Psychotherapy and Group Function* (New York: Basic Books, 1963).

23. A. L. Kadis, J. D. Krasner, and C. Winick, *A Practicum of Group Psychotherapy* (New York: Harper and Row, 1963).

24. H. Mullan and M. Rosenbaum, *Group Psychotherapy; Theory and Practice* (New York: Free Press of Glencoe, 1962).

25. Rosenbaum and Berger, *op. cit.*, p. 5.

26. E. W. Lazell, "The Group Treatment of Dementia Praecox," *Psychoanal. Rev. 8*: 168-179, 1921.

27. L. C. Marsh, "Group Therapy and the Psychiatric Clinic," *J. Nerv. Ment. Dis., 32*: 381-392, 1935.

28. L. Wender, "Current Trends in Group Psychotherapy," *Am. J. Psychother., 3*: 381-404, 1951.

29. T. Burrows, "The Group Method of Analysis," *Psychoanal. Rev., 19*: 168-180, 1927.

30. P. Schilder, "Results and Problems of Group Psychotherapy in Severe Neurosis," *Ment. Hyg., 23*: 87-98, 1939.

31. S. Slavson, "Group Therapy," *Ment. Hyg., 24*: 36-49, 1940.

32. J. L. Moreno, *Who Shall Survive?* (New York: Beacon House, 1953).

33. L. Bradford, in *Human Relations Training News, Vol. 1*, No. 1 (May 1967).

34. L. Horwitz, "Training Groups for Psychiatric Residents," *Int. J. Group Psychother., 17*: 421-435, 1967.

35. R. Morton, "The Patient Training Laboratory: An Adaptation of the Instrumented Training Laboratory," in Schein and Bennis, *op. cit.*, pp. 114-152.

36. I. Hendrick, "Instinct and the Ego During Infancy," *Psychoanal. Quart., 11*: 33-58, 1952.

37. D. E. Berlyne, "The Present Status of Research on Exploratory and Related Behavior," *J. Indiv. Psychol., 14*: 121-126, 1958.

38. K. Horney, *Neurosis and Human Growth: The Struggle Toward Self-Realization* (New York: W. W. Norton, 1950).

39. R. White, "Motivation Reconsidered," *Psychol. Rev., 66*: 297-333, 1959.

40. H. Hartmann, "Notes on the Psychoanalytic Theory of the Ego," *Psychoanal. Stud. Child, 5*: 74-95, 1950.

41. A. Angyal, *Foundations for a Science of Personality* (New York: Commonwealth Fund, 1941).

42. K. Goldstein, *Human Nature in Light of Psychopathology* (Cambridge, Mass.: Harvard University Press, 1940).

43. D. A. Hamburg and J. Adams, "A Perspective on Coping Behavior: Seeking and Utilizing Information in Major Transitions," *Arch. Gen. Psychiat., 17*: 277-284, 1967.

44. D. Bunker, "The Effect of Laboratory Education Upon Individual Behavior," in Schein and Bennis, *op. cit.*, pp. 257-267.

45. A. Stanton and M. S. Schwartz, *The Mental Hospital* (New York: Basic Books, 1954).

46. C. Rogers, personal communication, 1967.

47. J. D. Rockefeller, "In Praise of Young Revolutionaries," *Saturday Review of Literature, 51*: 18-20, 1968.

48. D. Wilbur, *Palo Alto Times*, October 24, 1968.

49. N. Kazantzakis, *The Odyssey: A Modern Sequel* (New York: Simon and Schuster, 1958), Book One, 1. 135-145, p. 6. © 1958 by Simon & Schuster, Inc.

50. I. Sarnoff, *Society with Tears* (New York: Citadel Press, 1966), p. 17.

51. L. Mumford, *The Myth of the Machine: Techniques and Human Development* (New York: Harcourt, Brace and World, 1967).

52. *Palo Alto Times*, October 12, 1968.

53. C. Argyris, "Conditions for Competence Acquisition and Therapy," *J. Appl. Behav. Sci., 4*: 147-179, 1968.

54. A. Freud and D. Burlingham, *War and Children* (New York: Medical War Books, 1943), pp. 99-104.

Editor's Comment. As Yalom suggests, therapy groups and encounter groups differ principally in their composition. Another way of describing the difference he notes is suggested by Maslow (1968) and Egan (1970). The therapy group focuses principally on the D-needs or the D-concerns of its members. D-needs (for "deficiency") arise when a person is deprived of basic psychological satisfactions such as the need for safety, for belonging, for intimacy, for respect, for recognition, and for competence. The principal focus of the encounter group, however, is on the M-concerns (for "maintenance") and the B-needs (for "being") of the participants. B-needs refer to what humanistic psychologists call "self-actualization" needs, which concern the development of one's human potentialities. M-concerns center about the energies involved in preserving the *status quo* in all areas of human living. Most of us invest too much of our energy in merely keeping the enterprise "afloat." It is not that D-concerns do not come up in the encounter group, nor is it that the members of therapy groups are in no way interested in or capable of B-functions; rather, D-needs are ordinarily so primitive, primary, and compelling that they obscure other concerns. The encounter group whose members are mired down exclusively in D-concerns should probably be called a therapy group. Still, we should not forget Bugental and Tannenbaum's complaint (noted in the Introduction) that even supposedly highly self-actualized group participants tend to deal excessively with the negative and the pathologic within themselves.

Therapy groups are not only problem-centered rather than growth-centered, but they are usually concerned with there-and-then problems.

Let me illustrate what I mean. One evening a girl in an encounter group said, when challenged on her poor participation: "Some really terrible things happened to me over the weekend." There were two ways for her to handle the confrontation: (1) to investigate the dynamics of her weekend or (2) to assess the impact of the weekend on her participation in the group. She herself chose the second, for she said a bit later: "I came into the group quite vulnerable, and what you said to me a little while ago, Dick, really crushed me." She chose to deal with the weekend insofar as it was affecting her that night in the group; that is, she chose to deal with it in a way that was appropriate to an encounter group rather than a counseling session. Counseling and therapy groups would be more effective, I think, if the interactions in such groups were more similar to the here-and-now interactions that typify encounter groups.

Personal Encounter in Higher Education

Sumner B. Morris
Jack C. Pflugrath
John R. Emery

Editor's Introduction. A teacher once told me that it is unfair to force students to come together in a classroom situation unless something takes place there that either could not or would not take place outside the classroom. Unfortunately, he often violated this principle in serious ways in his own classes. The use of the encounter group in education, as described in the following article by Morris and his associates, is a positive example of how to put this principle into effect.

Most of us, including the teacher mentioned above, have been the victims of "parallel" education. We have learned—for better or for worse—sitting next to our fellow classmates without ever really involving ourselves with them; consequently, we have been robbed of one of the greatest educational resources available—deeper contact with one another. Many teachers are beginning to use this resource in a great variety of situations in and out of the classroom ranging from elementary school through college. Morris and his associates describe a college course (Psychology 33: Personal and Social Adjustment) in which the encounter group was the principal focus.

Educational institutions, like most institutions, are conservative by their very nature. Educators are loathe to concede that experience-based courses such as the one described here are as authentically educational as content-based courses; thus, the use of encounter-like experiences in educational settings is bound to meet with strong resistance. The kind of research described in the present article will do much to dispel the fears associated with change. The authors describe some of the "classic" exercises currently being used in a wide variety of encounter groups. The results of their experiment indicate a student body come alive in deeply human ways.

The undergraduate course in the psychology of personal and social development at the University of California at Davis recently underwent some methodological changes. The changes were the addition of weekly encounter groups to traditional lecture during the fall and winter quarter and the substitution of the encounter groups for lectures during the spring quarter.

Reprinted from *Personnel and Guidance Journal*, 1969, 47, 1001-1007, ©American Personnel and Guidance Association. Used by permission of the publisher and the authors.

Students found that the addition of the encounter groups to the lecture increased their involvement in the course and made it a much more meaningful and relevant experience when compared with other college courses already taken. Students in the class where the encounter groups took the place of the lecture not only found their experience more meaningful and relevant when compared with the traditional lecture class but also scored as well as the lecture class on an identical final exam.

At a time when higher education is coming under increasingly critical attack for its "soul-less," technology-oriented, depersonalized ways (Billington, 1968; Goodman, 1962; Katz, 1968; Maslow, 1964; Sanford, 1967), it behooves us to reassess carefully and, if necessary, to reformulate our relationships with students and the experiences we offer them.

Many colleges and universities offer an undergraduate course in the psychology of personal and social development. The purview of this course is usually a kind of "understanding-yourself-and-others" psychology. Our own course at the University of California at Davis has recently undergone some marked methodological changes which we feel have contributed to a more meaningful and vital experience for our students.

The purpose of this paper is to describe what is happening in our class and to share feedback from the students involved. We are particularly pleased with some tentative outcomes because we believe they reflect an excitement and involvement not usually found in established college courses.

Method

At the University of California, Davis, the Psychology 33: Personal and Social Adjustment class offers four quarter units of academic credit and meets four times a week for the 10-week quarter. It is taught by the staff of the counseling center with 100-120 students usually enrolled. Traditionally, it has been a lecture course with an assignment to write a case study with the student himself as the subject. Some attempts were made to hold discussion groups once a week on course-related topics, but the discussions, while occasionally animated, seemed dominated by a few of the more verbal students. This dissatisfaction with less-than-optimum student involvement in a course that was to concern itself directly with their lives led to the approach described below.

In the fall and winter quarters of 1967-68, the Psychology 33 class was organized along traditional lines regarding the case study requirement, text and reference reading, and examinations. However, lectures were given at only two of the four class periods each week, with students spending the remaining two class hours in encounter or sensitivity-training groups (Rogers, 1967; Schutz, 1967). For this purpose the class was divided into groups of approximately 10 students, and staff members of the counseling center served as facilitators or leaders of the groups. One two-hour session each week was the modal treatment for the encounter groups with each group exposed to at least 20 hours of encounter-group activity.

The experience was structured as follows in an outline distributed to students at the beginning of the class:

The main focus of Psychology 33 will be small group experience. You will meet with a group of 8 to 10 fellow students once a week for approximately two hours (the time may vary somewhat between groups) in a kind of interpersonal laboratory in which personal encounter and sensitivity to self and others will be emphasized. This experience will provide an opportunity to bring down the conceptual and abstract (the content of the course) to a more personally relevant and meaningful level. The purpose is to stimulate self-examination and -awareness through the experience of listening and being listened to and receiving feedback about "how you come across to others." The emphasis is on growth and development.

The facilitators or leaders sought to establish something other than the typical class discussion. Since the course dealt with personal growth and understanding, the facilitators sought to create a group experience where students would use their senses more completely and effectively (listening, seeing, touching, etc.), be more aware of their inner selves (physical, as well as cognitive and affective), share with others what they were experiencing, and be more receptive to honest feedback from others. The idea was to establish a group climate that would permit students freedom to be themselves by experiencing all the variety and intensity of their feelings.

In the encounter groups students discussed personal issues such as what they wanted from the University, what was going on in their life at the present time, what they would like to change about themselves, their anxieties and fears, "here-and-now" feelings, and their reactions and impressions of other group members. In general, the issues dealt with were intended to stimulate an examination of their life, an interaction with others in their group, and a feeling of mutual trust.

Facilitators used group techniques that were both verbal and non-verbal. As the meetings progressed, the facilitators usually became a part of the group so that the responsibility for initiating various exercises and activities was increasingly shared. Non-verbal activities included such things as asking students to hold hands in two lines and simply hold eye contact with the person opposite them for approximately 30 seconds before moving to the next person and repeating the same thing. The idea here was to develop in the participants the trait of seeing another person and eliminating the usual verbal exchanges and cues (and defenses?)—with a resulting emphasis on seeing and observing while being in a physical "community" (holding hands) with others.

Body awareness exercises were structured wherein each person lightly slaps (or is slapped by another student) his arms, head, or back. Other non-verbal activities included, in encounter-group jargon, the "trust fall," "blind walk," and "cradling." "Indian wrestling" or simply pushing vigorously against the hands of a partner are other examples. The goal of this exercise is to increase the use of senses other than those commonly relied upon, to develop a feeling of trust with others, and to develop physical contact with others as a facilitator of communication. It was discovered that non-verbal exercises were an excellent way of up-ending usual classroom expectations (Shaw, 1955) by providing "official" sanction for new and different ways of interacting.

Various verbal exercises were interspersed with non-verbal ones. As an example, two-person dyads were organized with each person taking about three minutes to find out, as best he could, what the other student was like as a person. This task culminated in each student's introducing or presenting his "partner" of the dyad to the rest of the group. Also, students in the initial meetings were asked to give their general "first impressions" of each student in his group as he stood (or sat) directly in front of the student. Eye contact and directness between students were encouraged. Some students found this difficult and a good many superficialities were expressed, but more direct and real communication between students tended to follow this experience.

A micro-lab technique was used wherein students broke into groups ranging from three to five persons and talked for five minutes about the here-and-now and their present feelings. They then came together in the larger group and discussed what had transpired. This was usually repeated a second time. It seemed easier for more reticent students to express themselves and talk about real concerns in the smaller groups.

The "in-group—out-group" discussion model seemed especially effective for the application of certain issues from their reading and the lectures. The group was divided into two groups, and each student chose a student in the opposite group as a "counselor." One group became the in-group and was given a topic to discuss, with each counselor in the out-group observing his "client." Dealing with one's aggressive feelings and handling fears were examples of some of the structural tasks. After about 15 minutes, the discussion of the in-group terminated, and the pairs of students (counselor and client) privately discussed the experience. The student in the out-group was told to listen not only to what his partner said but to how he said it and to look for other cues as to how he functioned in the group. Frequently the role a student plays in the group is significant, that is, indicative of whether he is aggressive, defensive, passive, domineering, reflective, etc. After the interaction of the pairs, the process was reversed with the students in the observer or counselor roles becoming the in-group. It was felt that the listening skills of students developed further with this exercise in addition to the deepening of their relationships.

Various fantasy techniques were also used: for instance, "Close your eyes and imagine that you are climbing a mountain." Another is "Close your eyes and imagine that the rest of the group is coming toward you. What happens?" After the fantasy, each member of the group was invited to share his experience and discuss it with the group. Heavy interpretations were discouraged. The emphasis was on what this meant to each person phenomenologically, with some promptings and suggestions from the group. Who the person climbed the mountain with, how he went about it, what the view was, and which mountain he chose frequently provided rich material for group discussion and individual self-awareness. In one group, a student relating his fall into a crevasse with no one to help him get out, provided some significant cues to his feelings of alienation.

Evaluation

To assess student reaction to the course, questionnaires were completed by the students at the end of the fall and winter quarters. The following items comprised the questionnaire:

1. Compared to other college courses you've had, how would you compare this course on the following:
   (a) your degree of involvement in this course—Much more involved/More involved/Equally involved/Less involved/Much less involved
   (b) the relevance of this course to your life at the present time as a college student—Much more relevant/More relevant/Equally relevant/Less relevant/Much less relevant
   (c) the relevance of this course to your future life experience—Much more relevant/More relevant/Equally relevant/Less relevant/Much less relevant
   (d) your overall satisfaction with the course—Much more satisfied/More satisfied/Equally satisfied/Less satisfied/Much less satisfied
2. What part of the course was most satisfying to you? Lecture/Reading/Encounter group/Case study
3. What part of the course was least satisfying to you? Lecture/Reading/Encounter group/Case study
4. Do you think the encounter groups were Very worthwhile/Worthwhile/OK/Not worthwhile/Useless
   Any comments?

Further evaluation of changes in class methodology was obtained during the spring quarter of the same school year. Approximately 200 students had registered to take the course during spring quarter as compared with 71 students who had taken it during the fall quarter. (Apparently, word had gotten around. Many students told us that friends had suggested they take the class because of the encounter-group experience.) Since the Counseling Center staff felt it could handle only 120 students, it was decided to divide the course into two sections and to take "experimental advantage" of the situation. Thus, students were randomly assigned to either Section A or to Section B. Final tabulation showed 126 students assigned to Section A, and 51 students assigned to Section B.

Section A used the encounter group method described previously. However, rather than meeting for formal lectures as in the previous two quarters, the class met only once a week for organizational purposes and for informal discussion of matters of the students' own choosing, e.g., what was happening in the groups, personal experiences, etc. The idea behind this change from the previous quarters was to measure student performance on the informational part of the course (as measured by the final exam), given the condition of no formal lectures. The question here was, simply, Are lectures necessary at all in a course of this type? Attendance for the class meetings in Section A was voluntary, and the instructor intentionally avoided lectures. Section B was the traditional four-lectures-per-week course (without encounter groups) similar to that taught in previous years. It should be noted that previous student evaluation of the course (lecture only) had been generally favorable and that the instructor for Section B was an experienced teacher with a reputation for being a warm and helpful person.

At the beginning of the spring quarter, students in both sections were told that the final examination would cover the entire text. Students in Section A were informed that the encounter-group experience would be the main focus of the course and that there would be no lectures on the content of the text. For both Sections A and B, the final examination and case study each constituted one third of the final grade for the course. The other one third of the grade was determined by attendance in the encounter group in Section A and a midterm examination in Section B. Students from both sections were subsequently compared on their performance on an identical final examination comprised of objective test items taken from the instructor's manual of the text used.

Following the procedure used during the previous two quarters, the students were again asked to evaluate the course at the end of the spring quarter. The same questionnaire was given students in both Sections A and B asking them to compare the course with other college courses already taken as to (a) their degree of involvement, (b) the relevance of the course to their present life, (c) the relevance of the course to their future life experience, and (d) their overall satisfaction with the course. Responses were indicated on a five-point Likert Scale, e.g., from "much more relevant" to "much less relevant," and were assigned values from one to five so that a "total satisfaction" score was obtained for each student. Values were assigned to each response so that a lower score indicated a greater total satisfaction with the course. Comparison of student response between Section A and Section B was obtained.

Groups: Orientations and Structures

Results

Ninety percent (N=156) of the students enrolled in the class during the fall and winter quarters of the 1967-68 academic year returned completed anonymous evaluation sheets at the end of each quarter. Total enrollment in the class (N=173) consisted of 41 percent males and 59 percent females. Distribution by classes was 11 percent freshmen, 69 percent sophomores, 14 percent juniors, and 6 percent seniors.

Results (see Table 1) showed an overwhelmingly favorable response from the students to the first question. Eighty-seven percent of the students felt a greater degree of involvement with the class when compared with other college courses already taken. Fifty-two percent of these students said they were "much more involved."

Ninety-three percent of the students felt this course was more relevant to their lives as a student at the present time when compared with other college courses already taken. Fifty-nine percent of these students said the course was "much more relevant."

Table 1

Student Ratings of the Fall and Winter Quarter Course
Compared to Other College Courses Already Taken

Percentage of Student Responses (N=156)								
10	20	30	40	50	60	70	80	90

Degree of Involvement

Response	Bar extends to
Much More Involved	~52%
More Involved	~35%
Equally Involved	~13%
Less Involved	~7%
Much Less Involved	~7%

Relevance to Life at Present

Response	Bar extends to
Much More Relevant	~59%
More Relevant	~34%
Equally Relevant	~7%
Less Relevant	~5%
Much Less Relevant	~7%

Relevance to Future Life Experience

Response	Bar extends to
Much More Relevant	~34%
More Relevant	~48%
Equally Relevant	~13%
Less Relevant	~7%
Much Less Relevant	~5%

Table 1 (Continued)

Percentage of Student Responses (N=156)								
10	20	30	40	50	60	70	80	90

Overall Satisfaction with Course

	Much More Satisfied
	More Satisfied
	Equally Satisfied
Less Satisfied	
Much Less Satisfied	

Percentage of Student Responses (N=156)								
10	20	30	40	50	60	70	80	90

In addition, 85 percent of the students felt this course was more relevant to their future life experience when compared with other college courses already taken.

Also, 73 percent of the students were "much more satisfied" or "more satisfied" in their overall satisfaction with the course when compared with other college courses already taken.

Table 2 pinpoints student likes and dislikes about the course, showing that 74 percent of the students chose the encounter group as being most satisfying. In addition, it was found that 90 percent of the students considered the encounter groups to be "very worthwhile" or "worthwhile."

It was also discovered that 89 percent of the students found the traditional lecture and reading to be the least satisfying part of the course.

Table 3 compares the questionnaire evaluations and the final exam grades of students from the two sections in the spring quarter. As discussed previously, a lower score on the evaluation sheet indicates a greater total satisfaction with the course. Total possible score for the exam was 79.

Results show that students in the encounter section evaluated the course as being significantly more relevant and satisfying to them, as well as feeling themselves more involved with the course. It was also shown that there was no significant difference between either group in their performance on the final exam.

Implications

It is interesting to note the unpopularity of the more traditional learning methods used in college courses—notably lecturing and reading—in the presence of the encounter group. The encounter group assumes even more importance when it is shown that the instructor had been rated as an enthusiastic, interested, and well-prepared lecturer in past student evaluations.

Table 2

Other Student Ratings of Course During Fall and Winter Quarters

Percentage of Student Responses (N=156)								
10	20	30	40	50	60	70	80	90

Most Satisfying Part of Course

Lecture
Reading
Encounter Groups
Case Study

Rating of Encounter Groups

Very Worthwhile
Worthwhile
OK
Not Worthwhile
Useless

Least Satisfying Part of Course

Lecture
Reading
Encounter Group
Case Study

Percentage of Student Responses (N=156)								
10	20	30	40	50	60	70	80	90

Table 3

Comparison of Questionnaire Evaluations and Final Exam Grades
of Students in the Spring Quarter

		Mean	SD	z
Evaluation ("total satisfaction" score) Final exam grades	Section A (Encounter, N = 90)	8.23	3.15	
				8.28*
	Section B (Lecture, N = 37)	13.86	3.62	
	Section A (Encounter, N = 126)	56.73	7.14	
				0.87
	Section B (Lecture, N = 51)	55.75	6.63	

*Significant beyond the .001 level.

One possible limitation of the study is that it is not appropriate to ask a class composed of 80 percent freshmen and sophomores to compare the relevance and amount of involvement in this class with other college courses since most of them have taken only the basic freshman courses (e.g., English, history, mathematics, chemistry). Yet, it is somewhat of a sad commentary on higher education at present if one must wait until the second year of college to take a relevant course and become involved in it.

As a result of our exciting experiences over the past year, many more questions have been raised than have been answered.

The preliminary results indicate that a personal and social development course in higher education can be a more relevant and personalized experience for many college students. More specifically, the use of encounter groups in these courses can lead toward better and more meaningful feelings on the part of both students and the instructor, while at the same time maintaining a high level of transmission of knowledge.

The following are examples of many of the questions that have been raised:

1. Can encounter groups be incorporated successfully into other courses in the curriculum (e.g., sociology, anthropology, English, and mathematics)?

2. Can student-faculty relationships be improved through the use of encounter groups? What will the long-term effects of such relationships mean for higher education?

3. Can parents be included in these groups? What is the learning value of weekend retreat groups?

4. What types of students and professors aren't ready for encounter groups? What better methods are there than encounter groups?

5. How effective is the traditional lecture? Can it be replaced by a different, more personalized experience?

6. Just how do the students change who have been through the encounter groups? Can we specify different goals for different courses?

All of these areas are ripe for investigation and many of them are already being examined here on the Davis campus. Certainly more hard data need to be collected before any certain conclusions can be drawn. It is the hope of the authors that reporting of the preliminary research in this area will encourage others to search still further.

References

Billington, J. H. In U.S. universities 'the humanistic heartbeat has failed.' *Life*, 1968, 64, 32–35.

Goodman, P. *Compulsory mis-education and the community of scholars.* New York: Vintage, 1962.

Katz, J. *No time for youth.* San Francisco: Jossey-Bass, 1968.

Maslow, A. H. *Religions, values, and peak-experiences.* Columbus: Ohio State University Press, 1964.

Rogers, C. R. The process of the basic encounter group. In J. F. T. Bugental (Ed.), *Challenges of humanistic psychology.* New York: McGraw-Hill, 1967.

Sanford, N. *Where colleges fail.* San Francisco: Jossey-Bass, 1967.

Schutz, W. *Joy.* New York: Grove Press, 1967.

Shaw, F. J. Mutuality and up-ending expectancies in counseling. *Journal of Counseling Psychology,* 1955, *2,* 241-247.

Editor's Comment. Obviously, this course—personal and social adjustment—lends itself admirably to the use of the encounter group. However, some teachers, I am sure, see the emphasis on the encounter group here as anti-intellectual. Other teachers would deny this, seeing such an approach as transfusing lifeblood into the dying body of unimaginative higher education. Still others might be worried about certain ethical questions. For instance, even though such a course might be an elective, should a student be "forced" into an encounter-group situation if he does want to take such a course? Or should there not be two tracks, one providing group experience and one not? Questions such as these become easier to answer when the use of the encounter group is considered in the context of what takes place in the entire curriculum. For instance, consider the question of force. Students have been "forced" to follow stultifying curricula for years, and even today many of us are surprised and shocked at the harvest of rebellion we are reaping. In another context, is it evil to "force" a student taking a required speech course to get up several times a semester to speak before his peers and be videotaped even though he experiences great anxiety in doing so? That kind of "force" has been accepted by students and faculty alike. What is needed in such courses is the opportunity for the students to sit around and discuss the anxieties associated with the course so that they might deal with them more effectively. Certainly curricula should allow greater freedom for students, but is an educational system that urges its students to humanize themselves more fully by becoming involved with one another in both intellectual and affective ways infringing on the rights and freedom of its students?

Some of the exercises suggested for the course described by Morris and his associates involve some kind of physical contact. We live in a society in which many people fear physical contact, not because it is sexual, but because it leads to deeper psychological contact. This fear of intimacy is, it would seem, a kind of bondage in itself. Education should be a liberating experience, but what does an educational system do with those participants who do not want to be free?

Laboratory training in general and the encounter group in particular are not the "saviors" of education, but their judicious incorporation into a variety of educational enterprises cannot help but add a new dimension of vitality to a system desperately in need of vitality. Indeed, if educational institutions refuse to renew themselves from within in ways analogous to those suggested by Morris and his associates, their future seems bleak.

Interacting With Others:
Face to Face in a Small Group

J. W. Keltner

Editor's Introduction. The first three articles have dealt directly with encounter groups. Keltner's does not; rather, it explores the dynamics that are common to many different kinds of small, face-to-face groups, including encounter groups. One of the primary goals of the participants in any encounter group is to mold themselves into a cohesive community that supports the kinds of personal and interpersonal behavior that lead to human growth. In presenting a clear picture of the structure and inner workings of face-to-face groups, Keltner provides encounter-group participants with principles by which they can evaluate both the group process itself and their individual participation in this process. Each individual participant must learn to listen effectively to everyone else in the group. But each must also learn to "listen" to the group itself, that is, to become aware of what is happening in the group. Who is speaking to whom, and who is not speaking to whom? What is the mood or tone of the group (spontaneous or lifeless, etc.)? What kinds of interaction predominate (for instance, self-disclosure or confrontation)? Is leadership in the group diffused, or not? If the participants can learn to listen to the group itself and to process what is taking place in the group, then they can do much to make the dynamics discussed by Keltner work for them instead of against them.

In this chapter we are concerned with activities similar to what is often called group discussion. However, our frame of reference for dealing with speech-communication in small groups includes a wider range of interpersonal behaviors than most people think of when they refer to group discussion.

We will examine the differences between aggregations and groups. We will examine the differences between being alone in a crowd and being a member of a group. We will identify some of the key groups to which most of us belong.

A vital requirement for participating in small-group discussion is a sensitivity to our own and others' behavior in groups. We will explore some of the dimensions of this sensitivity.

From *Interpersonal Speech-Communication* by J. W. Keltner, ©1970 by Wadsworth Publishing Company, Inc., Belmont, California 94002. Reprinted by permission of the publisher.

As individuals we each face several problems upon entering a group. The problems of belonging, involvement, control, role, identity, and affection will be explored.

Any group has problems. We will look at some of the problems of identity, structure, norms, work, emotional factors, decision-making, leadership, problem-solving, argument, and group maintenance.

The basic social unit is an individual. You and I, alone and separate from each other, represent two isolated social units. In isolation from each other we do not exist as a group. If, however, some bond of communication should develop between us, the beginning of a group would have taken place.

What Makes a Group?

Aggregations and Congregations

George C. Homans describes the human group as "a number of persons who communicate with one another often over a span of time, and who are few enough so that each person is able to communicate with all the others, not at secondhand, through other people, but face-to-face. . . . A chance meeting of casual acquaintances does not count as a group for us."[1]

The collection of people at a football game is not a group in the sense that we will use the term here. This aggregation of people does not fit Homans' definition in that its members cannot communicate with all the others firsthand. Likewise, the congregation in a church may not be a group unless it is quite small. We shall refer to congregations and aggregations as collections of persons (individuals) without the necessary properties to be identified as a small group.

One Alone in a Crowd

No human infant could survive without other people, and no member of Homo sapiens develops into a *human* being unless he experiences interactions with human beings. Each of us has identity in relation to mankind. An infant cut off from human interaction may develop physically, but he may not become fully human. Helen Keller, for example, lost contact with humanity when she became deaf, dumb, and blind at age two. When Anne Sullivan became her teacher five years later, the child was physically healthy but no more than a little animal—not even a little savage. There are individuals afflicted from infancy with pathological disorders (physical and psychological) that isolate them from

[1] George C. Homans, *The Human Group* (New York: Harcourt, Brace & World, 1950), p. 1.

humanity, and these survive only with direct and constant human help. A fully formed adult human being can survive apart from humanity, and many—as hermits, prisoners in solitary confinement, and "lone wolves"—have done so. But they have been formed, however well or however badly, as human beings in the context of groups before they withdraw or are withdrawn from human society. By and large, we have survived and flourished as a species because man is a social animal and lives a group life; as a social unit the individual is rarely isolated from other people.

An isolate is a person who assumes a particular relationship to the groups to which he has belonged or now belongs, and his situation is defined with reference to the group from which he is isolated. Georg Simmel has discussed this problem of isolation:

> Isolation thus is a relation which is lodged within an individual but which exists between him and a certain group or group life in general. But it is sociologically significant in still another way: it may also be an interruption or periodic occurrence in a given relationship between two or more persons. As such it is especially important in those relations whose very nature is the denial of isolation. . . . It is clear that isolation is not limited to the individual and is not the mere negation of association.[2]

Freedom and Isolation

Freedom is not necessarily isolation nor is it achieved by isolation. Indeed, freedom may be restricted by isolation; that is, the freedom to develop relationships with other people in a particular group may be abridged by an isolation from that group. Conversely, *the freedom of an individual to act is a factor of his relationship with the other persons in a given group.*

Being alone, then, does not constitute isolation, for the spatial fact of aloneness does not necessarily destroy the communication bonds. Alone in my hotel room hundreds of miles from home, I may be writing to my family or talking by telephone to my secretary in my office. On the other hand, I can leave that hotel room to walk the streets of a strange city, jostled by strangers and physically near hundreds of people, and I can feel very much alone and isolated from that aggregation or from groups within the aggregation.

It is necessary that we be concerned with our functions within groups in order to increase our freedom to act and to choose the lines of action we may wish to take. The interaction within the group in the face-to-face relationship involves a most frequent and total use of the communication processes of speech.

---

[2] Kurt H. Wolff, ed. and trans., *The Sociology of Georg Simmel* (New York: Free Press, 1950), pp. 119-120.

Two or More Interacting Relevantly

When we establish the interaction bonds with another person, a group has formed. The nature of the interaction, which is determined by the two persons who become parties to its existence, exists because it is relevant to both. This relevant relationship suggests several properties of the interaction.

First, for any group of two or more, there is some joint focus of interest and of attention on a common problem or situation. It is most difficult to determine, sometimes, which comes first, the problem which causes common concern or the common concern that sees the problem.

A second property of this relationship is the behavioral claim of each member of the group relative to every other member. This claim is most readily perceived in the dyad (two-person group), because as two persons interact, each develops an expectation of how the other will act and react. Soon this expectation becomes a highly dependable property of the relationship and can be identified as a claim that one person has on the other's behavior. For example, if two persons work together on a project each soon becomes accustomed to the manner of the other in handling problems, using language, responding to different kinds of suggestions and interruptions. Thus, you could expect me to respond with accepting behavior when you would suggest that we take a lunch break. Each therefore has a claim on the other's behavior in that he can expect certain responses to events in the interaction. The presence of this claim is essential to the existence of a group.

Third, the establishment of the communicative bonds among the members of the group is one of the significant factors that transforms a collection of individuals into a group.

The Context of Small Groups

Actually, most of our social interaction is within the context of small groups. Charles H. Cooley refers to primary groups, which "are primary in the sense that they give the individual his earliest and completest experience of social unity."[3] The most obvious primary group is the family. Within the family group are found the more or less permanent relationships out of which more elaborate and complex affiliations develop as we move to other group memberships.[4]

From this home base of the family group, we join with other groups of varying significance to our social behavior. From the time each of us starts playing with other children—for most of us, at preschool age—peer groups, composed of friends and colleagues, are ubiquitous in our lives. In peer groups of children much social interaction takes place. As we grow older, we become involved with

[3] Charles H. Cooley, *Social Organization* (New York: Charles Scribner's Sons, 1909), p. 17.
[4] Cooley, p. 18.

other peer groups; such as the work group or the groups in which we perform in order to sustain our physical, psychological, and intellectual existence.

At one time or another, most of us belong to groups that have specific tasks to perform. The decorations committee for the homecoming dance has a specific task; a dormitory bull session on United States military policy has no such task. The discussion may have direction, but it is casually achieved by the group and is not imposed from the outside nor is it specifically and purposefully determined beforehand.

The distinction between a casual discussion group and a task group lies in the difference between goals of the two types of interactions. The particular goal and objective of the task group usually involves some anticipated action. The casual group has no such specific task but may have a more generalized goal that does not reach specifically beyond the meeting itself. In each group the essence of the interaction among persons in the face-to-face situation is the communication process.

The Individual in the Group

Effective interaction within a group requires that a person be sensitive to his own behavior and effects as well as responsive to the behavior and effects of others. There has been much work in recent years on the processes and condition of sensitivity to other individuals and to groups, including sensitivity training, which is aimed at aiding people to become more aware of themselves in relation to others and to the group. This training ranges from sensitivity awareness in self to group-process sensitivity. At one end, the emphasis is on developing awareness of the self and, at the other end, on developing awareness of the self and the group process. Such training has been variously effective, depending upon the skill and insights of the training staffs; but it has had no small impact upon individuals and organizations.[5] Reports on training programs indicate that there are at least two sectors of sensitivity development: the individual and the group. One must develop a sensitivity to himself in relation to others in the group, and he must also be aware of the problems and issues confronting the group as a group.

Problems of Individuals

Each member of a group confronts several problems upon his encounter with the group. These problems are belonging, involvement, desire to lead, role, identity, and affection. These problems are not always obvious and are often

[5] Mary Ann Coghill, *Sensitivity Training* (Ithaca: New York State School of Industrial and Labor Relations, Cornell University, 1967).

Groups: Orientations and Structures

unresolved. Many times the problems exist and are solved by individuals almost on the unconscious level of perception.

Belonging. One of the first issues that each of us as an individual faces upon entering a group has to do with the desire to belong to the group. Either before we encounter the group, immediately after we become involved with it, or at some later time in our relationship, we inevitably must deal with the question "Do I want to belong to this group?" In the family group we obviously do not have much choice, at least in the early years of life. The matter of choice is also restricted somewhat in vocational settings. But even in both of these, there are times when the issue of belonging is critical.

The resolution of the issue depends on the degree to which our perception of our needs and their fulfillment can be associated with the group as a way of meeting those needs. We seldom voluntarily join groups wherein we are not likely to receive any satisfaction of our own personal needs as we see them.

There are degrees of belonging, ranging from minimal to total involvement. At one end of the scale is the kind of belonging that is represented by simply having our names on the membership roll with nothing else involved. At the other end of the scale would be that kind of belonging wherin total time and energy are dedicated to the work of the group. Most of our group memberships fall somewhere between these two extremes.

Each of us has connections of greater or lesser degree with numerous groups. Beginning with the family group, the system of group affiliations spreads over the whole spectrum of our lives. When we anticipate affiliations with another group, the issue of wanting to belong arises. Sooner or later, each of us must make the decision about belonging to a group and about the degree to which we wish to become involved.

Involvement. Belonging does not necessarily imply involvement. As we noted above, one stage of belonging may consist of merely having our names on the membership list. Involvement has to do with the degree to which we are willing to commit ourselves to the deliberations, the performances, and the outcome of the group association.

The matter of involvement is critical for all of us as we take part in group life. At the one end of the scale is token involvement, which calls for the least amount of work or activity necessary to be considered party to the group decisions. At the other end of the scale, we are deeply committed and are party to every act, deliberation, and decision that the group makes. The issue is the degree of involvement acceptable to us.

Many of us shy away from joining organizations, saying that we just don't have the time. Essentially what we may be saying is that we do not wish to get involved. If a group has enough attraction for a person, he will find ways to become involved with it.

The issue of involvement arouses our concern for our own individuality. Some of us fear that too much involvement in any given group might smother us as individuals. Also, many of us feel that we do not want to be too closely associated with others for fear that we will lose our objectivity and our identity.

Decisions about involvement with the task and the people of a group are not always made consciously, and the decision point may be met several times. A person may at first be withdrawn or rather cold in his relationships with the other group members. Over time, this relationship may change, usually by degrees, and he becomes much more closely affiliated with the group task and with the members of the group.

Desire to lead or control. To what degree are we willing to assume leadership responsibilities in a group? Some of us have a strong desire to be leaders and to feel our influence spread over others; others tend to avoid leadership because of the burden of responsibility perceived as associated with the leadership of a group. Likewise, some of us may be leaders in other groups and have no desire to become involved at this level in a particular group. In any event, we are sooner or later faced with making a decision on this matter. The struggle over deciding this issue may run deep into our intrapersonal problems.

Function or role in the group. A further individual issue has to do with the role or roles that we will take in the group. In a sense, leadership is part of this problem, but we have separated it here because it presents a particular problem to each of us.

Abraham Zaleznik and David Moment have described role performance:

Role performances are the attributes that group members "know" about each other, the ways by which they characterize each other. These attributes become a force that provides the group with a basis for stable, predictable social and interpersonal relations on the one hand, and constrains members to behave consistently with others' knowledge and expectations of them on the other hand, sometimes at the expense of learning and development.

Role performance describes the individual's interaction with other individuals, the psychological conditions within him as he interacts, and his effects on other members before, during and after the interaction.[6]

The problem of roles incorporates what the other members of the group see and hear and what they feel about us, what we actually do, the things that the other members of the group do in response to what we do, and what we are attempting to accomplish with our particular performance. Our perception of

---

[6]Abraham Zaleznik and David Moment, *The Dynamics of Interpersonal Behavior* (New York: John Wiley & Sons, 1964), p. 181.

what we are doing may not be consistent with the perceptions of the others, and the incongruence of these perceptions causes difficulty in the process of group operation.

The nature of the role we take in a group is determined by many factors. Among them are the pressures of the other members of the group for us to behave in a certain way, our own desires to perform in a certain way, our own abilities to perform, the nature of the situation, and pressures from outside the group for us to perform in certain ways.

Difficulties often arise when other members of a group seem to want (put pressure on) a person to perform certain functions when he wants to perform others. This conflict causes serious disruption in the group efficiency. In order to deal with it, we must first recognize its presence. In order to be aware of its presence, we need that sensitivity to what is going on in a group, which will allow us to perceive what others are expecting of us and what we are expecting of ourselves.

Once we have recognized the existence of conflicting role pressures, we should then attempt to reduce the incongruence. We may cope with the incongruence by direct confrontation with the group about the differences or by adjusting our own behavior or by developing defense systems that will protect us from the attack of the other group members when we do not fulfill their expectations. Resolution of the role issue is best done through an interaction with all members of the group and through direct and perspective communication with and among all members of the group.

Identity. In Chapter 3, we discussed self knowledge. It is significant that for each of us the self revealed in one group may not be the same self that is revealed in another group. Our identity in our own eyes may differ from the identity perceived by others. This question of identity is closely related to role functions, which are based on a person's perception of himself, that is, on his perception of his identity.

William C. Schutz related identity to the issue of inclusion.

An integral part of being recognized and paid attention to is that the individual be *identifiable* from other people. He must be known as a specific individual; he must have a *particular identity*. If he is not thus known, he cannot truly be attended to or have interest paid to him. The extreme of this identification is that he be understood. To be understood implies that someone is interested enough in him to find out his particular characteristics. Again, this need not mean that others have affection for him, or that they respect him. [Italics added.] [7]

[7]William C. Schutz, *The Interpersonal Underworld* (Palo Alto, Calif.: Science and Behavior Books, 1966), pp. 21-22.

All of us are concerned with the kind of identity we have in the eyes of our colleagues. Upon coming into a new group, we often attempt to establish some characteristic identity that will enable others to separate us from the rest of the group. One of the principal issues which we must resolve for ourselves as we become involved in group situations is the identity that we will assume as members of a group.

Affection. Still another issue that an individual must resolve as he enters into a group interaction has to do with personal emotional feelings that he has for other individuals in the group. Schutz says that affection is based on emotional relationships between two persons (dyad). In the group situation, affection usually does not develop until the issues of inclusion, belonging, and control have been resolved for a person. The positive affection relationship is inferred in such terms as "friendship," "like," "love," "personal," "sweetheart," and "lover." The negative affection relationship is inferred in such terms as "enemy," "hate," "distant," and "dislike."

Schutz suggests that the development of affection is usually the last phase in the development of an interpersonal relationship. Thus, after people have encountered each other, have decided to become involved in joint interaction, and have confronted each other as to the nature of their relationship, then if they wish to continue the bond there must develop ties of affection where the essential behavior and thought involves embracing the other either literally or figuratively or both.[8]

The issue of affection has to do with the degree to which any of us will permit the development of this relationship as concomitant with our membership in a group.

One who has experienced too little affection for the best emotional development may tend outwardly to "stand off," to cling to an emotional distance and want others to do the same. Inwardly or unconsciously, however, he may be seeking a satisfactory affection bond. His fear of the closeness may stem from perceived personal rejection somewhere in his early experience. He perceives himself as being unlovable and is thus protecting himself from being further rejected. Sometimes a person with too little experience with affection seeks to be friendly with everyone, but on a superficial level, thus avoiding a personal confrontation with any one person. The resulting behavior is identified as *underpersonal.*

The same anxiety about acceptance can result in a different kind of overt behavior described as *overpersonal.* In this case, the person is trying to compensate for early failure in affection relationships. His behavior, then, seeks to get others to treat him on a highly personal affectional level. He seeks overtly for approval, is ingratiating and intimate. Unconsciously, however, he may be very

---

[8]Schutz, pp. 23ff.; see also William C. Schutz, *Joy: Expanding Human Awareness* (New York: Grove Press, 1967).

possessive, seeking to gather in friends and absorb them completely, punishing them if they attempt to relate to anyone else.

Those who have resolved the affection problem seem to have no difficulty with close emotional relationships with others. They can accept and deal with either closeness or distance. While it is important to have affection, this person can accept the lack of affection as a problem between him and the others. In other words, he feels secure in his knowledge that he is capable of loving and that there are things about him which can, in turn, be loved.

Sensitivity to group processes. A sensitivity to the problems of belonging, involvement, control, role behavior, identity, and affection is highly important for effective group membership. Thus, if we desire to become effective participants in the small-group processes, we should seek to become aware of and responsive to these problems that each person faces as he becomes a member of a group. Achievement of this awareness is not simple. Through the sensitivity type of speech-communication training many of these insights can be developed. A perception of and insight into the meanings of our own and others' behavior are keys to understanding many of the issues that each of us faces in the group experience.

We should also realize that each group develops its own particular standards and behavior norms. Certain jargon and word usages become particularly meaningful to the members of a given group. To understand the factors that are working in a group, much feedback is essential for each person in that group. Through this feedback we can increase our ability to observe the effects of our own behavior as well as that of others.

In order to understand some of the control and leadership issues, we need to understand the power structure of the group. We need to know where the status power exists and where the action power exists. We need to know who are the figureheads and who are the workers. We need to know who are those who influence the group behavior the most.

The mechanical processes of group discussion must also be understood by the individual. Each group has its own particular system of getting work done. What will work in one group may not work in another. One group may depend a great deal on a parliamentary procedure while another group hardly ever uses that system. One group may require formal speeches and another group may consider such communication taboo.

Problems of the Group

While each of us encounters a number of problems as we move into face-to-face interaction in group settings, the group also has problems, which are similar to the problems of the individuals in the group but are of a different genre.

Identity. What is the purpose and function of the group? What is the reason for its existence? What are the conditions under which this group exists? The answers to these questions help a group to identify itself. The members need to feel that the situation under which the group exists is clearly defined. To accomplish this definition there must be a common understanding of the attitudes of the members toward the group, the environment in which the group exists, the task of the group, the method of working that is unique to this group, and the nature and significance of the symbols of communication that are used.

Structure. No group exists without some kind of structure, which involves the leadership and influence system, the networks of communication, the patterns of roles, the subgroups, and the patterns of affection that exist among members of the group. In essence, the group structure has to do with the patterns of interaction among the members of the group, which represent the activity of the group.

The structure of a group begins to develop as the life of the group begins. The nature of structural factors and the manner in which they are developed raise critical problems that the group must face.

Standards. Each group develops a set of behavior and belief standards for its members. These standards are sometimes explicit and are expressed in the form of rules of behavior or conduct. At other times, they remain implied and are expressed by the actual behavior patterns of the group members.

Daniel Katz and Robert L. Kahn have identified the nature of group norms:

Norms refer to the expected behavior sanctions by the system and thus have a specific *ought* or *must* quality. . . .
Three criteria define system norms: (1) there must be beliefs about appropriate and required behavior for group members as group members, (2) there must be objective or statistical commonality of such beliefs; not every member of the group must hold the same idea, but a majority of active members should be in agreement, (3) there must be an awareness by individuals that there is group support for a given belief.[9]

Think of the various groups to which you belong. Identify the various norms of belief and behavior that exist for each of these groups. As you do so, you will discover that these norms appear to bind the group together and set standards of behavior for all who belong to these groups.

Management. In discussing the relation of the individual to a group, we referred to the issue of affection. Within a group, we need to develop a proper

---

[9]Daniel Katz and Robert L. Kahn, *The Social Psychology of Organization* (New York: John Wiley & Sons, 1966), p. 52.

balance of behavior that concentrates on the affective relationships between persons and the actual work or task functions that must be performed. A group with all work-centered behavior can hardly exist as a group for very long. On the other hand, a group that allows itself to become involved in wholly affective behavior will soon burn itself out with emotion. The establishment of an equilibrium and maintenance of this balance is an important function of any group.

This problem of balance between work and affection is dramatically demonstrated in our classrooms. When the class is so completely task centered that the personal feelings and individual problems are left unattended, the coherence and effectiveness of the experience will tend to be less effective than when there is opportunity for interpersonal interaction of class members with each other and with the teacher.

A task group may also be off balance in the other direction. Too much affective personal social activity can result in loss of task effectiveness, low morale, and general breakdown in the interpersonal support for the member.

Task-Group Processes

A small group with a specific task, which task is perceived to some degree by its membership, has a number of speech-communication processes that are critical or vital to its total effectiveness in completing the task successfully. These processes involve decision-making, leadership, problem-solving, argument, and group maintenance.

Decision-Making

In Chapter 8 we talked of the process of making a decision and the differences between decision-making and problem-solving in the large sense. We identified decision-making as a process of making a commitment. This commitment usually establishes future action or attitudes.

In a group, there are a multitude of decisions to be made; that is, there are many actions to be taken that require a commitment on the part of someone. At the beginning of the meeting, for example, someone, usually the chairman, must make such decisions as which items should be discussed first. Decisions involving the processes of the group, the subject matter of the discussion, and the individuals in the group are constantly being made by the group members alone and in concert with one another.

Any one of us has some difficulty in making a decision; when several people are faced with the problem of reaching a decision jointly, the difficulty increases. The essence of group discussion skills is based on the ability to develop our skill in joint decision-making.

The selection of a chairman for a group involves a decision that follows considerable interaction among the members of the group before the individual decisions of the several members coincide with each other to the degree necessary to allow a choice to prevail. Each individual member of the group makes a decision. The group decision becomes a reality when a number of individual decisions coincide with each other. This is not to say that the decision of one person does not influence the decision of another person. Indeed it does. In fact, this influence process makes possible much decision-making in face-to-face groups.

In the course of a session involving individuals in face-to-face discussion, the spectrum of decisions that must be made is a wide one. Each individual faces a number of questions and, in answering them, must make decisions. When do I wish to speak? What am I going to say? What is the purpose of my contribution? How much participation do I wish to have? What things do I want the group to do? Whom do I want as chairman? When should we stop discussing? What topics are germane to our discussion? To whom will I listen? How shall I let myself appear to the rest of the group? What goals should the group seek?

The questions represent an incomplete sampling and they are not organized in any particular way, but they are representative of some of the actual decisions that people make while engaged in a discussion group. Notice that some of them concern relation with the group. Others have to do with the functions and processes of the group. Obviously, decisions must be made on the personal level and on the group level. As we participate in any face-to-face group situation, we should be aware of the fact that every member of that situation is involved in making such decisions almost constantly during the time of the interaction.

While each of us is involved in making decisions that affect our behavior in the group, we are also involved in the larger decision-making function of the group itself. Among the decisions that a group must make are those that involve the nature of the procedures the group will use. Shall we use a majority vote to indicate the group decision? Should we have a formal chairman? What kinds of rules of procedure shall we follow in order to get our work done? What time shall we adjourn? These are examples of issues around which decisions by the group must be made in order to deal with its task.

In addition to the process type of decisions, the task group must make ultimate decisions that involve the completion of the task it set out to perform. A student appeals committee must eventually make a decision concerning any given appeal that may be brought to its attention. The homecoming dance committee must make those decisions necessary for commitments leading to the actual production of the dance. The board of directors of a corporation must make those decisions involving the financing, personnel, policies, and operational effectiveness of the corporation.

Decisions are being made with at least three dimensions: the personal dimension, as each one of us commits himself to certain behaviors; the group-process dimension, as the group struggles to establish or change its procedure to deal with the task at hand; and the task dimension, which involves the fundamental decisions necessary to reach the avowed and determined goals of the group.

Group Decision-Making

While the personal dimension is pretty much contained within each of us, the process and the task dimensions are shared by others within the group. Here the decision-making becomes more complex and difficult. Several forms of decision-making are possible.

In this realm of process and task decisions, each group must make a decision as to what conditions are to be acceptable as representing the group's commitment. If it is sufficient that only a majority of the group be involved in a decision, the majority-vote system may as well be used. In a situation where the total human resources of the group must be brought into the fulfilling of the commitment made by the decision, the obvious method of greatest merit would be the true consensus. Usually the free rides, the authority, and the "twofer" type of decision-making are to be avoided in a group where the fullest interaction between members is desired.

Majority Vote. This mechanical means permits the group to arrive at a decision, even though there may be some individuals who are not in accord with the majority decision. As a decision-making method, it has the value of reducing the time necessary to get a decision when there are variances of opinion. Its weakness lies in that it always leaves some members uncommitted to the decision. Thus if a group needs to have the full assistance of its total membership, the majority vote by no means guarantees such cooperation. Supposedly, once a group has made a decision, everyone in the group feels committed to that decision and acts accordingly. This outcome is doubtful. If I am not committed to the decision made by the group, I cannot, in honesty to myself, throw my energies and effort into following through on that commitment as would someone who was, in the first place, in agreement. Thus the majority-vote method often results in an incomplete decision.

Consensus. When everyone in the group agrees to the decision, we may say that a consensus exists. Some groups operate on this basis. A very sensitive executive committee of a large institution makes no decisions without consensus. If an action is necessary and the group cannot achieve a total agreement, the decision must be deferred until the complete agreement necessary develops or until someone capitulates and casts his vote in harmony with the rest "just in order that we may get action." The strength of the consensus system derives from its provision of more complete support of any decision. The method is weak because it often causes individuals to capitulate quite against their will in order that the group may move forward with the tasks before it.

We should recognize the difference between a true consensus and a phony consensus. The true consensus exists when everyone in the group actually agrees on the decision. A phony consensus exists when some in the group capitulate just in order that the group can move on but against their own choice or commitment.

Authority. Decisions are often made by a single individual, then imposed upon the other members of the group by force, by the influence of a man's prestige, by persuasion, or by manipulation of the group so that the members believe that they have no decision-making responsibilities in regard to the commitment that is handed to them by the single individual. This latter method is one of the more subtle ways to destroy group decision-making and group morale.

Free Ride. Often we may not care one way or another, and when someone suggests a certain procedure or task, we ride along with it because we have no objection. This is different from the majority situation where the persons opposing an idea make clear their opposition by their vote. In this case, there is no opposition, but neither is there unequivocal approval. The member simply has no feeling of commitment one way or another.

Twofer. "Twofer" is derived from "two for (fer) an idea" and implies that they "steamroller" others. Two people may decide upon a procedure, a task, or any other kind of decision that may be made in a given setting. Assuming that the other members of the group will "naturally agree with them," they act as if the decision had been made by everyone. For instance, after a couple of hours of a staff-group discussion of a very difficult personnel problem, one of the members (not the chairman) of the group says, "I think we need a break"; a second member says, "That's right, we do"; and the two get up and start out. In such a situation, usually the others in the group follow suit even though they do not know exactly why they fell in with the decision.

Problem-Solving. In Chapter 8 on decision-making and problem-solving we discussed the structure or sequence of the problem-solving process. A problem consists of (1) a goal or goals, (2) obstacles or barriers to that goal, and (3) a point of encounter. The solving of a problem proceeds from the point of encounter to an understanding of the goals and obstacles, setting criteria for a solution, examination of possible solutions, selecting a solution, and carrying out the selected solution.

The application of the problem-solving system to a face-to-face group situation becomes more complex than dealing with problems on a personal level. The interpersonal and intrapersonal communication functions become much more involved because of the various perceptions that are present in the group. In a group, a number of goals may be represented by the people present. Even though a given task seems quite clear, the varying perceptions of that task may be different. In order for a group to accomplish its task it must select and define its goal so that a direction can be taken. In order to arrive at a joint goal for the group, the goals of the various members of the group must be merged, coordinated, or rejected. Decisions must be made concerning the actual goal that the group would seek to secure. So the very process of identifying the goal can become a subject of controversy and problem-solving. How so?

Let's describe the subproblem:

Goal. To define the goals of the group.

Obstacles. Wide variation of individual goals of the members of the group.

Point of Encounter. A group meeting of the committee in which each person revealed his idea of the objectives of the committee.

We can assume that whenever a group faces a situation in which a goal or goals are involved and there is necessity to overcome barriers to the accomplishment of these goals, the process of problem-solving comes into play. While most of us generally muddle through the problems we encounter, an orderly approach to dealing with problems may lead to more efficient and effective solutions and to more powerful decisions in support of those solutions.

In discussing a problem, a group can increase its effectiveness in dealing with the problem if several steps or decisions are developed in somewhat orderly fashion:

Step 1. Identify and define the goal or goals of the group. (This means finding or reaching agreement on what these actually are.)

Step 2. Identify and examine the cause of the obstacles to reaching the goals.

Step 3. Examine the nature of the point of encounter; that is, just where is the group in relation to reaching its objective?

Step 4. Establish criteria, or standards, for reaching a solution to the problem.

Step 5. Seek out and describe as many solutions as appear to have some usefulness in the situation.

Step 6. Evaluate each solution in terms of its potential for meeting the criteria set up in Step 4.

Step 7. Determine which of the *solutions* are most likely to accomplish the criteria and thus reach the goals. Then proceed to work out a group decision on the matter.

Simply listing a series of steps through which a group should go in solving a problem is certainly no guarantee that it can be done. Most groups seem to jump from one point to another in the steps and sometimes with some success. The critical factor is that if all the information involved in the various steps is developed by the group, a more effective decision can be made.

Naturally, some things seem logically antecedent to others. It would seem quite stupid, for example, to try to evaluate the potential of any solution for meeting criteria when the criteria themselves had not been agreed upon, yet this fault is quite common in group deliberations.

All too often, shortly after a problem has been identified in brief, everyone present begins to suggest solutions. Lengthy arguments usually follow on the merits and demerits of the ideas, but there are no common criteria by which to judge them. Generally, no decision can be reached until some criteria or standards are accepted, either consciously or unconsciously, by the group as a whole.

There is no magic by which a group can solve problems. When the members of the group have sufficient skill and ability in communicating with each other, the problem-solving process of the group can be more effective than when such skills do not exist. The critical process of working out joint solutions to problems involves much interaction and understanding.

Leadership

Communication is the essence of the process of leadership. In no setting is this more apparent than in the face-to-face interaction among people. Notice that I have referred to the "process of leadership." Rather than speak of "leaders" I prefer to use the term "leadership," when examining that particular phenomenon of influence.

Robert Tannenbaum and his colleagues have defined leadership:

Interpersonal influence, . . . through the communication process, toward the attainment of a specified goal or goals. Leadership always involves attempts on the part of a *leader* (influencer) to affect (influence) the behavior of a *follower* (influencee) or followers in a *situation.*[10]

Viewing leadership as an interaction process requires that we examine the larger context in which this process takes place. This view of leadership also establishes a new approach to the preparation of persons for leadership functions. Research on leadership generally shows that the process involves the

[10]Robert Tannenbaum, Irving R. Weschler, and Fred Massarik, *Leadership and Organization* (New York: McGraw-Hill Book Co., 1961), p. 24.

Groups: Orientations and Structures

personality of the individuals, the nature of the group, and the situation in which the group finds itself.

Murray G. Ross and Charles E. Hendry summarize the research in this way:

Leadership is not something that can be imported from the outside. Leadership is something that emerges, that grows, and that is achieved. It is not enough to have certain qualities of personality and performance that one associates with leadership. Nor is it enough to have experienced leadership acceptance in one or more groups in the past. Leadership is a function of the situation, the culture, context, and customs of a group or organization, quite as much as it is a function of personal attributes and group requirements.[11]

In the face-to-face group situation (often called discussion), the issue of leadership is often critical. The struggle for the prime center of influence on the others in the group is often serious and bitter, even though it may be partially unconscious.

A group needs various kinds of influences in order to accomplish its tasks. In any situation that involves a group of people, any number of things need to be done. Who does these things? Who takes care of the mechanical problems of seating arrangement, having the proper materials at hand, proper ventilation, and the like? Who takes care of seeing tnat all participants in a group get acquainted with each other? Who sees to it that the discussion gets off to a good start and that the minds of the members of the group are focused immediately on the problems and tasks of the group? Who keeps the group moving along toward its goal? Who provides fresh ideas, coordination of ideas, mediation between differences, and so forth? Is one person capable of doing all of these things? Obviously not. It requires an array of talents applied at the proper time and in the proper way to have the greatest impact on the group.

Likewise, what one group needs at a particular time may not be the same as what another group needs. For example, a professor, who served on an important all-university committee, was impressed by the efficiency and effectiveness of the group. Each meeting was convened on time by the chairman, who promptly called for the first report on the agenda. That report was followed by other items on the agenda, and discussions were fruitful. When he was named chairman of another faculty group, he expected it to function in like manner. To his dismay, it was impossible to start that group in the same way as the first. In fact, the second group rarely convened on time; and when the committee finally gathered, no one seemed willing to assist the chairman in moving things along. As chairman, he had to tell the group what it was going to do. This necessity distressed him because he felt that he was abridging the responsibilities of his committee members by so doing.

---

[11] Murray G. Ross and Charles E. Hendry, *New Understanding of Leadership* (New York: Association Press, 1957), p. 28.

The needs of a group change with time and place. At the beginning of a discussion, a group may need someone to spark the problem or to define the nature of the situation. Later on, as the discussion grows heated and strong, the group needs someone to calm it rather than to stimulate it.

Many groups have several kinds of roles that create the leadership structure. These roles are determined largely by the group needs. However, the structure of a formal organization may determine one kind of leadership role, such as the club president. It is significant, however, that the person who fills this kind of leadership role is not expected to perform all the necessary influencing actions that a group needs.

In a group, one person may have considerable influence because he is a specialist in the subject area being discussed by the group and is perceived by others in the group as knowing more than they know about the subject problem. His influence results from his preeminence in attainment. Usually one member of a group is designated by election, appointment, or acclaim as the person with formal authority for the official responsibility of the group. Several persons may emerge in given situations as capable of helping the group to determine goals, achieve objectives, and maintain the strength of the group. All these can exist in a group at the same time and all have influence on the group. Taken together, they form an influence system which we call leadership.

When we look at this leadership process we find several components of prime importance: (1) interpersonal influence, (2) situation, (3) communication, (4) goals, (5) individual skills, (6) characteristic behavior, and (7) functions of group leaders.

Interpersonal Influence. Every person has a potential influence over others in the group. No two persons have the same potential; that is, the company president may have a great deal more influence potential than does a branch manager in the same organization. However, if this potential is to become a reality, actual attempts must be made to influence the thinking and behavior of the group. In almost all interpersonal discussion situations, these influence efforts are made through the various forms of speech-communication.

A person who is aware of his own potential chooses to use (or not to use) this influence for many reasons. He may choose to use it as a means of enhancing his own prestige or as a means of assisting the group to arrive at decisions. His use of his own power is a decision which he voluntarily makes or which the group may force or entice him to make.

In Chapter 10 on persuasion, we discussed credibility of sources. Thus, a person's influence in a given group has a relation to his perceived credibility. Persons with perceived high credibility are likely to have greater interpersonal influence than those with low credibility.

However, the matter of influence also hinges somewhat on the affection patterns that exist within the group. Within a group there are usually smaller

Groups: Orientations and Structures

subgroups formed by interpersonal affections; these are sometimes called cliques. Usually persons within these groups are more subject to influence by their friends in the same subgroup than by those outside the subgroup with whom they have weaker affection bonds. Sometimes this set of subgroup affiliations can be more powerful than high credibility sources from outside the group.

Situation. No influence potential is universal; that is, what may be influence power in one group may not be influence power in another group. Likewise what may be influence power at one time or in one situation in a group setting may not be influence power at another time or in another situation. The nature of the situation contributes to the leadership of the group. This situation consists of the physical things that are around us, the other people in our group, the nature of our organization, the larger culture and its norms and stereotypes, the goals of the group, the goals of the individuals in the group, and the goals of the larger organization of which the group is a part either formally or informally. This situation is constantly changing; and as it changes, so does the leadership structure of the group.

Communication. The communication processes represent the sole avenues through which a leader can function. This is not to say that speech is the only communication process that is used, but it does represent the greater part of the communication of any leader-group situation.

The communication of a leader involves more than merely developing an accuracy of message transmission. It requires that the messages themselves have action and attitude effects on the members of the group. It requires, therefore, that the leader be highly sensitive to the other members of his group and to the kinds of things that will affect them most.

Several functions of communication are of particular importance for the development of effective leadership. Among these are listening, giving orders and directions, stimulating and developing action, asking questions, guiding the process, gate keeping, evaluating performance, summarizing, and initiating ideas.

Nonverbal factors also play a significant part in group leadership. The physical behavior of the more influential members affects the group action. An influential member who sits apart from the group, stares out the window, and slouches in his seat, can influence the whole tone and atmosphere of the setting. Likewise, apparel seems to have some effect. Obviously, clothing that offends the group norms will cause some diversion of the group from its task and direction.

Goals. The purposes and targets of a group also contribute to the nature of the leadership. Each group has a wide spectrum of goals, conscious and unconscious, that influence its behavior. The group may be part of a larger group, as in a church group, and the larger group's organizational objectives influence the activities of the smaller group. The group also has the particular goals that represent its tasks and objectives. There are also the goals of each member of the group, particularly those of the persons who are in the more influential positions.

These various goals affect the nature of the leadership. In other words, those persons whose behavior is likely to assist the group and the individual members to satisfy their goals are more likely to have influence over the group. Thus, as the goals change, so does the leadership change.

Individual skills. While the nature of the leadership structure of a group depends on many of the factors we have mentioned, the skill of the individuals who have influence potential is important in bringing this potential into reality. In other words, everything may be just right for a certain person to have considerable influence on the group, but unless he has the skill to communicate and to perform those deeds necessary to bring this influence to bear he does not become a leader. Joseph E. McGrath and Irwin Altman report that the research studies they examined showed that "there seems to be a fairly clear picture of who will emerge as leader, or be an effective leader, in essence, the member with the highest status, skills, and training."[12]

Characteristic behavior. While we recognize that the process of leadership transcends any one individual, we cannot ignore the fact that individuals are performing leadership functions. It thus becomes important to look at the behavior of the individuals as they operate in leadership capacities. Doing so has led us to identify some of the more consistent behaviors that appear in the leadership role. Ross and Hendry summarize the current research on these factors.

The profile of the leader indicated by the research reported is that of a self-confident, well-integrated, emotionally stable individual, one who has a desire to lead and is willing, able and competent in a particular situation; who is identified with the norms, values, and goals of the group of which he is the leader; who is a warm, sensitive, and sympathetic person, and able to help members in a practical way; who is intelligent relative to other group members; and who is consistent in performing his leadership function. As an elected leader he will probably need to possess greater enthusiasm and capacity for expression than many others in the group. Different situations will undoubtedly demand more or less of these qualities, but in general terms this profile represents as accurately as can be described at the present time that which the "good" leader in our society must be.[13]

[12] Joseph E. McGrath and Irwin Altman, *Small Group Research* (New York: Holt, Rinehart and Winston, 1966), p. 62.
[13] Ross and Hendry, *New Understanding of Leadership*, pp. 59-60.

Groups: Orientations and Structures

Several points in this summary call for explication. One has to do with the identification with the group. Those persons who serve the group as leaders usually can identify and can respond to the emotional needs and norms of the group. It is not enough that the leader serve the mechanical and process needs. He must be able to relate to the individuals in the group, understand their personal needs and respond to them so that the members feel that he has their personal interests at heart as well as the interest of the group task. This capacity is related to empathy; that is, the leader is able to "feel with" the members of his group and to associate his feelings and emotions with theirs.

Another significant condition is the membership status of the leader. Generally, an effective leader must be considered a member of the group in the fullest sense. He identifies with the group; that is, his goals and his expectancies are related to the successes and failures of the group. He accepts the standards and norms of his group.

At the same time the more effective leader maintains a measure of social distance in order to be most effective. He does not become entirely "one of the boys" in the usual sense. To do so would allow him to be satisfied with the minimal achievement of the norms and goals. He maintains a certain social aloofness so that he can represent the idealized norms and standards of the group. He is able to push the group toward a realization of its creeds more effectively than other members would be willing or able to do. This is not to say that in his aloofness he removes himself from the group; such would be defeating his leadership. He maintains a sociable, friendly, helpful but not intimate relationship with his colleagues. The key relationship here is the degree of intimacy that he allows to develop. If he allows himself to develop a high intimacy with some members or all of the members of the group he may easily become lost in the personal variations from the group standards and cannot view the total task and function of his group objectively.

A third condition is the degree to which the leader gives practical help to his colleagues; that is, the kind of assistance that actually meets needs when they exist. There are too many would-be leaders who are imposing "help" on groups when that help is not needed or wanted. I'm always reminded of the fellow in a boys' club who claimed he was helping the group when he "finked" to the police about an impending battle with another gang across town. He claimed that he felt that his group members didn't know the significance of their acts and that they needed to be protected against themselves. As a matter of fact, his contention may have been valid, but for a member of that group so to violate the needs and the norms of their little society resulted in his being thrust out of the group forcibly. He was not meeting their needs as they perceived them, and that was all that mattered to them. On the other hand, the member who got his cousin, who was a national wrestling champion, to join the group was really meeting some of the perceived needs. The group needed physical manpower and that was what he provided.

A fourth condition of effective leadership is what has been called surgency. Those persons who are functioning effectively in leadership roles seem to have superior vitality and energy. They initiate more communication to and with other members of the group; they are more likely to be cheerful and to take setbacks without apparent great remorse; they are quite congenial; they have enthusiasm for what is being done and this enthusiasm commands a great deal of attention from the others in the group; they are most expressive of their feelings and thoughts; they show uncommon alertness to what is going on both within and without the group; and they show somewhat more originality than others in the group.

Those who are successfully leading groups appear also to have a higher-than-average level of emotional stability. They seem to be able to "ride with the punches," and to maintain objective attitudes toward the problems the group faces.

Those persons who are performing leadership functions have a condition of personal commitment to the group that affects their behavior in the group and their acceptance as leaders. It is quite possible that in any given group and for any given situation there may be several who can operate as leaders. For any activity, one person may have greater enthusiasm than another, therefore the one with the deeper enthusiasm could probably make a greater leadership contribution. With the leadership phenomenon, certain conditions stimulate specific persons to leadership; and, when these conditions pass, their leadership wanes and is transferred to others whose enthusiasm is more tuned to the new set of conditions. If we remember that the conditions of group experience are constantly changing, we then can begin to see the truly dynamic nature of this concept of leadership.

Functions of group leaders. Since we are focusing on the individuals who are part of the leadership structure of a group, it is appropriate that we try to identify the kinds of things that they do in order to meet the needs of the group. In doing so, we note again that in any group no one person does all these things.

Most effective leaders help the group to function as a unit. They integrate the various functions performed by other members and direct them toward the basic task. They help to concentrate the forces of the group on the goals and to resolve differences among the members of the group.

These leaders can bring the members of the group closer together in a cohesive unit, can maintain a high morale among the members of the group, can encourage a sociability that allows for freedom of expression and communication, and can help the members relate to one another.

Leaders seldom hold their positions unless they serve to bring the group closer to its goals. Indeed, it is the conscious and unconscious expectation of the members of a group that those who lead will assist in meeting the goals and, in some cases, will assist the group in clarifying and defining the goals so that they can be approached.

The leaders also provide initiative for the group. They often introduce new ideas or suggest different approaches to activities. Usually, they "start the ball rolling." For example, the leader performs an important leadership function when he starts the discussion at a meeting and helps the group get under way with the work on its task.

An effective leader is one who can help the group identify, analyze, and examine its needs. Since the needs of the group shift from time to time, the leadership that is effective brings these shifts to the attention of the group and helps to seek ways of meeting these requirements. The needs of a group cover a spectrum of possibilities involving the processes, the mechanical requirements, and the personal requirements of members in the group.

Effective leadership is useful in helping the group to establish structure for its procedures; that is, the organization of the group for effective work can be developed by good leadership. When a formal structure is required, good leadership senses the requirement and helps the group establish the necessary structure. When an informal framework is more useful, the effective leader helps the group rid itself of the formal trappings and get to the heart of the matter through more informal methods.

One of the most important functions a leader performs is to facilitate communication in the group. Those persons who can draw the untalkative ones out and get them to contribute are valuable to the group. Those persons who can help the group members understand one another and help them to share their meanings are performing some of the most important tasks a group has.

Ross and Hendry put it this way: "The leader who improves communication within the group probably makes for better morale, increased member satisfaction, and greater productivity."[14]

Fritz J. Roethlisberger, in an article in *Harvard Business Review*, suggests that interpersonal communication is at the heart of the administrator's function and problem. He presents a case study that is most effective in identifying communication problems. "A Case of Misunderstanding" involves a Mr. Hart and a Mr. Bing. Hart is Bing's supervisor and Bing is a highly skilled worker who is producing more output than the others by a unique method. Hart, having been on the same line with Bing before becoming a supervisor, becomes irritated by Bing's behavior. A struggle develops between the two men. In analyzing the case, Roethlisberger examines the problem from Hart's role as the supervisor (leader). He notes that Hart makes value judgments, does not listen, and assumes things that may not be so.

Roethlisberger concludes the case study with some remarks on communication:

[14]Ross and Hendry, p. 87.

Am I indulging in wishful thinking when I believe that there are some simple skills of communication that can be taught, learned, and practiced which might help to diminish misunderstanding? . . . Although man is determined by the complex relationships of which he is a part, nevertheless he is also in some small part a determiner of these relationships. Once he learns what he cannot do, he is ready to learn what little he can do. And what a tremendous difference to himself and to others the little that he can do—listening with understanding, for example—can make!

Once he can accept his limitations and the limitations of others, he can begin to learn to behave more skillfully with regard to the milieu in which he finds himself. He can begin to learn that misunderstanding can be diminished—not banished—by the slow, patient, laborious practice of a skill.[15]

Roethlisberger's comments and case demonstrate the function of communication in the leadership functions. That leadership is not reducible to a precise set of formulas and rules is obvious. To attempt to set out such formulas would be an exercise in futility.

The main thing to remember is that leadership and face-to-face communication are human spoken interpersonal symbolic interactions.

Argument

Few face-to-face discussions occur without some argument or difference of opinion. This is good. The exploration of difference of opinion is of great importance in the process of working out common understandings and agreements. At nearly every decision-making point, there are differences that must be resolved in some fashion. Throughout the whole system of problem-solving and joint deliberation there are constant differences that must be resolved through joint agreement if the group is to be effective as a group.

Argumentative discourse is a way in which the different points of view can be explored and tested. We should never assume that the discussion method eliminates the need for argumentation. In fact, the use of argumentation in discussion requires a much higher level of sophistication than it does in the formal debate, or "planned argument," situation.

We shall not discuss at any length the methods of argumentative discourse. However, we shall consider some of the particular adaptations to the face-to-face discussion.

Too often, in discussion, a raw assertion is mistaken for a full argument by both the sender and receiver. For example, in a committee session on student-faculty relations, a faculty member said, "There is no place for students in

[15] Reprinted by permission of the publishers from *Man-in-Organization* by Fritz J. Roethlisberger (Cambridge, Mass.: The Belnap Press of Harvard University Press, Copyright, 1968, by the President and Fellows of Harvard College), p. 174.

Groups: Orientations and Structures

curriculum planning." A student in the group retorted flatly, "You're simply not interested in what the student has to say." Soon the student and the professor were almost nose-to-nose in a heated exchange that contributed little of value to the deliberation. The two statements have a common fault. Neither the professor nor the student supported his assertion. Each picked up the assertion of his opponent without determining first what grounds or reasons existed for that position.

An argument contains an assertion backed up by reasons. Now, there are all kinds of reasons and they can be set up in the most subtle or the most blunt manner. An assertion can be supported by giving examples of instances that demonstrate the idea or dramatize the assertion. Naturally, when we cite one example in support of an idea, our opponent can say that one example is not sufficient to justify the proposition—and he may be right. So, part of the task, when we use an example, is to be sure that it is typical of a large number of cases, that it represents the actual character of the situation, and so on. Sometimes we can summarize examples by the use of statistics.

A proposition can also be supported by using analogies. That is, we can compare it to something similar; and, if the comparison is valid, our proposition is strengthened.

Frequently we support our assertions with other statements of a general and accepted condition or assumption. I may contend that student influence on the campus is limited because students have not been given a voice in making university policy. Each time we give reasons for our assertion, there must be an assumption that connects those reasons (examples, analogies, conditions) to the conclusion we state as our position. For my contention about student influence, the underlying assumption is that there is a clear relationship between participation in making university policy and influence on the campus. While this seems a reasonable assumption, we may discover that the making of policy is not actually related to influence in the campus community as such. For such generally accepted assumptions, we are not likely to be called on to justify them, unless some sharp opponent challenges the assumption and demands that it be proved.

In face-to-face discussion, the manner of argument is varied. Many times we start with the assertion. Such a statement as "I don't think students have a place in curriculum planning" is an assertion representing a conclusion or an assertion that opens up the argument. However, sometimes we start with the supporting materials, then lead to the conclusion, which is the fundamental proposition that we are trying to get the group to accept. A skilled advocate, working in a face-to-face discussion group, can use this method with a great deal of power.

Argument should not be ruled out of face-to-face discussion. Skill in handling evidence, reasoning, the style of discourse in order to convince others, and the like are extremely important in the framework of face-to-face interaction. In many instances, they constitute the major mode of that interaction.

It is unrealistic to assume that argument represents cold, analytical reasoning. The separation of reasoning from feeling seems impossible. The conclusions we seek through reasoning are usually goals that grow out of our goal-need systems. Even in the most objective scientific study, the process of working to a conclusion from the evidence and from prior knowledge is filled with personal feelings and interpretations. Most of us like to think that the positions we take, the propositions we would like others to accept, and the things we believe to be true are based on sound support. The nature of that support, however, may not be something that can be shared. The way a person sees his world is critical to the belief systems and conclusions which he holds about that world.

Summary

A group consists of a number of persons who communicate with each other over a span of time in a face-to-face situation. Freedom of individuals is not achieved in isolation from a group.

A basic group begins with a communicative bond between two persons, face-to-face. This is the fundamental of social interaction. Groups have distinguishing properties: such as joint focus of interest, behavioral claims among members, and bonds of communication.

Much of our interaction with others is in the small-group setting, in such groups as family, peer, ceremonial, and task.

Individuals within a group should be sensitive to their own behavior as it affects others as well as responsive to the behavior of others. Each individual faces certain issues in respect to his membership in a group: belonging, involvement, desire to lead, function or role, identity, and affection.

The group itself faces several issues that must be solved. It needs identity, structure, norms, and management of work and emotion.

The effective operation of a small task group depends on adequate use of several processes. Among these are decision-making, problem-solving, leadership, communication, goals, skills, and argument.

For Special Reading

Warren G. Bennis, Edgar H. Schein, David E. Berlew, and Fred I. Steele, eds., *Interpersonal Dynamics: Essays and Readings on Human Interaction* (Homewood, Ill.: Dorsey Press, 1964). This is an excellent collection of essays by some of the outstanding scholars of our time in the field of behavioral science. Much of the material covered here has direct application to small-group discussion.

Ernest G. Bormann, *Discussion and Group Methods: Theory and Practice* (New York: Harper & Row, 1969). Few books concerned directly with discussion methods deal with the findings of behavioral science in effective application. This book is an exception. Bormann has integrated some of the approaches of traditional methods with a good bit of behavioral science theory.

R. Victor Harnack and Thorrel B. Fest, *Group Discussion: Theory and Technique* (New York: Appleton-Century-Crofts, 1964). This is another of the books on method and technique that are tied closely to behavioral science theory. This clear, well-documented book is filled with excellent suggestions and explanations of the group processes involved in face-to-face behavior.

George C. Homans, *The Human Group* (New York: Harcourt, Brace & World, 1950). No one who presumes to make a study of small groups can ignore the work of Homans. His work, from the point of view of a sociologist, is almost definitive in terms of present-day theory. For those of you who really seek a basic understanding of group life, start with this book!

Joseph E. McGrath and Irwin Altman, *Small Group Research: A Synthesis and Critique of the Field* (New York: Holt, Rinehart and Winston, 1966). This is not a textbook or collection of essays. It is basically a cataloged summary of research in small-group work. Its greatest value is as a quick reference to the brief résumés of many of the key studies made in the past twenty years.

Robert Tannenbaum, Irving R. Weschler, and Fred Massarik, *Leadership and Organization: A Behavioral Science Approach* (New York: McGraw-Hill Book Co., 1961). The authors have gathered together their own writings and interpretations of other scholarly works covering theoretical, empirical, descriptive, and interpretative material dealing with leadership phenomena. Of importance is the section devoted to sensitivity training as a personal approach to the development of leaders.

Abraham Zaleznik and David Moment, *The Dynamics of Interpersonal Behavior* (New York: John Wiley & Sons, 1964). These authors have brought together various lines of thought about group processes and interpersonal interaction. They are concerned with helping students to learn more about the structure and dynamics of work groups and with the development of competence in the analysis of problems encountered in face-to-face group behavior.

Editor's Comment. Although Keltner discusses the kinds of structures, processes, and interactions that are common to a wide variety of face-to-face groups, almost everything he says is applicable either directly or indirectly to encounter groups. The participant who commits himself intelligently to the structures and processes of the group must surrender a degree of autonomy, but he also participates in the corporate freedom of the group—a freedom which allows him to involve himself in a wide variety of ways with his fellow participants. As Keltner suggests, the group member must allow others to make claims on his behavior, and he himself must make certain claims on the behavior of his fellows. The nature of these "claims" will be discussed in subsequent articles.

The "problems of individuals" which Keltner discusses certainly arise in encounter groups. With respect to the problem of belonging, the person who expects to benefit from membership in a group has to decide to become a psychological member rather than just a formal member. No one should be forced to join an encounter group; the forced member almost inevitably becomes a liability to the group.

Similarly, once a person decides to participate in a group, he tends to stifle the group if he is involved only in a token way. Token involvement deadens group interaction, for groups tend to move at the pace of slower members. As in the rest of life, the participant usually benefits to the degree he is willing to commit himself to the process of the group. The person who states before entering that he does not believe that much can come from the group usually fulfills his own prophecy and gains little else.

Even though members of encounter groups are encouraged to attempt to engage in "role-free" behavior with one another, individual participants often find themselves settling into nongrowthful role patterns—for instance, the silent observer, the continual confronter, the pacifist, and so forth. If this is the case, then conflicting role pressures arise—the one-who-supports versus the one-who-confronts. Only by engaging in a variety of interpersonal behaviors can the participant come to realize that he does not need rigid roles as a security measure and that seemingly conflicting roles can be integrated (for example, caring confrontation).

The question of individual identity in the encounter group is an extremely important one. Keltner quotes Schutz to the effect that the individual participant who is not known cannot be meaningfully attended to. Each participant, then, must take the initiative to venture out into the group in a variety of ways (for example, by self-disclosure, expression of feeling, confrontation, and so forth) if he expects to be attended to in the group and if he expects to find more creative ways of involving himself with others. One of the principal purposes of the encounter group is to give the members ample opportunity to exercise interpersonal initiative. Indeed, many groups die because of the collective apathy of the members. Feedback from others greatly facilitates the process of delineating one's identity, but the member who refuses to move out into the group can obviously expect little feedback.

Decision-making processes in encounter groups generally center around personal issues and group processes rather than specific tasks. The individual has much to decide: how much he is willing to risk, when and how to move into the group, and so forth. "Twofer" situations, authority problems, and "free-ride" participants are all characteristic of the ordinary encounter group and must be dealt with by the group as a whole. The group as a group may also tend to make "tacit decisions" about what may or may not be dealt with in the group. These "decisions" are made, for example, when individuals fear to bring up certain topics (for instance, sexuality) or when a topic is consistently ignored when it is brought up. Once such "decisions" are made, it is extremely difficult to reverse them. It is up to the participants to forestall such decisions before they discover that the group has been rendered sterile by its own unexamined, unchallenged regulations.

While groups may survive without an appointed leader, no group can survive without leadership. The encounter-group participant soon discovers that the process of leadership transcends any one individual—specifically, and especially, the trainer or facilitator. Leadership is a

Groups: Orientations and Structures

process in which all the members of the group must involve themselves. In the beginning of the group many members expect the trainer either to tell them what to do or to assume a directive leadership inconsonant with the goals of the group. They must learn, however, that leadership, like independence, is something that must be seized rather than conferred.

Finally, with respect to Keltner's section on argument, it is my experience that cooperative rather than competitive group cultures prove most fruitful. This does not mean that the group should be free of conflict. Conflict, if managed well, can open the group to unsuspected possibilities of growth.

The Group as a Unique Context for Therapy[1,2]

Morton A. Lieberman
Martin Lakin
Dorothy Stock Whitaker

Editor's Introduction. According to Lieberman, Lakin, and Whitaker, groups have six characteristics that serve as important influences on the therapeutic process. All six characteristics— cohesiveness, control of behavior, definition of reality, the generation of strong feeling, interpersonal influence, and feedback—are crucial in the encounter group also, for the encounter group is also a "unique context" for the stimulation of interpersonal growth. The authors suggest that the group therapist learn how to *utilize* the dynamics of the group situation. I have seen therapists who, while supposedly conducting group therapy, did nothing more than conduct individual psychotherapy in the presence of an audience. While perhaps little harm was done by such an approach, great opportunities were overlooked by the therapists. In the encounter group, the participants are expected to share leadership to become "facilitators" or "educators" (rather than therapists) to one another; thus, they should be aware of the dimensions of encountering discussed in this article.

A major impediment to the development of a theory of group therapy stems from the conceptual blurring of multi-person and dyadic relationships. One need only thumb through the journals in group psychotherapy to see that the predominant effort has been to build bridges between group and individual psychotherapy. This is not surprising, since most of us have cut our eye teeth as therapists in a two-person context. Even if this were not typical training experience, the two-person relationship would still be the likely model for the beginning group therapist. In our culture the expected setting for psychic help is a private, intimate relationship with one person—be he therapist, bartender,

Reprinted by permission from *Psychotherapy: Theory, Research and Practice,* 1968, 5 (1), pp. 29-36.

[1] An earlier draft was presented in a paper, "The Therapist Versus the Group," at the Tri-State Psychotherapy Society, Cincinnati, Ohio, October, 1966, and at the Illinois Group Psychotherapy Society, December, 1966, by Morton A. Lieberman.

[2] Some of the ideas presented here first appeared in a paper, "The Implications of a Total Group Phenomena Analysis for Patients and Therapist," presented at the 23rd Annual Conference, American Group Psychotherapy Association, Philadelphia, January, 1966, by Morton A. Lieberman. In press, *International Journal of Group Psychotherapy.*

Groups: Orientations and Structures

lawyer, doctor or clergyman. Even corporate bodies like the family or the church generally tender psychic relief in a two-person context, not through the corporate body as a whole. This cultural conditioning mediates the behavior of patients as well as therapists, and often obviates the employment of group properties for therapeutic objectives.

Most of us who do therapy in groups are successful the hard way. We swim upstream, against the forces of the group, depending on undefinable charismatic dimensions of our own personalities which, together with much sweat and toil, may illuminate some insight and may generate emotionally corrective trans-actions. We push and pull, to produce a climate in the group that will be conducive to therapeutic interactions. This engagement often produces bene-ficial effects. But does it maximize the potentials unique to the group situation?

Six characteristics of groups seem to us important influences on the thera-peutic experience of the patients. These are its capacities to:

1) Develop cohesiveness or sense of belonging.
2) Control, reward and punish behavior.
3) Define reality for the individual.
4) Induce and release powerful feelings.
5) Distribute power and influence among individuals.
6) Provide a context for social comparison and feedback.

The Relevance of Group Properties for Therapy

1) The capacity to develop cohesiveness. The fundamental ambivalence of the neurotic requires a force of some kind for keeping him in the treatment situation. In a dyadic relationship we think of positive transference as the force enabling the patient to undergo the anxiety associated with the therapeutic process. In a two-person context, the therapist may offer the patient exclusive attention and unconditional acceptance. He is always able to take the patient's side against his real or imagined protagonists. In the patient's fantasy, if he abides by the rules, the therapist can offer him deliverance.

The group therapy patient, whom we see as little different from the individual patient, also enters the treatment situation with expectations of deliverance conducive to feelings of positive transference, but the group context vitiates many of the preconditions for positive transference. The group therapist cannot offer exclusive attention to each patient. He is unlikely to express unconditional acceptance at all times, for his feelings inevitably will shift as first one patient and then another supports or sabotages the therapeutic effort or behaves con-structively or destructively toward the others. He cannot be each patient's ally uniformly, because the protagonists are not all outside but right there in the group, and share an equal right to his protection. The competing demands, shifting alliances and complex emotional structure present in the group context do not allow the patient to feel protected by the therapist as totally as in a two-person relationship. The therapist cannot be a fantasied deliverer in a group in the same personal sense that he can in a two-person relationship. What, then, binds the individual to the group? We suggest that the cohesive forces created in groups serve the same fundamental purpose as positive transference in the dyadic relationship. Feelings of belongingness motivate the patient to stay with the group and work with it and mitigate the pains associated with therapeutic exploration.

This is not to say that strong positive transference cannot take place in a group situation. The group therapist can, by considerable effort and charisma, establish and maintain attitudes and sets necessary for positive transference, but the style necessary to maintain such a stance in a group may interfere with strategies for inducing a therapeutic climate. Moreover, the likelihood of a charismatic therapist establishing such a relationship with all his patients is exceedingly small. Failures frequently drop out in the early sessions. On the other hand, for those patients with whom he succeeds in forming such a relationship, the therapist has restricted the range of interpersonal strategies available to him. Later changes are frequently achieved at the expense of patients experiencing profound disappointment and undue anxiety.

This does not imply that cohesiveness is entirely a productive quality in a therapy group. High cohesion lowers the willingness of patients to risk the disapproval of others—a fundamental condition in psychotherapy for discovery of new ways of behavior. Patients may come to value the group and membership in it above the gains potential in self-exploration and self-exposure. Thus it becomes important for the therapist to pay attention to the degree of cohesiveness in the group, to evaluate its relationship to the therapeutic process and to take responsibility for its management.

2) The capacity of the group to control behavior and to provide a system of rewards and punishments. In our previous work on focal conflict theory (Whitaker and Lieberman, 1965) we discussed the capacity of the group to establish norms and standards (and its tendency to pressure and punish those who violate or challenge these norms). The process of working out solutions to focal conflicts was seen as the dynamic mechanism through which norms and standards are built up in the group. It is evident that in a therapeutic context which includes such group-generated influences, the therapist cannot have the same degree of influence over the meting out of reward and punishment that he would in a dyadic relationship.

Groups have powerful means of enforcing the norms and standards they establish, making conformity an issue for both therapist and patient. The group therapy patient is almost inevitably confronted with pressure from others to change his behavior or views. For some neurotics, being open to influence is a frightening, overwhelming possibility. These people "dare not conform" and, therefore, resist any kind of influence. At the same time they feel they cannot influence their environment. The power of the group to control behavior, however, also implies that each member has a greater opportunity to shape the environment than the patient in individual therapy. Thus, one can recognize two kinds of conformity: the passive, inflexible conformity of the individual who does not attempt to influence his environment, and the active, functional conformity of a person who recognizes that others can influence and be influenced by him.

The normative need to be in step, to abide by the rules, is a powerful factor inducing conformity in a group. Disregard for the rules brings the potentiality of punishment. The ultimate punishment available to a group is the power of exclusion—either psychological or physical. In a dyadic relationship it is not exclusion the patient fears if he does not go along with the therapist, but loss of love. We are dealing, then, with two very different psychological experiences leading to similar behavior—conformity.

Pulling equally toward conformity is the group's most-prized reward—its power to offer the authenticating affirmation of one's peers. They are the ones whose acceptance, in the final analysis, is desired. The experience of consensual validation by persons who are important in a real and present world appears to be much more gratifying to the group therapy patient than the affirmation of the therapist.

This is not to deny that, as in individual therapy, the group patient wants acceptance from the therapist and fears the loss of his love. However, conformity to the *group's* values and standards and the influences of exclusion and peer affirmation are paramount.

3) The capacity of the group to define reality for its members. The group exerts considerable influence on how each patient views himself, the group as a whole and others in the group. A salient example of this influence was contributed in a group therapy course in which psychiatric residents observed two of their members working as therapists with an ongoing group:

The observers watched from a darkened observation room and discussed the proceedings afterwards with the two therapists. Before the eighth session began, we found that the window blinds had been removed for cleaning, so that the patients would be able to see the observers through the one-way mirror. The two student therapists felt that since all the patients knew they were being observed there was no need to call off the observation. As the patients arrived one by one each looked particularly closely at the large observation mirror and then took his seat. The meeting began with members talking about how difficult it was to communicate with people, "Particularly when you couldn't see them—in telephone conversations, etc." They referred to the observers (which they had not done in previous sessions) with statements like "It's uncomfortable." "I don't like being observed because it's one-sided. The observers can see the patients but the patients cannot see the observers." The meeting went on in this vein for about a half hour and then the topic shifted to other material. When the two resident therapists joined the rest of the students for a discussion of the session, the observers asked them why they had not intervened and brought some sense of "reality" to the group by pointing out that the observers could be seen for the first time. They answered that the light had shifted and the observers couldn't really be seen. Their belief was so strong that several of us had to accompany them into the therapy room and demonstrate that obviously the group could see the observers—perhaps not every facial gesture, but clearly at least their outlines.

This to us was a dramatic instance of a group's capacity to define its own, special reality. The two therapists, who had gone into the meeting knowing the observers could be seen, and the patients collectively upheld as "reality" the illusion that the observers could not be seen.

In this case the group defined an illusion as reality. In other instances the group-generated reality destroys or challenges illusions of individual patients—as for example, convictions about one's own unattractiveness, or the untrustworthiness of others, or about the facts of any given matter.

In dyadic therapy a major task of the therapist is to define reality for the patient. The therapist's view of reality is often accepted rather readily by the patient—perhaps because of the therapist's status as an expert or perhaps because the process of identification forms so strong an element in the patient's relationship to him. In the group, reality grows out of the multitude of interactions and counteractions, and frequently one can see a struggle between the group and the therapist over who is the arbiter of reality. This is particularly true of therapists who have a highly developed model, because these more articulate theories emphasize "rules" for translating patient productions into more abstract categories. Therapists who employ a theory that emphasizes primitive, unconscious feelings frequently engage the group in struggles over the "real meaning" of a particular event. Similarly therapists who emphasize particular transactions will often engage the group in a struggle to "correctly" label a particular interaction, for example, as "game playing." Labelling such occurrences as "therapeutic resistance" all too frequently obfuscates a detailed examination of the phenomenon and its potential therapeutic possibilities.

The group therapist can, of course, attempt to impose his version of reality on the group, but the price may be to create a gross dependency state or to generate unexpressed reservations or rebellion. Another pitfall for the therapist is to participate in the consensus about a perceived "reality" that is in fact an illusion. Groups frequently establish dangerous illusions as in scapegoating, where an individual in the group becomes the focus of particular feelings. Some of the group's "realities" are illusions that need to be dealt with therapeutically. We believe the error of attempting to be the sole definer of reality is made more frequently by therapists than the error of taking too little responsibility for this process. The most appropriate stance is that of monitor of the group's realities, challenging consensus when it seems necessary, but also recognizing that most group definitions of reality are useful.

4) The capacity of the group to induce, stimulate and release powerful feelings. Historically, emotional contagion was the first phenomenon to interest investigators of groups. LeBon, MacDougall and Freud pointed out that powerful primitive affect can be released in groups. Individuals may be carried away, may experience feelings which they later believe are uncharacteristic of themselves, and may act on feelings without displaying their typical controls. This potential in groups can have either positive or negative effects on therapy. An individual may experience previously-denied feelings not with enduring terror but with growth—the corrective emotional experience of finding that the feelings are not overwhelming or that the feared consequences do not occur. Negative effects may occur when an individual is overwhelmed by affect and must defend against the group situation by literal or psychological withdrawal, or by the invocation of undesirable defenses.

Since contagion occurs in groups, but not in individual therapy, the process of circumventing defenses may be quite different in the two settings. In individual therapy the sequence involves first analyzing the resistance in order to release the feared affect. In group therapy, participation in group-generated affect may allow the patient to by-pass defenses so that the feared affect may be experienced first, thus rendering the resistance less necessary.

It is also possible that the kinds of affect are rather different. Feelings of solidarity with others, empathy toward peers, ganging up against a common enemy are not experienced in individual therapy. Moreover, a particular affect may have a different quality in the two therapies. For example, the patient in individual therapy who intimates his innermost feelings to a benign professional person undoubtedly risks far less than the group therapy patient, who may undergo feelings of extreme exhilaration or fear as he reveals himself "in public."

The managing of group affect becomes one of the essential skills of the therapist. This skill involves tamping down contagion where necessary, protecting individuals who need to be exempted from participation in group affect, breaking up group resistance in order for affect to emerge, sensing when to let the affect run on and develop and when to introduce cognitive reflection about the affect.

5) The distribution of power and influence in the group. Power is distributed unevenly in groups. Some members have great influence over the course of group events, standards, the way the group defines reality; others have not. Power is fluid—it does not consistently remain in the same hands, but fluctuates with the state of the group.

The power of the therapist, for example, is rarely discussed perhaps because it is not a problem in the interpersonal setting of two-person therapy. The individual therapist has considerable influence on what is talked about and how it is talked about. The group therapist, on the other hand, senses differences at times in his degree of control or influence. His power vacillates because, singly, he cannot effect the "therapeutic contract." The therapist in a group setting must pay attention to the area of power and influence and realize that, no matter how sensitive or skillful he is, he cannot have the same degree of influence on the interpersonal situation that he would in a two-person relationship.

Associated with the group therapist's experience of power are attitudes he may hold towards his patients. He may feel less personal responsibility for his charges in the group setting. The amount of influence we have with another human being is related to the amount of responsibility we feel for him; groups, no matter what their purpose, tend to blur the lines of individual responsibility, making it more difficult for any single person, no matter what his role, to feel that what happens to the group or to individuals in a group is directly related to his own behavior.

The group therapist, for example, has difficulty seeing any one-to-one correspondence between his interventions and therapeutic benefit to a particular patient. Group therapists indicate that they have difficulty perceiving what they have done to help a particular person in a group; that is, they find it difficult to articulate the relationship of a specific intervention to a particular response in an individual patient. The group therapist can point to effective interventions, but he sees them as part of a long chain of events in which they are interwoven with the interactions of a group of patients. The fate of a particular patient in a group depends upon many factors and, although the therapist influences all of these factors, he cannot experience the direct causal relationship between his behavior and the patient's therapeutic gains that he does in individual therapy. Others have put it that in a group there are "multiple therapists"; whether or not one agrees with this formulation, it illustrates how the group therapist experiences his role.

What are the consequences of giving help in a situation where it is difficult to relate one's own efforts directly to the help received by the patient? Does it limit the types of gratification the group therapist can experience in the role of the help-giver? His inability to articulate a direct connection between his intervention and the ultimate therapeutic benefits to individual patients would seem to mean that he cannot experience the same kinds of legitimate gratifications that are possible in a dyadic relationship. Expecting rewards similar to those experienced in the individual setting is a frequent cause for the neophyte's sense of frustration in a group.

6) *The capacity of the group to provide a context for social comparison and feedback.* During group therapy patients frequently compare their attitudes

toward parents, husbands, wives, children; their feelings about immediate events in the group; the things that make them sad, happy, guilty, angry; the ways that each typically deals with and expresses anger, affection, and so on. Such comparisons occur naturally and facilitate revisions of the patient's identity by confronting him with new possibilities in feeling, perceiving and behaving.

Another kind of interaction which is possible in groups is commonly called feedback. One patient says to another, "When you went on and on just now I felt like giving up," or "You just said something sarcastic to me and I felt hurt and resentful." Such comments allow the recipient of the feedback to understand better the impact of his behavior on others. Feedback contributes quite directly to the therapeutic goal of helping each person to recognize and accept responsibility for the interpersonal consequences of his behavior.

Asking for and providing feedback does not come naturally; or rather, it may be imbedded in potentially destructive behavior. Patients sometimes try to "help" one another by offering interpretations: "You dominate the group because . . .," or "you are sarcastic because you are afraid to be angry in any more direct way." Sometimes interpretations are apropos, useable, and offered in a helpful spirit, but often they are heavily invested with projection, or function as a personal defense or a safe way of expressing hostility. The group therapist must teach the group to utilize feedback appropriately. Social comparison and feedback occur in individual therapy only occasionally as deliberate tactics, never as major avenues toward therapy.

Some Implications

For Therapeutic Outcomes

These six group properties create conditions that engage the group therapy patient in a number of activities and concerns which differ from those of the patient in dyadic treatment. In comparison with the latter, the group patient gets little practice in reflecting about himself and his interactions with others, in associating about his own feelings, in analyzing dreams, in linking present and past experiences or penetrating covert meanings; he is too busy actually interacting and finding a viable place for himself in the group. But he gets greater practice in expressing his feelings to peers, in noting the consequences of such expressions, in attempting to understand and empathize with others, in hearing from others about his impact on them and in comparing himself with others.

Does this differing balance in experience lead to differences in outcome? It is commonly assumed that the group patient should end up getting help of much the same order as he would have obtained in a dyadic relationship. It is perhaps helpful to test this assumption against, first, the end-state of the patient at the close of therapy (symptoms, conflicts, defenses, interpersonal patterns and the like); and second, the meta-learning achieved (learning how to approach problems, how to confront and resolve conflicts and how to cope with anxiety).

Three aspects of the patient's end-state are relevant: (1) the symptoms or presenting complaint; (2) the revision of maladaptive patterns, the relinquishment of neurotic defenses or the resolution of neurotic conflict; and (3) the unsought, ancillary gains. Symptom relief, for example, may be achieved at different rates. (The "placebo" effect, critical in many instances of rapid symptom relief, seems to us unique to the dyad.) Particular behavior changes or conflict resolutions may be accomplished better by one of the two settings depending on the nature of the problem, the composition of the therapy group, and so on. For example, a therapy group whose composition encourages a patient to maintain an established neurotic pattern may be less effective for that patient than individual therapy. On the other hand, a group which, say through emotional contagion, led a patient to experience a previously-feared affect may be more effective than individual therapy.

Finally, the two treatment situations may be conducive to rather different ancillary benefits. For example, difficulty in giving to others may be only peripherally related to the patient's presenting complaint or core conflicts, but nevertheless an issue. Since giving to others is often a focal concern in a group, many opportunities appear for each patient to note the nature of his anxieties about giving and to try out giving behavior. Thus, changes in giving behavior may occur sooner or more directly than in individual therapy. The two therapies may also call attention to different aspects of man—in group therapy, for example, patients are likely to be struck by the basic kinship, the sharing in the human condition, of persons who may appear quite different. They may be impressed both by the difficulties in communicating meaningfully to others and by the profound rewards experienced when such communication proves possible. The dyad, in contrast, does not directly facilitate such experiences.

The differences for meta-learning may be even greater than the differences in end-state outcomes. In any form of therapy the patient often adopts a style of approaching problems which reflects the characteristic processes of the therapy. It is not unusual for a patient to emerge from a psychoanalysis with an increased tendency to pay attention to his dreams, to deduce emotional meaning from forgetting, to search out unrecognized feelings when he notes inconsistencies in his behavior. A patient who has undergone group treatment may be more likely to seek out feedback from others, to make social comparisons, to test out behaviors interpersonally.

For Selection of Patients

Patients may vary in their aptitude for therapeutic gains within the two environments. Some patients may "take to" the processes characteristic of individual therapy readily. They may be highly reflective, more investigatively inclined, interested in searching out their own feelings and in speculating about links with past life. Similarly, some patients may enter more readily into the fluid round of interactions characteristic of group therapy. They may need a present arena for trying out new behavior, comparing themselves with peers, asking for and receiving feedback. Patients who may be comparable in terms of diagnostic category, severity of impairment, conflict area, and so on, may not be comparable in aptitude for the two therapeutic situations.

For the Therapist

May not the same reasoning apply to therapists? If the two settings involve quite different processes, the therapist's task, the potential stresses upon him, even his way of understanding the patient may all be different. A therapist may be unevenly suited for the two roles. The person of the therapist is important in the dyad because he is the instrument that creates or induces the climate in which psychotherapy will take place. His warmth, his understanding and his strength are paramount. Conditions of intimacy and non-judgmentalness are required to create the therapeutic milieu. Trust and faith in the person of the therapist permits the patient to undergo the risks and pain of the process. The patient's wish to be like the therapist is an important element of the dyadic process.

These personal qualities are less important for the group therapist, whose central role is to manage the group conditions to effect a climate for therapeutic encounters. Warmth, understanding, symbolization of strength are not paramount. They are not totally unimportant, for group therapy must include some aspects of charisma. Nevertheless, the group is ultimately the salient psychological body for the patient; in the long run the personal qualities of the therapist are not critical in shaping the therapeutic climate, or inducing appropriate identifications.

Self-understanding also may play a different role in the two therapies and different kinds may be required. The dyadic therapist must know his own vulnerabilities, conflicts, biases and predispositions, so that his responses are less likely to be insensitive, destructive, or inappropriate. Self-understanding is also expected to sharpen his perception of "what is going on."

The group therapist, too, must be aware of "what is going on," but this includes group and interpersonal phenomena which are not present in individual therapy. Self-knowledge does not take the group therapist as far as it does the individual therapist since he is not a direct participant in all that is going on. The kind of self-knowledge he needs concerns how vulnerable he is to various kinds of group contagion, how threatened he is by unanimous attack and what defenses he is likely to invoke against it, what it means to him to maintain a deviant position in a group and much else that is irrelevant for the individual therapist.

A therapist must come to know his patients. For some, understanding of another human being comes from knowing what he has experienced, what he thinks and what he feels. Others understand another human being through seeing how he behaves and what he does. The first type of person may make a poor group therapist or may find the role distasteful because the kind of information he needs about others may not be available in a group—at least not without fighting against the character of the group itself.

Finally, the special characteristics of the group as a context for therapy may generate differing views of human nature. The moral pessimism associated with the psychoanalytic tradition may be generated by the analyst's experience of the patient in the analytic setting, which emphasizes such features of the personality as the primitive character of impulses, the intractable nature of defenses and the like. In contrast, the group therapeutic process emphasizes capacity to settle differences, interpersonal sensitivity and communication, which may lead to an image of man cast in terms of competence.

For Training

What has all this to do with training the group therapist? In our view, the special qualities of the group context suggest that a critical training need is to help the group therapist adopt the perspective of a "social engineer," a term that perhaps seems cold and manipulative, but is meant rather to underscore the management of social forces and the mining of group resources as the essential skills which the group therapist must develop. Most training relies on an apprenticeship relationship which utilizes the process of identification—a tool of the charismatic leader—to teach the novice how to become a group therapist. The trainer points out what is "really occurring" in the group, thereby relating to the student therapist in the same fashion as he relates to his patients—incorrectly. The training tradition, in other words, duplicates with the student the very errors he is to correct as a group therapist. But are there any ways out of this quandary? Part of the answer may lie in our paying closer attention to certain aspects of the personality of the trainee. If it is true that people differ in how they acquire understanding of their fellow men, then some people may have less aptitude as group therapists than others. There are other personal qualities that may make considerable difference in how well a person can function as a group therapist. The model of social engineer, which we suggest is appropriate to the group therapist, is alien to the tradition from which most therapists stem. The medical model, which all the helping professions share, is a cure model in which the patient is seen as sick and needing something to be done for him; there is also a "hothouse model" in which psychotherapy is seen as an artificial situation designed to stimulate growth and, finally, a "powerhouse model" wherein positive persuasion is used to deal with the patients' problems. All three, or any combination of them, involve the therapist in certain psychological relationships to the patient. They involve forms of deliverance and intimacy which are external to the natural processes that occur in groups. Training programs must take into account the impact of these traditional conceptions about the role of help-giver and the needs of the help-giver. Otherwise they will create therapists who unwittingly align themselves against the inherent forces in the group setting which can contribute most to therapeutic gain.

Reference

Whitaker, D. S. & Lieberman, M. A. *Psychotherapy through the Group Process*. New York: Atherton Press, 1965.

Editor's Comment. Most people who seriously commit themselves to the encounter-group process find it a powerful force. This article spells out the foundations of this power.

Optimal cohesiveness in the encounter group is achieved when the participants forge themselves into a community that supports strong interactions. If cohesion (in the sense of "liking") is too high in the group, it can lead to stagnation, to the feeling that "Nothing is happening here because we all seem to 'like' one another too much." Group members must learn to strike a balance between (a) the need to affirm one another because they like one another and (b) the types of behavior (self-disclosure, confrontation) that entail running the risk of disapproval. If the group is cohesive in the sense that the members are solidly "for" one another, then they can risk more with one another.

There is no doubt that groups, including encounter groups, "have powerful means of enforcing the norms and standards they establish." In the encounter group, rules are more facilitating if they are arrived at by some kind of explicit (rather than tacit) consent. Conformity to rules is, in a sense, a neutral phenomenon. If a person conforms because he is the pawn of the group, then conformity is counterproductive. But if conformity means that a participant positively commits himself to norms that he sees as facilitating the work of the group, then such conformity is a sign of integrity rather than a violation of it. The rules and norms of the group should be as highly visible as possible so that the individual participant knows to what he is committing or refusing to commit himself.

In the encounter group the participants help one another define reality by interacting with one another in a wide variety of ways and by giving one another direct and immediate feedback with respect to the impact they have on one another. Other persons, simply because they stand outside me, have a vision of me that I cannot have. Their willingness to share this vision is one of the most powerful dimensions of the group.

Encounter-Group Models. Whether one approves or disapproves the use of a medical (mental-sickness, mental-health) model in the practice of individual and group psychotherapy, such a model seems peculiarly inappropriate in dealing with encounter groups, for the group members can in no way be considered patients. However, a combination of the "social engineering," the "hothouse," and the "powerhouse" models referred to by the authors seems to be appropriate for several reasons. First, the trainer is a "social engineer" in that he both models and promotes the kinds of interactions that put people in growthful contact with one another. Second, the encounter-group situation is contrived and thus resembles the "hothouse" model. The question, however, is not whether the group situation is contrived but whether it works—that is, whether it benefits the participants. The encounter group is a laboratory in which the participants are free to experiment with different styles of interpersonal behavior. Third, since responsible confrontation (as opposed to hostile attack) is usually an important dimension of the group experience, the encounter group also follows the "powerhouse" model, wherein something akin to positive persuasion is used to deal with participants' problems.

Finally, perhaps one of the reasons I personally prefer group experiences to individual counseling and therapy is that, as the authors suggest, there is relatively little interpretation in groups. Interpretation deals with the conjectured foundations or sources of a person's behavior and thus tends to be hypothetical, abstract, and often boring. Lengthy interpretations, especially, rob the interaction of a sense of engagement and immediacy—a quality that is important to the functioning of the group. Lieberman and his associates merely note the different role that interpretation plays in individual as opposed to group therapy; they do not evaluate that role or pass judgment on it. I would tend to speak more evaluatively, at least with respect to the encounter group, and say that the group in which there is a good deal of interpretation of behavior is a group in flight. Interpretation in such a group is most likely being used by the participants as a means of insulating themselves from one another. (See *E:GPFIG,* pp. 297-301.)

Groups: Orientation and Structures

Part Two.
Goals

Many groups and organizations in our society fail to perform effectively because they have continually and consistently refused to establish and review the criteria for judging their own success or failure. That is, they have refused to establish and review their goals. Business organizations are forced to do so. The degree of their success or failure, to put it somewhat simplistically, is measured monetarily—by their profits or losses. But what criteria can we use to judge whether educational enterprises have been successful or not? At the end of any given year, how do we know whether congress has been successful or not? How does a parish determine whether it has been religiously successful or not?

The encounter-group participant, too, has to ask himself what, for him, constitutes success and failure in the group experience. Can he say, for instance, that it has been a successful experience, if, at the end of the experience, he can say that he "liked" it? Should an encounter group induce certain specific changes in his style of interpersonal living, and, if so, what should these changes be? The encounter-group movement is young, and there are no definitive answers to these questions, but they are questions that should be asked. The following articles and comments are not meant to outline definitive goals for encounter groups; rather, they are meant to stimulate the participant to start thinking about goals so that he might determine precisely what he wants from the group experience. (A more systematic treatment of encounter-group goals may be found in *E:GPFIG*, pp. 68-103.)

Goals and Meta-Goals of
Laboratory Training

Warren G. Bennis

Editor's Introduction. Goals in encounter groups are usually meaningful to the degree that they are concrete and are internalized by group members; but establishing clear goals is not the same as dictating how participants should behave. Even concrete goals allow individual participants ample opportunity to structure the experience according to their own needs. For instance, self-disclosure—especially disclosure of the here-and-now feelings, attitudes, and motivations that affect a member's participation in the group—is essential to the life of the group, but the individual must determine just when and how he should disclose himself and at what depth. Goals, then, should be facilitating rather than binding; they should be stimuli rather than edicts.

Bennis (1964) and Benne (1964) promote "planned goallessness" in laboratory-training groups; such groups start without any specific goals because one of the overriding purposes of the group is to create its own goals. The theory is that the interactions involved in this creative process contribute to the growth of the participants. When "planned goallessness," or the formulation of an operational contract for the participants, is a primary value, however, the group often ends with just that—a well-formulated contract that cannot be fulfilled because time has run out. Generally speaking, there is no reason to place more value on "planned goallessness" than on the establishment of relatively explicit and concrete goals that are known to all the participants (and not just to the facilitator). They are different kinds of experience, each with its own set of values, each emphasizing different dimensions of the interpersonal-learning process. It is undeniable, however, that both kinds of groups possess certain communalities. I generally opt for high visibility in group experiences as a safeguard against manipulation and as a means of providing a degree of general psychological safety for the participants.

Editor's References

Benne, K. D. From polarization to paradox. In L. P. Bradford, J. R. Gibb, & K. D. Benne (Eds.), *T-Group theory and laboratory method.* New York: Wiley, 1964, pp. 216-247.

Bennis, W. G. Patterns and vicissitudes in T-Group development. In L. P. Bradford, J. R. Gibb, & K. D. Benne (Eds.), *T-Group theory and laboratory method.* New York: Wiley, 1964, pp. 80-135.

I think there is general agreement about the goals of laboratory education. The "take-home" booklets, the promotional material, the opening lectures of laboratories generally reflect this consensus. And while there are some variations of the stated goals, depending on the staff and participant composition (e.g., Church Laboratory, School Administrator Laboratory, and so on), they usually include objectives such as these: (a) self-insight, or some variation of learning related to increased self-knowledge; (b) understanding the conditions which inhibit or facilitate effective group functioning; (c) understanding interpersonal operations in groups; and (d) developing skills for diagnosing individual, group, and organizational behavior.

But beyond these explicit goals, there rests another set of learnings which shall be referred to as "meta-goals" (or "values," if you would prefer). These meta-goals transcend and shape the articulated goals. They are "in the air" at every laboratory and undoubtedly guide staff decisions ranging from laboratory design to trainer interventions. More crucial is the realization that the meta-goals, if internalized, lead to a set of values which may run counter to the participant's sponsoring ("back-home") organization. I would like to suggest four pivotal meta-goals for discussion; the hope being that, if reasonable, they can be integrated into future human relations training more explicitly.

1. Expanded Consciousness and Recognition of Choice[1]

Extracting men in organizations from their day-to-day preoccupations and transplanting them into a culture where they are urged to observe and understand personality and group dynamics creates conditions where "givens" become choices—or at least create potentials for choice. Laboratory training—if anything—is a device which de-routinizes, which slows down for analysis, processes which are "taken for granted." It is a form of training which questions received notions and attempts to "unfreeze" role expectations (the Lewinian re-educational and change process of "unfreezing, restructuring, and refreezing"). The impulse for this cognitive restructuring comes about primarily because the control mechanisms taken for granted in institutionalized behavior are decisively absent in a laboratory. I am referring to control mechanisms which serve to regulate behavior, such as mission, authority patterns, norms regulating intimacy and control, decision apparatus, communication, traditions, and precedents. The ambiguity of norms, of behavioral constraints, of anticipatory

Reproduced by special permission from *NTL Human Relations Training News*, 1962, **6** (3), "Goals and Meta-Goals of Laboratory Training," Warren G. Bennis, pp. 1-4. Copyright 1962 by NTL Institute for Applied Behavioral Science, Washington, D.C.

[1] The author acknowledges his debt to Jack Glidewell who, in a lecture at NTL's Management Work Conference at Arden House, February, 1961, alerted him to the importance of "choice" and "choice points."

rewards, creates what Lewin referred to as a "primitivization" of behavior due to the regressive climate. And the happy necessity of this human existence, to paraphrase T. S. Eliot, is for men to find things out for themselves, i.e., to create order, clarify one's identity, establish norms and a sense of community. In fact, one can look at laboratory training as the formation of norms and structure which build a community—except that, unlike most communities, the constituent members are present at its birth.

There are many analogies to this process; psychotherapy, perhaps, is the most obvious. According to one of its proponents, Karl Menninger, a regressive situation is evoked whereby the patient is deliberately forced to re-experience situations which bind and immobilize present choices. The indoctrination and socialization practices of many institutions, particularly "total institutions" where attempts are made to reshape normative patterns, bear a close resemblance to this unfreezing process. The "insight culture" of mental hospitals,[2] the "coercive persuasion" and "thought control"[3] programs used in Korean P.O.W. camps, military indoctrination programs,[4] and even some management development programs[5] are all to some degree exemplars.

Laboratory training, then, realizes its meta-goal of "expanded consciousness and recognition of choice points" by way of a very complicated process: extracting participants from their day-to-day preoccupations, cultural insulation, and de-routinization. Parallel to, and combined with this unfreezing process, is an emphasis on awareness, sensitivity, and diagnosis, all of which encourage the participant to think about his behavior—most particularly to think about how he chooses to behave.

2. A "Spirit of Inquiry"

Closely related to the meta-goals of choice—and, in fact, only conceptually separable—is an attitude of inquiry associated with science. It is a complex of human behavior and adjustment that has been summed up as the "spirit of inquiry" and includes many elements. The first may be called the hypothetical spirit, the feeling for tentativeness and caution, the respect for probable error. Another is experimentalism, the willingness to expose ideas to empirical testing. The exigencies of the laboratory situation help to create this orientation. For the ambiguous and unstructured situation creates a need to define and organize the

---

[2] Alfred Stanton and Morris S. Schwartz, *The Mental Hospital* (New York: Basic Books, Inc., 1954).

[3] Edgar H. Schein, *Coercive Persuasion* (New York: W. W. Norton & Co., Inc., 1961).

[4] Sanford M. Dornbusch, "The Military Academy as an Assimilating Institution." *Social Forces*, May, 1955. Pp. 316-21.

[5] Edgar H. Schein, "Management Development as a Process of Influence." *Industrial Management Review*, M.I.T., May, 1961.

environment. In addition, the participants are prodded and rewarded by staff members to question old, and try new, behaviors; they are reinforced by concepts to probe, to look at realities unflinchingly, to ask "why."

Again this bears a kinship with the methodology—although *not*, notably, the symbolic interpretive system—of psychoanalysis. Nevitt Sanford has said in this connection (in an S.P.S.S.I. Presidential Address at an American Psychological Association meeting in August 1958) that it appears "...most notably in Freud's psychoanalytic method of investigation and treatment. (This method is, in my view, Freud's greatest, and it will be his most lasting contribution. By the method, I mean the whole contractual arrangement according to which both therapist and patient become investigators, and both objects of careful observation and study; in which the therapist can ask the patient to face the truth because he, the therapist, is willing to try to face it in himself; in which investigation and treatment are inseparable aspects of the same humanistic enterprise.)"

In laboratory training all experienced behavior is a subject for questioning and analysis, limited only by the participants' threshold of tolerance to truth and new ideas.

Both meta-goals, the "spirit of inquiry" and the "recognition of choice," imply that curiosity about and making sense of human behavior are as legitimate and important (if not as "sanitary") as non-human phenomena. (I have always been perplexed and sometimes annoyed at observing the most gifted and curious natural scientists and engineers stop short of asking "why" when it touched on the human condition. Part of laboratory education, I suspect, is to expand the range of curiosity and experimental attitude to "people.")

3. Authenticity in Interpersonal Relations

An important imperative in laboratory training has to do with the relatively high valuation of feelings: their expression and their effects. The degree to which participants can communicate feelings and in turn evoke valid feelings from other members is regarded as an important criterion of group growth. One theory postulates that "group development involves the overcoming of obstacles to valid communication,"[6] i.e., where valid communication is defined as interpersonal communication free—as far as humanly possible—of distortion.

Authenticity, "leveling," and "expressing feelings" comprise an important part of the laboratory argot, all of which can be summed up in a passage from *King Lear*: "Speak what you feel, not what we ought to say."

[6] Warren G. Bennis and Herbert A. Shepard, "A Theory of Group Development." *Human Relations* 4:1956.

This tendency toward authenticity should not be surprising when we consider that so much time and attention are devoted to the analysis of interpersonal behavior, to understand the effects of a participant's behavior on other group members. Measurements of changes during these training programs, indeed, suggest personal growth resembling that seen in psychotherapy;[7] i.e., the participant, as he knows himself, will be much the same person as he is known to others.[8]

4. A Collaborative Conception of the Authority Relationship

Permeating the atmosphere of laboratory training is a concept of the authority relationship which differs substantially from the legalistic Weberian emphasis on legitimacy of position. The contractual elements are understressed, and the collaborative and interdependent elements are accentuated. In McGregor's writings we can identify the major elements in this conception of authority: (a) Management by objective, i.e., the requirements of the job are set by the situation (they need not be seen by either party as personal requirements established by the superior),[9] so that the authority relationship is viewed as a collaborative process where superior and subordinate attempt to develop ground rules for work and productivity; (b) the recognized interdependence between subordinates and superiors; (c) the belief that subordinates are capable of learning *self-control*, i.e., to internalize and exercise standards of performance congruent with organizational objectives without reliance on controls from exogenous sources.

Underlying this conception of authority is the "double reference" held toward superiors and subordinates based on person and role ingredients. For the subordinate and superior have to view each other as *role incumbents* with a significant power differential (even taking into account the interdependence) as well as *human beings* with strengths and weaknesses. Most theories of organization deny the personality elements of role and thereby fail to come to terms with the basic antagonism and tension between role and personality in organizational behavior.

How this conception of authority is internalized during laboratory training is beyond the scope of this paper; moreover, the process is not altogether clear. Readings and lectures cover the material somewhat, and identification with staff members undoubtedly contributes. But most important is the realization that *the teaching-learning process of laboratory training is a prototype of the*

[7] Richard L. Burke and Warren G. Bennis, "Changes in Perception of Self and Others During Human Relations Training." *Human Relations* 2:1961. Pp. 165-82.

[8] Marie Johoda, *Current Concepts of Positive Mental Health*. New York: Basic Books, Inc., 1958.

[9] Douglas M. McGregor, *The Human Side of Enterprise*. New York: McGraw-Hill, 1960.

collaborative conception of authority. Putting it differently, we can say that learning is accomplished through the requirements of the situation and a joint, collaborative venture between the trainer and participants. Also, there is the belief that participants can exercise self-control in the learning process; i.e., the participant accepts influence on the basis of his own evaluation rather than reliance on outside controls, such as rewards and punishments. Internalization, through credibility—rather than compliance, through exogenous controls—is the type of social influence employed in laboratory training.[10] It is precisely this form of influence which holds for the collaborative conception of authority we have been discussing.

These four meta-goals, then—expanded consciousness and recognition of choice, spirit of inquiry, authenticity in interpersonal relations, and a collaborative conception of authority—represent what I think to be the most important results gained from laboratory training. (Another important meta-goal not discussed here is the professionalization of the manager's role.)

It is interesting that critics of this approach regularly misconstrue or fail to understand these meta-learnings. Dubin, in an otherwise thoughtful analysis of this training, wonders whether it doesn't train managers to be "other-directed," or to become "permissive leaders."[11] From other sources, charges are made about "togetherness," brainwashing, and "group-thinking." It is not entirely the fault of the critics, for the writing in the field has generally stressed the purely "group dynamics" aspects while slighting the meta-goal emphasis presented here.

I think we trainers, too, have colluded in this misunderstanding from time to time. We become preoccupied with matters of "expressing feelings" or "shared leadership" or "manipulative behavior" or "giving feedback" or "democratic functioning," or with "people who talk too much *vs.* people who remain silent" or with "cohesive *vs.* fragmented groups," and so on. These are, of course, legitimate matters and should concern trainers. But they've gained a hegemony which I want to question.

For I care much less about a participant's learning that he talked too much and will, in the future, talk less, than I do about his recognizing that choice exists and that there are certain clear consequences of under- or over-participation. I care much less about producing a "cohesive" group than I do about members' understanding the "costs" and gains of cohesiveness, when it's appropriate and worth the cost and when it may not be. I care far less about developing shared leadership in the T-Group than I do about the participants' recognizing that a

---

[10]This formulation of social influence is taken from Herbert C. Kelman's "Processes of Opinion Change," *Public Opinion Quarterly* (Spring 1961), reprinted in Warren G. Bennis, Kenneth D. Benne, and Robert Chin (editors), *The Planning of Change.* New York: Holt, Rinehart, & Winston, 1961. Pp. 509-17.

[11]Robert F. Dubin, "Psyche, Sensitivity, and Social Structure," in Robert Tannenbaum, Irving Weschler, and Fred Massarik, *Leadership and Organization.* New York: McGraw-Hill, 1961. Pp. 401-15.

Goals

choice exists among a wide array of leadership patterns. In short, I care far more about developing *choice and recognition of choice points than I do about change*. Change, I think, is the participants' privilege, but choice is something trainers must emphasize. (This goes right across the board. I will try doggedly to create valid conditions for "giving and receiving feedback," for example. I will doggedly insist that the members "experience" it so that they have a basis for choice. Then I will just as doggedly insist that a choice remain open, to continue or not, to modify or not.)

Emphasizing the meta-goals has another importance with respect to organizational change. For they represent what the participant internalizes and transfers to his organization. "Everything the child learns in school he forgets," goes an old French maxim, "but the education remains." Similarly the meta-goals remain. These internalized learnings have profound implications for the individual and for the organization because they deeply affect and modify the value and motivational commitments which determine the individual's orientation to his role. I think we have to keep them explicitly in mind in our training and in our future designs.

Editor's Comment. The goals and meta-goals spelled out in Bennis' article are not as concrete as some might desire. There are at least two reasons for this. First, he is discussing laboratory training in general rather than the encounter-group experience. A laboratory in interpersonal relations is, of its nature, much more highly personal than a laboratory in the consultation process. The general goals of laboratory training have to be adapted in different ways to the various species of laboratory training. One of the mistakes that has been made on the part of some in the development of the laboratory movement has been to impose encounter-group goals on a wide variety of laboratory experiences (for example, managerial laboratories) instead of allowing goals to develop naturally from the needs of the experience itself. Second, Bennis' statement is a relatively early one (1962) in the history of the development of the encounter group. The encounter-group movement has been expanding so rapidly (see Clark's article in the section dealing with expression of feeling) that earlier statements of goals sound somewhat conservative today.

I would like to emphasize some of the goals that Bennis either discusses directly or at least implies. First, the participants must work toward establishing a community in which it is possible for members to be highly personal with one another. Second, the participants are to strive to engage in "new" forms of interpersonal behavior. "New" behavior is obviously a relative term. If my tendency is to remain relatively quiet in groups, "new" behavior for me would mean speaking out more frequently. The participants experiment with human behavior that is not part of their ordinary interpersonal style. Third, Bennis talks about "collaborative authority," which refers to another important goal of the group—the diffusion or democratization of leadership. Leadership is related to the needs of the group. Whenever anyone in the group satisfies any of the needs of the group, he is at that time participating in the leadership function of the group.

TORI Community

Jack R. Gibb

Editor's Introduction. In the following somewhat schematic article, Gibb explains briefly the spirit of what he calls a TORI experience, "a radical experiment in high-trust living." The term TORI comes from the words *trust, openness, realization*, and *interdependence*. The article does not describe specific steps in the formation of a TORI community but rather describes what can happen in such a community. Although Gibb is concerned mainly with larger groups (100 to 2000), much of what he describes can also take place in an encounter group if the members come to trust one another deeply. As I have suggested before, if the encounter-group experience is to be fruitful, the members have to risk venturing out of themselves in order to contact one another in a variety of ways. In the section entitled "The Process of Growth and Learning," Gibb describes a number of concrete ways in which participants might develop a sense of interpersonal agency in order to grow. (The question of agency is dealt with in *E:GPFIG*, pp. 359-362.) I stress the importance of the participant's initiative because so many of the people I meet in groups are deficient in this respect. Too many participants wait passively for the group to do something for them; instead, they should be wondering what they can do for the group. The same participants then wonder why they have a poor experience. In the encounter group the participant, almost literally, gets the kind of experience he deserves.

The TORI community is a radical experiment in high-trust living. It may vary in size from 100 to 2000 or more persons, depending on the space available and the purpose. The aims are to build greater trust in an organization and to enhance the growth of participants. The community lives together from 12 to 50 hours, in a one- to three-day session, and may meet several times.

We have created the experience for such diverse groups as congregations, college faculties, national conferences, residents of college dorms, freshman orientation programs, high school student bodies, and the staff and management of companies. It is appropriate for any group of any size that wishes to build a more humanistic climate.

The TORI community is a design for personal growth and for human relations training. We have discovered that it can be created by any interested person, whether or not he has had professional training, and with or without professional consulting help. Ministers, teachers, parents, managers and psychiatrists have tried numerous and often inventive variations of the TORI community. We do not view it as therapy, sensitivity training, or counseling. It is an experience in living—in being and doing (5).

We have used these community experiences as major events in organizational development programs. Sometimes intensive small-group experiences increase the fragmentation and departmentalization of the organization. The intensive TORI community has a unifying and wholizing effect, increasing the awareness of, and loyalty to, the total organization. Large organizations may build up forces that counter growth—i.e., that move toward depersonalization, covert strategy, passivity, and dependency (7,19). The TORI experience releases powerful intrinsic forces toward greater personalization, openness, self-determination, and interdependence (1).

The community is in part a derivation from the TORI theory that my wife, Lorraine, and I, together with numerous associates, have formulated from several years of experimentation (1,2,3,4,9). During the past two years Sandra La Boon has been working with me in formulating a theory of community and in doing research upon the effects of the TORI experience upon participants and their organizations.

I have prepared this informal article in response to requests for information from participants and from those interested in using the experience in their organizational settings. The theory underlying the community experience is described in the publications listed at the end of this paper, cited here by number where relevant, and in other publications not as yet available.

I see myself, and others see me, as growing in significant ways from my own TORI community experiences. My first T-groups in the late 1940s changed my personal and professional life in many ways (4,17,22). The TORI experiences are for me an even more significant turning point. Each community is for me a unique experience—something like meeting a new person, and *really* meeting him. I have corroborated some of my theories. And I've been surprised a lot. The TORI community is the most powerful growth and learning milieu that I have as yet seen. Man's capacity for achieving love and creative interdependence is even greater than I had imagined.

What Happens

Each community is an organism that creates its own life-style. It emerges from some initial common experiences designed to create a climate of greater trust, and then it flowers in a unique way. What we try out are partly derivations from

TORI theory and partly educated guesses. Perhaps the best way to describe what happens is to present the critical aspects of community as we now see them.

1. Emergence and flow. The community flows from the merging of inner forces seemingly discovered by members as they experience each other in depth. Particularly at the beginning, I suggest activities that we have found to be developmental. I try to sense what is happening, get in touch with the "flow," and try to help it happen sooner and better. This is helpful when I'm really in touch with myself and with others. As more activities emerge I do less initiating.

2. Trust. The community grows as trust develops and as fears are reduced (6,16,17). Especially effective are activities that help participants see their fears and trusts, how they arise, how they are expressed, and how they affect others. While there are many well known experiences that illuminate fears and trusts (e.g., trust walks, exploring the dark, running into space), emergent activities are most effective. We are moving away from techniques and methods as fast as possible in favor of spontaneous happenings (2). Members of the community may suggest activities that they have tried before or heard about. Often groups will invent spontaneous and flowing things that feel right to them. Activities are especially effective when they involve everyone, are nonritualistic and nonrepetitive, and allow individual freedom of expression. The standard training and therapy games and exercises are less effective than those that people create for themselves. What goes on in the creating is the key to the growth process.

3. Fluidity of structure and boundary. As the community grows, physical and psychological structure emerges from the flow. Form follows function. Members feel free to join activities or to be alone. Physical movement is frequent and easy. We have tried to provide as much free and open space as possible. Open space allows the community to be visible to itself and to become aware of itself as an organism, permits contagion to enhance the flow, encourages members to be open to as many people as possible, allows much physical movement, and enhances the feeling of community.

4. Wisdom of the community. The community takes care of itself. What needs to be done gets done. "Decisions" are often made on the basis of nonverbal community sensing. People get more and more in touch with each others' momentary and more enduring needs. "Doing it together" comes from a growing sense of caring and excitement. Occasional brief meetings of the total group to voice feelings of the moment are helpful, and may lead to awareness of unmet community needs, an emerging new direction of action, or to a community decision (6,21).

5. *Freedom and self-determination.* Community members gradually come to feel that they are allowed by each other to be and become more of what they are, to "do their own thing," to make their individual choices with minimal constraints. Diversity increases and seems to be nurtured and valued (7). Because freedom seems to be a matter of inner achievement and awareness of choice, members are strongly encouraged to participate in whatever way they wish rather than to "take the role of observer" (2,3).

6. *Personal responsibility.* A member comes to feel responsible for himself and for his own experience. More and more persons make their needs clear to themselves and to others. Care and concern emerge and are shared, replacing advice-giving, helping (15), and therapy (14). At some point I usually say something like, "I am here to learn and to grow, to take responsibility for myself, to experience me and to experience you, to help create the environment I want for me, to increase the range of people and activities that I can love and enjoy." Though I have many feelings of concern for others, I refuse to "take responsibility for" the community experience or any of the members. I am there to grow and learn (2,3,8), not to teach and lead (10,12).

7. *Awareness of interdependence.* Members feel a heightened sense of belonging to the whole, of doing spontaneous things together. Reciprocal dependence and wanting to be close seem to come from inner impulse rather than from expectation or feelings of responsibility (16). The community may come together to sit close, share feelings, have a happening, or play. Sometimes a community of as many as 150 or 200 will form something akin to an intense T-group for several hours. This becomes a powerfully moving experience and opens up new vistas for everyone as to what an intimate community might become.

8. *Openness.* Members become increasingly transparent to the total group. They share impulses, attitudes, and feelings in depth. I suggest many nonverbal and physical activities because they produce rich and visible expressive behavior, allowing people to show feelings rather than talk about them.

9. *Touching.* Touch comes to be important in communication and validation of feelings. Members hug, tussle, cluster, and show feelings in physical ways. Fear and trust are visible to self and others through expressive activity. A person's feelings about touching relative strangers usually reveals to a person some of his fears and trusts.

10. *Importance of the person.* Members come to feel important and influential. Persons can cause things to happen. Others listen and respond when feelings and perceptions are expressed.

11. Freedom from role. Persons feel increasingly free to be impulsive and spontaneous and to act on their inner feelings and perceptions. They become increasingly free from role prescriptions, role obligations, responsibilities, and other demands that persons seem to make on them (2,3).

12. Transcendence. Participants often speak of the experience in spiritual, mystical and cosmic terms. Community activities, particularly in later stages, may become sacramental in quality.

13. Celebration. The experience can become celebrative, joyful, and festive. Members become intensely aware of the emerging joy in depth communication with others. People enjoy people.

14. Humanness. Members expand their awareness and appreciation of a wider band of attributes that they consider part of the human condition. They come to appreciate people who are angry, gentle, petty, loving, rejecting, fearful, uncontrolled, euphoric. Especially impressive is the growing appreciation of vulgar, primitive, and earthy qualities: body smells, uninhibited language, less elegant or attractive vagaries of feeling and behavior (16,17).

15. Love. There is an increase in availability of warmth, caring and love. Persons become more aware of loving feelings and less frightened in showing them. As fear of the community disappears, love and warmth are released (5,17).

The Process of Growth and Learning

The following are optimal conditions for personal learning and growth:

1. Doing on one's own initiative. I learn what I do. Growth occurs when a person, on his steam, does things which embed the action in his body. Changed behavior results from showing feelings rather than talking about them, from doing things rather than thinking about or observing them, from letting me happen rather than examining my motives, and from physically carrying out an impulse or making a choice. After growth I look different (11,12).

2. Intrinsic genesis. My learning starts in me. I grow when the impulse for action is generated from within, when I take full responsibility for my own learning, when the rewards are within the process itself, and when I am my own teacher and model. Growth is its own reward (2,8). A growing person doesn't have to be rewarded—or punished.

3. *Trying out.* I am in the process of continually creating a new me. I learn by trying out the things I deeply want to do and by experiencing the effects upon myself and others (12).

4. *Authenticity of tryout.* I have to do what I am. Permanent and genuine growth comes when I am finding the me I like and when I am doing in the community what I deeply, organically, and bodily want to do. It's good for me when my gut tells me it's good. The growing person comes to trust himself.

5. *Augmenting a strength.* I grow by building on me. Growth is best when it adds to what I and others see as my strengths. It is *not* a remedial or corrective process. I learn by doing something else, not by *stopping* something.

6. *Social interaction.* I learn and grow in interaction with others—in *community*. I cannot grow alone. Learning to be personal, open, self-realizing and interdependent is a social process (16).

7. *Embedding in a natural setting.* I am a total being, relating totally to my life flow. The most enduring growth comes when I make hot decisions, "real" choices, in situations that *matter to me*. The large community, with its compelling reality and its multiple options for action, is superior to the small group, which is more effective than the clinical dyad. The community becomes important and "real," and more powerful for behavior change than simulations, role playing, exercises, and other contrived experiences (18,20).

How It Affects People

We are doing research to determine the effects of the TORI community upon the organization and the participant. Preliminary analysis of the data suggests that the experience is a powerful one, somewhat similar in impact to two weeks of sensitivity training (18,20). The research includes an analysis of how the participants see the experience. The following comments are corroborated by the quantitative data and illustrate the range of responses:

Persons speak of changes in their feelings about themselves: "I have never been more confident, accepting and comfortable with my *self*," "I have come to feel I am a warm, likable and attractive person." There is an increase in feelings of responsibility for self: "I am *me*, and I can do my own thing," "I do things because I want to, not because I should," "I have given me to me." People get in touch with their feelings and "make them known to myself and others," become "willing to share and give to others." One said, "You know, it's hard to know what you *are* feeling, and expecially to put it into words." Some experience a growing sense of freedom: "I feel free because of what you have allowed me to do and be" (2,22).

Meaningful and enduring relationships form during the experience: "I found beauty in other persons when I took the risk to approach them openly," "I was able to ask for help, and received it," "I found a new friend whom I value." A young girl said, "I have come to love a person of another race." Deep gratitude is expressed for those who "made the effort to know me," "helped me find so much of the good in me," or who "listened and cared as my own family doesn't do."

"I can allow persons to come close enough to care about me, and I care for them." It is lovely when a person discovers he can let someone express care and affection for him in a physical way: "There are people I can touch, and who are able to touch me." It is especially meaningful when deep caring and physical affection is shared between persons of the same sex. A withdrawn and gentle man told us he had felt so alone at first, but had "found a brother." A woman was "grateful for the existence" of her woman friend, saying, "She has given me life" (16).

Persons may rediscover a joy in their physical being: "I feel a greater ease with my body," "I realize I have to first be a woman who loves and is loved," "I feel alive!"

Members have spoken of the "power of the Holy Spirit" in the community and of a "spiritual happening." A feeling of transcendence might be expressed in oneness, a sense of "knowing all are involved—I with you and they with us—together." One said, "I was born this weekend" (16).

Some report feeling disturbed: "I was frightened to find it was so easy for me to get angry," "I came to observe and got caught up in it," "You really shook me up. People had been saying things like that to me for years, and now I understand what they mean," "I came to be with people, but have never felt so alone," "I was frightened at how easy it was for some people to get out of control."

Some make changes in their subsequent behavior, their personal lives, their marriages, or their professions (10,13,14). "I was able to say 'I love you' to someone I had loved for a long time," "I have to have a more close, intense, open relationship with my husband. It is proving difficult and painful to create," "I no longer depend on my husband for strength and reassurance," "My job has become one of being human while managing." A little boy identified his mother's experience as "that was when mother quit punishing us so often" (18,20).

Our research shows that significant changes occur in the community and in the members following the experience. However, one aim is fully accomplished if the participants see themselves as having a full and rich experience *during the process*. This, in itself, is a great improvement over most conventions—cocktail parties, weekend retreats, receptions, small groups and other more traditional efforts to create community. We think we are making some progress in finding out what a community might become.

References

1. Gibb, J. R., & L. M. Emergence therapy: The TORI process in an emergent group. In G. M. Gazda (Ed.), *Innovations to group psychotherapy.* Springfield, Ill.: Thomas, 1968.

2. Gibb, J. R., & L. M. Role freedom in a TORI group. In A. Burton (Ed.), *Encounter: The theory and practice of encounter groups.* San Francisco: Jossey-Bass Publishing Co., 1969.

3. Gibb, J. R. The counselor as a role-free person. In C. A. Parker (Ed.), *Counseling theories and counselor education.* New York: Houghton Mifflin, 1968.

4. Gibb, J. R. Climate for trust formation. In. L. P. Bradford, J. R. Gibb, & K. D. Benne (Eds.), *T-group theory and laboratory method.* New York: Wiley, 1964.

5. Gibb, J. R. Group experiences and human possibilities. In H. A. Otto (Ed.), *Human potentialities.* St. Louis: W. H. Green, 1968.

6. Gibb, J. R., & L. M. Humanistic elements in group growth. In J. F. T. Bugental (Ed.), *Challenges of humanistic psychology.* New York: McGraw-Hill, 1967.

7. Gibb, J. R. Fear and facade: Defensive management. In R. E. Farson (Ed.), *Science and human affairs.* Palo Alto, Calif.: Science and Behavior Books, Inc., 1965.

8. Gibb, J. R., & L. M. Leaderless groups: Growth-centered values and potentials. In. H. A. Otto & J. Mann (Eds.), *Ways of growth: Approaches to expanding awareness.* New York: Grossman, 1968.

9. Gibb, J. R. Defense level and influence potential in small groups. In L. Petrullo & B. M. Bass (Eds.), *Leadership and interpersonal behavior.* New York: Holt, Rinehart & Winston, 1961.

10. Gibb, J. R. Dynamics of leadership. In *Current Issues in Higher Education.* Washington, D.C.: American Association for Higher Education, 1967.

11. Gibb, J. R. Sociopsychological processes of group instruction. In N. B. Henry (Ed.), The dynamics of instructional groups. *Yearbook of the National Society for the Study of Education.* Part II. Chicago: University of Chicago Press, 1960.

12. Gibb, J. R. Learning theory in adult education. In M. S. Knowles (Ed.), *Handbook of adult education in the United States.* Chicago: Adult Education Association of the U.S.A., 1960.

13. Gibb, J. R. Communication and productivity. *Personnel Administration,* 1964, 27, 8-13.

14. Gibb, J. R. Defensive communication. *The Journal of Communication,* 1961, 11 (3), 141-148.

15. Gibb, J. R. Is help helpful? *Association Forum and Section Journal* (YMCA), 1964, Feb., 25-27.

16. Gibb, J. R. Search for with-ness: A new look at interdependence. In W. G. Dyer (Ed.), *New dimensions in group training.* New York: Van Nostrand, 1970.

17. Gibb, J. R. Some psychological aspects of faith and trust. In J. A. Waterstradt (Ed.), *Festschrift for P. A. Christensen.* Salt Lake City: University of Utah Press, 1970.

18. Gibb, J. R. Sensitivity training as a medium for personal growth and improved interpersonal relationships. *Interpersonal Development,* 1970, Vol. I.

19. Gibb, J. R. Managing for creativity in the organization. In C. W. Taylor (Ed.), *Climate for creativity.* New York: Pergamon Publishing Co., 1970.

20. Gibb, J. R. Effects of human relations training. In A. E. Bergin & S. L. Garfield (Eds.), *Handbook of psychotherapy and behavior change.* New York: Wiley, 1970.

21. Gibb, J. R., & L. M. The process of group actualization. In J. Akin (Ed.), *Language behavior: Readings in communication.* The Hague, The Netherlands: Mouton & Co., 1970.

22. Gibb, J. R. The small-group experience: What does it mean? In L. N. Solomon & B. Berzon (Eds.), *The encounter group: Issues and applications.* In press.

Editor's Comment. Gibb, in discussing counseling and counselor training elsewhere (1968), describes the behavioral goals that he thinks would greatly concretize the encounter-group experience. He suggests that the counselor (and, by implication, the group member) learn how to be as personal as possible. Specifically, this means: (1) expressing directly to another whatever I am presently experiencing, (2) communicating without distorting my messages, (3) listening to others without distorting their messages, (4) revealing my true motivation in the process of communicating my message, (5) being spontaneous and free in my communication with others rather than using habitual or planned strategies, (6) responding immediately to another's need or state instead of waiting for the "right" time or giving myself enough time to come up with the "right" response, (7) manifesting my vulnerabilities and in general the "stuff" of my inner life, (8) living and communicating about the here-and-now, (9) striving for interdependence rather than dependence or counterdependence in my relationships with others, (10) learning how to enjoy psychological closeness, (11) being concrete in my communications, and (12) being willing to commit myself to others.

A lack of concreteness is one of the principal causes of boredom in groups. If the members are willing to risk the kinds of interaction described by Gibb, they will be amply rewarded.

Part Three.
Leadership

Leadership in the encounter group is a complex phenomenon, for success in the achievement of the group's goals depends not only on the leadership of a good trainer but also on the quality of leadership exercised by the group as a whole.

In the past, one of the failures of some studies of leadership was the tendency to consider the leader and the situation (the circumstances in which leadership is exercised) as separate—that is, as having no influence on one another. The trend among researchers now, however, is to study leadership as a *process* of social influence involving three interactive components: a leader (or leaders), those who are led, and some shared situation.

With respect to small groups, opinions vary on what the "compleat" group leader should do and even on how important it is that there be a leader at all. Gibb (1964) claims that his finest experiences with groups have been with "leaderless" groups. Clearly, however, leaderless groups are not necessarily groups without leadership. A group without an appointed leader may flourish, but a group without leadership will die. Even in the so-called leaderless groups it is apparent that the group prospers to the degree that its members assume a sense of agency—a sense of responsibility for "leading."

The encounter group is a laboratory in which the members learn how to exercise the components of leadership humanly, but skillfully, in a process that is productive of richer interpersonal living. Every encounter group, then, is a leadership-training group, for it is designed to make its members leaders (in some sense) in interpersonal relating.

Reference

Gibb, J. R. Climate for trust formation. In L. P. Bradford, J. R. Gibb, and K. D. Benne (Eds.), *T-group theory and laboratory method.* New York: Wiley, 1964. Pp. 279-309.

One Small-Group Leader's Paradoxical Problems of Becoming a Member of His Own Group

David Nyberg

Editor's Introduction. In describing the process by which the trainer or facilitator ceases being a leader in order to become a member of the group, David Nyberg gives an account of the trainer's traditional role and of typical interactions that take place between the trainer and the participants. The thesis of this article is that the trainer must be rejected by the group in his role as trainer and that this permits him to enter the group as a member.

Many of the participants' problems with the leader, as Nyberg indicates, stem from what he calls the "anonymous authority" of the facilitator. In the "traditional" encounter group, the participants have to grapple with the problem of the ambiguous authority of the facilitator. If the trainer is also very nondirective in the group, his authority can seem even more ambiguous and problematic. The reader should be cautioned, however; there are more facilitator styles in encounter groups than the one described by Nyberg, even though the style he describes might be the most common. In *E:GPFIG* I suggest a style of leadership which involves high visibility rather than ambiguity, active participation on the part of the trainer rather than nondirection, and explicit working toward the diffusion of leadership among the group's members (pp. 123-140). Nyberg, too, is for the diffusion of leadership, but his approach is less direct than the one I suggest. Like Slater (1966), he discusses leadership in terms of dependency, counterdependency, revolt, and the exclusion of the leader. While the existence of such phenomena cannot be denied, I prefer to discuss leadership in terms of group goals, means to these goals, and a climate of cooperation rather than competition.

Editor's Reference

Slater, P. E. *Microcosm: Structural, psychological, and religious evolution in groups.* New York: Wiley, 1966.

During the last twenty years the small group context, as a means for management training, task achievement, therapy, academic learning, and many forms of personal growth, has been subjected to the rack of scientific investigation. The character of published information on small groups (under many aliases) has become more and more that of the formal research report. The study of small groups now has a certified place in several fields of social science, and as a consequence of the empirico-scientific measurement paradigm assumed by most social scientists, the nature of the information sought and reported is naturally skewed toward controllable, statistically analyzable unit variables. One of these "unit variables" is thought to be the group leader, and because his variations are defined restrictively for research purposes, some questions about his place in the group have virtually been ignored.

In the medley of information now available to us about small groups there are only a few notes about the problems a group leader has in becoming a *member* of his group, if he wishes to do so. We usually read either about techniques available to him for manipulating circumstances to produce desired effects or about differences between "leaderless" groups and "led" groups. Both techniques and categories of leadership are viewed in light of the concept of leader effectiveness, derived from functional role theory.* The basic question was then and remains now: What is the relationship between leader behavior and group performance?

Some of the ideas that go with this question help in understanding why *membership* as a focus of inquiry is reserved for group participants and not for group leaders. Generally the leader's *membership* in the group is not considered at all. His *role* takes the attention of investigators. When his membership is considered, it is in terms of *acceptance*, which is tacitly equated with membership. Acceptance relates to the key notion of effectiveness.

It is my view that becoming an accepted leader, which I see as a role function, is to be distinguished from becoming a group member, which I see as a transactive quality; moreover, I feel that a leader has more difficulty than a "registered participant" in becoming a member. Very briefly, the situation I wish to explore is this: at the beginning of a group the leader is automatically in the group by virtue of his role as a leader, but he is out of the group as a person-in-himself by virtue of the same role (which is assigned to him by the participants, either in compliance with or against his wishes). To be in the group as a person, he must be ousted from the group as a leader: re-entry into the group following this ouster assists the leader in becoming a member.

From *Tough and Tender Learning* by David Nyberg (Palo Alto, Calif.: National Press Books, 1971), pp. 91-110. Reprinted with the permission of the publisher.
*The prototype study in this area is often considered to be Lewin, Lippitt, and White's work of 1940 on "Leader Behavior and Member Reaction in Three 'Social Climates,'" as reported in Cartwright and Zander's *Group Dynamics* (1967).

Let me sharpen some terms. I am thinking mainly about "growth" groups, as opposed to "task" or "training" groups, and about "leaders" who are interested in their own involvement in groups more than in merely overseeing the involvement of others. I am motivated by a desire to better understand what has happened to me in groups over the last few years, rather than by an ambition to establish a theory about small group dynamics with regard to leadership. I will be grateful if this chapter is not mistaken by the reader as a prescriptive declaration, but taken instead for what it is intended to be—a description of personal involvement in a certain context which I believe has implications for many types of personal doings and dealings in other contexts, such as "teaching" in classrooms.

Perhaps the best way to begin is with a definition of group membership. This is unfortunate because I can't do it. The second best way may be to explain why I can't begin in the best way. I know what membership is in much the same way that I know what love is. This sort of knowing is felt more than cognized. I know membership or love every time it happens, and I know it with a certainty which simply cannot be overcome by attempts to prove it false. Just as surely, I know when membership or love that was certain at one time is *not* happening anymore. No one who has experienced loving or being loved can reasonably deny that such experience exists, no matter what name he gives the experience. Poets, philosophers, psychologists, and mothers have tried to define love so those who haven't experienced it could understand it. The definitions fall short. There is in all of us who thought we knew what love was before we felt it sufficient conviction later that we really didn't know what to expect. Moreover, we are helpless when we do know to explain it fully to others, much less to define it. So it is with membership. I could try forever to define it and perhaps always be right, but I'd never be done and therefore, in the end, the "definition" would be misleading. I can suggest that group membership is like love; it is a pleasure and an honor, it is altogether a good feeling, and it is important.

I am *not* trying to suggest that the phenomenon of membership is incapable of being induced and shared among many. Rather, it is a superverbal phenomenon which has its potence and meaning *in a context.* Since the context of its occurrence and growth cannot be fully recreated through language (though it can be abstractly represented), the phenomenon itself cannot be completely reproduced verbally, either.

Even though I cannot define it, I can describe membership with some validity if I consider it as an object in its own right, that is, as an event-in-context. Membership has an object status by virtue of a general characteristic of events that Dewey (1960) elucidates in his revaluation of context. His argument, briefly, is this: All existences are *also* events, by virtue of their temporal character, but that they are *only* events is a position that can be maintained only by ignoring context. His position is that an event is both "eventful and an eventuation." It is characterized by a "from which" and a "to which." These characteristics qualify any given event and make it distinctly the event which it is with a quality of its own. An event with a distinctive quality is no longer *only* an event; it becomes an object in its own right.

The context that concerns me is small "growth" groups, and the "from which" elements of this context give me a starting point for a discussion of leader membership.

Four conditions are necessary for membership to occur. I will discuss these four roughly in their own natural sequence: they would never, of course, appear in isolation in the experience of a leader. The conditions are: submission to anonymous authority, trust, risk, and acceptance.

Before proceeding, I would like to describe in more detail the type of group leader for whom membership is a problem. There are essentially two modes of leadership commonly found in current practice. The first is the *model* mode wherein the group leader will assume the role and posture of the ideal member as he conceives the animal. He will demonstrate the ideal by acting out what he expects of each participant in terms of group behavior. The idea is that perfect imitation will produce another living model—an idea at the foundations of certain religious institutions, Bandura's theory of social learning, and many phases of military life. In this model the leader is seen primarily as a teacher and only secondarily, if at all, as a learner. This type of leader would not necessarily want to become a member of his group in the sense I have in mind; therefore, this discussion is not directed toward him.

The other mode is one that may be referred to as *scanning*. In this mode, the leader may unconsciously be acting as a model, but his intention is to facilitate and encourage everyone in the group to scan (through interaction) the persons and the attitudes present in order to construct an eclectic indigenous model for all to understand. The model is a product of the group's efforts, rather than a product of the leader's experience alone. This mode is akin to the Socratic and experimental methods of philosophy, and to the fundamental starting point of existential thought, namely, that philosophy begins with an experience of the whole person rather than with the products of sensation, cognition, or affect in isolation. In this mode it is difficult to distinguish the teacher from the learner, and it is to this type of leader that membership is an issue.

Submission to Anonymous Authority

From the moment a commitment is made to attend a group, a client-professional situation is produced. There is the one who comes and the one who is come to. The mere presence of a leader is fulfillment of the expectation for authority. The assumptions which experience provides, that when something is organized it is controlled and that what is controlled has a controller, are packed up and brought along without a second thought. When the leader is introduced, these expectations are secured; that he is the leader is learned immediately, though his name may fade out of mind in thirty seconds.

Generally, the first thing a leader says to the group is that he does not want to be a leader, but a participating observer, as he hopes all of the group will become. He will deny that he wants power over the group. It is significant to note that no one else in the group has any cause to make such a humble statement. The trainer becomes a gift-giver, he offers his status, and by so doing he creates suspicion, discomfort, bewilderment, scorn, and other varied reactions in the gift-getters. Rarely is there gratitude in return for this gift, as it is seen more in terms of abnegation than generosity or respect.

The fact of his being accepted as *a* leader is unavoidable, but he may become an unacceptable leader with whom the group feels stuck. Because expectations developed by most people over a lifetime lead them to seek behavior-clarifiers in new situations, and because group leaders are commonly reluctant to provide overt satisfaction for these expectations (one of the things to be learned in a group is how to decide on and develop one's own preferences in behaving), model needs arise. The leader offers no verbal information as to what "proper" behavior is, so people seek covert information in the behavior of a perceived model who is usually the leader, the old-timer.

Model needs are quite high at the beginning of a group. If denied a model then, the more dependent members will become hostile in active (whining) or passive (withdrawal) manners. The more independent members will begin voting for themselves as the most acceptable alternative leader, running overt or covert campaigns for the office. As political camps develop, the leader can point out the split and thereby re-establish his expertise and his model potential. But he will be seen as a model no matter what he does, for he is perceived as having the corner on authority and experience. The behavior the leader chooses to manifest at this time will inevitably fashion the mold of the model.

A conflict is inevitable at this point: the leader wishes to divest himself of authority so the group will learn how to handle itself, and the group participants wish to invest authority in the leader in order to submit to it and relinquish responsibility for what will happen (or, as is often suspected early in a group's life, what will *not* happen since no one seems willing to organize and plan). Authority, even in its most vague conception, is a strong determinate of attitudes, and in an almost childlike way the group participants demand that they have some.

The leader is desired as a protector. The people in the group borrow strength from him, seek permission and reinforcement from him, and ask him to absorb their feelings as he seems to absorb his own. They use him as a counselor, either by attending to his words or by noting subtle behavioral cue systems as they did when they were students and had to guess the "right" answer by watching the teacher's eyes and the tilt of her head, by discriminating the tones of her voice, and the like. Insofar as the leader is aware of these practices, he will deliberately confuse the group by responding either at random with what seem to be inappropriate behaviors or by following a cue system of his own which has to do with the feelings and appearances of the group, rather than the questions or issues on the floor. On one hand the participants are struggling with questions of organization and expectation, while on the other the leader is already struggling with feelings and attitudes of which the group is largely unaware. At this point the leader is outnumbered—he is the only one who does not appear to be concerned about structure—and in a sense he is an alien in the group, at least with reference to this particular issue. He has become the authority of the group in an anonymous way, for the group participants do not know who he is yet or what he is really up to, though they are willing to obey him even if they have to make up their own commands and attribute them to him. This attribution is a sort of super ego function. It is not uncommon in children as they begin to wander out from under the constant gaze of their parents to explore the world. Old constraints remain to haunt the "good conscience."

In different ways and for different reasons the leader is seen at once as a professional, a seducer, a gift-giver, a model, a director, and an unwilling organizer. All of this adds up to his being an alien in the group, an authority cloaked and inscrutable, an authority who is frustratingly difficult to obey since he issues no demands.

Trust

To me, trust is what makes risk less risky and more possible. Having trust is being assured that one can rely on another, at least under certain conditions. Unconditional trust is rare, for very few people have the capacity to fulfill all conditions for reliability in all circumstances. We generally learn whom we can trust under specific circumstances. In a group situation the leader is usually trusted from the outset as a competent professional and as an experienced group-maker. This trust is largely of a desperate nature for it is produced by suspicion and anxiety. Undergoing a group confrontation for the first time is a threatening business because it is a new experience, because it brings fear of exposure, and because of the popular fantasies of eroticism in groups which plague so many imaginations. Suspicion and anxiety are roused to a high level and need to be allayed by some sort of commitment to something or someone. The leader is needed as a keeper of the group's safety; he is needed as a source of trust.

There is by now no doubt that needs influence perceptions. When we are deprived of something we need we search it out. In this case when we do not trust ourselves or the strangers in the group, or for that matter the group process itself, a high need for trust in something is aroused. Any potential source of trust becomes flagrantly apparent to the perceiver, and in a group that source is the leader. He becomes a trustee, not yet a person who also needs trust. He is at first perceived as a source only. This cannot help from setting the leader apart from the rest of the group. If he is using a nondirective approach to the group growth process, he will make himself appear as an unwilling source for need satisfaction in an effort to become inessential to the nourishment of the group's development. He wants to become unnecessary (the aim of a good teacher) and is thus unwilling from the start to let the group depend on him.

The leader's reluctance to function as a source for need satisfaction is sometimes interpreted as a secretive, manipulative "technique." When it is so perceived, a common group reaction is mild rebellion, a testing of what limits exist, and an oblique denunciation of confidence in the leader. The rebellion seldom goes far, however, and the leader begins to be treated as a spy—a reticent observer who is compiling a mental dossier on every participant. We tend to be suspicious of potential sources of trust for we have all had the experience of certain behaviors in school going on "the permanent record" via reports by our teachers and some of our more socially ambitious peers. Early in the life of a group, the leader is trusted as a professional (and this trust is tested by asking the leader in many ways to please perform as he is expected to), but also mistrusted as a spy who is collecting information but not sharing it.

The spy role is partly a product of the leader's timing of his responses. It is true that he has a lot to say about the way a group is forming, but it is also true that providing this information too early creates a dependence which is difficult to overcome later on. His timing of his responses is intended to foster the growth of the group for it keeps questions open, and with the questions, curiosity. Curiosity has a tension of its own and this tension moves a group to explore what in fact it is up to. The same effect of timing applies to almost any individual learning situation.

Now the leader is leading a double life within the group (as the group perceives him) and thus is not to be completely trusted. A consequence of this is that the participants band together in their common plight, namely, that the "psychologist" won't tell them what is going on or what he thinks of each of them although they know he is observing them. The leader is to a degree ostracized from the group, for while the participants are trying to be more honest with each other (a function of tension created by curiosity and uncertainty), the leader is perceived as being dishonest—or at least as refraining from honesty. The leader has become an alien in an added sense. He remains "outside" the group because he is still seen in part as a traditional leader—someone who is needed to lean on for authority-support but not allowed to lean himself—and he is also "outside" the group because he now seems to be refraining from honesty while the others are becoming quite involved with it.

Risk

Risk as it applies here is most properly a function of exposure, of self-disclosure. The physical analogy of dying of overexposure to the elements or to the environment suggests that exposure of the emotions or feelings carries a threat of psychological or ego death. To march unguarded and unprotected among the elements (strangers, enemies, etc.) one needs courage and some confidence that survival or strengthening will result from the efforts made.

There are two facets to risk in a group. The first is risking to expose oneself, and the second is risking to expose another.

A group leader naturally accumulates experience at both kinds of risk-taking during the course of his work. The more he is exposed to such behaviors and the more he is involved with them himself, the less threatening they become to him. Being familiar with one's reactions in risky situations and having experienced the relief and often the joy of its results tend to make such risk-taking desirable, and therefore less risky in terms of ego protection. A successful experience with personal risk tends to strengthen the ego, which in turn makes ego less of an issue altogether.

There is no more interesting topic of conversation than oneself. The person who does not want to talk about himself is rare: either he has no interest in himself or he has explored himself sufficiently to reduce the need and the pressure to *get at* the exploration. The first of these possibilities is so uncommon that there is nothing much to say about it. The second is, however, very important for the membership potential of a group leader.

Trust and risk are related in a very close way: they seem almost mutually dependent. It is difficult to risk anything unless you can trust to some degree, and it is difficult to develop any trust without risking something of yourself and coming out with more confidence than you began with. Assuming that when a group begins the participants have no reason to risk anything of themselves because they have no reason to trust anyone present (except the leader as a professional), the leader again finds himself in a position unique to the group. He has risked before. He has exposed himself and others in similar group situations.

These two facets of risk (exposing self and exposing another) reflect two distinctly different behaviors. Exposing oneself at the risk of rejection by others is perhaps the less threatening of the two sorts of risk. One reason for this is that *you* have the privilege of choosing what *you* think *you* can deal with at any given time. The surprise aspect of exposure of self is reduced almost to insignificance. There is an anticipation process of working and warming up to a point where you are ready and anxious to reveal something, and this does not happen when some other tries to do the exposing for you. As confidence of acceptance by the group grows with experiences of risking personal exposure to a group, more and more of one's private doubts and questions become public and significant tensions are resolved. As these cathartic pressures are relieved, exposure or "acting out" needs dissipate and are replaced with certain comforts and assurances which lead to a desire to expose others so they can experience the same "settling growth." A desire to share comfort with others motivates prodding, encouragement, and sometimes goading which is often misunderstood as aggression. It is true that aggressive behaviors occur in groups, but trying to expose another is not always aggressive; it can be supportive and compassionate.

A group leader who has been through self-exposure many times is likely to feel that what he could say about himself again is rather repetitious and therefore feel no immediate need to get into it. For the most part, group participants have not had this experience (which is why they are in a group in the first place), and they are frightened of it. As they find themselves exposing more and more of themselves to each other they will eventually come around to telling the leader that he has not said much about himself. He is again seen as an "outsider," this time in a nonrisking sense. As will become apparent later on, those who do not risk self-exposure in the group are the ones who have least chance of becoming full members of the group. To become a member one must be known by the group, and if one does not expose himself, one will not be known.

The second kind of risk-taking, exposing another, is what a leader spends most of his time promoting, though not necessarily by doing it himself. Whereas the first kind of risk has a relatively brief attraction for a group leader, thus making it progressively harder for him to get his membership in the group through it, the second kind remains a viable means for him no matter how long he works in groups. Each group is different, and encouraging exposure of others is always appropriate and never repetitious. The leader gradually gravitates to this exposure-of-another kind of risk while the participants are more naturally concerned with the first kind of risk, the personal exposure. In this way, the leader is separated from the group because he appears to have more courage in "getting at" the other members of the group. Each member senses this, prepares himself to meet the challenge with whatever armor he has available, and develops a sympathy with the other members.

Whenever one person exposes another and the exposure provokes deep feelings, the nonexposed participants rush to comfort the person whose feelings they have shared. Often this comforting takes the form of temporarily rejecting the person who provoked the response. As was suggested above, the leader is most generally the one rejected, either for doing the deed himself or for allowing it to be done. This situation always seems to resolve itself, mainly through a new strength the exposed person gains from the experience: it is often he who invites the rejected one (the exposer or leader) back into the group as a sort of thanks and as an extension of friendship. When this is perceived by the other participants, they realize the difference between a friendship born of a significant personal experience shared with some risk, and the kind of mere acquaintance with each other that they have had from the beginning. New pressures to participate in a meaningful and personal way are generated from a sort of envy of the friendship, which amounts to a desire to share a sense of personal meaning with others. I believe that literally every individual seeks and needs experiences with (intense) personal meaning. Such experiences are scarce among us information-oriented, busy people, and are all the more alluring for their rarity. When it becomes clear that one's present context is supportive of such experiences, one finds it difficult to give up the (another!) chance to share in them.

If the leader is perceived as directly involved in such a breakthrough, and he generally is so perceived, he gains a compatriot in his uniqueness within the group, and this is one of the first steps toward membership. Two people have shared something of themselves with each other.

Acceptance

I view acceptance as personal and explicit, not as a general "love thy neighbor" feeling. In the discussion about submission to anonymous authority I might have included submission to gentility or to "just good manners" or to the most flaccid sense of Christian charity, which is an impersonal sort of deference. Genuine personal acceptance is based on knowledge and experience shared with the person who is accepted, and it may include the internal struggle we sometimes have in coming around to accepting someone who is not like ourselves. At this point, I'm willing to suggest that it is this *felt* acceptance originating from intimate experiences with another that is the basis of membership in a group.

Membership

All four elements that develop in the context of group activity reduce the likelihood of the leader's being accepted in the same way as the rest of the participants. As long as he remains an authority of some sort, is only half trusted (i.e., remaining half-spy), and is perceived as a nonrisk taker (of the self-exposure type), the most he can hope to become in the group is an accepted leader.

My own experience in groups leads me to speculate that a leader may be accepted as a full member of the group only if he is first rejected, thrown out completely from the "group life" once that has been established. When the group feels or tells the leader that they can get along without him or that they would prefer to get along without him because of something he has done, then he is in the position of having to get permission for re-entry into the group. He no longer doles out permission, he *asks* for it himself. It is only when he is no longer *needed* that he can be sure that he is *wanted*. If being wanted is being accepted for what you are as a person, not as a leader, then being wanted is being a member.

It should be clear that being a member of a group is quite different from being a vital functionary within the group. It is different from being a teacher, trainer, guide, or counselor. These are all names of roles, not of any person. In the governing of the group the leader must be deposed from his seat as patriarch and elected to the house of commons, the group itself, which is the supreme governing body. No one else in the group has ever held the chair, so no other member has the same route to travel for getting into the group. In a sense, the leader has more to overcome than the other members of the group *because* he has been in other groups before.

Ordinarily the leader elicits faith from the participants—faith in his authority, in his knowledge, in his control—and this faith makes risking and trusting possible. But as long as others have faith in him in this manner, he is kept apart, for the object of faith is a source of strength, and a source of strength cannot be seen as weak (i.e., as one of the faithful) for then he would cease to be a source of strength. The leader must break this faith to gain acceptance as a full and equal member of the group.

In summary it might be said that unless a group becomes strong enough in its own life, in its own sense of itself, to dispense with its leader, the leader will not have a very good chance of becoming a member. And a sense of membership on the leader's part may be his most vital proof that he has indeed helped make a group.

A Note on Re-creational Research

I have a rather uneasy (and familiar) feeling that any one part of what I have written above is vulnerable to the scrutiny of tough-minded researchers, but a distant voice reminds me that "all particulars become meaningless if we lose sight of the pattern which they jointly constitute" (Polanyi, 1958, p. 57). And it is the pattern that is important to me. This pattern is not a given in my view, but an elusive product of transaction between me and several similar contexts, an unintended product that emerged out of an experience. In Dewey's phrase, it is an event-in-context.

A research problem is suggested here. In following a research design to validate my hypothesis, I would first have to assume the hypothesis and then concentrate my observations on the effects all relevant actions, behavior, etc. had on the hypothesis. But by doing this I would be denying the unintended, emergent quality of the pattern. I would have an unspoken goal for the group and thereby I would be guilty of a manipulation that would alter the situation I meant to research. Instead of focusing on the actions of the group in their particularity, I would focus on the actions that seemed to lead toward or away from my hypothesis. The new situation may be researchable, but that is not my concern. Perhaps Polanyi (1958, Chap. 8) can help make my problem clear:

. . . our attention can hold only one focus at a time and . . . it would hence be self-contradictory to be both subsidiarily and focally aware of the same particulars at the same time.

The pattern I have tried to describe I became aware of subsidiarily, and if I were to focus on it during the experience I would change it insofar as I am involved in the group from a different perspective or point of view. In reading this sentence, you are focusing on its *meaning*, and you are aware of each word, each bit of punctuation only subsidiarily. You do have the opportunity, however, to try it again, this time focusing on each word and ignoring the overall meaning. The experience of reading the sentence will be different for you and the meaning different as well because your new interest leads you to different things. The sentence itself is available for yet more readings: it stands there waiting for you, ready to be viewed in whatever way you want. A group of living people, though, are not a very reasonable parallel to a group of typed words. The people are affected and thereby changed by each "reading," by each experience, by each moment. One cannot read the *same* "human sentence" (group in relation) twice, and it is impossible for one of the words (individuals) in this sentence (group) to jump out of his place in it to read it without changing it.

In brief, the membership I have described cannot be the subject of customary psychological research. To know that membership has taken place, one must experience it—be an intimate part of it and not merely an observer. I agree with Polanyi's notion that there is a vital component of knowledge which is the (passionate) contribution of the person knowing what is known. This contribution is not opposed to "knowledge," nor is it an element to be overcome in "objectifying" what is known. The thing "known" that I have been trying to describe is essentially a feeling, a "had" feeling. I know I had this feeling, and I have tried to re-create in language an experience which was re-creational in itself—clear only after it had happened. I would suggest that this attempt is research, very like what Moustakas calls heuristic research (Moustakas, 1961).

This sort of research may be tough-minded in its own way. A reasonable starting point for doing such research well is the researcher himself. This beginning entails more than merely accepting the fact that at least one person is always present in research; it entails the introspective process of experiencing oneself as an instrument to the point where one can see and accept comprehension and compassion mingling. Traditionally, we have separated these two elements or concepts of experience to refine and clarify each of them. Perhaps it is time to explore in research one implication of transaction theory, namely, that we reconsider the effects of our using pairs of distinct concepts (Thomas, 1968), especially those concerned with personal experiences.

References

Cartwright, D., and Zander, A. (Eds.) *Group dynamics.* (3rd ed.) New York: Harper and Row, 1967.

Dewey, J. *Experience, nature, and freedom*, edited by R. J. Bernstein. New York: Bobbs-Merrill, 1960.

Polanyi, M. *Personal knowledge.* Chicago: University of Chicago Press, 1958.

Thomas, L. G. Implications of transaction theory. *The Educational Forum*, January 1968. Pp. 145-55.

Editor's Comment. Nyberg claims that it is as impossible to define good group membership as it is to define love. But leadership is meaningless unless it is related to helping the participants become good members. Therefore, if good membership cannot be defined or described, then neither can effective leadership. I believe that both can be adequately described without putting either leader or member in some kind of conceptual straitjacket. *E:GPFIG* is an attempt to outline the basic elements of good group membership.

I contend that the participant has a right to know the functions of the trainer in the group as well as something about the dynamics of leader-member interaction. Since most groups start with a great deal of ambiguity or "planned goallessness," the average participant—especially if this is his first experience—knows little about the function of the facilitator in the group. In most groups, the facilitator is an enigmatic figure for the participant. The ambiguity under which he works makes him an "ink blot" for the participants, and he should not be surprised if they spend a good deal of time in projective activities toward him. If, as Nyberg suggests, the facilitator wants to become unnecessary (as leader or facilitator) and does not want the group to depend on him, then he should clarify his function right from the start. Nyberg admits that the ambiguity of the group situation and especially the "anonymity" of the facilitator make things difficult for the facilitator. Nyberg's article helps "blow the cover" of the trainer; as such, it should be read by prospective group members and not just by trainers. Participants are becoming more and more sophisticated about the nature and inner workings of groups. This fact should have some impact on the way that facilitators present themselves to group members.

I am not trying to suggest here that an encounter group avoid handling leader-member problems or that they can be avoided in such groups. In many ways it may well be quite growthful for a person in a group to work through his feelings about the leader; but group members who become preoccupied with the facilitator and with their relationships to authority figures in general can be dodging the real work of the group: mutual self-involvement.

In some group situations (see *E:GPFIG*, Chapters 2 and 5) the major dimensions of the encounter-group experience—including the nature of leadership—are outlined for the participants before the group experience begins. The prospective participants are told outright that the facilitator, like them, is interested in participating in the growth processes of the group. The resources he has because of his expertise and experience he places at the service of the group, but he claims no special privileges because of these resources. His principal task is to see to it that the leadership he is capable of exercising becomes diffused among the members of the group. In the beginning he is relatively more active, perhaps both modeling behavior and using exercises to stimulate the participants to interact with one another; but, as more and more members get a feeling for the encounter process and participate in the leadership function of the group, the facilitator becomes more and more like the other members of the group.

I do not think that the leader should be (or that he should allow others to cast him in the role of) an unwilling organizer, counselor, father, teacher, professional, seducer, gift-giver, or director. Nyberg says that the leader who is a model would not necessarily want to become a member of the group in the sense that he (Nyberg) has in mind. He suggests that a "model" is not in the group primarily as learner. However, a facilitator, even though he models good membership behavior, need not be artificial when he does so and he can be as sincere a learner as the rest of the participants. Furthermore, I think that a good facilitator can be both a model and a "scanner" in Nyberg's sense.

I have used what I call "low threat" facilitators in encounter groups to try to avoid some of the leader problems discussed here. These are paraprofessionals who are still in a training situation. Since they are less "distant" from the other members of the group in terms of experience and professional qualifications, the problems of the diffusion of leadership are lessened. Group members are ready to see them "in process" more readily than they see professionals in this light. Perhaps some group leaders are overtrained for the function they are to fulfill in the group. Their status, rather than making them more effective, stands in the way of the leadership-diffusion process.

It is too early in the history of encounter groups to claim that one style of leadership is universally preferable to another or that highly structured groups are either more or less growthful than those characterized by high ambiguity and goallessness. In high-ambiguity groups the leadership process outlined by Nyberg probably characterizes the interaction. The leader must be ousted as leader in order to return as member. In group experiences characterized by high visibility, the problems of dealing with the leader tend to be minimized and, at least in some cases, the participants quickly get down to the work of dealing with one another.

Building Leadership Skills

John L. Wallen

Editor's Introduction. If all the members of the encounter group are to become leaders in some sense of that term, then they must know the kinds of behaviors that make groups centers of growthful human interaction. Leadership behaviors have to be spelled out, operationalized, given clear definition. Although Wallen's article is concerned specifically with education, his discussion of a humane and democratic kind of leadership is directly applicable to participants' behavior in the encounter group.

Education is one of the largest industries in our country and one of the most criticized. It is an industry that is highly resistant to change, for it is an industry that is highly bureaucratic. There seems to be a great need for decentralized leadership, but this means that many teachers are needed who are willing to risk the disapproval of their superiors (and their peers) in exploring alternatives to our present educational system. Wallen urges experimentation with role-free behavior in educational situations and suggests that teachers must be role-free if they are to be creative. Teachers and students are "role-free" when they consider themselves first as persons who have needs to think, feel, communicate, and make decisions; but when they look upon themselves primarily as fulfilling roles with respect to one another, education is lifeless because it does not include an interchange of feelings and emotions.

How many secondary school leaders at some time have experienced laboratory training? It might have been called "sensitivity training"; it might have been a group at one of the National Training Laboratories like Bethel, or Cedar City, or Lake Arrowhead.

How many secondary leaders enjoy the music played by the Jefferson Airplane, the Buffalo Springfield, The Grateful Dead, or "Sgt. Pepper's Lonely Hearts Club Band"? To how many secondary principals are those names strange and unfamiliar?

From *Humanizing the Secondary School*, Norman K. Hamilton and J. Gaylen Saylor (Eds.). Reprinted with permission of the Association for Supervision and Curriculum Development and John L. Wallen. Copyright ©1969 by the Association for Supervision and Curriculum Development. An edited printscript of an address presented at the Secondary Education Council Conference, "Humanizing Secondary Schools," St. Louis, Missouri, November 1-4, 1967.

I ask these questions because the theme I will develop here relates to a kind of experience of learning which grows out of laboratory training, and because readers of this booklet who happen to be secondary school people deal daily with the people who like the Jefferson Airplane and the Buffalo Springfield. I really wonder as I raise these questions if part of any secondary conference should not have time set aside for listening to the words that these groups sing in their songs. Here we are speaking about a question of humanizing, and the theme that I see being repeated over and over in many of these songs is a desperate request that somebody let them become human. I do not know whether I can remember exactly, but the Buffalo Springfield has one song ending with "Those of us who run to catch a moment in the sun always seem to find we weren't supposed to run."[1] Another phrase from that song is "Finding what you sought with all the time you bought leaves you with the thought that perhaps you've just been bought."[2] I suspect that maybe some of us, too, feel that way.

I have heard a lot of discussion about humanizing the student. As a matter of fact, I hear so much discussion that the word begins to lose meaning for me. While I listen to talk about this process in rather general terms, I suddenly feel that the key is that *you cannot humanize anybody but yourself*, and I think that this is where we must start.

With all the talk about how we are going to humanize other people, I would like to put the shoe on another foot and say, how humane are your interactions? I guess I would give another slogan to remember—possibly a cliché. Some may be familiar with Marshall McLuhan's[3] work on understanding media in which he says "The medium is the message." He goes on to point out that far and above what television has to present, television itself as a medium is a different kind of message. He gives as an example that, when the child who has grown up watching television is presented with print, he looks at the page and tries to get the message from the whole page as he does with television. He has learned a certain attitude toward how you get experience. Reading is a very different kind of thing. I do not want to belabor McLuhan's point, but I believe that when you come to the question of humanizing the school, *the person is the message.*

I am no specialist on curriculum; I do not know anything about the use of space in schools; I do not know anything about scheduling in modular blocks or flexible schedules. Yet I do have a very strong conviction that the place in which any child will develop his potentialities as a person is through contact with somebody who is more than a role—*who is himself a person!*

[1] Stephen Stills, songwriter, "Everybody's Wrong." Ten East Music and Springale Tunes. *Buffalo Springfield.* ATCO Record #SD33-200.
[2] *Ibid.*
[3] Marshall McLuhan. *Understanding Media.* New York: McGraw-Hill Book Company, Inc., 1964.

The Person and the Role

If I asked you to write three sentences beginning with the word "I," some of you would write sentences of this type: "I am a teacher." "I am a principal." "I am a man." "I am a husband." "I'm an American." Others would write: "I feel resentful at having to write this." "I'm anxious to go home." "I wish this were over." "I feel good today."

These two types of responses point up a distinction between the person as a role and the person as a person. This distinction between the role and the person is a crucial one when dealing with the question of humanizing secondary education.

When you go to the restaurant and the waitress comes and takes your order, you deal with her as a role, essentially. You do not really care what her name is; you do not really care whether she is married or single; you do not really care how many children she has or whether she left home crying this morning because her husband said something unkind to her. You do not really care very much as long as she gets your food to you on time and does not overcharge you. In short, as long as she performs within the role there is a satisfactory relationship established. Likewise, we may say she does not really care about you as a person. You are the other complementary role, the customer. The waitress waits on the customer, and there is a very restricted and circumscribed set of behaviors that can take place between the two of you.

All of us have roles that we play in life. Some roles have a high degree of deference in them as, for instance, a bellboy, but whatever they are, they are impersonal. Do not be mistaken—I do not want to say we should never play roles, for obviously that is impossible. What I am speaking about is the fact that a role, in many cases, tends to swallow up and destroy our quality of being a person, our personality; and to the extent that this happens, we have less humane interactions with other people because the interaction is often dictated by the role and not by the fact that persons are simply present at a given moment and relating to each other.

There are several ways in which a person differs from a role. First, a person has uniqueness, a sense of self—self-identity, self-concept. There is a flavor to a person; he has a style. The role implies that the behavior should be interchangeable. Anybody else, put into that role, should be able to operate and carry out the requirements of the position. Second, the person wants the feeling that he runs his own life; he is not a puppet; he is not manipulated; he is not directed or coerced by others. A third characteristic of the person, and the one to be emphasized in our work and in everyday life, is that a person can reason and process information logically and arrive at conclusions which may be more or less sound.

Roles Within the School

More important to me in looking at the person is the fact that he has feelings; he feels anger, joy, affection, sadness, humiliation, surprise, discouragement—the gamut of emotion. Yet the part that I usually find missing in our interactions is the ability to deal with feelings, both mine and those of the other person.

We should begin by thinking about the roles within the school systems. We have a principal, which is a role; we have a teacher, which is a role; we have a student, which is a role; and much of what takes place in the schools is an attempt to keep each person in his role as others see it. For instance, if the teachers are accustomed to a principal role which is rather directive and a principal comes in who would like to have more of a free-swinging school with more responsibility and initiative taken in the classroom, he encounters all kinds of resistance. He is not being a good principal because he is not fulfilling the expectations that the teachers have of his role. In short, any time you violate a role expectation, the other person becomes somewhat uneasy because he does not know how to deal with the situation. Each of us is much more comfortable as long as each one predictably stays within his role, but the role itself is dehumanizing.

Sidney Jourard's book, *The Transparent Self*,[4] stresses the point that failure or inability to know one's real self can make one ill. He is talking about self-alienation. His book makes reference to nurses. My observations from the work I have done with nurses and physicians convince me that the role has swallowed up so much of their person that there is literally little person left. They now have this professional mannerism, "Well, have we had our orange juice this morning?" Jourard says that "they have repressed or suppressed much of their own real or spontaneous reactions to experience and that they replace their spontaneous behavior with carefully censored behavior which conforms to a rigid role definition or a highly limited self-concept. They behave as they should behave and feel what they should feel." When roles or self-concepts exclude too much of what he calls "real self," a person soon experiences certain symptoms such as vague anxiety or depression, and sometimes boredom.

"If the person has come to neglect the needs and feelings of his body, then such physical symptoms as unwarranted fatigue, headaches, and digestive upsets will arise. So each of us pays a price for not being able to be truly himself."

Would people in schools act any differently if they responded as they really felt about what takes place in the school? What kinds of differences, if any, would you expect to find if people were to be more personal, more genuine, and less role-like as they interact in the school? Think about faculty meetings, about conferences between a principal and a teacher, and about student-teacher interaction.

[4] Sidney M. Jourard. *The Transparent Self*. Princeton, New Jersey: D. Van Nostrand Company, Inc., 1964.

Can a teacher be a person and play a role at the same time? Can one separate role from person? Why cannot the person modify and influence his role so that his personality is expressed in his performance? Does being a person mean that each expresses whatever he feels when he feels it, even if at the expense of dignity? Does playing a role produce boredom? What is the difference between role and function? Are these words synonymous?

The Position and the Role

When we speak of a position we think of the particular duties that the individual has to carry out in that position, the things that he must do. When we speak of a role we speak of the expectations that others have of him. It is very much like the situation in a play, a drama. A teacher once said to me, "I can't go into a liquor store without feeling guilty because somebody will see me and they'll hear that a teacher has bought liquor." This feeling very much points out awareness of the perception of the community's expectations, but it does not have anything to do with the duties of filling the position of being a teacher. It has no relation to whether he is a good teacher or a poor teacher. It has to do with the way he feels in relation to the rest of the community, and the way the community might feel about him.

There is a continuing reference to the relation between the role and the person. I think that what needs to be isolated is the key problem that we all face—how to make our performance within our role fulfilling and meaningful to ourselves. That is the problem the student has—how he can fulfill his role as a student in a way which is personally meaningful to him. He is not going to stop being a student; that is a role in which he is cast when he comes into the school. Yet can he be a person as a student, and can the teacher be a person as a teacher?

If you have read a recent article by Carl Rogers[5] you are familiar with this point of view. His article alerts me to that kind of education in which the interaction between persons is most delicate, namely, in psychotherapy. The general trend in the field at the present time is for the therapist to get away from techniques, to stop hiding behind a nondirective mask, to stop simply reflecting what is going on outside, to stop only interpreting behavior and, instead, to start to interact as he himself is at this particular moment. Ten years ago a psychotherapist would never have said, "I don't see where this is getting us; I'm so bored with what you're telling me I can hardly stay awake." This would be much more apt to happen with a therapist today, and it may be that he will get

[5]Carl R. Rogers. "The Interpersonal Relationship in the Facilitation of Learning." In: *Humanizing Education: The Person in the Process.* Robert R. Leeper, editor. Washington, D.C.: Association for Supervision and Curriculum Development, 1967, pp. 1-18.

the response that one person gave a therapist who said this, "I'm so glad you said that because I'm bored, too."

Toward Being a Person

Over and over again I am reminded of the story of "The Emperor's New Clothes." It is a kind of mutual charade which is what an excessive emphasis upon role enactment does to us. My favorite story along this line is of the husband and wife who had been planning for many, many years to take a trip abroad, but they never could find the time. Finally, the husband came home and he said, "Well, dear, I think I have things in such shape that we can take six months off this summer and go to Europe for the trip we have always wanted to take. Is it going to be okay with you?" She said, "I have been waiting for ten years. This is fine." The husband looked through the doorway across to another room where he saw a little old gray-haired lady knitting and rocking, and he said, "While we are away you will have to find someone to take care of your mother." The wife said, "I thought she was your mother!"

The condition that makes that kind of situation possible is pluralistic ignorance—when each person does not know something but thinks he is the only one who does not know. I submit that many of the difficulties in schools stem from this kind of situation. Everybody at a faculty meeting may be bored, may be feeling it is a waste of time, but each thinks that he is the only one. Besides, a good teacher should not say this, or a good principal should not say that; thus they go on enacting a charade which results in wasting everybody's time and in increasing the tension in the school. Nobody cares enough to get up and say, "I'm bored; I wonder if anybody else is."

If people were to be more themselves as persons, would there be more hurt feelings? I think this is probably true, but what do we do when we relate to other people? A great deal of our effort goes into avoiding hurting feelings or having them hurt. If the proper climate is established, hurt feelings are the first step in learning, for if we spend all of our time protecting ourselves from having hurt feelings, we will never find out why our feelings were hurt, and that is where inquiry starts.

When we relate with others, should there always be the element of complete trust? In order to be involved interpersonally, do we have to open all the intimate avenues of our private feelings? Openness with other people is not an end in itself; it is a means to an end. In many cases we are not open with the other person because of a lack of concern for him. In Herbert Thelen's article[6] he introduces the definition of *humane interaction* as an interaction that would be enlightened and compassionate; an interaction that is based upon caring; but I

[6]See Thelen's chapter, pp. 17ff.

think that he did not stress sufficiently another aspect of caring which might be misinterpreted as only sentimental kindness or superficial affection.

A person who learns how to use his own angry feelings instead of withdrawing in anger is indicating a concern. I know my wife cares for me when she is willing to tell me how angry she is about something I have just done. What it says to me is, "I don't like the way things are going, and we can't work it out unless you know what my reaction is." On the other hand, when she becomes angry and withdraws, this is a far more difficult situation, because at that point the contact has been broken. I am not saying that at all times—in order to be a person—you must express all the feelings you have. But one ought to be able to express those feelings that are *relevant* to the other person's performance.

I look upon human feelings, particularly negative feelings because we have most difficulty with negative feelings, as key factors in human relationships. They play what I call the fuse-function in interpersonal relations. When you build a house, you just do not put the same capacity in all the wiring. You put in one part of the wiring which is more apt to burn out; that is the fuse. When the fuse blows, you then check the circuit to find out where the overload is and correct it. This is the function that anger, depression, boredom, irritation, and resentment play in interpersonal relations. Before a relationship goes completely sour, before it goes completely bad, before trust is completely broken, one or the other or both parties will begin to experience some kind of negative feelings. If you ignore these feelings and say, "No good teacher has these kinds of feelings, or no good administrator has these kinds of feelings," you are ignoring the fact that the fuse is blown. This indicates that there is something wrong in the relationship and that you had better check your communication circuits.

If administrators react to feelings in this way, it is possible to say to a teacher, "You know, I am really becoming quite concerned and would like to discuss what this means for the ways we are working together." It may be that he will discover, as a principal, that he is doing certain kinds of things which lead to the behavior of the teacher. It may be that the teacher will modify his behavior or that neither will modify their behaviors, but that each will understand the other better as a person. This cannot occur without the use of negative feelings as a signal.

Several years ago an experience brought home to me, rather vividly, the poverty of our behavior in our roles. At a time when I was serving as a clinical psychologist, I received a call from a young man who said that he had a difficult family situation. He wondered if I would be willing to sit in with the family while they had a meeting. I accepted. We gathered in the home of the elderly mother, whom we will call Mrs. Johnson. There were the grown son and daughter, who were talking about a third child who was a grown daughter, Dorothy. Dorothy had gotten to the point where she would have to go to the state mental hospital, and the task that the son and daughter were attempting to undertake was to explain to the mother what was going to happen. They anticipated that she would be very upset by this and would not permit it.

As we gathered, there was a rather tense and strained conversation for a half hour during which nobody brought up anything relevant to Dorothy's situation. The mother then said, "I think I'll prepare some coffee and cookies." When she went out, the two who were left said, "You tell her." "No, you tell her." So, when she came back in, I started the conversation by saying, "I understand that there was a reason for this meeting; I wonder if we can get to it."

The son immediately began to describe what the psychiatrist said about Dorothy and what needed to be done. I still have the picture of the mother looking like a pioneer woman—white hair, very erect, sitting in her rocking chair with her hands folded in her lap. She did not respond at all as they expected her to. She did not break down; instead, she merely asked, "Who is going to go to the hospital with her?" The son said, "Well, the attendants will meet her at the psychiatrist's office, and they'll take her to the hospital." The mother replied, "Do you mean a member of our family is going to the hospital without another member of the family with her?" At this point, the son said, "Well, yes, I get the point, Mom. I'll go with her." There was some further discussion and the arrangements were worked out. If the reader had been watching, he would have thought, "What a stalwart person this old lady is!"

To this day I do not know why I did it, but after the meeting was over and as we were walking to the door, she walked past me, and I found myself putting my arms out. She put her head on my chest and she sobbed and sobbed. Now, this was not part of the role of being a psychologist, but it was important for her. I know it was important for me because of the tension we had been under that evening. I have a suspicion it may have been important to her son and daughter also who could not reach out to her. Things like this are not planned. You do not make a plot of it and say, "Now two minutes of hand-holding." It is a response which comes from the person, and as I reflected on it, I had to struggle with the fact that I felt guilty for having done what I did. What psychiatrist or psychologist goes around embracing his clients?

Are You "For Real"?

Can you trust your own impulses? Do you feel that "your self" will be constructive to other people? At this point, we run into a dilemma that we ought to face. I am not attempting to say that if everybody were always to be open and express his feelings and respond as he feels, this would be the best of all possible worlds. There are many of us who would be very cruel, very hurtful if we were to be ourselves. We cannot just be sincere and be ourselves. We do know that there are certain ways of behaving which are more apt to be helpful to other people than other ways. Why do we not develop a method in which we can train people in these ways of behaving? Yet that would be to deny each person's individuality. The behavior is not helpful if it is not *your* behavior. The behavior is not helpful if it is a mask, if it is a gimmick, if it is not sincere. So, we face the dilemma of how to be spontaneously the kind of person who will be helpful to the other person.

One of the things you will find when you begin to depart from your role, or to remake it into a role which is compatible with the style of person you are, is the question you are asked in one way or another, "Are you for real?" I get asked that with regard to my beard, for instance. Many people, when they feel free enough, will ask if I have a beard because I am a psychologist, or if it is a gimmick to get some kind of response from the audience. The last thing that enters their minds is that my wife and daughter might like it.

When you act in a way which does not fit the stereotype or role expectation, you may expect that other people will begin to question, "Are you for real?" When a teacher leans over Johnny at his desk and says, "Johnny, that is an excellent paper you have done," Johnny really has to ask himself the question, "Is he for real, or is this just his way to manipulate me to get me to do something else?" It is very different, for instance, from a teacher's really speaking for himself by saying, "I liked what you wrote. It was meaningful to me."

I had a lab experience with a nursing staff of 25. We worked in small groups. I assumed right at the beginning, of course, that since we were going to be working closely together, we would be on a first-name basis. I said, "As soon as you feel comfortable, drop the name Dr. Wallen and refer to me as John. I feel so much more comfortable on this basis, and I'll expect to take the same liberties with you." I then discovered that some of these people who had worked together for 15 years did not know each other's first name. In the hospital they had always been Miss Jones or Miss Smith. Some had never seen each other in street clothes—only in uniform. It became a central issue in the group which contained the staff's administrator. They could not feel comfortable calling her Betty, even though the administrator said, "I'm perfectly comfortable in being called Betty."

There was all of this old residual feeling about the role. Well, they worked that through and by the time the conference was over, these old role stereotypes had disappeared and they began to discover that all of them had areas in which they felt inadequate. Each had ways in which her feelings were hurt. All had experiences which made them feel angry. They became able to express affection for each other much more openly. But the thing that intrigued me was that the administrator called me a couple of weeks later and said, "I had occasion the other day to call one of the head nurses to say I wanted to have a conference with her. The head nurse said, 'Okay, is this going to be a "Betty" conference?' " That was the term they developed for talking as persons, each with a stake in the situation—not just in some kind of role jockeying.

Laboratory Training

I have mentioned laboratory training. I would like to say more about it because if you think about the dilemma I have just mentioned (the dilemma of being yourself, on the one hand, or, on the other hand, of acting in ways with a higher probability of being helpful and more constructive to other people), the whole question of how you learn this type of behavior is extremely important. You cannot learn it by drill or rote, as I have said before. This could destroy your individuality. On the other hand, you cannot simply say, "Find it out for yourself," because you may spend the next 100 years and not find it out.

We must have some kind of an educational context and experience in which an individual can be helped to discover the constructive aspects of his own behavior in relation to other people. That is essentially what is meant by the laboratory method of interpersonal relations or human relations training. We sometimes call it *experiential learning,* or we sometimes speak of it as *communication by experience* and not just by words. The key essence of laboratory training (learning) is that you examine the behavior that occurs in the learning situation and try to find out what it means, and that any particular thing that happens, any interaction, is fair game. This requires the development of a kind of skill that most of us do not have. And this, I would emphasize, may be the central point of this chapter.

When we talk about developing leadership, the central skill that I think the instructional leader must develop is the ability to talk about behavior as it occurs, or shortly thereafter. The factor which will make a difference between one year of experience as a principal on the one hand, repeated 18 times, and 18 years of experience as a principal, on the other, is the ability to learn from that experience. You learn by examining it. Any particular thing which happens in a lab is grist for the mill. In a typical T-Group (training group), for instance, an unstructured style of leadership is used. Perhaps twelve people get together and the leader may say, "We're here to learn about human behavior; we're here to learn how people interact; we're here to learn about ourselves. We can go about this any way we please. I will not be a lecturer; I will not be an instructor; I am not the chairman of this group. When I have skills that are helpful, I will try to make contributions that will be helpful."

Then he sits back and the group becomes totally unstructured. Participants usually begin to become somewhat anxious and the people do what they typically do when they become anxious. There are some who start to talk a lot because that is the way they handle their anxieties. There are others who withdraw and do nothing, because that is the way they handle *their* anxieties. This behavior then becomes the material that they will examine to try to see what it tells them.

Typically, there is an increasing dissatisfaction, and as people get more and more dissatisfied, they handle their anger and dissatisfaction the way they typically handle it. Those who withdraw when they get angry, withdraw and have their feelings hurt; those who blast out and attack, blast out and attack. Again, the lab consultant will ask them to look at what is happening in the lab situation and how they feel about it at that time. Gradually, the structure begins to develop in the group and they begin to learn how to interact, and they learn which of their behaviors are helpful and which of their behaviors are destructive. Nobody tells them how they should change, but they get information about how other people see them, and how other people respond to them, and they are able to take that information into account.

The kind of skill that a principal ought to develop is the kind of skill that would enable him to sit down with teachers and talk about what happens between them. For example, a little incident was reported to me recently by a principal which is typical of the kinds of problems he was currently worrying about. It seems that there was a piano in one of the homerooms, and the music teacher wanted to use the piano in the afternoon, but another teacher was using the room. I asked if he really cared how the problem was solved as long as the people involved were satisfied, and he said that he did not. So I suggested that his role then was to enable the people to solve it and not to solve it for them. But the question that comes back is, does he have the kind of skills that would enable him to sit down with those involved, not as the heavy who is going to make the decision, but as one who is going to help them understand what the goals of the school are in relation to students, and to see how they arrive at the kind of decision that would work for them?

Another teacher came to me after being in an interpersonal relations group to say his whole style of dealing with children had shifted in one regard. Before, when Susy came up to tell him that Billy had hit her, he would go to Billy and find out what the situation was. Now, he says, what I do is to get Billy and Susy to sit down together and they work it out, so that Susy is encouraged to tell Billy how she feels about what he did to her, and Billy is encouraged to tell Susy what he thought happened. In short, the teacher moved away from a pattern in which he played a highly directive role all the time to one in which he played a facilitative role by asking people to look at the way they interact and at what it means to the two of them.

Interpersonal Interactions

Now a few words about the way we as human beings look at our interactions with others. One of the things that appalls me is that we find it so easy to build buildings and so hard to build teams and organizations. Recently in southern Oregon I talked with two principals who had moved into new schools, in which they were going to use team teaching, ungraded classrooms, and an openbuilding approach. They had teachers who had come from situations in which each had his own classroom and was supreme. Yet when they came together in the new schools there were no walls in the buildings except for a little central office which the teachers had, and they were expected to work together.

The design was beautiful with all kinds of great theory behind it! Yet it is asking the almost impossible to throw six people together and expect them to form a team by themselves, when they have not had the necessary background to form a team. When I commented on this, the principal said, "That's exactly the kind of problem we're getting; we're hearing bickering and fault-finding; and people are running to the principal's office to complain about somebody else."

I heard an example a couple of years ago about a high school where they started team teaching in the English section. They took an excellent teacher and made him team chairman. The end result was that the team was so ineffective that by the end of the year they had destroyed this person as a classroom teacher. He could no longer go back to his own classroom because he had lost his confidence.

I am continually alarmed and surprised that we know so little about human beings; if we want a committee to work, we simply appoint it and then we drop the members in a room and say, "Now do a job," as if there were no problems of establishing trust, of learning to be open, and of relating to each other.

One of the ways I personally would define the role of the administrator, whether it is that of principal or superintendent, is that he might very well see his job as a coach to those who report to him. I get the impression—I can say this because I am so naïve in the field of education that the reader may forgive me if I am mistaken—for instance, that many principals do not understand the difference between being a teacher in a classroom and being a principal of a school. This may be one of the reasons why the principals do so much with the pupils, and why they have so many pupils coming to their offices, rather than regarding their main responsibility as one of helping teachers to develop humane interactions among themselves as teachers and to be able to learn from each other. You would not have a very high regard for a coach who insisted on playing quarterback on his own team. We have the most respect for a coach who is able to train people so that the quarterback really runs the game without having to have all the signals given from the bench. I think the same thing is important in a manager's job.

I have been impressed with a recent article about a professional football team. The writer pointed out that every Saturday they take movies of their game and they study these in detail, even though they are not going to play the same opponent next weekend. They study, look at their own interactions, and see which kinds of interactions might be improved; then they spend all week practicing and improving for a new opponent. I suddenly became aware of the fact that here is an instance in which a collection of human beings spend about 95 percent of their time practicing how to be a team and only 5 percent performing. Yet, a typical business executive or a typical school administrator spends about 99-44/100 percent of his time performing and the remaining small fraction actually looking at the way he performs and practicing how to perform better.

I suggest that it might be possible to build in, with appropriate help, some ways of looking at "How well do we operate as a team?" "How well do we interact?" I hear complaints from teachers about such mundane things as the fact that every teacher handles playgound duty or hall duty in a different way. So, the teacher who tends to be more strict gets the hard looks from some of the pupils because someone else is too lax, and the end result is that the child has to learn to adjust to five or ten different sets of standards.

I would say that one of the responsibilities in a school, if you are really concerned about humanizing, is to help develop a climate which is consistent in some way. That is, the principal, as a leader, needs to find ways to help the teachers develop common understandings. What happens when a teacher shows up a half-hour late for duty, and somebody else has to take it and is upset about it? How do they handle that? Do they discuss it among themselves, or do they merely build up hard feelings or do they go to the principal and complain? All of these are very important things with regard to the climate of the school.

Climate for Humaneness

What would be a climate conducive to developing fully functioning human beings? We have some guides to this matter from the work of Chris Argyris in the Yale School of Industrial Management.[7] He describes three basic kinds of norms that ought to exist in a good climate. I will not use the same terms he does, but they are adapted from his formulation. The first is the norm of *openness,* which he calls *individuality.* Here you have a range, from openness on the one hand, to closedness on the other hand. By openness we mean that people are able to report their feelings about what is relevant. The second norm he calls *concern.* I prefer to call it *receptivity,* and at the opposite end of receptivity is indifference or antagonism. To what extent do I want to know what you see in my behavior? To what extent do I want to know what you feel? To what extent am I interested in your problems? In short, am I receptive to your being open?

The third norm he calls *trust,* but I think it is more clearly described as a *risk-taking* norm. The spirit is "Let's try it and find out." At the opposite end would be "Let's not rock the boat; let's play it safe." You can imagine, then, a school in which the principal has built and helped the teachers to build norms in which they were *open* with each other, in which they were *receptive* to each

---

[7]Chris Argyris. *Organization and Innovation.* Homewood, Illinois: Richard D. Irwin, Inc., 1965.

other, and in which it was the norm to *take risks* and try out things and evaluate them instead of playing it safe. This is a picture of the kind of school in which the children would be open and receptive and also risk-taking.

Recently two principals said to me, "We feel that more important than the new building we are moving into is the staff that we move in. Will you help us put on something that will enable us to begin to build a kind of open inquiry into the way we work together, that will enable us to work better together? In short, can we have some kind of practice at being a team before we have to go onto the field?" They did not have much money and the conditions under which we had to carry out the workshop were far from the best. They were able to find an old, abandoned army barracks, which is owned by a college and is kept for a few summer courses. The teachers worked all day Thursday, and drove two hours, without dinner, to come to this abandoned army camp, with the desolate wind sweeping in from the ocean. They came in to find a cold meal of potato salad and cold meat. Many of them had been resistant to coming. One of the fellows said, "You know, the only reason I'm here is because I respect my principal. I don't think there is any benefit in this, and I am quite resistant to the whole idea."

The principal was willing to stick his neck out; he believed in the idea. We all stuck our necks out. You can imagine the moods of these people as they came in. I was intrigued by one of the young teachers who said to us, about a day and a half later, "When I came that first night, I was tired; I'd never seen such a God-forsaken place; the beds were lousy; there were too many women for too few showers. Everything was wrong, and the thing that I wanted most was to go home and have a bath and go to bed. I didn't know what the program was going to be; I was scared to death about all this unknown. Now that I've been here for a day and half, you know, I'm delighted that I don't know what's going to happen this afternoon."

For three days, morning—afternoon—evening, during scheduled sessions and free time, at meals—at work—at play, we became our own laboratory in humane relations. Our own interactions created the subject matter for our inquiry in which we were simultaneously participants and observers. In many different activities occurring spontaneously or by prior planning we followed the three steps of laboratory inquiry: act—understand—apply. (a) *Act:* Our interactions provided shared, or public, data. (b) *Understand:* We described what happened and tried to understand it by finding out what each person had seen, how he felt about it, what he thought influenced him to act as he did, how he reacted to the actions of others. Thus, the private data from individuals supplied meaning to the public data. (c) *Apply:* Each person drew conclusions (emotional as well as intellectual) for himself and tried these out in new situations. The group drew conclusions about itself as a group and about how to move toward more humane interactions.

Over the three days the norms within these school faculties moved toward openness, receptivity, and toward a willingness to take risks in trying new ways of relating to others. People began to experience themselves and act as persons rather than restricting their behavior to what they believed was appropriate to the role of "teacher."

By the end of the workshop this group had developed such an open climate that the members were reluctant to leave. They were now expressing some fear—"I'm afraid we'll lose this when we get back home." Another of the changes that took place over this period of time was that they were now able to express affection openly, which they had never been able to express before. For them, it was a great element of support to know that they could be themselves with the other people in this particular group.

One last vignette, which was very touching to me: One of the assistant principals was talking to me, after the conference had broken up, and he was saying that he thought that the last session had been somewhat of a let-down. We had been talking about carry-over back home. "Gee, there just weren't many ideas. It was so passive; not much interaction. I wonder why that is?" At this particular point, I looked over and saw one of the older teachers, I suppose in her late fifties. She had given the appearance of being a bold sort of person—a good sport and a good egg. She came over and said with feeling, "This is the first time in five years since my husband died that I felt that anybody cared about me." I turned to the assistant principal and I said, "Can you see why they weren't interested in talking about carry-over back home?"

Training in Human Relations

I used to think that achieving change was just a matter of freeing people to be themselves. I now really feel that one must create the right kind of educational situation to bring about change. You may say, "Well, some of this has been interesting to me. I'd like to know more about it. I'm not thoroughly sold that this is the way to go, but there's something to speculate about. What could I do?"

The first thing that I would suggest is that if you have not attended a human relations laboratory or a sensitivity training laboratory, or an interpersonal relations laboratory, whatever it is called, you ought to attend one for your own education. You can get information about these from the National Training Laboratories.[8] So, the first suggestion I would make is to attend a lab. In the Pacific Northwest we are attempting to develop a program to help schools train the entire faculty and staff in interpersonal relations. One of the requirements is that we will not go into the school unless the principal has had laboratory

[8] National Training Laboratories, 1201 Sixteenth Street, N.W., Washington, D.C. 20036.

training. If he does not know what it is all about, the process could be too threatening.

A second suggestion I would make is that you might find out from NTL who the associates are in your neighborhood, and get someone to come in as a consultant to work with you in developing some kind of program of upgrading your own leadership skills and developing the kind of human climate you really want in the school. There are some 350 associates in what we call the NTL network throughout the country.

Another source of assistance is The Human Development Institute[9] in Atlanta, Georgia. The reason I am mentioning The Human Development Institute is that this organization has started an approach that is unique. It has attempted to develop programmed materials for interpersonal relations. Believe it or not, a student of Carl Rogers teamed up with a student of B. F. Skinner, and they decided to use Skinner's method of programmed learning to teach Carl Rogers' concepts of human interrelations. They have made a breakthrough in this by making a programmed book which is intended to be used by two people, carrying them through a series of experiences.

I will summarize by saying that I believe these approaches establish the climate for a trusting relationship and build openness and honesty. Without some such approach which can help school personnel become a team, changes in schools are apt to be administrative in nature without true support and participation by the total staff in identifying and reaching the common goals of the school.

Editor's Comment. Teachers who intend to use laboratory methods in the classroom need solid schooling in group dynamics, and they need a variety of high-level group experiences. Teachers, obviously, are always dealing with groups. It thus seems strange that most of them learn little or nothing about group dynamics in their formal education. They would like to have cohesive classrooms, but they know little or nothing about group cohesiveness and the laws that govern it. They would like to encourage leadership, but they base their teaching practices on theories of leadership that not only are twenty years out of date but never were valid.

Drucker (1968) has an interesting theory of adolescence which is relevant to educational practices. He suggests that adolescence is a cultural creation. Years ago it simply did not exist. By the time the young person was relatively physically and mentally mature (the period we now call early adolescence), he had to leave home, perhaps start his own family, and begin to make his way in the world. If he could count on living only until about age forty, he had to start early. His wife had to go through eight to ten pregnancies in order to have three children. But today most adolescents do not go out to found families and make a

[9] The Human Development Institute, 34 Old Ivy Road, N.E., Atlanta, Georgia.

living; they stay in school. Thus, Drucker defines adolescence as the period lying between the onset of physical and mental maturity and the time when the young person becomes productive. Since in our present educational systems one cannot really "be productive" but can only "show promise" of future productivity, it is only natural that all the problems we associate with adolescence arise. One reason laboratory training is needed in the schools is that it allows students to *do* things. One learns how to involve himself more effectively with others by actually involving himself with others, not just by listening to lectures about human adjustment. Teachers who feel threatened by laboratory learning situations are the victims of their own education and training, but their fears should not be used as a justification for robbing the present generation of students of a richer, more personal education. Laboratory training may not be the salvation of education, but it can be a powerful tool, both in teacher-education programs and in the classrooms of teachers who have been adequately trained to use laboratory methods with their students.

Editor's Reference

Drucker, P. F. *The age of discontinuity: Guidelines to our changing society.* New York: Harper & Row, 1968.

Prescribed Games: A Theoretical Perspective on the Use of Group Techniques[1]

Joan Ellen Zweben
Kalen Hammann

Editor's Introduction. The tendency of a group more or less unwittingly to establish nonfacilitative rules for itself has already been mentioned. Since one of the functions of a facilitator or trainer is to "keep the system open," to prevent the introduction of entropic elements into the group process, he usually confronts the group in its attempts to legislate constraining rules. Since he has a good deal of experience with groups, he views what is happening from a special vantage point. This does not mean that he legislates for the group, but he makes sure that the group is aware of its own legislation. Ideally, this skill should become more and more diffused among the members of the group in the course of the interaction so that the facilitator need not continually bear the odium of being the group's gatekeeper.

Zweben and Hammann's article suggests certain "exercises" or "games" that the facilitator can use to confront group members with their constrictive interactional processes. These exercises can prove quite diagnostic, for they highlight interactional styles and uncover the whole pattern of rules by which interaction in the group is governed at a given point in time. The article is one of the first attempts to provide a theoretical basis for the use of exercises in the group.

The past few years have seen a proliferation of ingenious techniques for encounter, sensitivity, and therapy groups. Unfortunately, such techniques often lack a broad conceptual rationale for their application; instead they are discussed as relatively isolated "things to try" with overly specific purposes. The following is a theoretical perspective on some of the techniques. First we shall discuss the place of rules in human interaction. Next, encounter groups and the like ("self-analytic groups") will be presented as structured situations in which the impact of rules can be

From *Psychotherapy: Theory, Research and Practice*, 1970, **7** (1), pp. 22-27. Used with the permission of the publisher and the authors.
[1]The authors wish to express their appreciation to Cora Bierman and Jessica Hammann for editorial assistance.

explored. Finally, we shall present a rationale for "Prescribed Games" as techniques for such exploration within groups.

Rules and Roles in Human Interaction

Most human interaction is governed by implicit or explicit "rules" (Watzlawick, 1967) specifying what participants may and may not, must and must not do while they are together. Rules about behavior associated with some position in social space (father, leader, etc.) specify a "role;" a set of such roles constitute a "social system," and a social system typically involves an overarching set of rules ("norms") which apply to the behavior of all participants in the system. The rules each participant has for his own behavior are not limited to his own conceptions of his various roles.

In the initial encounters of a group (social system) the rules are tested out and defined by the participants. Later they become stabilized and relatively harder to alter as members become comfortable with established ways of interacting. People are generally unaware of this process and of the rules themselves, but if the rules are excessively constraining they may limit severely what sorts of persons participants can be with each other. Of crucial importance is the fact that the rules affect not only what people can do but also what they can experience. Hence changes in the rules both reflect preceding changes in experience and constrain or open new areas of future experience for those influenced by them.

The Link to Self-Analytic Groups

Despite their differences, therapy, sensitivity, and encounter groups provide opportunities to (1) experience the effects of rules by which they habitually limit their interaction with others, (2) become aware of how such rules are established and changed, and (3) experience what it is like to live under rules allowing greater freedom. It seems likely that such groups are more effective (lead to greater insight, behavior change, etc.) when they focus more directly on these kinds of rule-exploration.[2] How does such exploration take place?

Much of a leader's energy in this sort of group goes into explicitly or intuitively diagnosing the existing rules. He may focus more on the rules individuals have for themselves, as psychotherapists typically do, or on the rules the group is establishing for all members, but in either case he is likely to come

---

[2] For example, though he conceptualizes it somewhat differently this seems to be much of what Eric Berne is doing through "transactional analysis." His thesaurus of *Games People Play* represents a significant, though not usefully organized, compendium of the relatively constraining sets of rules which form the basis of many relationships.

across some rules that are quite constraining. He may then attempt to change such constraining rules in one of several ways.[3] A common approach is to point them out or to make an interpretation and hope group members will alter their behavior in appropriate ways.

For example, group members often initially express their feelings in the form of questions instead of statements, as if they had a rule against the open expression of feelings. Questions beginning with "Why . . ." (e.g., "Why did you do a crazy thing like that?") illustrate the functions such a rule performs. These questions lend themselves well to being employed as double binds, since it is impossible to pin down what the asker intends by his communication. Consider the question (asked tensely), "Why are you so angry with him?" Responding to the affect by saying something like "You seem to object to my being angry with him" can evoke the reply, "Oh no, I was just curious." Responding to the question as if it were indeed a request for information is likely to evoke further angry questioning or accusations, since not dealing with the affect leaves unfinished business. "Why . . ." questions, then, are very well suited to evasion of responsibility for one's own "negative" reactions. Their appearance is therefore likely to signify that people are operating as if there were a rule against expressing negative affect directly or "unreasonably" and are seeking to avoid being blamed for such expression. Such a rule may, of course, be an internal one: a person may feel guilty if he allows himself to express anger directly "without a good reason."

In order to help group members become aware of the consequences of such a rule, the leader might focus their attention on the group's communication pattern by saying: "We seem to be expressing our feelings in the form of questions instead of statements; perhaps we're developing a norm against the open expression of (negative) feelings."

Prescribed Games

An alternative and, in our view, a more useful approach is the use of a "Prescribed Game."[4] The techniques subsumed under "Prescribed Games" go one step further than interpretations such as the above in that they permit participants to translate these interpretations directly into their own immediate experience. In a Prescribed Game the group leader structures interaction for a

[3]Whitaker and Lieberman (1964) have spelled out this notion that a group therapist's main function is to help a group establish "enabling" rather than "restrictive" rules.

[4]We are using "game" here in the sense of "rule-governed interaction." We regret the additional connotations the word "game" may carry for the reader, from "frivolous competition" to "(un)conscious manipulation" to mathematical "Game Theory," but no other word seemed to serve as well. We hope our addition of the adjective "prescribed" will help in this regard: it seems to us to connote serious purpose and conscious participation, as well as a pleasing sense of being "just what the doctor ordered."

delimited period by prescribing what the norms and, sometimes, the roles for participants and the task will be during that time. Afterward, members discuss what they experienced during the game: what they saw, became aware of, and felt while interaction was governed by the rules the leader set up. In prescribing a game the leader may be following either or both of two main strategies: that of Caricature and that of Set-Breaking.

The Strategy of Caricature, or More of the Same

In the strategy of Caricature (also referred to as symptom scheduling, negative practice, reactive inhibition, and therapeutic paradox or paradoxical intention), the essence is to ask group members to behave deliberately in accordance with a rule they were already following implicitly, under conditions which allow its experiential impact to be heightened. To foster this heightening, the leader may ask members to exaggerate the behavior. For example, a member who seems to allow himself only ingratiating, self-deprecating behavior may be requested to "Get on your hands and knees and apologize for yourself to every member of the group." Or he may be asked to "Get a compliment from each member of the group and immediately find some way to refute or disqualify each one." Alternatively, the leader may request members to translate the behavior into another modality (e.g., two members who are using words to keep one another at a distance may be asked to push each other away physically). This exaggeration or translation allows the members to experience more fully the impact of what they are doing, both on themselves and on others, and to decide for or against change on the basis of this experiential understanding. In addition, the experience of doing deliberately something which they may previously have been doing unconsciously or involuntarily can help members gain both awareness of and control over the behavior. (Cf. control of muscular tics gained by practicing them, and Jackson's "prescribing the symptom" to help a patient learn to eliminate it.)

Other Examples:

1) In a situation like that described above in which members seem to be expressing their feelings in the form of questions rather than as statements, the leader might prescribe a game such as the following to bring it to members' attention through the strategy of Caricature:

"Members may communicate for the next five minutes *only* by asking questions. Once you have been asked a question, you may ask one to someone else in the group, but no one may answer any questions during the Game. You may not question the person who questions you more than twice in succession (so that the interaction will not focus on two people for very long).''

This exercise very rapidly elevates the tension level and may reveal many content issues previously hidden as it becomes obvious to participants that questions are also statements. In addition, members become attuned to the affect-laden nature of questions in general and particularly to the accusatory quality of "Why . . ." questions.

2) Almost anything members are doing verbally can be highlighted by asking them to do it nonverbally. For example, a member who is seeking to dominate others may be asked to push them to the floor and stand triumphantly over them, a group of newcomers who have been trying vainly to become full members of the group may be asked to break into a circle of old members, etc. In nearly all such cases, the impact of rules by which people were seeking to limit the range of their own or others' behavior is clearly demonstrated.

The Set-Breaking Strategy, or Highlighting by Contrast

The second strategy a leader may use involves prescribing a game which gives group members a taste of interacting under very different rules. The sudden change in what participants experience may then demonstrate the effects of the previous rules quite clearly by contrast. For example, members may be asked to do exactly the opposite of what they have been doing. If they have been expressing their feelings in the form of questions, as above, the leader may prescribe a game with the rule that no one may ask a question until he has made a statement committing himself to a position. Members often find that once they have made the statement, there is no need for a question after all. They can then use their experiences to explore the use of questions to evade responsibility for feelings.

Other Examples:

1) Even if they do not hide behind questions, many group members initially communicate in highly tentative ways, surrounding all expressions of feeling with immense amounts of protective and distancing verbiage. Such verbiage helps them to disown controversial remarks, and hence reduces the risk of their being criticized or devalued for expressions of feeling or ideas which others cannot accept. Often such members seem to believe that only the most cautious kinds of approach and the most limited sorts of vulnerability to others will be safe for them to risk. The leader may help them explore the degree of reality in these assumptions through a Set-Breaking game such as the following:

"Pair up, and carry on a dialogue in which each of you speaks only one sentence at a time before the other responds." (After members have done so for a short time:) "Now communicate using only one phrase before the other responds." . . . "Continue your dialogue using only one word before the other responds." . . . "Now use only gibberish." . . . "Now communicate nonverbally."

Members typically experience a heightening of emotional intensity in the interaction and greater contact with the other person as the game proceeds. Those who find this game extremely anxiety arousing are often able to gain meaningful insight into their reliance on words for distancing and control.

2) Gestalt therapists often make a rule "No Why-Because games" ("Why did you do that?" "Because I'm hung up on my mother, I guess." . . .). This rule has the effect of discouraging members from relating to one another through a detailed examination of how their psyches work. Such a rule is often particularly effective in enhancing professional therapists' capacity to relate! (Levitsky and Perls). For groups without a great tendency to intellectualize, one may prefer to allow or even prescribe why-because games in order to facilitate intellectual understanding. The rule against them can always be invoked as a Set-Breaking game if the group becomes too involved in amateur psychoanalysis.[5]

An Example of Mixed Strategies: The "Systems Games"

Other, more complicated Prescribed Games can be used for working with various dimensions of interpersonal style. Among the most powerful of these are the "systems games" (Satir, 1966; Zweben and Miller, 1968). They are based on the notion that the rules for interaction (norms) which characterize a social system depend in important ways on the set of roles which make up the system.

The systems games are efficiently played in subgroups of four, three participants and an observer. Participants suggest one of four interactional rules for their own behavior (roles). These are: # 1—agree or placate. All negotiations or expressions of feeling must be cast in these terms. Actor behaves as though his feelings are not worth considering. E.g., "Whatever you want is fine with me." "Don't you think we could do it better another way?" or "Let's not get upset about it; I'm sure you two can get along without fighting." # 2—blame or attack. Others are treated as though their feelings did not matter. E.g., "You *always* change the subject whenever we try to talk about sex." or "If you would only stop doing that, we could begin to accomplish something around here." # 3—be

---

[5] Or what Gestalt therapists describe somewhat more colorfully as "mindfucking." Another useful bit of Gestalt argot is "mindbending," which refers to behavior aimed at getting someone to invalidate his own perceptions. E.g., "Don't say that. You're not *really* angry with your sister. Tell her how you love her. Tell her you're sorry."

correct or reasonable. All disagreements are decided on the basis of pronounce-ments about what "authorities" (such as the *Bible* or a psychology text) say; the actor behaves as though neither he nor others have feelings worth considering. E.g., "It's not appropriate for a girl your age to wear lipstick. All the child-care manuals agree." or "I understand it is good to ventilate one's feelings. You seem upset; perhaps you should shout at me. (Of course, it will not touch me, but) it may prove therapeutic for you." #4—being irrelevant. All significant interactions are disrupted by changing the subject or being in some way inappropriate or incongruous, making jokes, or diverting attention by nonverbal means. E.g., "(Argument? What argument?) I'm just sitting here, groovin' on the lights." Or "We've had spaghetti at our house four times this week." #5—commit self to a position and include the other person. E.g., "I would like to do this; what would you like to do?" This way of relating is also characterized by congruence between what the person expressed verbally and in other modalities, i.e. there are no mixed or hidden messages.

Each participant in a group of four plays one role at a time, in combinations chosen at random or prescribed by the leader. (Rule #5 is usually saved for later, as one purpose of the games is to bring the hidden rules into awareness and under conscious control.) Participants are then encouraged while taking the roles to make a decision of some sort or to discuss a controversial issue. The observer helps the participants in his group of four stick to the role they select and also comments on the interaction as an onlooker. Non-verbal means, such as voice tone, gestures, posture, and expression can and should be used to enact each role. Participants are asked to play until they have a sense of the payoffs and the constraints and frustrations of both the role they are enacting and the social system that is evolving. Everyone is then encouraged to comment on what he experienced. Both the Caricature and the Set-Breaking strategies can be employed by instructing participants to be sure to try the role they think they usually play and also the one that comes hardest for them. The leader can also use the games to highlight a group pattern by assigning a particular combination of roles. For example, if the group members are dealing with each other in a very gingerly fashion, having all members play the placator simultaneously usually effects a very rapid transformation.

An Additional Use for Prescribed Games: Finding Out What the Rules Are

In addition to those already mentioned, group leaders occasionally use prescribed games of a third type. These are games aimed at bringing out the effects not of one specific rule or cluster of rules, but rather of the whole pattern of rules by which interaction in the group is governed at a given point in time. They can also be used to help clarify for the members or the leader just what the rules are at that point. For example, the leader may ask members to think of things they would like to say to other members which they do not feel it is "appropriate" to say, or of things which previously seemed inappropriate but which could be said now. A discussion of what sorts of things these were can help clarify both what "autistic" rules individuals are using to limit their own behavior and what the norms of the group are perceived to be.

Other Examples:

1) Secrets: In a variant of the game just presented, the leader may request members to think of a secret they would not wish to tell at this time, to imagine telling it, and to then share their fantasies of what it was like to tell their secrets. This process may bring out clearly the nature of the rules (and attendant fears) which are currently making it difficult for members to share certain kinds of thoughts or feelings.

2) Group fantasy: The leader may begin a fantasy about the group and different members' roles in it, then suggest the rule that people add to the fantasy by saying whatever comes into their mind when another person finishes speaking. As in psychoanalytic "free association," such a rule may help members to talk about constraints or conflicts about what to do which they had not previously acknowledged.

3) Ranking: The leader may ask members to stand in a line representing their rank order on some dimension such as "influence in the group," "frankness," etc. How they place themselves may provide a rich source of data not only about perceptions of influence but also about rules concerning competition (Do people fight freely for the top spot? Do they fight politely for the bottom spot?), how much influence is it acceptable for people to suggest that they have (Do people seem to assume that only men can legitimately have the top spots?), and the like. The leader may then suggest that anyone who believes someone else is incorrectly placed can move him to another place in the line. This phase can similarly bring out rules about what parts of the dimension are seen as "legitimate" for men, older members, etc. to be in (e.g., are all the older members moved to the top?). In addition, it may bring out such rules as "It is all right to suggest that a person has more influence (is better) than he thinks, but not that he has less (is worse) than he thinks," or that "One must accept the leader's estimate of a member's position," etc. (This game can also be prescribed as a Set-Breaker if the group seems to be operating on the rule that all members are to be treated exactly alike, as if there were no important differences among people.)

Leaders seem to use fewer prescribed games of this last type than of the Caricature or Set-Breaking types. This may be in large part because the whole format of a self-analytic group often amounts to a prescribed game of this type writ large: members are presented with a relatively unstructured situation (on which they tend to impose their habitual rules for dealing with others) and with rules for their interaction (either explicit or implicit in what the leader says) such as "limit your discussion to what is occurring Here and Now" and "Talk about what you are feeling." Talking about "the Here and Now" often leads to identification of patterns of rules as they are established; talking about feelings supplies a constant stream of data about the effects of those rules as they form and change.

Summary and a Look Ahead

We have attempted to provide a theoretical perspective within which can be placed many of the growing number of exercises, "nonverbals," etc. used by leaders of self-analytic groups. We have pointed to the central importance of implicit and explicit group rules, both for individuals (roles) and for group interaction (norms), in determining what happens when people come together. We have suggested that exploration of these rules and their effects provides a central task for groups which hope to help individuals become aware of and change maladaptive or unnecessarily constraining ways of relating to others.

We see two main needs for the future in this area, a conceptual one and a practical one. The conceptual need we see is for a useable typology of the rules people use to structure their relationships. Such a typology would help practitioners think more clearly about the situations they encounter in groups and devise appropriate prescribed games to clarify those situations for participants. The practical need is for a compendium of prescribed games which are useful in the ways we have suggested. (The authors would be glad to serve as a clearing house for such games: readers who send descriptions of innovations they run across or originate will receive collections, brought up to date occasionally, of all prescribed games we have received.)

It may be that groups aimed at fostering human growth are on the verge of moving beyond a dependence for their methods on the intuitive flashes of brilliant artists, into an era of techniques firmly based on tested theories of human interaction. If this is true, a rich and exciting time lies just ahead.

References

Berne, Eric, *Transactional Analysis in Psychotherapy*. New York: Grove Press, Inc., 1961.

Berne, Eric, *Games People Play*. New York: Grove Press, 1964.

Garfinkel, Harold, *Studies in Ethnomethodology*. Englewood Cliffs, New Jersey: Prentice Hall, 1967.

Levitsky, Abraham, & Perls, Frederick, "The Rules and Games of Gestalt Therapy." Available from the San Francisco Gestalt Therapy Institute, 3701 Sacramento St., San Francisco, California 94118.

Satir, Virginia. Paper presented at the American Psychological Association Convention, New York City, 1966.

Watzlawick, Paul, Beavin, Janet, & Jackson, Don D., *Pragmatics of Human Communication*. New York: W. W. Norton, 1967.

Whitaker, Dorothy Stock & Lieberman, Morton A., *Psychotherapy through the Group Process*. New York: Atherton Press, 1964.

Zweben, Joan Ellen & Miller, Richard Louis, "The Systems Games: Teaching, Training, Psychotherapy." *Psychotherapy: Theory, Research and Practice*, June 1968, 5(2), pp. 73-76.

Editor's Comment. To say that leadership is a function of the entire group and not just of the facilitator does not mean that the facilitator has no specific leadership functions to perform. His expertise makes him a resource person with a special value to the group. His function is to put his skills at the service of the group and its goals. On the one hand, he should not be a manipulator fulfilling his own needs for power and influence; on the other hand, he should not apologize for intervening in both ways suggested by the authors: (1) telling the participants what he thinks is happening (or not happening) in the group and (2) suggesting ways in which the group might move ahead. Zweben and Hammann indicate that exercises or games fulfill the first of these functions, but it is evident that exercises can be ways of actually initiating growthful kinds of interaction such as self-disclosure and confrontation. The number of different games or exercises available is limited only by the imagination of those involved in the sensitivity-training movement.

Facilitators differ radically in their use of exercises: some seldom use exercises but rather expect the group to find ways of moving forward and of extricating itself from the impasses it devises; others use exercises almost as a matter of course at every group meeting. I have experienced facilitators who handled exercises so authoritatively or so awkwardly that resistances among group members were merely heightened. If the facilitator is not skilled in using exercises, or if he is uncomfortable with them, then he should omit them; if they are used, they should be suited to the temper and needs of the group. It also seems better to ensure that the members know why certain games are being used and to have them consent to their use. The rule of thumb is simple: if exercises are helpful and suited to the group, let them be used; but they should not take the place of free interaction among the participants. Some members depend too much on exercises; they participate well within the structure of the game, but when the game ends so does their participation. The game has not served to increase their sense of agency or initiative. Other members always resist exercises, claiming that they are contrived. Quite often, however, this is just another sign of members' resistance to the goals of the group and to the group process itself. On the other hand, members *should* complain if games are forced on them indiscriminately. One quality is absolutely essential in the facilitator: social intelligence. He should be in touch with his own experiencing and the experiencing of others and should know something about the interaction of the two. Exercises in the hands of such a person can be important stimuli to growth.

Part Four.
Interactions: Communication Processes, Self-Disclosure, Expression of Feeling, Support, and Confrontation

The articles in this section deal with the various modalities of interaction that constitute the heart of the encounter-group experience: communication processes, self-disclosure, the expression of feeling, support, and confrontation. The encounter group is a laboratory that has two general purposes: diagnosis and experimentation. By interacting with others and receiving feedback with respect to the impact he makes on them, the participant comes face to face with the many dimensions of his interpersonal life-style. In very concrete ways he comes to know his interpersonal strengths and deficits. This diagnostic process then serves as a stimulus for the group members' experimentation with "new," more creative ways of being with one another. This does not mean that the participants invent new forms of interpersonal behavior. "New" here means untried modes of involvement. For instance, the participant might find new ways of translating himself into non-cliché language, reveal areas of himself which he has previously feared to reveal, deal directly with his anger instead of trying to ignore it, learn how to give support by sharing his experiences with others, confront others because he cares and wants to get involved with them, and respond to confrontation by self-exploration in the community of the group rather than by increased defensiveness or counterattack.

The Anatomy of a
Message

Ernst G. Beier

Editor's Introduction. We spend a great deal of time communicating with one another, both verbally and nonverbally. Quite often, however, communication is not a way of making deeper contact with another person but a way of fending the other off under the *guise* of making contact. It would be impossible to become intimate with everyone we meet, of course, and no one suggests this as an ideal. The language we use in our contacts with waitresses, insurance men, gas station attendants, and sales personnel is necessarily "commercial." It is not the language of involvement, and it is not expected to be. But quite often, even in noncommercial situations, language is nothing more than psychological or interactional filler: it is used to fill interactional space and time, but it hardly puts one human being into any type of deep contact with another. In fact, if we were to do a kind of time-and-motion study of our communication processes, most of us would probably be shocked at how much time we spend in this form of noncommunication.

The encounter-group participant is expected to lay aside superficial modes of communication in his effort to translate himself effectively to the other members of the group. He is expected to drop his communication defensiveness, to put fewer filters between himself and others. This means that he must both talk and listen with greater intensity. He might find that he is uneasy when he cannot engage in the filler, the cliché-talk, that characterizes so much of his ordinary day. He must also listen much more actively than he usually does. Total listening is, in a sense, nonselective: it encompasses all the cues emitted by the other, even those that the other would rather conceal and those that, as a listener, one finds uncomfortable to hear. The active listener goes out of himself in search of significant cues. The ultimate value of such active listening is to translate what is heard into effective interaction.

We often use communication processes in order to control and manipulate one another. In the first article in this section, Ernst Beier suggests that we do this both knowingly through what he calls "persuasive" messages and unwittingly through "evoking" messages. Both kinds of message control the respondent by arousing in him certain feelings and emotions which in some way constrict or direct his response. In neither case does the message-sender admit to the subtle emotional impact of the covert message. The encounter group, as a laboratory in which communication styles are examined, tries to get at the "meta-messages" embedded in the communications of its participants.

Beier's article is one of those taken from the literature on psychotherapy. However, it is not only the disturbed person who uses evoking messages in an attempt to control others or keep them at a distance. The neurotic might have a more desperate need to control others and his communications might be more heavily laden with evoking messages, but even those of us who are burdened only with a greater or lesser degree of the "psychopathology of the average" play our share of communication games with one another. One goal of the encounter group is to establish a climate of game-free interaction. What Beier says here, then, is applicable not only to therapy but to the encounter group and to day-to-day living.

The Persuasive Message

We can distinguish two different types of messages, one persuasive and the other evoking. This differentiation helps us analyze the communication process in the therapeutic hour. First we will discuss the "Persuasive Message," the elements of which contain both contextual and nonverbal (paralinguistic) cues. In the persuasive message the sender codes his message in full *awareness* of what he is doing. The purpose of his message is to create in the respondent an emotional climate favorable to the sender's intent. For this purpose to be achieved properly, the respondent must not have any awareness of the sender's intent. He must be made to feel, not to think.

The Persuasive Message:

Sender	*Message*	*Respondent*
conscious coding	contextual and nonverbal cues	choice made on basis of emotional climate, not awareness

The persuasive message can be illustrated with examples from advertising, though this is only one of its many uses. A sender wants to sell soap. In order to persuade the prospective buyer to purchase it, he tries to create a favorable emotional climate. He finds that he sells more soap by packaging it in yellow paper; this works only so long as he keeps his manipulation hidden. Once aware of the device, the respondent (the buyer) at least has a choice, and may use criteria other than package color to make up his mind.

Reprinted from Ernst G. Beier, *The Silent Language of Psychotherapy* (Chicago: Aldine Publishing Company, 1966); copyright © 1966 by Ernst G. Beier. Used with the permission of the publisher and the author.

We use this type of message frequently in daily exchange. It is surprisingly effective. A lover sends flowers to his beloved, a student slips the proverbial apple to the teacher—these are behaviors designed to gain the ends of the sender by arousing favorable emotional climates in the respondent.

The goal of a persuasive message can be stated as follows: to impose a condition on the respondent under which he behaves as the sender wishes without becoming aware that he has been led to that particular choice with a certain message. The respondent should be persuaded to (1) make the choice desired by the sender and (2) believe that he made the choice on his own judgment. Once a sender is successful in achieving these two ends he is a "persuader." With the persuasive message the sender increases the probability of the occurrence of a specific response by constricting the respondent's response activity. The persuader literally does not permit the respondent to use his head.

Persuasion is also used for the purpose of producing an emotional response where no particular action (such as purchasing soap) is required. An existentialist type of play such as *Waiting for Godot,* by Samuel Beckett (1954), is made up of persuasive messages. The overt component of the message does not make any sense—the plot is without meaning—but the covert component achieves a strong emotional impact. These covert cues cause the respondent to emote and, just as dream symbols make him feel uncomfortable, he does not quite know why he feels the way he does. It is not clear whether or not the author wrote with an awareness of what emotions he wanted to elicit, but his highly skillful use of covert cues to elicit an emotional response in the absence of an identifiable source is worth mentioning. When the play was banned in Spain, the author could say "what silliness," as he had not committed himself to any purpose.

The persuasive message is often used as a "testing" device, precisely because it evokes responses without accountability. A boy "accidentally" touches the hand of his beloved and fearfully waits for the desired response—always ready to defend the "accidental" nature of his forwardness if challenged.

The persuasive message is also put to use in the educational process: the young child is manipulated into beliefs and attitudes by planned covert cues, which he will prehend rather than comprehend (Sullivan, 1953). Family and religious practices often include such planned covert communication. The little boy asks a question about sex and his mother changes the topic. The child is affected by the response. He may be "reinforced" in feeling that sex is something to avoid, without ever knowing why he feels this way. Or the child hits his sister and the parent diverts him by offering to play with him. The child here is persuaded to avoid aggression by the new emotional climate set up for him. Repeated persuasive messages will create certain value systems in the child without his ever becoming aware of where he learned these values. This is an emotional part of the process of *introjection.*

In the therapeutic process, too, the therapist uses persuasion to help the patient discover new choices. The "Hm, hm" and many other responses act as powerful tools to emphasize and reinforce certain values. Psychotherapy can be seen as an act of counterpersuasion. (See Chapter XVI, "The Ethical Problems of Control of Behavior.")

The Evoking Message

An important variation of a persuasive message is the "Evoking Message." The difference occurs in the state of awareness of the sender. The sender of the persuasive message knows what he wants from the respondent and gets it through the use of subtle cues which reduce the respondent's awareness that he has been "set up" or persuaded. The sender of the evoking message has no awareness of his wish to persuade. He codes information without awareness and consequently obtains responses for which he cannot account, even though he himself evoked them.

The Evoking Message:

Sender	*Message*	*Respondent*
		choice made on basis
	contextual and	of emotional climate,
unconscious coding	nonverbal cues	not awareness

As an illustration of the evoking message we can consider an individual who thinks of himself as lonely and without any friends. In a careful analysis of his messages, we discover the coding of very subtle cues that are likely to create an emotional climate in the people he addresses, resulting in negative and angry feelings. The sender evokes this negative response but is nevertheless able to see himself as the victim of circumstances. As he was not aware that he coded this information, he does not have a feeling of responsibility for the response he obtained. Indeed, the evoking message seems to be the type of communication which maintains the patient's present state of adjustment. With this message he helps to create those responses in his environment which confirm his view of the world. Through the responses he elicits, he constantly obtains proof that the world is exactly the place he thinks it is!

One can see the therapeutic process as one in which the therapist refuses to reinforce the patient's present state of adjustment by refusing to make the response the patient forcefully evokes in him. The patient makes an ambiguous statement which in his experience has the effect of making the respondent feel uncomfortable. The therapist, however, responds with an asocial response (such as "Hm, hm") rather than confirming the patient's expectations; this gives the patient a sense of uncertainty—and the possibility for new choices. Historically, the therapist has learned to respond to the social expectations of the patient's message empirically, rather than through a theoretical stratagem. The most frequent responses found in psychotherapy (such as "Hm, hm," "Go on," etc.) are simple, asocial responses.[1]

The evoking message is probably one of the basic tools used by individuals to maintain their consistency of personality. With this message an individual can elicit responses without being aware that he is responsible for doing so. To a certain extent he can create his environment without feeling that he is accountable for the responses which come his way. If a given individual does not have overwhelming problems, we call the fact that he creates a peculiar, idiosyncratic environment for himself his "character" or his "eccentric" behavior. The person with emotional conflict, however, creates a world in which he typically feels victimized by others, in which he experiences great unhappiness, though he has little awareness that he is often the creator of this world.

The evoking message gives us clues to characteristic differences among people. Once we understand the kind of response an individual repeatedly evokes in his environment, we can gain a beginning understanding of his psychological dynamics. A businessman evokes fear in his employees by means of such cues as *setting, words,* and *gestures,* but he is surprised that he is not loved for all the good he does for them. He gives us some tentative information about the nature of his conflict. We could speculate that while he thinks of himself as a person who is sacrificing himself for his men, he acts as if he should be feared by them. Message by message he elicits a different emotion than he thinks he elicits, reinforcing in himself a feeling that his "true nature" is understood.

Another example is the dentist who gives his patients the message that he is unconcerned about their pain by many subtle hints at their being "sissies." He may not be aware of this behavior and is surprised that his practice does not flourish. Message by message, perhaps with the *conscious* intent of helping them, he creates an emotional climate in which he makes the patients ashamed of their expressions. He is surprised to learn that instead of returning, the patients reject him. Observing that he does not learn from the feedback (rejection), we can speculate that perhaps this dentist has a conflict about being in the profession of dentistry.

This is not to say that all environmental responses are elicited, but a great many are, and when one is concerned with the prediction of behavior, a careful analysis of the evoking message is often accurate and helpful in prediction.

---

[1] Dr. Arnold Bernstein in New York reported to us that he placed conventional responses such as "Hm, hm" and "Go on" on a tape and had an experimental volunteer patient alone in a room turn a switch which activated a tape recorder, whenever she wanted the therapist to respond. She was given the understanding that the therapist would be sitting next door. After six hours the patient was asked to describe the therapist and she said that she thought of him as "most understanding, warm, and considerate."

People live in a fairly consistent world because, to some extent, it is a world of their own creation even if they do not consciously want it that way. The responses people obtain through the use of the evoking message are likely to be rewarding and meaningful to them within their total psychological economy; consciously, though, they may reject such an implication. They may not always want to pay the price of their unaware "manipulation," but they nevertheless use all their skill to maintain their present state of adjustment.

Reason and Emotion

The *manifest* cues of the message contain information which the sender consciously wants to give and for which he assumes responsibility. "Give me this book" manifestly means that the sender wants the respondent to act in a certain way and that he is willing to be held accountable for his manifestly expressed wish. With the *covert* component, on the other hand, the sender may convey information for which he does not want to be held accountable. Though his effort is not always successful, the covert cues of a message are coded to leave the respondent without recognition of the covert message but still subject to an emotional impact. We shall introduce another illustration of the relationship between reason and emotion. An unkempt juvenile says to a stranded motorist: "Can I give you a hand with your car?" The overt cues of the message are clear; the conventional meaning of the statement is one of solicitude. But the boy's unkempt appearance and perhaps his intonation keep the motorist in doubt; the emotional impact may be "danger," and so he responds, "No, thanks." The answer may perhaps be quite against his immediate interests and given with only the general rationale: "I wonder what this boy really wants from me."

When one considers the sender of the message, the unkempt juvenile, it appears that there is some dissonance between the overt and covert cues he conveys to the motorist. Disregarding whether the boy is in fact honest or dishonest, it can be inferred that he wants to be recognized for offering help (overt) and most likely does not wish to be recognized as a doubtful or criminal character. Even if he had dishonorable intentions, it would not be plausible to assume that he wants to alert the motorist to that fact. Assuming for the moment that the boy has again and again had the experience of creating doubts in respondents and having his friendly gestures of help rejected, it is quite likely that he has some conflict about his identity. He maintains behaviors which permit him to hold on to the opinion that he is a helpful person, but that the *world* is hostile and rejects even his worthwhile efforts.

One could speculate that the boy's psychological economy requires the maintenance of his discordant messages: he elicits and obtains the type of response that he has found to be an acceptable compromise between various needs. The conflict seems to be his need to see himself as both helpful (overt) and threatening (covert) at the same time; it is expressed in such a manner that the response (rejection) is typically elicited and serves to reinforce not only his use of such a message, but also his feeling that he lives in a world filled with injustice. After all, his good efforts are not recognized or rewarded. It is quite possible that this sense of living in an unjust world also gives this boy an alibi, a sense of freedom to engage in retaliatory acts. With the discordant message he can maintain his psychological adjustment.

To generalize, through the covert component of his message a person may code his information in a way that impedes another person's recognition of certain of his needs. Yet though he does not want to be recognized or held accountable for expressing these needs, he does want to have an emotional impact on other people, an impact that elicits a specific constricted response from them.

A person may want to impede recognition of certain of his needs because he wants to avoid having a respondent bring judgmental processes to bear on the message. The person who is trying to avoid being fully understood in what he says is possibly afraid that if he were understood he would then obtain responses which do not fit his self-image, responses with which he feels he cannot cope.

On the other hand, to use a message for an emotional impact allows a person to obtain a response which is at least partially determined by the emotional climate he has created, with which he can cope precisely because he has succeeded in impeding recognition of *some* of his wishes. There seems to be a negative relationship between "recognition" and "emotional impact." Information that creates an emotional impact seems to constrict recognition in the respondent. This suggests that the stronger the emotions in which a person becomes engaged, the less active are his cognitive processes. A respondent facing direct aggression such as a fist in his face is likely to react to the source of the aggression and then fight back, talk, run, or whatever else he does as his typical reaction to aggression. It is unlikely, however, that he has the time or the inclination to try to understand and recognize the full context and meaning of the aggressive act. It is also unlikely that he can use his best judgment to fight it. (Japanese soldiers learn how to yell during an attack for this reason.)

The emotional impact of a strong gesture is likely to deprive one of the use of cognitive processes: the emotion occurs at the cost of one's judgmental processes. The loss of adequate judgment becomes even more obvious in a case of covert aggression in which the respondent has no awareness that he has been aggressed against. He cannot find the object and merely feels discomfort. Since he cannot identify the source of his discomfort, he is thus deprived of an object he can fight. The use of covert cues had created an emotional impact which effects and controls the respondent's behavior precisely because his recognition, his discriminative cognitive process, and his judgmental powers are constricted. We may say that, for purposes of communication, the modes "to know" and "to feel" are separate and, to some extent, mutually exclusive states. That is not to say that these two modes of behaving *must* be mutually exclusive, but merely that one can be used to the exclusion of the other. It is our suspicion that a persuasive message that uses covert cues to create an emotional impact in a given respondent is probably more effective in reaching this goal than a message that tries to persuade by the power of reason. The use of emotions constricts the choices. The use of reason, however, gives the individual freedom to make his own choice and so is not likely to have an equal degree of persuasive power.

Some field researchers would support this conjecture. Some social scientists (Watson, 1947) placed some "Jewish-looking" persons in such a manner that they blocked the sidewalk. Pedestrians who had to detour into the street to pass by made various comments about the Jews. The social scientists, camouflaged as pedestrians, engaged these people in conversation and used, among others, rational and irrational methods of approach. To give an example of the rational comments, people who made a negative comment were approached with: "How do you know they are Jews?" or "You should not call all Jews names when you find some annoying." One of the emotional comments was: "This is a very un-American thing to say." The report stated that the emotional-impact statements created more uncertainty in the respondents than statements of any other category. It appears that emotional-impact statements constrict the respondent's response activity and are persuasive, while rational-impact statements are more easily disregarded.

A message designed to arouse an emotional impact must be based on redundancies, i.e., cues which have been overlearned by the respondent. These cues have to convey emotional meaning without benefit of thought. The words or gestures used for such a purpose must, in addition, be transmitted in the right setting and with some concern for timing.

To call a person "a Communist" at a Communist gathering is ordinarily not threatening and may even have a favorable meaning ("comrade"). However, it can be threatening when it is done in a different setting, such as at a meeting of the House Committee on Un-American Activities. A redundant cue designed to create an emotional experience in the respondent must be overlearned before it is effective. It will often include three different sources of information in its coding: words, adjuvant cues (tone of voice, choice of words, sequence of thoughts, pauses, timing), and setting cues. The stick-up man, in order to arouse the designed response in the bank teller, may need a determined voice, the supporting gesture of a threatening pistol, and the ability to convey the information that he is serious about his task. A father, in order to impress others with his authority, may raise his voice and, as Machotka (1966) pointed out, he may also raise his head!

These subtle cues are important elements of the message, often determining the nature of the response in a more significant way than the manifest component of the message. By shifting the emphasis from one component to the other, a person can choose to what extent he wants to constrict the response activity of the respondent or to what extent he wants to allow judgmental processes to enter in the choice of a response. The above distinctions are made to remind us of the great lability in human communication and the large number of possible connotations a person can code into his message.

We have been looking at the message from one particular viewpoint, its consequences on the respondent. We distinguished between the manifest or lexical component and the covert or hidden component. We found that with a different emphasis on each of the message components, a sender can determine the degree of restriction he wishes to impose on the response activity of a given respondent. This task is accomplished through the creation of an emotional climate (engagement) in the respondent which produces responses favorable to some of the wishes of the sender. We distinguished the persuasive message, in which manipulation is conscious, from the evoking message, in which the manipulation occurs without awareness. We believe that in the evoking message we have found the means by which a person is able to maintain consistency of behavior as well as his state of maladjustment. We believe that our analysis of the message in terms of the consequences on the respondent will help us in the understanding of the psychotherapeutic process.

Editor's Comment. One of the goals of the encounter group is to enable members to use communication as a means of cooperating with others rather than controlling them. Therefore, the underground communication implied in the sending of both persuasive and evoking messages should be challenged in the group. Clear rather than cloudy communication is the ideal. Beier suggests that, by our covert messages, we tend to create the kind of environment we want or feel we need and that we avoid being fully understood because we fear that we could not cope with the response we would receive if we were understood. The encounter group provides a climate of safety and support in which such unproductive patterns of communication can be diagnosed and dealt with.

Beier makes an extremely important point in discussing the emotional dimensions of our messages. He suggests that an emotion-laden message constricts the ability of the respondent to reply. If this is the case, then the laboratory has two functions with respect to the communication process. First, the message-sender should become aware of the effects of the subtle emotional dimensions of his messages and learn how to use emotion openly and constructively in the communication process. Second, the respondent should become aware of the ways in which emotions embedded in the sender's messages tend to constrict or immobilize him. This may signal a general inability to deal with the emotional issues of life. The encounter group can thus serve as a laboratory in which the participants learn to deal more effectively with their own emotions and those of others.

The Eloquence of Action:
Nonverbal Communication

J. W. Keltner

Editor's Introduction. Communication among the members of an encounter group consists of more than words. Keltner cites studies indicating that only 35 percent of the social meaning of a communication is carried in the verbal message; the rest is carried by various forms of nonverbal behavior. I once videotaped the last session of a semester-long encounter group. During the session one young man, while claiming that the course had been a "great" experience in which he had been vitally interested, sat slouched in his chair, speaking in a rather desultory way to no one in particular. Later, when he saw himself on the screen, he said: "What a liar I am." Many people in encounter groups "lie" in ways similar to this: their verbalizations simply do not correspond to their normal behavior. It is impossible *not* to communicate in the group. If we do not communicate by our words, then we do so by our silences, our posture, our whole bearing. In this article Keltner summarizes current findings in the area of nonverbal communication. The encounter group can be a laboratory in which the participants discover the often overlooked richness of such communication.

Speech-communication involves more than just voice and diction. The body, as an instrument of communication, tells almost as much as and sometimes more than the words we produce through sound and articulation. Some of the more subtle and significant meanings derived from speech-communication are developed through the nonverbal systems. Starting from the general concept of a culture defined by its nonverbal more than its verbal communication systems, we explore the various areas of nonverbal communication behavior as they relate to speech-communication. Starting with the assumption that it is practically impossible for a human being not to communicate in some way, we examine several channels of nonverbal speech-communication behavior. Among them are the voice as a tonal code, physical activity as a verbal cue, space and distance as a cue, and time as a cue.

From *Interpersonal Speech-Communication* by J. W. Keltner, © 1970 by Wadsworth Publishing Company, Inc., Belmont, California 94002. Reprinted by permission of the publisher.

In his book *Sense Relaxation,* Bernard Gunther describes nonverbal communication as follows:

Shaking hands
Your posture
Facial expressions
Your appearance
Voice tone
Hair style
Your clothes
The expression in your eyes
Your smile
How close you stand to others
How you listen
Your confidence
Your breathing . . .
The way you move
The way you stand
How you touch other people

These aspects of you
affect your relationship
with other people, often
without you and them
realizing it. . . .

The body talks, its message
is how you really are

not how you think you are . . .
There are some girls
who lack support
and are push-overs. Many
in our culture
reach forward from the neck
because they are anxious
to get a-head. Others
hold their necks tight;
afraid to lose their head.
Body language is literal.
To be depressed is, in fact,
to press against yourself.
To be closed off
is to hold your muscles rigid
against the world. Being open
is being soft.
Hardness is being up tight,
cold, separate,
giving yourself and other people
a hard time. Softness
is synonymous with pleasure
warmth, flow, being
alive.[1]

Nonverbal Behavior

We have frequently referred to nonverbal factors that influence the communicative interaction between persons. The extent to which these nonverbal behaviors are a part of our communicative effort is, according to Andrew W. Halpin, deserving of more attention.

Communication embraces a broader terrain than most of us attribute to it. Since language is, phylogenetically, one of man's most distinctive characteristics, we sometimes slip into the error of thinking that all communication must be *verbal* communication. . . .

Unfortunately, the very nature of higher education forces all of us to place great store by the *word*, whether oral or written. What passes as education often consists of little more than having students regurgitate to the professor the same words that he has given them—untouched in the process by human thought. But

[1] Bernard Gunther, *Sense Relaxation: Below Your Mind* (New York: Collier Books, 1968), pp. 90-91. Copyright ©1968 by Bernard Gunther.

the language of words is only a fragment of the language we use in communicating with each other. We talk with eyes and hands, with gestures, with our posture, with various motions of our body.[2]

Let's take a closer look at the body and its contributions to speech-communication. "It has been estimated that in face-to-face communication no more than 35 percent of the social meaning is carried in the verbal message."[3] How, then, is the other 65 percent of the message carried?

Dean C. Barnlund's review of the literature on nonverbal communication led him to the following conclusion:

Many, and sometimes most, of the critical meanings generated in human encounters are elicited by touch, glance, vocal nuance, gesture, or facial expression with or without the aid of words. From the moment of recognition until the moment of separation, people observe each other with all their senses, hearing pause and intonation, attending to dress and carriage, observing glance and facial tension, as well as noting word choice and syntax. Every harmony or disharmony of signals guides the interpretation of passing mood or enduring attribute. Out of the evaluations of kinetic, vocal, and verbal cues decisions are made to argue or agree, to laugh or blush, to relax or resist, to continue or cut off conversation.[4]

Note that Barnlund finds that "many and sometimes most of the critical meanings" are stimulated by the nonverbal factors. The scope and depth of these nonverbal messages are too frequently overlooked.

Edward T. Hall, in his landmark commentary, *The Silent Language*, starts with the assumption that "What people do is frequently more important than what they say."[5] From this base, he develops a broad theory of interpersonal, intergroup, and intercultural communication. In fact he takes the position that a culture is its communication.

Hall's thesis is that every human culture is constructed on ten primary message systems. The *interactional system* involves linguistic communication, vocalization, kinesics, and the like. The *organizational system* has to do with the social structure: class, caste, and government. The *economic system* deals with work in maintenance occupations. The biological, social, and cultural relations between

[2] Andrew W. Halpin, *Theory and Research in Administration* (New York: Macmillan Co., 1966), pp. 253-254.

[3] Randall Harrison, "Nonverbal Communication: Exploration into Time, Space, Action, and Object," in J. H. Campbell and H. W. Hepler, eds., *Dimensions in Communication* (Belmont, Calif.: Wadsworth Publishing Co., 1965), p. 161.

[4] Dean C. Barnlund, *Interpersonal Communication: Survey and Studies* (Boston: Houghton Mifflin Co., 1968), pp. 536-537.

[5] Edward T. Hall, *The Silent Language* (New York: Doubleday & Co., 1959), p. 15.

male and female fall under the *sexual message system*. The *territorial message system* concerns space, boundaries, formal and informal position relationships, places, property, and the like. Such cultural activities as teaching and learning, enculturation, education, and rearing children are dealt with by the *temporal system*. The *instructional system* deals with teaching and learning. The *recreational primary message system* has to do with participation in the arts and sports, with entertainment, games, and fun. The *protective system* involves the processes of protecting and being protected; formal, informal, and technical defenses; self-defense, and care of health. The *exploitation message system* relates to material systems that allow human contact with the environment and involves the technology of equipment and materials in dealing with property and human behavior.[6] Of all these systems, Hall identifies only the first as directly including verbal or linguistic communication. The others are areas of nonverbal communication.

The coexistence in the United States of diverse subcultures (the "jet set," the WASP middle class, the many ethnic subcultures, the culture of poverty, the various black subcultures, the radical right, the anarchistic left, the youth subcultures—to name but a few) communicates some significant messages about America to those without and to those within. The antagonism—and cooperation—between organized labor and management convey much about our economic system. The overt and covert emphasis on sex in the communications and entertainment media expresses considerable information about American culture. The political divisions of the country (regions, states, counties, urban complexes) and the whole history of public and private domain in the United States are territorial messages. Our free public education system communicates another highly significant message about our temporal culture. Attendance figures for sports contests and for symphony concerts and sales figures for recreational equipment contribute more information about the country.

All these and many more, according to Hall, tell something about us to ourselves and to others. At the same time, they represent areas in which our own communicative efforts are personally involved. Thus, when we become involved in the recreational message system, we can use certain common terms and experiences to interact with each other. For example, we use such terms as "behind the eight ball" (from pool), "four-flusher" and "ace in the hole" (from poker), "Monday-morning quarter-backing" and "carry the ball" (from football), "stalemate" and "gambit" (from chess), "couldn't get to first base" and "threw me a curve" (from baseball). Baseball and football are major spectator sports in the United States; in countries of the British Commonwealth, cricket, soccer, and rugby football are favored; in Spain and Mexico, bullfighting brings out the crowds—and there was a time in Rome when "everybody" turned out to

[6] Hall, *Silent Language,* p. 174.

watch the Christians and the lions. Such national recreational preferences make for differences in the recreational message systems of various countries.

Impossibility of Noncommunication

Another assumption is vital to the understanding of nonverbal communication. The authors of *Pragmatics of Human Communication* take the position that it is impossible *not* to communicate.

There is no such thing as nonbehavior or, to put it even more simply; one cannot *not* behave. Now, if it is accepted that all behavior in an interactional situation has message values, i.e., is communication, it follows that no matter how one may try, one cannot *not* communicate. Activity or inactivity, words or silence all have message value: they influence others and these others, in turn, cannot *not* respond to these communications and are thus themselves communicating. It should be clearly understood that the mere absence of talking of or taking notice of each other is no exception to what has just been asserted. The man at a crowded lunch counter who looks straight ahead, or the airplane passenger who sits with his eyes closed, are both communicating that they do not want to speak to anybody or be spoken to, and their neighbors usually "get the message" and respond appropriately by leaving them alone. This, obviously, is just as much an interchange of communication as an animated discussion.
Neither can we say that "communication" only takes place when it is intentional, conscious or successful, that is, when mutual understanding occurs. Whether message sent equals message received is an important but different order of analysis.[7]

So, when the postulates of the impossibility of not communicating are joined with the principles of nonverbal communication, we include a considerable portion of human behavior. It would seem, therefore, that when we deal with the interpersonal interaction level, we are dealing with one of the key building blocks of total human society.

The speech-communication event, therefore, involves a continuous many-channeled process of communication. The systems into which it fits are numerous, and it is a constant process. In speech-communication, messages are being coded and transmitted through physical movements and attitude; through voice rate, tone, quality; through gesture; through dress and cosmetic facades; through the use of objects; through the control of space; and through an ordering process in time. In fact, the act of human speech-communication is a multimedia process of almost infinite dimensions, many of which are nonverbal.

[7]Paul Watzlawick, Janet H. Beavin, and Don D. Jackson, *Pragmatics of Human Communication* (New York: W. W. Norton & Co., 1967), pp. 48-49.

Classes of Nonverbal Communication

Jurgen Ruesch and his colleagues pioneered in research on nonverbal communication. Their studies led them to the conclusion that nonverbal language may be identified as sign language, action language, and object language.[8]

Sign language includes forms of codification of written systems into gestural systems. For example, the hitchhiker's gesture may be almost "monosyllabic." The tone of voice may serve the function of an exclamation point, a question mark, or a period.

Action language involves those movements that are not used exclusively as signals. Walking, running, sitting, and the like meet personal needs, but they also say something to those who are sensitive to the message of activity. The actual manner of physical movement may carry a considerable load of information.

Object language comprises the display of material objects including the human body and its raiment. The arrangement of furniture conveys information about the persons who live with the arrangement. The clothing we choose and the way we wear it tells much about us and may at the same time be a form of message we are sending to others.

Communication About Our Communication

As we talk with others, we not only speak words to send messages but also provide clues, usually nonverbal, about how the messages are to be taken; that is, we communicate about our communications. The metacommunication aspects of our messages indicate how the receiver should interpret the message proper. Suppose I say to you, "That music is great"; and, as I speak the words, I put my hands over my ears and shake my head. My nonverbal communication says something to you about how you should interpret the message possible from my words. When we are speaking together and I lean forward, look you in the eye, and point a finger at you, I indicate that the verbal message should be interpreted as having some special importance. In both instances my *metacommunication* conveys some instruction as to how you should deal with the verbal message. In effect, I am communicating to you through at least two different channels. One channel may reinforce, emphasize, or contradict what is coming through the other channel. In speech-communication, these messages coincide in time; therefore, they must be developed through different channels.

---

[8] Jurgen Ruesch, "Nonverbal Language and Therapy," in Alfred G. Smith, ed., *Communication and Culture* (New York: Holt, Rinehart and Winston, 1966), pp. 209-210.

Mixed Communication

Nonverbal messages transmitted simultaneously with verbal messages generally reinforce the spoken communication. "Man, am I glad to see you!" in a given situation would be reinforced by a broad grin; a warm, hearty voice tone; a firm handshake; and an arm thrown across the other's shoulders. In fact, with these nonverbal communications, the words merely sum up an integrated, honest message.

"I hate his guts!" can be honestly said in a tone of loathing, with a curl of the lip, and a hand gesture dismissing the despised individual.

When we are able to communicate honestly, we don't send out mixed communications, that is, nonverbal messages that contradict what we say in words. We sometimes, for whatever reasons, lie in our teeth; and when we do, truth may be revealed through nonverbal messages simultaneously transmitted.

Some of the reasons for mixed communication provide comfortable livings for many psychiatrists. A woman said repeatedly to her husband, "I love you," and she believed that she did. But she scorched his breakfast eggs and decorated the living room in green (a color he detested) and overstarched his dress shirts. She was not aware of her deep hostility toward him. Her nonverbal messages contradicted what she said in words.

Some mixed communication results from requirements of the social games we play. As we interact with others in social situations, particularly those required by business, political, and community involvements, we use accepted verbal formulas: "Glad to see you," "So glad you could come," "We had a delightful time," "Delighted to meet you," "It's a pleasure"—the list could be nearly endless. We don't always mean what we say; and some of us are occasionally betrayed by simultaneous nonverbal messages: the listless voice, the dead-fish handshake, the deadpan expression, the spineless slump, the deep sigh of bored forbearance.

A small boy says, "Nice doggie—I'm not afraid" and hurriedly crawls into the safety of his father's lap. A student says, "Sure, I understand" and continues to look puzzled. A cat-hating woman says, "Oh, what a lovely kitty!" and shudders slightly. A woman quarreling with her lover says, "I never want to see you again!" and leans slightly toward him.

Albert Mehrabian has reported a study of attitudes revealed through head and body movements of persons as they addressed others. The findings indicate that when information communicated through nonverbal channels contradicts information communicated through the verbal channel, the nonverbally communicated information seems to predominate in the interpretation of the person receiving the two sets of information.[9] Such contemporary research merely confirms age-old proverbial wisdom: "Actions speak louder than words."

[9] Albert Mehrabian, "Orientation Behaviors and Nonverbal Attitude Communication," *Journal of Communication,* Vol. 17 (December 1967), p. 331.

Mixed communication creates confusion for the receiver. Which message should he respond to, the words he hears or the contradictory nonverbal communication? In many instances, social custom dictates a "proper" verbal response, which may also involve mixed communication. Anyone who must transmit verbal messages that are subject to contradiction by nonverbal messages must be aware of the hazards of mixed communication. Successful politicians and successful hostesses, for example, must often say the "proper" words in the "proper" way, regardless of their own personal feelings; and those who are successful have schooled themselves to avoid betrayal by nonverbal contradictions. In reality these clever ones have learned how to "lie all over."

Glaringly obvious contradictions between verbal and nonverbal messages are relatively rare; most are obvious only to sensitive observers; some are so subtle that only a lie detector could catch them. People differ markedly in their sensitivity to nonverbal communication. Some take the spoken message at full face value, regardless of nonverbal information. Others can truly say, "What you do speaks so loud, I can't hear a word you say."

If we are to be effective speech-communicators, we must be aware of mixed communication so that we can evaluate feedback consisting of contradictory messages. If we modify to accommodate only verbal feedback, we may be diverted from our purpose, which is that the other person should receive our message as we want him to receive it. We should be alert for nonverbal communication; and when this contradicts the verbal message, we must decide how much we should believe of which message.

The Voice as a Nonverbal Cue or Tonal Code

Through practice, the voice, which reflects much of a speaker's inner reaction and attitude, can be controlled and developed to provide proper reinforcement for verbal messages. The actor, in preparing himself for developing characterizations, learns how to bring his voice into focus as a positive reinforcement of the verbal and physical cues he uses in the performance.

Most of us do not have clear perceptions of how our voices sound to others. Inadvertently, many times, inner feelings that contradict verbal messages are revealed by the voice, thus confusing our speech-communicative efforts. While constructive criticism from friends can be useful as we learn to control the characteristics of our voices, frequent use of a tape recorder is generally more effective.

Pitch

Pitch, of course, is the relative highness or lowness of voice tone, as in musical notes. Few of us, fortunately, consistently speak in monotones; most of us indicate surprise, for example, by a higher pitch of voice tone and disappointment by a lower pitch. But few of us effectively use variety of pitch in speech-communication. Varied pitch usually indicates interest in and concern for the listener and can be a valuable reinforcement of the verbal message. A few problems connected with pitch should be noted.

Tenseness of body and particularly of throat will not permit maximum use of the pitch range of which the voice is capable.
Variations in pitch should correspond with meaning; otherwise, the voice tone transmits a message that contradicts the verbal message and serves to block communication.
Too much prestructuring of the pitch changes to be used in a speech-communication situation will tend to destroy spontaneity.

Quality

The physical and emotional state of the speaker affect the quality of the voice. A voice of clarity, resonance, vibrancy, and richness depends on a physical and emotional state of being that allows the speaker to breathe properly, to form words with precision, to open up the passages of the nose and throat to permit maximum resonance, and to avoid unnatural and tense stridencies that contradict the verbal messages.

Volume

Loudness, also, is a factor in vocal reinforcement of the verbal message. The volume of our verbal productions affects our listeners. Through varying the loudness we can emphasize certain ideas. Through adjusting the volume to the size of the room we can demonstrate that we are willing to accommodate our communication to the listener.

Rate and Rhythm

Rate and rhythm are also significant in the system of vocal cues. Relentless rapidity of delivery soon bores an audience and suggests that the speaker is rushing to get through rather than seeking to transmit information.
Changes in the speed of delivery of our speaking reflects changes in our attitudes and orientation toward our listeners. With psychiatric patients, "faster rates, shorter comments, and more frequent pauses have been found to be associated with anger or fear while opposite tendencies indicate grief or depression. Increase in the number or length of pauses may be symptomatic of indecision, tension, or resistance."[10]

[10]Barnlund, *Interpersonal*, p. 529.

Physical Activity as a
Nonverbal Cue

Movements of the body provide significant cues either to reinforce verbal messages or to contradict them. Such cue movements may involve the whole body (slumped in dejection, lax in indifference, tensed in apprehension) or some part of the body (the lift of an eyebrow, the tilt of the head, a clenched fist). Birdwhistell has worked out a system for identifying action in relation to the verbal messages.[11] His concept of kinesics involves the development of representative patterns of action so that they can be analyzed for their message significance. While his contributions to an understanding of the significance of bodily action are great, we are yet a long way from being able to codify behaviors of the body as precisely as some verbal behavior has been identified. However, the movements of the body unquestionably contribute much to the total face-to-face communication process.

Eye contacts alone transmit volumes of meaning between persons. A person who is assured of his position in the interaction may be more inclined to provide direct eye contact with his partner.[12] Anyone who has observed the eyes of others recognizes that much is communicated through their movement. We understand the expression "if looks could kill . . ." because we have sent (and received) such eye messages or at least have observed them. We exchange glances with friends in unspoken commentary on situations.

Gross movement of the body in communication situations does more than reinforce verbal messages. Most of us are inhibited to greater or lesser degree in terms of bodily movements in communication. If we can use the body to assist in communication, we are rewarded by a release of energy and an increasing freedom of expression which apparently cannot be achieved by other means.

Freeing the body from the conditioned restraints of bodily activity is one of the greatest problems in developing effective person-to-person speech-communication. Our society has generally relegated active physical movement to such places as the gymnasium, the athletic field, or the dance floor and discourages exuberant physical activity in communication situations. Different cultures and subcultures have different standards of physical activity in communication. In some such as the British upper classes, the use of the hands and body to communicate is considered shocking bad form. In others, such as the French, Polynesian, and Italian, there is a great deal more physical activity associated with speech. In few cultures, however, is much attention focused on the body as a communicative instrument.

[11] Roy L. Birdwhistell, "Backgrounds to Kinesics," *ETC.*, Vol. 13 (1955), pp. 10-18.
[12] Georg Simmel, "Sociology of the Senses: Visual Interaction," in Robert E. Park and Ernest W. Burgess, eds., *Introduction to the Science of Sociology* (Chicago: University of Chicago Press, 1921), p. 358.

Mime artists like Marcel Marceau and Francisco Reynders show us the tremendous possibilities of the body as an instrument of communication. The movement of a finger, the bend of the back, the position of a foot, the tilt of the head, and uncounted movements and positions carry information in various contexts. Communicative interaction that involves free use of bodily movement carries impact, with a high level of accuracy in transmission of the total message.

For generations, speakers have been instructed about how to stand, what positions of the hands should be used to express given emotions and feelings, how the feet should be placed, how to sit, how to rise, and so forth ad nauseum. All these instructions were set down in rules and systems designed to establish rigorous sameness of movement. Now we believe that such standardization is undesirable. *Each person should develop his own mode of physical expression in respect to his intent, the situation, and the context and nature of the message.*

Physical movement that inadvertently contradicts or intrudes on the message should be avoided. Thus, erratic movement of the hands, shifting of the feet, repetitive and meaningless facial movements and the like will tend to distract the listener from the actual communicative purpose. The body should be used to reinforce rather than to confuse or to inhibit communication.

Further, *bodily movements that serve for nonverbal communication should develop from internal feeling associated with the message being transmitted.* Assuming that primary concern is with reinforcement of the verbal message, we should allow our bodies to reflect the physical components of our messages as freely as possible. Of course, when we intend to send a double message, the body serves as a special instrument. External expression of internal feeling is of great importance in effective communication.

Space and Distance as a Cue

Where a person sits or stands during a communicative interaction has message value. There is a difference in the message of an interviewer when he sits behind his desk in comparison to the message he suggests when he comes around his desk and sits closer to you. The physical distance between persons in the communication situation tells a great deal about the nature of their message.

Hall relates space to the vocal message and to the character of the communication in an intriguing scale:

1. *Very close* (3 in. to 6 in.)	Soft whisper; top secret
2. *Close* (8 in. to 12 in.)	Audible whisper; very confidential
3. *Near* (12 in. to 20 in.)	Indoors, soft voice; outdoors, full voice; confidential

4. *Neutral* (20 in. to 36 in.)	Soft voice, low volume; personal subject matter
5. *Neutral* (4½ ft. to 5 ft.)	Full voice; information of nonpersonal matter
6. *Public distance* (5½ ft. to 8 ft.)	Full voice with slight overloudness; public information for others to hear
7. *Across the room* (8 ft. to 20 ft.)	Loud voice, talking to a group
8. *Stretching the limits of distance*	20 ft. to 24 ft. indoors; up to 100 ft. outdoors; hailing distance; departure[13]

While this range is suggestive rather than prescriptive, it does give an interesting perception of the use of space in speech-communication.

The space factor is particularly noticeable in small-group meetings. I recently worked with a seminar, the first few meetings of which were in a regular conference room, which was so arranged that members of the group sat at long tables arranged in a hollow square. There was open space in the middle, and a number of unused chairs allowed the group to break down into subgroups separated by empty chairs. While the group was meeting under these conditions, there was a very low level of close personal interaction in the sessions. At the suggestion of one of the members, we moved across the street to a dingy little cellar, less than one third the size of the conference room, in which old end-up cable drums had been arranged closely together in a tight circle. There were just enough stools, and all members could gather around the drums only if they sat very close together. Almost immediately after moving to this setting, the tone of the meetings changed from impersonal to a highly personal interactive atmosphere.

Time as a Cue

Hall said that "space speaks" and "time talks."[14] Time does communicate much. *The rate at which we speak, move, and gesture tells of our inner intensity of feeling.* The cadence of our walking communicates something of our personal feeling and character. Each of us seems to have an inherent basic rhythm which is uniquely his. Our movements also reflect extrinsic rhythms imposed by situation and context. The heavy, slow movement of the ceremonial procession contrasts sharply with the movement on a dance floor.

Those of us who are exactly on time for appointments reveal something about ourselves and our perception of the importance of the situation. Halpin has pointed out some meanings associated with promptness:

[13] Hall, *Silent Language*, pp. 163-164. Copyright ©1959 by Edward T. Hall. Reprinted by permission of Doubleday & Company, Inc.

[14] Hall, *Silent Language*, pp. 15ff. and pp. 128ff.

When a meeting is scheduled, whether between two or more people, who waits for whom and for how long says important things about relationships to the people concerned. Most organizations or cultures develop informal tolerance ranges for lateness, to keep a person waiting beyond the tolerance limit is a subtle way of insulting him. However, the handling of promptness and lateness can vary with the subculture and with the functions of the meeting. Thus military officers are likely to arrive a few minutes ahead of the appointed time, whereas professors usually arrive from five to ten minutes after the set time. In the social sphere, only a yokel will arrive at a cocktail party at the stipulated time; whereas good manners require a guest to arrive at a dinner party not more than ten minutes late.[15]

The pause in verbalization is also a factor of timing, as well as of vocalization. A break in the verbal output may provide opportunity for physical reinforcement cues to be made with some strength. A pause is often a method of creating anticipation, as when a speaker, after being introduced, strides to the platform, glances over his notes, looks calmly over the audience as if sizing it up, then stands for a moment looking hard at approximately the center of the audience. By the time he starts to speak, he probably has the attention of the audience; he has sent it the message that he is at ease, in command of the situation, and expects it to respond.

Summary

The nonverbal cues of speech are of utmost importance to the total act of speech-communication. Much of the message of the interaction is carried by voice, by movement, and by the use of time, space, and objects. As we attempt to communicate with others, we should so integrate these many elements to create strong reinforcement for the basic verbal message; or, if we wish to provide a cover-up or protection, we can use nonverbal means to send messages contrary to the verbalization. The old adage "What you are speaks so loud I cannot hear what you say" is indeed consistent with contemporary understanding of human communication.

For Special Reading

Edward T. Hall, *The Silent Language* (New York: Doubleday & Co. 1959). How people talk across cultures and societies as well as within these systems has long been a subject of professional study. But Hall takes on a tough task of examining the nonverbal communication within and between people and cultures. When he says "communication is culture" and "culture

---

[15] Halpin, *Theory and Research*, pp. 255-256.

is communication" he really means it. The rationale he uses to develop this concept is most provocative as well as stimulating.

Marshall McLuhan, *The Mechanical Bride: Folklore of Industrial Man* (New York: Vanguard Press, 1951). This one will make you hot and cold, mad and glad. McLuhan takes a healthy slug at the manipulation and control of the collective public mind. His book is a collection of advertising gems with his own subtitles and textual analysis of them. Here you will see how the nonverbal works in the areas of the subconscious and the supraconscious.

Jurgen Ruesch and Weldon Kees, *Nonverbal Communication* (Berkeley: University of California Press, 1956). One of the first solid attempts to examine nonverbal communicative behavior in a way that can be understood. If you are at all interested in the nonverbal aspects of communication, you must read this book. While the authors bring their interest in communication from the field of psychotherapy, their analysis and application is outstanding.

Editor's Comment. Keltner quotes Gunther as saying that "body language is literal." Body language is immediate, direct. We reveal ourselves, whether we want to or not, through a host of nonverbal cues. Put more positively, nonverbal behavior can be an important way of expressing personal identity and uniqueness. The kinds of nonverbal language discussed in this article can either reinforce or belie the verbal content of the participant's interactions. For instance, there are many nonverbal signals for noninvolvement, disinterest, boredom. Ideally, a member should speak out if he is bored. But if he does not, then it is up to the other participants to read the nonverbal signs of his noninvolvement. If they fail to do so, then the interaction can lose some degree of its immediacy.

A failure to be aware of the nonverbal dimensions of communication in the encounter group is uneconomical. Often, the discrepancy between what is being said and what is being communicated nonverbally muddies the communication process and too much energy is wasted trying to deal with the discrepancy. This is true both of individuals and of the group as a whole. The participants must become aware of the "mood" or "tone" of the group by becoming aware of all the forms of nonverbal communication in the group. If the group atmosphere is speaking louder than the verbalizations of the participants, this should be explored. Nor should it have to be the facilitator who addresses the question of nonverbal communication in the group. Diffusion of leadership means that all group members should listen and react to all the communication taking place.

Changing the physical or nonverbal arrangements of the group can sometimes have an impact on the verbal communications among the members. For instance, simply moving the participants' chairs closer together can raise the level of intimacy of verbal communication in the group. Since the physical arrangement is one of intimacy, most members find that it is almost impossible to talk about abstract or inconsequential issues.

Perhaps many of us would be surprised if someone were to observe our participation in several group discussions and then present us with a graph of our interactional patterns and style. Some encounter-group members are quite involved in the sense that they try to get other people to reveal themselves and express their feelings, but they do little revealing themselves. Then they are "surprised" when challenged for their lack of participation. Feedback from other participants is essential for anyone trying to get an objective view of his interactional style. For instance, some people tend to remain silent while others, when they do talk, talk either to the whole group or specific individuals or to the floor. The encounter group, in order to remain engaging, needs a high degree of immediacy. While it is evident that both the silent member and the participant who talks to the ceiling or the floor leave something to be desired in terms of immediacy, the member who usually addresses the whole group also has problems with immediacy. When a person addresses everyone, he runs the risk of not contacting anyone. In my experience, the most immediate and engaging encounter groups are those in which individuals speak directly to individuals—or to the group through specific individuals. Discourse to the entire group tends to become abstract and deal more with the there-and-then rather than the here-and-now.

A word about interruption. In the encounter group, if interruption is synonymous with a failure to listen, then it is obviously harmful to group interaction. However, if interruption signifies an eagerness on the part of members to contact one another, then it can be quite constructive. Groups which are too "polite" often lose a degree of immediacy. Letting the other "finish" is often a sign of a constrictive group culture rather than an atmosphere of civility or a concern for the individual.

What Price Privacy?

Chester C. Bennett

Editor's Introduction. One thing people in encounter groups do is talk about themselves, that is, reveal themselves to one another. Bennett's article is the first of several dealing with the benefits—and some of the perils—of self-disclosure. Bennett challenges current thinking on the value of privacy. He argues that privacy is not as important as we have been led to think and that we should investigate the human-growth possibilities that lie in self-disclosure. It may be that the consequences of self-revelation (for instance, rejection by others) are not as disastrous as we fear they might be. Bennett suggests that what we need on all levels of interpersonal living is more interpersonal communication, better managed, rather than more effective ways of hiding ourselves from one another. One may not agree with all that Bennett has to say, but his article gives the reader an opportunity to rethink consciously and deliberately the issues of privacy and self-disclosure. Self-disclosure of some kind *is* a value in the encounter group. The person who is not ready to experiment responsibly with some degree of openness about himself is not ready for fruitful participation in the group. (For an extended discussion of self-disclosure, see *E:GPFIG*, pp. 190-245.)

The fashionable strategy for the crusader these days is to invoke some "inalienable right" in support of his favorite cause. Ipso facto, he seems to be wearing a white hat, his particular motivations are beyond suspicion, and any real consideration of the values at issue becomes impertinent. We are thus importuned by a whole array of alleged rights—the *right* to counsel and the *right* to bear arms, the *right* to criticize a policy and the *right* to defy a law, the *right* to subsistence and the *right* to strike, the *right* to use smutty language and the *right* to take intoxicating drugs, the *right* to bare the bosom in public and, paradoxically, the *right* to privacy.

It is not my intention to suggest that all these "rights" are wrong; but claiming them as rights does not make them right—and certainly they are not inalienable. Privacy, for example, is a graceful amenity, generally to be fostered, but with

Reprinted from *American Psychologist*, 1967, **22** (5), pp. 371-376, © American Psychological Association, Washington, D.C. Used with the permission of the publisher and the author.

discriminating restraint and with due recognition of obligations as well as privilege. It is the writer's contention that the moral imperative is more often allied with the surrender of privacy than with its protection.

It should be recognized at the outset that the right to think one's thoughts in private is not at issue if one elects to keep them to himself. No psychological test reveals information which the subject cannot conceal by the simple expedient of not responding to the questions. There are no bugs, no listening devices capable of tuning in on the mind and reporting the substance of a meditative process. No one can see the thoughts that are not expressed. No one can overhear what is not said. The right to think (to feel, to wish, to judge, to plan) is inalienable. Even in the presence of a crowd, one's freedom to commune with himself remains inviolate if he chooses to keep it so.

Strictly speaking, the invasion of privacy is a contradiction of terms—like turning on the light to see what the dark looks like. The real issue is not the right to experience privately, but the right to communicate selectively. When the right to privacy is invoked, it usually means that someone feels he is being forced, or persuaded, to communicate against his will, or that his willing communications are being misused. Often it means simply that he wants to transmit some kind of message to a second party without being overheard (or overseen) by a third. In any case, the values involved can best be understood in terms of the management of communication rather than the sanctity of privacy.

To bring the issue into focus, a few words about communication are in order; for the distinctive genius of the human organism is its dependence upon communication. The growing child has little use for privacy. Born with the most adaptable of nervous systems, he is, by the same token, relatively unconstrained by patterned instincts—predetermined solutions to his problems. With a maximum capacity to learn, nature gives him maximum latitude to test and choose alternatives. Thus the human infant enters life peculiarly helpless, peculiarly ill fitted to survive. Hairless and incoordinate, sensitive to heat and cold, he must be fed, swaddled, moved about, and even burped. In the process, he is utterly dependent on other human beings, first for sheer survival, and later for guidance and education. Everything that happens to the young child, pleasant or unpleasant, is experienced in the context of interpersonal transactions. He can learn to love, and he can learn to hate, but he can never be indifferent to people. With the acquisition of language, it becomes abundantly clear that all his skills, his concepts, his values, his very humanness and selfhood are generated through the medium of interpersonal communication.

Communication is not forced upon the child; he welcomes it and seeks it out. His need for companionship is unbounded. There are times when he will want to be let alone (not left alone), but he will probably use the pause to assimilate some recent message and to formulate his next question. The child who really "keeps to himself" is an unhealthy child—an alienated child deprived of warmth and sustenance. The adolescent, of course, may want a room of his own, and a diary to hide from his parents. But secrets are for sharing—with another adolescent, at least. The tragedies of adulthood—the broken homes, the estranged neighbors, the irrational tensions, and mental illness—reflect our ineptitude in the management of interpersonal communication.

Primitive man, like the child, had little use for privacy. The compelling demands of survival and defense gave rise to communal living. One man might kill a rabbit, but it took the whole clan to tackle a herd of mastodons or to fight off another clan. With the discovery that one man could make a better spear while another could throw it more effectively, we have the emergence of vocations and a system of exchange. The group became dependent upon cooperation; the system dependent upon communication. With the development of more sophisticated skills and equipment, communal clans united to form the communal community and the communication network became increasingly elaborate. True, the community is held together partly to defend itself against other communities, and the communication system is devoted in part to keeping the community's secrets from other communities. But secrecy within the community is incompatible with cooperation, inimical to the welfare and progress of the ingroup. And as the world shrinks, we see with increasing clarity the incompatibility of secrecy with peaceful coexistence among communities.

The right to cultivate privacy by isolation has never been a problem. The lone woodsman, the hermit, the monk in his cell, can have privacy and to spare. Studies of stimulus deprivation have shown, however, how few people can tolerate privacy on this basis. Most of us want to have our secrets and someone to share them with too. We want the benefits of communal living and the fruits of cooperation, along with the pleasures of solitude. Privacy becomes a concern with the development of city living.

According to Mumford (1938), privacy emerged as a privilege of the upper class family with the establishment of the "private home" apart from the place of business; which also created the professional housewife and the commuting breadwinner. With separate rooms and doors instead of curtains, privacy invaded the family itself. By the seventeenth century, the woman in her boudoir, the man in his den, the children and servants in their cubicles could keep secrets from each other, and the fluid communication of one-room living began to deteriorate.

As Mumford points out, the heated house with indoor plumbing permitted the embellishment of sex for recreational rather than purely utilitarian purposes, and the fulcrum of activity shifted from the kitchen stove to the bed. At first, the private bedroom emancipated sex. It was a place to entertain, to court, to revel—a veritable wellspring of communication. It was later, much later, with the rise of the Puritan ethic with its violent deprecation of the physical organism, that the bedroom became an asylum—a hideaway for shameful rituals. The closed door, in most households, is not so much a guardian of privacy, as a symptom of prudery; a barrier between the generations, an obstacle to fluent sex education, a reinforcement of guilt and repression. Strictly speaking, of course, sex is not ordinarily a private experience, but a peculiarly delicate and intimate transaction between at least two people. I submit that even in this sensitive area, more serious problems stem from mismanaged communication about sex—partners who cannot discuss it, children who must not be told, and alienation of the deviate—than from mere breaches of privacy.

As any Plymouth visitor can testify, there was precious little privacy aboard the Mayflower. The colonization of America has never represented a flight from human association. With a continent to get lost in, the Pilgrims clustered along the seaboard and built stockades around their communities. They were seeking freedom, but freedom to live *together* as they chose. The American freedoms—freedom of speech, freedom of press, freedom of assembly, and freedom of petition—are by definition inconsonant with privacy; they bespeak the right to communicate. Indeed, freedom of worship is not concerned primarily with private devotions, but with the right to worship publicly, to share beliefs and rituals with a congregation of one's choice. America is the "melting pot." Assimilation is our boast. Segregation is our shame.

There is no reference to privacy in the United States Constitution. The Bill of Rights, designed to safeguard the rights of individuals, makes certain provision for the protection of private property and for the security of the person, and it specifies that no person "shall be compelled in any criminal case to be a witness against himself." But there is no general sanction of privacy as a right. According to Ernst and Schwartz (1962), the word "privacy" did not appear in legal literature until 1890 when it was discussed by Samuel Warren and Louis Brandeis in the *Harvard Law Review* (1890-91).

By and large, both the law and the mores have had more to say about the surrender of privacy than about its protection. Certainly the occasions when one is required or expected to divulge personal information are numerous. With proper authority the police do search and seize. The witness in court must tell the truth and the whole truth. Communicable diseases are reported, and the physician must report a gunshot wound. The driver must report an accident. Few secrets are kept from the Internal Revenue Service with impunity. In these and many other situations, the invasion of privacy has been justified by a more or less explicit consensus that the interests of the common good outweigh the rights of individuals to withhold information.

There is also a basic acceptance of the moral obligation to be an informer if one has knowledge of significant antisocial activities. We are supposed to report a crime to the appropriate authority. The impulsive rejection of the tattler is really associated with a perverse respect for the special morality of the delinquent. There is "honor among thieves" because the squealer may be told on next. Sober judgment recognizes being one's brother's keeper as the higher ethic.

The confidentiality of communications in certain dyadic relationships is generally respected, sometimes with legal sanctions. Tampering with the mail is a

Federal offense. Bugging devices are for the most part illegal. No one is required to testify against his spouse. The physician is supposed to treat his patients in confidence, although if the patient happens to be the President of the United States, or a unique medical anomaly, this privilege may be preemptorily invaded by the press.

The prototype of confidential relationships, of course, is that of the defendant with his lawyer. It is based upon the fundamental principle that a person accused is deemed innocent until he is proven guilty and the burden of proof rests upon his accuser. Accordingly he may not be compelled to testify against himself and the attorney who represents him may retain his confidences. It should be noted that this privilege applies to a specific situation in which someone is accused of crime and subject to punishment if found guilty. The charges must be made explicit in open confrontation and the adversary trial procedure is intended to ensure a fair defense. No one questions the importance of protecting innocent people from false accusation, but it is not always clear that the lawyers' insistence on preventing any voluntary confession of guilt is in the public interest. It is not always clear that the adversary trial with its complex rules of evidence is the most effective method of reaching the truth and administering justice. Less devious communication might better serve these ends.

The confessional is also respected as a confidential relationship. It should be noted that this, too, is a communication; a revelation, in fact, of the most private secrets to at least one other person. Its premise is the ancient dictum that "confession is good for the soul." The reference, in many religions, is to public confession. The Protestant sinner must bear witness "before men" to achieve absolution. Indeed, it is recognized in Catholic circles that the traditional confessional, intent on making peace with God, leaves unresolved the problem of making peace with the community.

The mental health professions have been greatly concerned about the confidentiality of the psychotherapeutic relationship. Generally speaking, therapists feel the revelations of the patient should be sacrosanct. The practical issues are complex, however, and their solution far from self-evident. If the patient reveals antisocial tendencies, what are the therapist's obligations to the general welfare? If the patient is a public ward, or a committed criminal, has he lost the right to privacy along with other civil rights? Are his records public property? If the therapist is employed by a public institution, what are his responsibilities to his employer, ultimately the taxpayer? To what extent may he violate confidence in teaching other therapists or contributing to the professional literature? To what extent do his obligations to the patient involve the transmission of private knowledge to the patient's employers or associates in the interest of better understanding? None of these questions can be answered by rule of thumb. In practice, there is considerable reporting of psychotherapeutic communication to third parties when therapists feel, for one reason or another, that it will benefit the patient, or will serve other constructive ends with minimal damage to the patient. In all probability, moreover, the secrets of the therapeutic hour are as often divulged by the patient as by the therapist. Patients have published their own accounts of psychoanalysis. The readiness of people to discuss their personal problems with neighbors, and even with strangers, makes one wonder, in fact, whether confidentiality is so necessary to the privacy of the patient as to the comfort of the therapist. There are therapists who believe the therapeutic process is facilitated in the presence of an audience. The popularity of group therapy reflects a similar assumption that patients find help in sharing personal problems—that confession is good for the psyche as well as the soul.

The explicit defense of privacy as a moral issue is a contemporary phenomenon. There was little concern over privacy in rural America a generation ago. The recent furor in Boston over the discovery that technicians spot-check telephone calls to see that the system is working properly strikes a chord of amusement for anyone who has shared an old-fashioned party line. As a matter of course our conversations were monitored by a gaggle of neighbors, and the girl at the switchboard was the steward of everyone's affairs. She could tell you where the doctor was calling, who was getting engaged, and why Aunt Hattie would not be home for Christmas. There were tensions, of course, but basically there was security in knowing everyone's business—and in having yours known. The traditional place to find solitude was the big city. Only in its teeming crowds would you be left alone—and lonely.

With the technological development of communication, today we have organized gossip, and the city no longer permits escape. The keeping of records engulfs us. As a matter of fact, the average citizen has few secrets that are not recorded somewhere and more or less available to anyone with a serious interest in probing. The Bureau of Vital Statistics, the hospital where he was born, schools, colleges, and employers keep records. The credit bureau knows where he has lived, whom he has married, and whether he chooses to stall the plumber or the sporting goods store. If he has ever been on relief or worked for the Government, been arrested or joined an association, there are quasi-public records of his activities. Directories and newspaper files are other sources of information, and of course the Internal Revenue Service and Social Security have him tagged. There has even been talk of late of pooling all these records in a single master file of computerized microfilmed social histories of the American citizenry. Perhaps it is the impersonal nature of this programmed snooping which has generated the heat over privacy.

On the other hand, there is reason to feel that the public welcomes as much as it resents the invasion of privacy. Certainly it is demanded of public figures. Thanks to aggressive reporting and efficient transmission, the news is no longer limited to public events. The President's operation and his favorite barbecue sauce are headlines. Any candidate for office forfeits the privilege of keeping secrets. The entertainer's private life is often more entertaining than his performance. Intimate stories of prominent people crowd the news. An amazing assortment of people hire press agents and distribute their own releases in order to achieve prominence. Many a criminal would rather be caught than ignored. The popularity of biographies and of biographical TV programs like Ralph Edwards' *This is Your Life* and Edward R. Murrow's *Person to Person* reflect a basic urge to know and to be known—the universal mark of the gossip.

Thus the contemporary concern over privacy parallels a pervasive need to communicate; the individual's right to secrecy is counterbalanced by the public's right to knowledge. The explosion of communication networks, moreover, is only one phase of vast and growing systems of world-wide interdependence. I have no idea how many people in how many remote places may have contributed to my possession of a refrigerator—an alloy from Bolivia, a process discovered in Sweden, a bookkeeper in Schenectady? The total production team may run to millions. Less obvious, perhaps, is our psychological interdependence, our reliance on the integrity of other people. Time was, a farmer picked a mess of beans and the family ate them. Today, an army of food handlers has opportunity to poison our meal. Time was, a careless workman let the horse escape. Today he can plunge the whole Northeast into darkness; or even push The Button. More to the point is our dependence on the integrity of decision makers, the political, intellectual, and scientific leaders who affect our welfare at every turn.

Our dilemma will not be resolved by hiding away from each other in separate caves, but through more and more interpersonal communication, better managed. There is no escape from the ties that bind us together—none, at least, if we wish to enjoy the amenities of communal living, the products of cooperative enterprise, and the power that comes with knowledge. And despite all our tensions and anxieties, it is my conviction that our knowledge of personality, along with other things, is on the increase. I think the man in the streets knows more today than ever before about the dynamics of behavior, the management of emotions, and the secrets of mental health. He has been exposed to a tremendous amount of psychological indoctrination from Peyton Place to televised group therapy. He does not always use his knowledge to the best advantage but he is familiar with the lingo and will give you some perceptive interpretations of his children, his neighbor, and Bobby Kennedy.

The critical problem we face is not how to keep secrets from each other, but how to facilitate this readiness to communicate. The overriding question is how to maintain an atmosphere of trust and confidence which will enable us to talk about personal affairs as freely as we talk about automobiles; to share experience as we share the weather. There will always be people who abuse confidences— people who would "get the lowdown" on someone to do him harm or to achieve selfish ends at his expense. We need restraints to curb vicious people who misuse communications as well as other privileges. But history tells us again and again that the witch hunters are more to be feared than the witches. The prevailing tendency to restrain any and all investigation of personal attitudes, feelings, and habits as unwarranted invasion of privacy engenders suspicion of everyone's motives. Sincere and constructive efforts to understand people may be outlawed along with meddlesomeness. The moral imperative is not to protect privacy, but to foster communication and to treat personal confidences with respect.

When the right to privacy is invoked, I find it appropriate to examine the motives of those who would withhold information. There are hermits, of course, people with a genuine distaste for human association who simply want to be left alone. Let them have their privacy. So long as they do not bother others, there is no need to bother them. Their secrets are probably unimportant anyway. There are prudes who find embarrassment in every personal disclosure. They are more bothersome, because they tend to inhibit other people and their communications are not much fun. But we can let them draw the shade. Their secrets are not nearly as salacious as they think. Then there are the paranoids who see themselves being spied upon from every bush. They suspect the motives of others as the prudes suspect their own. They isolate themselves and, as every clinician knows, the more they cherish secrecy, the more important it becomes to help them learn to communicate.

Finally, there are the rascals. These are the people who do have something to hide, from outright crime to malevolence. These are the people who cheat when no one is looking, who pretend to competence they do not possess, who measure success in terms of the necks they have broken, whose standard of ethics is not getting caught. As might be expected these are some of the most ardent defenders of privacy. Their secrets impinge on the welfare of others and the moral imperative may often demand their exposure.

While the problem is admittedly complex, it should be possible to develop criteria for a rational evaluation of the relative propriety of privacy and communication. As a point of departure, I suggest that the right to privacy depends upon the nature of the secrets it protects. We can ignore the preservation of official secrets. The penalties for divulging military or diplomatic information are well defined. We can also pass quickly over the secrets of business and the signals of the football team. In our competitive society these secrets of tangible value are fair game. If you have not stolen the other fellow's first, you have legal recourse. The secrets that concern us are the personal secrets—the false pretensions, the peccadillos, the skeletons in the closet. I suggest that we examine first how important the secrets are to the person involved. How damaging will their revelation be? To what extent can they be used by someone else to do him harm? Next we should examine how important the secrets are to others. How many may be harmed, and in what way, by their disclosure? How many may be harmed, and in what way, by silence? Finally we should consider how the secrets may affect the general welfare. Is it of any importance to the community as a whole whether they are kept or revealed?

The analysis of situations in these terms will not immediately resolve the problem of privacy, but it may provide the basis for a rational assessment of the values at issue. For example: The use of psychological inventories and questionnaires in job selection has been challenged. The clinical application of these procedures is generally accepted by clients seeking professional help, and the job applicant may be quite willing to entrust his secrets to the psychologist. He fears they may be misused by the employer, however. The fact that he was once confined to a mental hospital is an unimportant secret; at least it should be. In our present stage of enlightenment, it may be seen as important by the employer and the applicant may be rejected. There may be no compelling reason for disclosure, but if the knowledge is to be abused it may be just as well for the employer to have it now instead of discovering it later. An enlightened employer, on the other hand, might use this information constructively in fostering good employee relationships. On balance, the moral imperative is not to protect this particular secret, but to educate the employer. Perhaps, this is where the psychologist should bend his efforts. I suspect a comparable analysis of many secrets would lead to similar conclusions.

By contrast, the fact that a job applicant is actively psychotic may be an important secret. It may be genuinely disqualifying for sensitive or responsible employment and may have far-reaching implications for the welfare of many people. The privilege of privacy must be weighed against potential hazards for associates, programs, and even the community. Here again, the moral imperative is not to protect the secret, but to direct the psychotic to more suitable employment—and to treatment. Perhaps again this is a task for the psychologist.

There are secrets that we have no right to withhold when they infringe the rights of others. Even when disclosure is less vital, it may still be generally desirable if it fosters understanding and the uninhibited flow of interpersonal communication. There is, in fact, an overriding imperative to create and maintain an atmosphere of trust and confidence such that secrets can be told, that personal information will be treated with respect and used constructively. It is the writer's conviction that the importance of honest communication in our interdependent relationships outweighs the sanctity of privacy as a social value. I would lay the burden of proof upon the keeper of secrets to show that his silence is not inimical to the welfare of others. Of course a burden of proof lies also on his inquisitor to show that his interest is not vicious, vengeful, nor idly curious.

The person who would shape the destiny of others accepts a special obligation to communicate. I find the attitude expressed by one witness at the Congressional hearings on privacy that, "I would rather have somebody looking in my window than in my mind," disqualifying for any position of social responsibility. I shall not labor the philosophic proposition that the "mind," being the product of interpersonal communication, belongs to the society. In more pragmatic terms, anyone who undertakes to influence the lives of other people must accept an obligation to let them know where he stands, to reveal his motives, to share his purposes. The attorney owes this to his client, the teacher to his student, the parent to his child, the statesman to his public. An honest mind should be an open window.

References

Ernst, M. L., & Schwartz, A. U. *Privacy: The right to be let alone.* New York: Macmillan, 1962.

Mumford, L. *The culture of cities.* New York: Harcourt, Brace, 1938.

Warren, S. D., & Brandeis, L. D. The right to privacy. *Harvard Law Review,* 4, No. 5, 1890-91, 193-220.

Editor's Comment. Encounter groups are not for the hermits, prudes, paranoids, or rascals that Bennett describes—that is, unless they are looking for ways to change their behavior. Rather, the group is a laboratory in which the participants learn how to manage interpersonal communications. Bennett suggests that secrecy within a community is incompatible with cooperation. If people have to hide things from one another, they do so because they do not trust one another. The encounter group is a community in which cooperation helps provide a climate of mutual trust in which deeper levels of disclosure become possible. There is a kind of circular causality: a climate of trust encourages deeper disclosure, but risked disclosure also engenders trust.

If privacy is not an absolute value, neither is its opposite. The encounter group is caricatured in many ways; with respect to self-disclosure, the caricature is the group as an arena of psychological exhibitionism. Psychological nudity, however, is no more a virtue than prudery. Responsible self-disclosure is a way of making contact with another; it is an invitation to the other to "come in." Deeper levels of disclosure should be reached, not for their own sake, but because people desire more intimate contact with one another.

In the encounter group, then, it is not essential that the participants immediately disclose the "shadow" side of their existence. In the beginning it is more important for people to be honest and open about the here-and-now realities of the group: their feelings about being in the group, their reactions to one another's behavior, and so forth. Deeper disclosures involving behavior outside the group should not be avoided, but they should not become a substitute for here-and-now realities. Even when the participants do talk about behavior outside the group, it should in some way be made relevant to *these* group members in *this* situation. Self-disclosure, then, is not an end in itself, but a means of interpersonal contact.

The Johari Window and
Self-Disclosure

Joseph Luft

Editor's Introduction. This selection begins with a short explanation of the Johari awareness model (sometimes called the Johari window), a theoretical tool that Joseph Luft uses to represent the person in relation to others and to explain the value of self-disclosure in human interaction. Luft maintains that interacting with others is facilitated when people have adequate knowledge of one another's behavior, feelings, and motivations. In this he seems to agree with Bennett's supposition that secrecy within a community is inimical to cooperation. Luft also claims that, in order to disclose himself effectively to others, a person must first be in contact with his own experiencing. If a person, for one reason or another, ignores what is going on within himself—if he is not in contact with his own feelings—he is hardly in a position to translate himself to others. Luft in no way makes an absolute value of self-disclosure. He describes both the underdiscloser and the overdiscloser and lays down a number of rules for engaging in appropriate self-disclosure.

Brief Summary of the
Johari Awareness Model

The four quadrants [in the figure below] represent the total person in relation to other persons. The basis for division into quadrants is awareness of behavior, feelings, and motivation. Sometimes awareness is shared, sometimes not. An act, a feeling, or a motive is assigned to a particular quadrant based on who knows about it. As awareness changes, the quadrant to which the psychological state is assigned changes. The following definitions and principles are substantially the same as those in *Group Processes* (Luft, 1963, pp. 10-11). Each quadrant is defined:

1. Quadrant 1, the open quadrant, refers to behavior, feelings, and motivation known to self and to others.

From *Of Human Interaction* by Joseph Luft (Palo Alto, Calif.: National Press Books, 1969), pp. 13-14, 19-22, 56-59, and 127-134. Used by permission of the publisher.

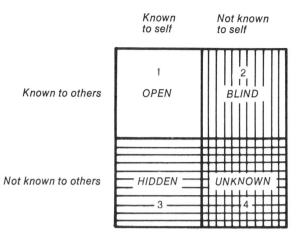

Known to others   Known to self / Not known to self

2. Quadrant 2, the blind quadrant, refers to behavior, feelings, and motivation known to others but not to self.

3. Quadrant 3, the hidden quadrant, refers to behavior, feelings, and motivation known to self but not to others.

4. Quadrant 4, the unknown quadrant, refers to behavior, feelings, and motivation known neither to self nor to others.

There are eleven principles of change:

1. A change in any one quadrant will affect all other quadrants.

2. It takes energy to hide, deny, or be blind to behavior which is involved in interaction.

3. Threat tends to decrease awareness; mutual trust tends to increase awareness.

4. Forced awareness (exposure) is undesirable and usually ineffective.

5. Interpersonal learning means a change has taken place so that quadrant 1 is larger, and one or more of the other quadrants has grown smaller.

6. Working with others is facilitated by a large enough area of free activity. It means more of the resources and skills of the persons involved can be applied to the task at hand.

7. The smaller the first quadrant, the poorer the communication.

8. There is universal curiosity about the unknown area, but this is held in check by custom, social training, and diverse fears.

9. Sensitivity means appreciating the covert aspects of behavior, in quadrants 2, 3, and 4, and respecting the desire of others to keep them so.

10. Learning about group processes, as they are being experienced, helps to increase awareness (enlarging quadrant 1) for the group as a whole as well as for individual members.

11. The value system of a group and its membership may be noted in the way *unknowns* in the life of the group are confronted. . . .

Enlarging Quadrant 1

The idea that we all wear masks is as old as history itself. And it is equally well known that we are at times painfully transparent despite the effort to hide. These qualities, the need to cover up and the inevitability of inadvertent disclosure, immediately set the stage for the drama of human interaction. (See in this regard Goffman, 1955 and 1959).

Artists, writers, people sensitive and skillful in working with others, know about these conditions of human interaction. They are preoccupied by what they see and know and by what eludes them. The contrast between what a man hides and what he reveals without awareness stirs curiosity in all of us. And this is just what is captured in the photographs by Walker Evans in *Many Are Called* (Agee and Evans, 1966). In effect he has seen and photographed the faces of all of us, and James Agee describes how rigidly and permanently we are locked in from ourselves, from others, from openness to the world.

Charlotte Selver is not quite as pessimistic as Agee. She is interested in "Sensory Awareness and Total Functioning" (Selver, 1957). She quotes from Ernest Schachtel (1947): "The average adult . . . has ceased to wonder, to discover. . . . It is this adult who answers the child's questions and, in answering, fails to answer them, but instead acquaints the child with the conventional patterns of his civilization, which effectively close up the asking mouth and shut the wondering eye." Schachtel continues, "Even if, in modern civilization, the capacity for such fresh experience has largely been deadened, most people, unless they have become complete automatons, have had glimpses of the exhilarating quality that makes fresh experience, unlabeled, so unique, concrete and filled with life." Charlotte Selver goes on to talk about her own work. She sees people, a cross section of the adult population, who come to her for help; they appear to have lost touch with themselves, their bodies, their feelings. They characteristically ask for direction, instruction, and guidance because they have learned too well the lessons in growing up: do not trust yourself, others know best, tune in to the important people around you, ignore your own promptings (Selver, 1957):

People who come to the studio to have me tell them what to do to get a good posture—how to move, how to stand, how to sit—or in order to be exercised, are quite astonished at first, when they are invited to become more restful, to give up the "doing" so that they can listen better to what their body has to tell them. We need quiet for self-experience—quiet and awakeness. We need permissiveness too, permissiveness to all the subtle changes which may be needed.

It is easier at first for people to lie down on the floor, permitting time to perceive, or, as we say, to "sense" themselves. We ask, "What can one feel of one's own organism, what of happenings within—not what one *knows* of one's body, or what one *thinks* about it, or believes *somebody else expects one to feel of it*, but what one *actually senses*, no matter what comes to the fore?"

Sensations come gradually; one can not force them. The more one expects, the less will come. We learn gradually not to expect anything at all, but to register what is happening in our organism. This physical self-experience is for many people entirely new, often stirringly so.*

Selver's work could be illustrated in Johari terms. Internal behavior, tensions, needs from within, are attended to, so that they become recognizable in Q1. Various exercises and activities, such as deliberate breathing, feeling one's weight on the floor, moving one's limbs, are done in a way that helps the person to receive ongoing sensations from his own body. These inner impressions are always there but become walled off and lost. Eventually, by restoring contact with self through exploration and sensing, one rediscovers more of one's selfness. In this way, one may restore part of the lost openness to the world, the world of inner life.

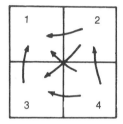

Repeatedly, people report how good it feels to be in touch with oneself. For Selver, this experience is valuable because she believes that all tensions and anxieties, indeed all feelings, are physically and psychologically present simultaneously. Awareness of and sensitivity to inner states is therefore fundamental to being a person instead of a robot. I refer to Charlotte Selver's work because it so clearly expresses a key aspect of the intrapersonal equation without which interpersonal perception and behavior make little sense.

One of the figures here shows constriction and a greatly reduced open quadrant. Behavior and feelings for the individual represented would be limited in range, variety, and scope. Stereotypy and inflexibility would characterize this person's relationships. Generally, interaction would tend to be conventional and limited, and the person's upbringing would be psychologically deprived and unfree. However, the interaction model assumes that all humans are responsive to *present* groups and individual relationships, and that change or learning could follow if opportunities for new interaction occur. The degree of rigidity is a function both of the size of Q1 and of the boundaries between quadrants.

*From "Sensory Awareness and Total Functioning" by Charlotte Selver in *General Semantics Bulletin*, numbers 21 and 22, published by the Institute of General Semantics. Reprinted by permission.

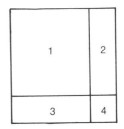

<table>
<tr><td>1</td><td>2</td></tr>
<tr><td>3</td><td>4</td></tr>
</table>

Psychological constriction and openness, hypothetical extremes

The other figure represents an individual whose interactions are characterized by great openness to the world. Much of his potential has been developed and realized. The simple square design distorts this fellow because it is obvious that, if anything, the area of the unknown for him may be even larger than it is for the average person, and that his blind and hidden quadrants might be very complex. Since he has a high degree of awareness of self, he is less preoccupied with defensiveness and distortion. He has more access to inner resources. He is not overly involved in self-scrutiny or soul-searching. As described earlier (Portmann, 1965, p. 40), openness to the world implies a developed and ever-growing state, an experiencing, doing, enjoying, struggling, changing, creating, dreaming, agonizing, renewing, problem-solving, appreciating state of being with self and with others. Large tolerance for anxiety in self (especially in doing original things and in confronting many kinds of unknowns) and for the acceptance of differences in others are qualities in persons with a large first quadrant. Boundaries between quadrants are flexible and permeable. The flow of feelings and of ideas suggests a high capacity for all kinds of experience, conflict, enjoyment, and personal productivity. . . .

Self-Disclosure

You are in charge of the third quadrant, the hidden area. What you reveal is pretty much up to you, though not entirely so. Sometimes pressure from conflicting forces in all the quadrants forces accidental disclosure. Slips of the tongue, unusual associations of thought, and all kinds of mistakes may occur which reveal what you don't want to reveal. It takes energy, attention, and perhaps a good imagination to do an able job of hiding. Not disclosing could be a form of lying, obliquely by an act of omission. Selective disclosing could do a fine job of misleading, too.

William Blake wrote in his *Songs of Experience:*

A Poison Tree

I was angry with my friend:
I told my wrath, my wrath did end.
I was angry with my foe:
I told it not, my wrath did grow.

And I water'd it in fears,
Night and morning with my tears;
And I sunned it with smiles,
And with soft deceitful wiles.

And it grew both day and night,
Till it bore an apple bright;
And my foe beheld it shine,
And he knew that it was mine,

And into my garden stole
When the night had veil'd the pole:
In the morning glad I see
My foe outstretch'd beneath the tree.

Mowrer (1964), Jourard (1964), and Culbert (1967) find that transparency is not necessarily a mark of soundness in a person nor an indication of depth in a relationship. The key issue is appropriateness in self-disclosure, the balance of spontaneity and discretion reflecting the nature of the relationship.

Disclosing too much creates at least as many problems as disclosing too little—but of a different kind. Strict control over Q3 disclosure tends to create distance in relationships. Lax control means relationships either too close (smothering) or too demanding. The plunger, who discloses a great deal from his private, hidden sector, may be seeking to impose himself on others or may be asking others to take over control or may be wishing for closeness that is not necessarily desired by others. A child may show this most clearly. Since he has not yet developed a self strong enough and discriminating enough to cope with complex social situations, he deals with everyone by disclosing a great deal. This may be charming and enjoyable and humorous in children, but hardly so in adults.

Does self-disclosure mean the person is open, free, and trusting? Perhaps. The overdiscloser may be trying to behave openly, freely, and trustingly. Or he may be unable to differentiate relationships in which such disclosure is appropriate. Superficially, he looks free and spontaneous, but he may actually be demanding more of your care, your time, and your feelings than you are prepared to offer. The overdiscloser appears to trust everyone because he has not yet learned to discriminate the qualities of different relationships. It is the other person in the relationship who must take the responsibility for defining the nature of the relationship. In appropriate disclosure, behavior is reciprocal or mutual, and persons take their proper share of responsibility for defining what the relationship is and what it is becoming.

"We do not need to reveal ourselves to others, but only to those we love. For then we are no longer revealing ourselves in order to seem but in order to give."—Albert Camus (1963).

The underdiscloser reveals too little; he reserves control for himself. He may feel more threatened than others. His third quadrant is large, and he is not moved easily to reciprocate disclosures. He is more comfortable when others disclose more than he does. He tends to quell spontaneous reactions, holding back in order to double-check what is revealed. Facial and bodily expression, the natural concomitants of feelings, are constrained to not reveal. It takes a long time to learn to mask.

The low self-discloser is preoccupied to prevent leakage from Q3. He gives expressions of personal opinions and attitudes cautiously, frequently using cliches and platitudes so as to avoid idiosyncrasy. He appears to be emotionally self-sufficient even when he is not. In groups, he is one of the last to recognize the development of trust. But he may be greatly surprised and relieved to find out that he can disclose more freely and more spontaneously than he imagined. It comes as a great and refreshing relief to learn that he *can* let go without being hurt and without giving up control. In exercising a bit more freedom in the group, the low self-discloser may feel as if he were being wanton and unrestrained to even admit he has feelings.

Sad to say, one sees group participants who have indeed become so impacted in Q3 that they have lost touch with themselves altogether. Only extreme feelings seem to register. When this happens, Q3 feelings and behavior may slip over into Q2 or Q4, areas unknown to the person and unavailable to him. A condition of emotional and intellectual impoverishment sets in over time. I say intellectual as well as emotional because the walling-off process does interfere with such basically intellectual resources as imagination and fantasy life.

Behavior in a learning group is inevitably a sample of one's behavior on the job or at home. Frequently, participants learn that work behavior is duplicated in the group.

A highly capable scientist discovered in the learning group his own techniques for keeping people at a distance. He was strenuously objective with everyone at all times. Recreational activities, having a beer with a colleague, even going to parties were carried out objectively and dispassionately. Although efficient as a scientist, he had become a caricature of a supervisor. Fearful that any relationship might get out of control, he had adopted the role of a perennial critic—and he was exactly the same way in the group. As the group developed and persons levelled with him about the effect he was having on them, he began to change in response to them. He was so starved for companionship that he literally cried with pleasure when he described how important the new, more open relationships in the group had become. Months after his return to his job he wrote of changes he experienced as he permitted himself more openness with his colleagues as well as with his own family. In addition, he reported that his colleagues saw him as a more effective team member as well as a more enjoyable human being. . . .

Trust and Appropriate Self-Disclosure

Some self-disclosure, Q3 to Q1, is essential before new learning about the blind area, Q2, can begin. Why then are universal trust and universal self-disclosure not advocated?

Warnings come from all quarters, from *caveat emptor*, let the buyer beware, to *cave canem*, beware the dog, and these admonitions have come up through the history of human experience. Our coins tell us, "In God we trust." On matters of life and death we trust our physicians, politicians, airline pilots. We have little choice. Advertisers implore us to trust their products. Attractive people on television tell us in effect to trust them and not our own sense data.

The real issue is trust in human relationships, and here everyone runs scared. People are afraid of people at least as much as people need people; perhaps it is because people need people that they are afraid. In most new groups there is a mixture of excitement and anxiety. In new social groups, new classes, new encounter groups, or new business contacts, the most predictable reaction is a rise in tension. A clear illustration of the meaning of interpersonal tension is the mother who discovers that the days when company drops in is the time when her infant is most apt to throw up his food. The child is breast fed and apparently responds to both the physiological and psychological changes in the mother and in the rest of her household. In one experiment (Luft, 1966 . . .), two students who did not know each other were asked to sit across a room from each other in silence and to note their reactions on a piece of paper. Initially, the most conspicuous feeling was tension or anxiety. This was reported in private interviews with each subject (*S*) after each experiment. Later, even without words, the subjects "came to terms" with each other and were more comfortable. When a stranger was introduced to this dyad, again anxiety rose and negative feelings were expressed by the *S*'s toward the stranger on the rating sheets. There was no customary or conventional set for occasions such as this experimental one, and the *S*'s had no easy way to check each other out. Had they been permitted to talk with each other, it would not have taken very long to reduce tension and to find some basis for at least a modicum of trust.

This experience in nonverbal interaction offers a clue both about trust and about self-disclosure. In this respect humans are not much different from other species. Animals become suddenly alerted at the presence of another animal and begin to sniff at each other cautiously. It takes a while for them even under the most favorable circumstances to become less vigilant and more relaxed.

Disclosures from the hidden quadrant (Q3) are ordinarily done gradually and reciprocally. Under special circumstances such as a crisis or an emergency, the acquaintance process may be speeded up. A regional power failure, an earthquake, an acute illness in a neighborhood, or an accident may radically change interpersonal processes and produce new disclosures. The releasing effect of public crises puzzles many people who cannot understand why a catastrophe may have such satisfying effect on interpersonal exchanges.

It would be of value to examine more closely what occurs as two or more persons grow in trust and become more open about themselves. Perhaps an element of risk-taking paces the process of change. By risk I mean the chance you take in having your feelings hurt, such as becoming more anxious or embarrassed, insulted, belittled or in other ways offended. There are other kinds of psychological assaults that make one a bit wary. How much does it take to make you feel foolish, irritated, annoyed, angry, ashamed, or guilty? Waiters, bellboys, and others who rely heavily for their income on eliciting gratuities from customers are sometimes highly-skilled in letting a patron know that he will not be let off easy if he violates the level of tipping. Or perhaps experience with the general public has not always been pleasant and the waiters and bellboys have had to learn to protect themselves. In brief, there are real psychological hazards in even the most perfunctory relationships and the hazards are increased to the extent that one's openness makes him vulnerable.

What about the risks of not being open, or not disclosing? Is it true that one is psychologically safer by keeping his third quadrant to himself? Isn't it foolish to let people know what you feel and think?

The answer is no, quite the contrary. I say this unequivocally even though there must be times when everyone regrets having been too transparent. I cannot recall a single group of persons who came together to learn about people, about themselves, and about groups who did not discover that they were too closed off from people in everyday life in their families, on their jobs, and with friends. Sometimes this discovery is expressed in words like feeling lonely, isolated, alienated. Most of the time participants experience deep satisfaction with their feelings of greater openness and intimacy after working through some of their common group problems. They begin to see direct connections between their initial behavior in a group and their behavior at home.

Another set of risks involved in not sharing selectively from your hidden third quadrant has to do with learning about your own self. As mentioned earlier, if to know yourself is of interest to you and if appropriate self-disclosure to others is an integral part of the learning-about-self process, the risk you run in not being open is clear.

In addition, there is the risk of loss of personal flexibility. As mentioned in the original description of the Johari Window, it takes energy and attention to hold back reactions. Spontaneity is reduced and others then see you as more inflexible. It also takes considerable energy to set the face into a rigid mold, a mask, and then to hold the mask in place.

But feelings and expressions, not only of face but of the whole body and of the voice as well, are difficult to disguise and perhaps impossible to control totally. Sometimes in holding back, the best you can do is to distort what comes through, thereby interfering with communication and with other interpersonal transactions.

Finally, the risks of being more open and more transparent must be borne not only for the satisfactions and enjoyment of people and of self, but for increased realization of self. Lest that last phrase slip by as just another platitude, I'd like to rephrase it something like this. Your talent and your potentials have a better chance of being developed if you as a person have access to your own feelings, your imagination, and your fantasy. If you can be open and free even with but one other person there is greater likelihood that you can be in touch with self. In Johari terms, *a change in any quadrant affects all quadrants*, and since you have direct awareness in the first and third quadrants, the behavior and motivation here are subject to your control. Regardless of other risks, the greatest risk therefore would come from not exercising the awareness and control you do have.

A middle-aged woman who holds an important job and has a pleasant, dignified appearance became increasingly dissatisfied with her behavior in a learning group. Frequent misunderstandings of what she tried to say plus patronizing reactions from others bothered her. It took quite a while before she became aware of the fact that she was overcontrolling her own reactions to what was going on. She was finally stung by the remark made by an influential member who lumped her together with two other persons who were seen as "nice," meaning bland and ineffectual. She had enough confidence in the group by this time to express her annoyance in what was for her a strong outburst. To her surprise she found that this free expression made the group take notice of her in a new way. She then admitted that she felt she had to be diplomatic at all times, that she thought her face was too transparent, and that it was all she could do to try to keep people from knowing what was going on within. It was only then that she learned in new exchanges with others that she could well afford the risk of being herself more. Further, she became aware that her expressive face, instead of being an unfortunate handicap, was actually a lively and colorful aspect of her whole bearing. In the next few days she was much more relaxed and more expressive too. She seemed to have shed a tightness of visage; she acknowledged feeling freer and more buoyant than she had for a long time. She became a more active person as well as a more enjoyable group member.

There are certain persons who plunge into a relationship. (Samuel Culbert [1967] refers to these as revealers. As I use the term, a plunger is a high revealer.) Lewin (1948) has observed that Americans are far more casual and open about the acquaintance process than Europeans. He does add, however, that once a European develops a close relationship, he is more apt to go deeper both in his disclosures and in his involvement than the American. But surely in both populations there are the plungers who, relative to the general norm, tend to be both more open and more trusting than others. Though I do not have the evidence at hand I would guess that where this openness is expressed with due consideration for what is going on with the other, there is indeed apt to be a quicker development in the pattern of relationships. However, for many the plunger or quick self-discloser is anathema, to be avoided at all costs. A plunger when he proceeds without due consideration for you is one who discloses the hidden or private area at a rate that usually is too rapid for your comfort.

Since it is possible to move too slowly or too rapidly in disclosing Q3, what principles govern appropriate disclosure? . . .

In a study of "self-disclosure and interpersonal effectiveness," Halverson and Shore (1969) evaluated fifty-three Peace Corps trainees on a series of personality dimensions, including authoritarianism, sociometric choice, interpersonal flexibility and adaptability, and conceptual complexity. The latter is a measure of ability to appreciate alternative ways of viewing a social situation. Self-disclosure was negatively correlated with authoritarianism and positively correlated with conceptual complexity. "A person of a higher level of conceptual complexity interacts in an interdependent manner (i.e., assuming mutuality and equality in relationships), whereas one at a low level presumably interacts unilaterally (e.g., dominant and submissive roles). It follows that there should be more openness in communicating to others in an interdependent rather than a unilateral interaction" (1969, p. 216). In addition conceptual complexity correlates significantly with interpersonal flexibility and general adaptability, in the findings of this research.

Halverson and Shore also found that "self-disclosure assumes importance in the development of more stable and less superficial interpersonal relationships" (p. 216). That is, the trainees disclosed self in growing relationships selectively. Another interesting finding by the researchers supports the idea that intelligence itself (as measured by two different intelligence tests) is not related to openness or accessibility. Other personality variables, such as those mentioned above, determine the degree of self-disclosure. It should be noted that conceptual complexity as the researchers define it (the capacity to process interpersonal information in a flexible way) is not significantly correlated with intelligence.

The question remains: When is self-disclosure appropriate?

In an earlier discussion bearing on Q3 it was pointed out that the person has some choice in disclosing himself because the hidden area is known to self and not to others. Principles governing what is disclosed, where and when and to whom, have only recently begun to be studied systematically. These questions bear closely on the meaning and quality of interpersonal relations, and are tied in with wide-ranging issues in the teaching-learning process, psychotherapy, leadership, encounter group practice, and intraorganizational life. It is apparent that what is considered appropriate self-disclosure will vary with each individual, his life style, his social environment, and other important and unique variables. Still it may be of value to characterize appropriate self-disclosure through a series of hunches from which testable hypotheses may be drawn. Self-disclosure is appropriate:

1. *When it is a function of the ongoing relationship.* What one shares with another belongs in the particular relationship; it is not a random or isolated act.

2. *When it occurs reciprocally.* This implies that there is some degree of interdependency and mutuality involved.

3. *When it is timed to fit what is happening.* The self-disclosure grows out of the experience that is going on between or among the persons involved. The timing and sequence are important.

4. *When it concerns what is going on within and between persons in the present.* Some account is taken of the behavior and feelings of the participants individually and of the persons collectively. There is recognition of the relationship as an emergent phenomenon in addition to the individual selves.

5. *When it moves by relatively small increments.* What is revealed does not drastically change or restructure the relationship. The implication is that a relationship is built gradually except in rare and special cases.

6. *When it is confirmable by the other person.* Some system is worked out between the persons to validate reception of that which has been disclosed.

7. *When account is taken of the effect disclosure has on the other person(s).* The disclosure has not only been received; there is evidence of its effect on the receiver.

8. *When it creates a reasonable risk.* If the feeling or behavior were really unknown to the other, it may have been withheld for a reason bearing on differences which have yet to be faced by the participants.

9. *When it is speeded up in a crisis.* A serious conflict jeopardizing the structure of the relationship may require that more Q3 material be quickly revealed to heal the breach or help in the reshaping of the relationship.

10. *When the context is mutually shared.* The assumptions underlying the social context suggest that there is enough in common to sustain the disclosure.

The fact that persons will sometimes use casual meetings as the social setting for disclosing rather important personal information suggests that the need to reveal personal matters is not always gratified. Persons may be trapped in social relations such that the perceived risk prevents freer interaction. Since most social relations do not have built-in conditions for clarifying the bases for risks or the nature of mutual entrapment, stalemate sets in. The individual looks elsewhere, hardly aware that he is in a trapped state or that he can work out of it. Sometimes a bartender or plane passenger can help by just listening. More often than not, such contacts with friendly strangers are less than satisfying and the individual is still in a stalemate in his usual social relations. Encounter groups at times offer an opportunity to learn about characteristic hangups, with a chance for new awareness and different behavioral experience to carry over to back-home situations. Again, the encounter group is not a panacea, but it does demonstrate repeatedly that under competent guidance many participants learn significant things about people and groups in general and about their own relationships in particular.

Editor's Comment. Luft suggests reasons why a person might fear, and therefore avoid, self-disclosure. Perhaps one or two more reasons could be added. Self-disclosure is a form of interpersonal contact and, as such, leads to intimacy. The person who fears intimacy, even though he rationalizes his refusal to disclose himself under a number of rubrics (including the fear of shame), will avoid self-revelation. Second, most of us fear change or, at least, the effort that is involved in self-improvement. When a person reveals forms of behavior with which he himself is dissatisfied, he puts himself under some pressure to change. However, if he is not ready to undergo the pain of change, he will refrain from discussing such behaviors (and perhaps from even thinking about them). To disclose oneself is, often enough, to confront oneself, and such self-confrontation can be too painful to risk.

Perhaps it can be said that we live in a culture in which intimate self-disclosure is not popular. It is as though we need some kind of cultural permission to talk about ourselves freely, and we grant ourselves this permission only rarely—for instance, in counseling and psychotherapeutic situations. It is almost as if the need to be open were a sign of disturbance rather than integration. If, as Luft claims, healthy sharing is held in check by custom, social training, and diverse fears, then the encounter group can be a laboratory in which such constricting taboos are challenged.

Luft's rules for appropriate disclosure imply that disclosure must take place in an atmosphere of mutual support. The encounter situation itself makes certain demands for openness, but this does not mean that the members should try to force one another into self-revelation. Extorted disclosure usually benefits no one. Disclosure is a way of making contact with another and must, therefore, be engaged in freely. Silent members hinder the progress of the entire group. They remain "unknowns" and thus prevent the development of a climate of trust. They should, therefore, be confronted; but responsible confrontation should be based on respect for the person being confronted—even the person who is not as open as others.

Healthy Personality
and Self-Disclosure

Sidney M. Jourard

Editor's Introduction. Jourard's thesis in this article can be stated both positively and negatively. He suggests that "every maladjusted person is a person who has not made himself known to another human being and in consequence does not know himself." More positively, self-disclosure is an important avenue to personal and interpersonal growth. Another theme in the article is reminiscent of one of Gibb's theses (1968): although roles are essential in social living, a person needs time to be role-free if he is to avoid self-alienation. Jourard claims that self-disclosure is a way of being role-free. Everyday life, then, should include the kind of disclosure that is ordinarily associated with counseling and psychotherapy. Such disclosure is possible, Jourard suggests, only in a context of love.

For a long time, health and well-being have been taken for granted as "givens," and disease has been viewed as the problem for man to solve. Today, however, increasing numbers of scientists have begun to adopt a reverse point of view: disease and trouble are coming to be viewed as the givens, and specification of positive health and its conditions as the important goal. Physical, mental, and social health are values representing restrictions on the total variance of being. The scientific problem here consists in arriving at a definition of health, determining its relevant dimensions, and then identifying the independent variables of which these are a function.

Scientists, however, are supposed to be hard-boiled, and they insist that phenomena, in order to be counted "real," must be public. Hence, many behavioral scientists ignore man's self, or soul, since it is essentially a private phenomenon. Others, however are not so quick to allocate man's self to the limbo of the unimportant, and they insist that we cannot understand man and his lot until we take his self into account.

I probably fall into the camp of these investigators who want to explore health as a positive problem in its own right and who, further, take man's self

Reprinted from *Mental Hygiene,* 1959, vol. 6. Used with the permission of the publisher and the author.

seriously—as a reality to be explained and as a variable which produces consequences for weal or woe. In this chapter, I would like more fully to explore the connection between positive health and the disclosure of self. Let me commence with some sociological truisms.

Social systems require their members to play certain roles. Unless the roles are adequately played, the social systems will not produce the results for which they have been organized. This flat statement applies to social systems as simple as one developed by an engaged couple and to those as complex as a total nation among nations.

Societies have socialization "factories" and "mills"—families and schools—which serve the function of training people to play the age, sex, and occupational roles which they shall be obliged to play throughout their life in the social system. Broadly speaking, if a person plays his roles suitably, he can be regarded as a more or less normal personality. *Normal personalities, however, are not necessarily healthy personalities* (Jourard, 1958, pp. 16-18).

Healthy personalities are people who play their roles satisfactorily and at the same time derive personal satisfaction from role enactment; more, they keep growing and they maintain a high-level physical wellness (Dunn, 1958). It is probably enough, speaking from the standpoint of a stable social system, for people to be normal personalities. But it is possible to be a normal personality and be absolutely miserable. We would count such a normal personality unhealthy. In fact, normality in some social systems—successful acculturation to them—reliably produces ulcers, piles, paranoia, or compulsiveness. We also have to regard as unhealthy those people who have never been able to enact the roles that legitimately can be expected from them.

Counselors, guidance workers, and psychotherapists are obliged to treat with both patterns of unhealthy personality—those people who have been unable to learn their roles and those who play their roles quite well, but suffer the agonies of boredom, frustration, anxiety, or stultification. If our clients are to be helped, they must change, and change in *valued* directions. A change in a valued direction may arbitrarily be called growth. We have yet to give explicit statement to these valued directions for growth, though a beginning has been made (Fromm, 1947; Jahoda, 1958; Jourard, 1958; Maslow, 1954; Rogers, 1954). We who are professionally concerned with the happiness, growth, and well-being of our clients may be regarded as professional lovers, not unlike the Cyprian sisterhood. It would be fascinating to pursue this parallel further, but for the moment let us ask instead what this has to do with self-disclosure.

To answer this question, let's tune in on an imaginary interview between a client and his counselor. The client says, "I have never told this to a soul, doctor, but I can't stand my wife, my mother is a nag, my father is a bore, and my boss is an absolutely hateful and despicable tyrant. I have been carrying on an affair for the past ten years with the lady next door, and at the same time I am a deacon in the church." The counselor says, showing great understanding and empathy, "Mm-humm!"

If we listened for a long enough period of time, we would find that the client talks and talks about himself to this highly sympathetic and empathic listener. At some later time, the client may eventually say, "Gosh, you have helped me a lot. I see what I must do and I will go ahead and do it."

Now this talking about oneself to another person is what I call self-disclosure. It would appear, without assuming anything, that self-disclosure is a factor in the process of effective counseling or psychotherapy. Would it be too arbitrary an assumption to propose that people become clients *because they have not disclosed themselves in some optimum degree to the people in their life?*

An historical digression: Toward the end of the 19th century, Joseph Breuer, a Viennese physician, discovered (probably accidentally) that when his hysterical patients talked about themselves, disclosing not only the verbal content of their memories, but also the feelings that they had suppressed at the time of assorted "traumatic" experiences, their hysterical symptoms disappeared. Somewhere along the line, Breuer withdrew from a situation which would have made him Freud's peer in history's hall of fame. When Breuer permitted his patients "to be," it scared him, one gathers, because some of his female patients disclosed themselves to be quite sexy, and what was probably worse, they felt quite sexy toward him. Freud, however, did not flinch. He made the momentous discovery that the neurotic people of his time were struggling like mad to avoid "being," to avoid being known, and in Allport's (1955) terms, to avoid "becoming." He learned that his patients, when they were given the opportunity to "be"—which free association on a couch is nicely designed to do—would disclose that they had all manner of horrendous thoughts and feelings which they did not even dare disclose to themselves, much less express in the presence of another person. Freud learned to permit his patients to be, through permitting them to disclose themselves utterly to another human. He evidently did not trust anyone enough to be willing to disclose himself *vis a vis*, so he disclosed himself to himself on paper (Freud, 1955) and learned the extent to which he was himself self-alienated. Roles for people in Victorian days were even more restrictive than today, and Freud discovered that when people struggled to avoid being and knowing themselves, they got sick. They could only become well and stay relatively well when they came to know themselves through self-disclosure to another person. This makes me think of Georg Groddeck's magnificent *Book of the It (Id)* in which, in the guise of letters to a naive young woman, Groddeck shows the contrast between the *public self*—pretentious, role-playing—and the warded off but highly dynamic *id*—which I here very loosely translate as "real self."

Let me at this point draw a distinction between role relationships and interpersonal relationships—a distinction which is often overlooked in the current spate of literature that has to do with human relations. Roles are inescapable. They must be played or else the social system will not work. A role by definition is a repertoire of behavior patterns which must be rattled off in appropriate contexts, and all behavior which is irrelevant to the role must be suppressed. But what we often forget is the fact that it is a *person* who is playing the role. This person has a self, or I should say he *is* a self. All too often the roles that a person plays do not do justice to all of his self. In fact, there may be nowhere that he may just *be* himself. Even more, the person may not *know* his self. He may, in Horney's (1950) terms, be self-alienated. This fascinating term "self-alienation" means that an individual is estranged from his real self. His real self becomes a stranger, a feared and distrusted stranger. Estrangement, alienation from one's real self, is at the root of the "neurotic personality of our time" so eloquently described by Horney (1936). Fromm (1957) referred to the same phenomenon as a socially patterned defect. Self-alienation is a sickness which is so widely shared that no one recognizes it. We may take it for granted that all the clients whom we encounter are self-alienated to a greater or lesser extent. If you ask anyone to answer the question, "Who are you?" the answer will generally be "I am a psychologist," "a businessman," a "teacher," or what have you. The respondent will probably tell you the name of the role with which he feels most closely identified. As a matter of fact, the respondent spends a great part of his life trying to discover who he is, and once he has made some such discovery, he spends the rest of his life trying to play the part. Of course, some of the roles,—age, sex, family, or occupational roles—may be so restrictive that they fit a person in a manner not too different from the girdle of a 200-pound lady who is struggling to look like Brigitte Bardot. There is Faustian drama all about us in this world of role playing. Everywhere we see people who have sold their soul, or their real self, if you wish, in order to be a psychologist, a businessman, a nurse, a physician, a this or a that.

Now, I have suggested that no social system can exist unless the members play their roles and play them with precision and elegance. But here is an odd observation, and yet one which you can all corroborate just by thinking back over your own experience. It is possible to be involved in a social group such as a family or a work setting for years and years, playing one's roles nicely with the other members—and never getting to know the *persons* who are playing the other roles. Roles can be played personally and impersonally, as we are beginning to discover. A husband can be married to his wife for fiteeen years and never come to know her. He knows her as "the wife." This is the paradox of the *"lonely* crowd" (Riesman, 1950). It is the loneliness which people try to counter with "togetherness." But much of today's "togetherness" is like the "parallel play" of two-year-old children, or like the professors in Stringfellow Barr's (1958) novel who, when together socially, lecture *past* one another alternately and sometimes simultaneously. There is no real self-to-self or person-to-person meeting in such transactions. Now what does it mean to know a person, or, more accurately, a person's self? I don't mean anything mysterious by "self." All I mean is the person's subjective side—what he thinks, feels, believes, wants, worries about—the kind of thing which one could never know unless one were told. *We get to know the other person's self when he discloses it to us.*

Self-disclosure, letting another person know what you think, feel, or want is the most direct means (though not the only means) by which an individual can make himself known to another person. Personality hygienists place great emphasis upon the importance for mental health of what they call "real-self being," "self-realization," "discovering oneself," and so on. An operational analysis of what goes on in counseling and therapy shows that the patients and clients discover themselves through self-disclosure to the counselor. They talk and, to their shock and amazement, the counselor listens.

I venture to say that there is probably no experience more horrifying and terrifying than that of self-disclosure to "significant others" whose probable reactions are assumed, but not known. Hence the phenomenon of "resistance." This is what makes psychotherapy so difficult to take, and so difficult to administer. If there is any skill to be learned in the art of counseling and psychotherapy, it is the art of coping with the terrors which attend self-disclosure, and the art of decoding the language, verbal and non-verbal, in which a person speaks about his inner experience.

Now what is the connection between self-disclosure and healthy personality? Self-disclosure, or should I say "real"-self-disclosure, is both a symptom of personality health (Jourard, 1958, pp. 218-221) and at the same time a means of ultimately achieving healthy personality. The discloser of self is an animated "real-self be-er." This, of course, takes courage—the "courage to be." I have known people who would rather die than become known. In fact, some did die when it appeared that the chances were great that they would become known. When I say that self-disclosure is a symptom of personality health, what I mean really is that a person who displays many of the other characteristics that betoken healthy personality (Jourard, 1958; Maslow, 1954) *will also display the ability to make himself fully known to at least one other significant human being.* When I say that self-disclosure is a means by which one achieves personality health, I mean something like the following: it is not until I *am* my real self and I act my real self that my real self is in a position to grow. One's self grows from the *consequence of being.* People's selves stop growing when they repress them. This growth-arrest in the self is what helps to account for the surprising paradox of finding an infant inside the skin of someone who is playing the role of an adult. In a fascinating analysis of mental disease, Jurgen Ruesch (1957) describes assorted neurotics, psychotics, and psychosomatic patients as persons with selective atrophy and overspecialization in various aspects of the process of communication. This culminates in a foul-up of the processes of knowing others and of becoming known to others. Neurotic and psychotic symptoms might be viewed as smoke screens interposed between the patient's real self and the gaze of the onlooker. We might call the symptoms "devices to avoid becoming known." A new theory of schizophrenia has been proposed by a former patient (Anonymous, 1958) who "was there," and he makes such a point.

Alienation from one's real self not only arrests one's growth as a person; it also tends to make a farce out of one's relationships with people. As the ex-patient mentioned above observed, the crucial "break" in schizophrenia is with *sincerity,* not reality (Anonymous, 1958). A self-alienated person—one who does not disclose himself truthfully and fully—can never love another person nor can he be loved by the other person. Effective loving calls for knowledge of the object (Fromm, 1956; Jourard, 1958). How can I love a person whom I do not know? How can the other person love me if he does not know me?

Hans Selye (1946) proposed and documented the hypothesis that illness as we know it arises in consequence of stress applied to the organism. Now I rather think that unhealthy *personality* has a similar root cause, and one which is related to Selye's concept of stress. It is this. Every maladjusted person is a person who has not made himself known to another human being and in consequence does not know himself. Nor can he be himself. More than that, *he struggles actively to avoid becoming known by another human being.* He *works* at it ceaselessly, 24 hours daily, and it is work! The fact that resisting becoming known is *work* offers us a research opening, incidentally (cf. Dittes, 1948; Davis and Malmo, 1951). I believe that in the effort to avoid becoming known, a person provides for himself a cancerous kind of stress which is subtle and unrecognized but none the less effective in producing, not only the assorted patterns of unhealthy personality which psychiatry talks about, but also the wide array of physical ills that have come to be recognized as the stock in trade of psychosomatic medicine. Stated another way, I believe that *other people come to be stressors to an individual in direct proportion to his degree of self-alienation.*

If I am struggling to avoid becoming known by other persons then, of course, I must construct a false public self (Jourard, 1958, pp. 301-302). The greater the discrepancy between my unexpurgated real self and the version of myself that I present to others, then the more dangerous will other people be for me. If becoming known by another person is threatening, then the very presence of another person can serve as a stimulus to evoke anxiety, heightened muscle tension, and all the assorted visceral changes which occur when a person is under stress. A beginning already has been made, demonstrating the tension-evoking powers of the other person, through the use of such instruments as are employed in the lie detector, through the measurement of muscle tensions with electromyographic apparatus, and so on (Davis and Malmo, 1958; Dittes, 1958).

Students of psychosomatic medicine have been intimating something of what I have just finished saying explicitly. They say (cf. Alexander, 1950) the ulcer patients, asthmatic patients, patients suffering from colitis, migraine, and the like, are chronic *repressors* of certain needs and emotions, especially hostility and dependency. Now when you repress something, you are not only withholding awareness of this something from yourself, you are also withholding it from the scrutiny of the other person. In fact, the means by which repressions are overcome in the therapeutic situation is through relentless disclosure of self to the therapist. When a patient is finally able to follow the fundamental rule in psychoanalysis and disclose everything which passes through his mind, he is generally shocked and dismayed to observe the breadth, depth, range, and diversity of thoughts, memories, and emotions which pass out of his "unconscious" into overt disclosure. Incidentally, by the time a person is that free to disclose in the presence of another human being, he has doubtless completed much of his therapeutic sequence.

Self-disclosure, then, appears to be one of the means by which a person engages in that elegant activity which we call real-self-being. But is real-self-being synonomous with healthy personality? Not in and of itself. I would say that real-self-being is a necessary but not a sufficient condition for healthy personality. Indeed, an authentic person may not be very "nice." In fact, he may seem much "nicer" socially and appear more mature and healthy when he is *not* being his real self than when he is his real self. But an individual's "obnoxious" but authentic self can never grow in the direction of greater maturity until the person has become acquainted with it and begins to *be* it. Real-self-being produces consequences which, in accordance with well known principles of behavior (cf. Skinner, 1953), produce changes in the real self. Thus, there can be no real growth of the self without real-self-being. Full disclosure of the self to at least one other significant human being appears to be the means by which a person discovers not only the breadth and depth of his needs and feelings, but also the nature of his own self-affirmed values. There is no necessary conflict, incidentally, between real-self-being and being an ethical or nice person, because for the average member of our society, self-owned ethics are generally acquired during the process of growing up. All too often, however, the self-owned ethics are buried under the authoritarian morals (Fromm, 1947).

If self-disclosure is one of the means by which healthy personality is both achieved and maintained, we can also note that such activities as loving, psychotherapy, counseling, teaching, and nursing, all are impossible of achievement without the disclosure of the client. It is through self-disclosure that an individual reveals to himself and to the other party just exactly who, what, and where he is. Just as thermometers and sphygmomanometers disclose information about the real state of the body, self-disclosure reveals the real nature of the soul, or self. Such information is vital in order to conduct intelligent evaluations. All I mean by evaluation is comparing how a person is with some concept of optimum. You never really discover how truly sick your psychotherapy patient is until he discloses himself utterly to you. You cannot help your client in vocational guidance until he has disclosed to you something of the impasse in which he finds himself. You cannot love your spouse or your child or your friend unless those persons have permitted you to know them and to know what they need in order to move toward greater health and well-being. Nurses cannot nurse patients in any meaningful way unless they have permitted the patients to disclose their needs, wants, worries, anxieties and doubts, and so forth. Teachers cannot be very helpful to their students until they have permitted the students to disclose how utterly ignorant and misinformed they presently are. Teachers cannot even provide helpful information to the students until they have permitted the students to disclose exactly what they are interested in.

I believe we should reserve the term inter*personal* relationships to refer to transactions between "I and thou" (Buber, 1937), between *person* and *person*, not between role and role. A truly personal relationship between two people involves disclosure of self one to the other in full and spontaneous honesty. The data that we have collected up to the present time have shown us some rather interesting phenomena. We found (Jourard and Lasakow, 1958), for example, that the women we tested in universities in the Southeast were consistently higher self-disclosers than men; they seem to have a greater capacity for establishing person-to-person relationships, inter*personal* relationships, than men. This characteristic of women seems to be a socially-patterned phenomenon which sociologists (Parsons and Bales, 1955) refer to as the *expressive* role of women in contradistinction to the instrumental role which men universally are obliged to adopt. Men seem to be much more skilled at *im*personal, *instrumental* role-playing. But public health officials, very concerned about the sex differential in mortality rates, have been wondering what it is about being a man which makes males die younger than females. Do you suppose that there is any connection whatsoever between the disclosure patterns of men and women and their differential death rates? I have already intimated that withholding self-disclosure seems to impose a certain stress on people. Maybe "being manly," whatever that means, is slow suicide!

I think there is a very general way of stating the relationship between self-disclosure and assorted values such as healthy personality, physical health, group effectiveness, successful marriage, effective teaching, and effective nursing. It is this. A person's self is known to be the immediate determiner of his overt behavior. This is a paraphrase of the phenomenological point of view in psychology (Combs and Snygg, 1959). Now if we want to understand anything, explain it, control it, or predict it, it is helpful if we have available as much pertinent information as we possibly can. Self-disclosure provides a source of information which is relevant. This information has often been overlooked. Where it has not been overlooked, it has often been misinterpreted by observers and practitioners through such devices as projection or attribution. *It seems to be difficult for people to accept the fact that they do not know the very person whom they are confronting at any given moment.* We all seem to assume that we are expert psychologists and that we know the other person, when in fact we have only constructed a more or less autistic concept of him in our mind. If we are to learn more about man's self, we must learn more about self-disclosure—its conditions, dimensions, and consequences. Beginning evidence (cf. Rogers, 1958) shows that actively accepting, empathic, loving, non-punitive response in short, love—provides the optimum conditions under which man will disclose, or expose, his naked, quivering self to our gaze. It follows that if we would be helpful (or should I say *human*) we must grow to loving stature and learn, in Buber's terms, to confirm our fellow man in his very being. Probably, this presumes that we must *first* confirm our *own* being.

References

Alexander, F. *Psychosomatic medicine.* New York: Norton, 1950.

Allport, G. *Becoming. Basic considerations of a psychology of personality.* New Haven: Yale University Press, 1955.

Anonymous. A new theory of schizophrenia. *J. abnorm. soc. Psychol.,* 1958, *57,* 226-236.

Barr, S. *Purely academic.* New York: 1958.

Buber, M. *I and thou.* New York: Scribners, 1937.

Davis, F. H. & Malmo, R. B. Electromyographic recording during interview. *Amer. J. Psychiat.* 1951, *107,* 908-916.

Dittes, J. E. Extinction during psychotherapy of GSR accompanying "embarrassing" statements. *J. abnorm. soc. Psychol.* 1957, *54,* 187-191.

Dunn, H. L. Higher-level wellness for man and society. *Amer. J. Pub. Health,* 1959.

Freud, S. *The interpretation of dreams.* New York: Basic Books, 1955.

Fromm, E. *Man for himself.* New York: Rinehart, 1947.

Fromm, E. *The sane society.* New York: Rinehart, 1957.

Groddeck, G. *The book of it.* New York and Washington: Nerv. & Ment. Dis. Pub. Co., 1928.

Horney, K. *Neurosis and human growth.* New York: Norton, 1950.

Horney, K. *The neurotic personality of our time.* New York: Norton, 1936.

Jahoda, Marie. *Current concepts of positive mental health.* New York: Basic Books, 1958.

Jourard, S. M. *Health personality. An approach through the study of healthy personality.* New York: Macmillan, 1958.

Jourard, S. M. & Lasakow, P. Some factors in self-disclosure. *J. abnorm. soc. Psychol.,* 1958, *56,* 91-98.

Maslow, A. H. *Motivation and personality.* New York: Harper, 1954.

Parsons, T. & Bales, R. F. *Family, socialization and interaction process.* Glencoe: Free Press, 1955.

Riesman, D. *The lonely crowd.* New Haven: Yale University press, 1950.

Rogers, C. R. *The concept of the fully-functioning person.* (Mimeographed manuscript, privately circulated, 1954).

Ruesch, J. *Disturbed communication.* New York: Norton, 1957.

Selye, H. General adaptation syndrome and diseases of adaptation. *J. Clin. Endocrinol.,* 1946, *6,* 117-128.

Skinner, B. F. *Science and human behavior.* New York: Macmillan, 1953.

Snygg, D. & Combs, A. W. *Individual behavior.* New York: Harper, 1949.

Editor's Comment. Mowrer (1968a) has assembled a good deal of evidence indicating that concealment—especially the concealment of irresponsible behavior—can lead to emotional disturbance. He sees the neurotic as a person who is undersocialized rather than oversocialized, as a person who must invest too much of his energy in constructing and preserving a facade in his interpersonal contacts. Mowrer (1968b) has also elaborated an approach to therapy called integrity therapy, or integrity training, to which disclosure—especially disclosure of one's areas of irresponsible living—is central. It is important to stress that self-disclosure is not just "confessing one's sins" (although that may be part of the process). It involves sharing the intimate dimensions of one's real self—hopes, joys, fears, aspirations, anxieties, and so forth. In a more positive vein, Jourard claims that a willingness to disclose oneself to significant others endows one with a certain freedom to be. If a person does not have to invest a great deal of energy in presenting a "proper" image of himself to others, especially to those who are most meaningful to him, then he has energy to invest himself in others in more productive ways.

I would suggest that the *way* in which a person discloses himself to others is also important. I have seen people in therapy groups rattle off in a kind of actuarial way a good deal of quite intimate information about themselves. They revealed themselves because they were asked to or because they thought they were supposed to do so. I call this kind of self-disclosure "history," as opposed to the more personal and effective "story" (see *E:GPFIG*, pp. 234-238). Such an actuarial approach to self-revelation often constitutes a barrier rather than a bridge to interpersonal contact. On the other hand, a person who is interested in contacting others is not preoccupied with merely retailing information for the sake of information, no matter how intimate. He is selective in what he tells, not because he wants to conceal anything, but because his first concern is the interpersonal realities of the group. He wants to translate himself to the other members in ways that are relevant to *these* people in *this* situation. This is "'story." The person who deals in history rather than story does not have a feeling for where the group is with respect to self-disclosure. Such a person is probably quite self-centered and is inevitably a poor listener. The person who is too preoccupied with his own needs finds it difficult to engage in the kind of self-sharing that leads to the climate of trust and mutual support so necessary for the well-being of the group.

Editor's References

Mowrer, O. H. New evidence concerning the nature of psychopathology. In M. J. Feldman (Ed.), *Studies in psychotherapy and behavioral change.* Buffalo, N.Y.: University of New York at Buffalo, 1968 (a). Pp. 113-193.

Mowrer, O. H. Loss and recovery of community: A guide to the theory and practice of integrity therapy. In G. M. Gazda (Ed.), *Innovations to group psychotherapy.* Springfield, Ill.: Charles C. Thomas, 1968 (b). Pp. 130-189.

Permission to Grow: Education and the Exploration of Human Potential

Don Clark

Editor's Introduction. This article could well serve both as an introduction to the spirit of encounter groups and as an indication of the possibilities for the renewal of education in the United States through the human-potential movement. Clark's article bursts with feeling and enthusiasm. It is a report permeated with the personality of the author and his feelings; for some in academe such a report is heresy, for others it is a refreshing change. Armed with a grant from a large foundation, Clark set out to see what was going on under the rubric of sensitivity training and the human-potential movement. In the course of his wanderings, he became "unfrozen" himself in ways in which he had not anticipated. He found that education need not be the staid, lifeless process that usually goes on in universities. Assuming that one of the goals of education is better affective contact among people, Clark saw this goal being achieved more effectively outside than inside formal educational institutions—for instance, in "growth centers" and in a wide variety of group experiences. What he saw during his odyssey was both an affirmation of and a challenge to the human-potential movement.

Introduction and Outcome

This study started in the autumn of 1968, but it is the offspring of personal and professional interests that go far back in years. As an undergraduate at Antioch College (1948-53) I had a heavy dose of what was then being called "group dynamics." It seemed bothersome at times to thrash out a small problem in a "town meeting" or to find myself pushed into involvement in an instant "buzz session," but there was no doubt about the excitement generated or the

This report was made possible in part by funds granted by Carnegie Corporation of New York. The statements made and views expressed are solely the responsibility of the author.

Don Clark, formerly a professor at City University of New York, is a writer, clinical psychologist, and educator in private practice in the San Francisco Bay Area. His books include *Those Children* (Wadsworth, 1970), *The Psychology of Education* (Free Press, 1967), and *Emotional Disturbance and School Learning* (S.R.A., 1965).

promise held for a genuinely democratic society, so I was hooked by the human potential that showed itself when a group set out in search of truth.

During my graduate training in clinical psychology I was walking the usual mental-hospital, guidance-clinic path, but my attention was repeatedly diverted by the newly developing profession of school psychology and the newly developing set of clinical techniques called "group therapy." By the end of my training I was a clinical psychologist with a professional investment in group therapy who was keeping an eye on the field of education. When I started work at Hunter College in 1961, I was feeling a need to pull together my interests in a teacher-training setting. During the next four years I developed a kind of educational discussion group that left me dissatisfied because participants seemed unnaturally glued to their chairs even though they were *talking* about feelings, about themselves, and about people in and out of the room. Role-playing helped, but group interaction leaped into color at the moments when bodies touched and words were momentarily unimportant. I had long been familiar with T-groups, group therapy, and psychodrama, but sometime around 1965 I started hearing stories about Esalen and WBSI, where highly unusual procedures were being tried out. I first smirked at the West Coast fadists and the Los Angeles charlatans but slowly began to suspect that there were kindred souls who were doing a more active job of searching than I.

I visited Esalen and WBSI in February 1968. By the following summer (1968) I had started to converse and correspond with professionals around the country who were working under such banners as "humanistic education," "humanistic psychology," "human-potential movement," "Gestalt therapy," "encounter," "growth center development," "theater games," "guided fantasy," "nonverbal communication," and "sensory awareness." All were involved in a seemingly more inclusive category called "sensitivity training" and all had some interest in formal education.

When the present study was funded in the autumn of 1968, it was my intention to visit perhaps ten geographical "centers" where there was a lot of interest and activity in some kinds of sensitivity training in education. I also planned discussions with perhaps forty leaders in the field. I would then write a book describing the key workers, their work, and their technical vocabularies. I was heading for a surprise.

It did not take me long to suspect that I had entered an Alice-in-Wonderland world where all my running would barely keep me in place. An example of the rate of expansion is that in January 1969 there were approximately thirty-seven identified "growth centers" in the United States. In August 1969 there were approximately eighty-seven such centers. I changed my "comprehensive survey-study" to an "impressionistic survey-study." I kept my eye and ear alert for the "new" and "different" that might have something to say to education. I found my share of disheartening blind alleys, but I also had my moments of joy.

I participated in groups in California, Washington, D.C., New York, Philadelphia, and Boston while clothed and nude, indoors and out, mute and verbal, with eyes open and closed. I interviewed the leaders of the field at deskside in the NTL headquarters, in airplanes while sipping scotch and soda, and in the hot sulfur baths at Esalen. I found there was always more to learn about.

"Why is everyone running to these groups?" I am often asked this and am ultimately forced to answer in terms of my personal needs and experience. "I am attracted because I need the stimulation of new techniques and ideas in order to get on with my personal growth," I answer. Why did I not satisfy these needs in the university where I was a faculty member or in the professional organizations of which I am a member? "Because the university and professional organizations are stuck with the restrictive rules of yesterday's style of inquiry while some 'under-thirty' students, Black militants, and hippies have shown me that there can be a freer kind of inquiry." The focus and findings of this study came clear finally as I started to write the report. I am reporting my good fortune to have seen the birth of a new style for centers of learning.

My intention was to produce a comprehensive book describing sensitivity training in relation to education past, present, and future. This report, written in September 1969, was a compilation of impressions and recommendations. The book needed more time for digestion and reflection. I am at work on it now and hope to publish it early in 1972.

I had intended to present this report in a more pedantic style, but a black-and-white photo does not adequately present a colorful scene. At the risk of drowning the reader in a sea of mixed metaphor, I have yielded to my impulse to put emotional life into the abstract prose wherever possible. I hope that the chosen style does not lessen the report's credibility.

Impressions

Faced with the task of describing what I have seen and heard during the months of this study, I feel like an explorer just returned from a tour of a little-known continent. Oh, there have been a handful of explorers and visitors there before me, but not one of us has seen the whole continent and not one of us can give a comprehensive picture of it. First I must tell you that it is a very big continent and that it is very rich in natural resources. I saw a lot being taken from the land. Some pioneers are harvesting food and sinking wells that may provide food and drink to a human race that is suffering the malnutrition of misunderstanding and dying from a thirst we call alienation. Some pioneers are mining precious gems never before seen by men in Western civilization, while some are busily mining fool's gold. Some are prospecting for profit and some for fun. If ever there was a "dark continent," this is it. Though I am far from it as I sit here writing, it has captured me. Rarely an hour of my waking life now passes without some memory of my exploration crowding to the surface or some fantasied expectation making me look ahead to a return visit.

I've given up using the term "sensitivity training" because what is afoot here is more than sensitizing or making one aware of his own feelings and the feelings of others. That is a part of it. But there is also the exploration and discovery of new facets of human experience and new human skills that can be developed. Terms like "exploration of human potential" are more inclusive and accurately descriptive.

People are becoming declassified. We are getting over the orgy of categorization and diagnostic labels that failed to explain human experience. In the human-potential movement, a person is seen as unique and is given the opportunity to explore himself as unique and unlike other people. At the same time he is offered the chance to touch the core of his "humanness," or the essence of what he shares with all other human beings. He can learn to be proud of his individuality and of his bond with other humans instead of being pressured to conform and shamed by his categorically labeled differences. He is not seen as a "borderline schizophrenic" or an "emotionally mature" individual but as a man who can find growth in meditation or who enjoys his work when he puts all of himself into each small task.

Conservative guardians of civilized virtues like "patriotism" and "religious duty" are very worried about this new movement. In Los Angeles there is a telephone number that you can dial day or night (reputedly sponsored by the John Birch Society) that warns of the dangers of sensitivity training as a tool of the *Communist conspiracy*. Ironically, it may be America's fantastic concern for materialistic property rights that has pulled us into the massive exploration of human potential. We hold it a great sin to cheat someone of his property or to tamper with his inheritance. The beatniks and then the hippies came along and tantalized us with the nagging possibility that each of us is being cheated of some of his inner wealth. Many of us started thinking: "Maybe that accounts for my feeling a little restless and dissatisfied and sour. Maybe those youngsters have gotten hold of some truth about how you find happiness, even though they claim that happiness is a byproduct rather than a goal." Mass media have convinced most Americans that happiness can be attained and that it is the *right* of every citizen. If that is so, we reason, and if those damned hippies have it and I don't, then somebody has been cheating me of my rightful inheritance. Once that seed is planted, it is a short step to trying out some kind of group experience that offers a lure of "personal growth." It is a matter of protecting one's property and not being cheated out of the full happiness that TV says can be attained.

At the end of August 1969 I participated in the annual meetings of the Association for Humanistic Psychology (AHP). At the opening session, a huge ballroom was quite literally *packed* with humans sitting on the floor. There was no furniture and one could see little of the carpeting. It looked like a late summer garden of human bodies, pressed against one another in a wild array of colors. There was an air of expectation and hope mixed with religious dedication. Participants self-mockingly spoke of "this carnival" and "the flesh market" but their voices contained concern lest "the search" be sidetracked or contaminated. The meetings were supposed to end with a very regular dance in the same ballroom two nights later, but most of the people found their way to the hotel's truck-unloading platforms where two clarinets, a bongo, trays, spoons, soda-pop cans, hands, and voices provided such an intense human melody that the kitchen employees flew dancing through the doors that held them captive as if they were being carried joyfully to the sea by an unseen river. If I had any doubts before the AHP meetings about whether this movement will continue to grow in membership and intensity, I have no such doubts now. It is only a matter of *how* it will grow now, the paths it will take, and whether it will unknowingly be swallowed and digested during growth by the society it is reacting against.

The nagging question in my mind is whether the human-potential movement will offer individuals permission to grow or whether it is possible that it will be rendered impotent by the clamor of too many consumers ready to change costume and vocabulary but unready to stop doing "business as usual" in a newly decorated arena that reeks of the same old dissatisfactions.

Education, Psychotherapy,
and Growth

When people discuss the human-potential movement, they are usually talking about encounter groups. There is a wide variety of techniques used in encounter groups and considerable confusion results from talking about "it." Carl Rogers, Bill Shutz, and Paul Bindrim run different kinds of encounter groups as do the hundreds of other leaders in the country.

To further complicate matters, some groups are primarily exploration oriented, some are educational (a prototype being an NTL industry group), while still others are psychotherapeutic in orientation. I believe that the techniques holding the most promise for education in the future are those that center around exploration, whether or not in an encounter group format. In such groups I have felt myself come alive as techniques were provided for searching the self in new areas or in new ways but no clues were offered as to which discoveries could be considered "right," "good," or "worthwhile." In groups that were traditionally "educational" or "psychotherapeutic" in orientation, I got the feeling that one was searching for Easter eggs and that the group leader presumably knew where they were hidden and could tell an egg from a stone. The new "encounter" language and games were being used but the "patients" were searching, as usual, while the therapist subtly directed the search through evaluative reactions to the patients' discoveries or the teacher helped the students jump through the discovery hoops leading to the final answer, already written in the lesson plan. Priests, teachers, therapists, and parents know too many answers about what is "right," "wrong," "good," and "bad." They are not in a position usually to encourage the kind of exploration that leads to unpredictable growth.

In the exciting exploration groups (one led by Ed Maupin comes to mind), I made *my* discoveries—discoveries that were valid and valuable for *me* at that point in my growth. If my discovery could be put into words, I was free to share it with the group or keep it to myself. Other members of the group were available as actors for my drama or as guides through their sharing of their own understanding of truth if I cared to enlist their aid in my search.

Encounter vocabulary and exercises can add a refreshing and entertaining new twist or facade to dreary old psychotherapy and to pseudo-discovery teaching, but it is disheartening to me to see this exciting possibility for a new kind of human self-understanding get ground into the familiar teacher's and psychotherapist's sausage.

The main reason why the *psychotherapeutic* and *educational* orientations in the human-potential movement keep getting mixed up with one another is that both contain a heavy dose of human *growth*. We are made anxious by the prospect of a quack doctor practicing psychotherapy with no license and no applicable training, but few are made anxious at the prospect of someone "practicing education without a license." We know that stimulating and urging human growth is educational, but we also know it is a part of most healthy everyday relationships. Most of us can take it or leave it when educational assistance is offered, depending upon our needs of the moment. This is not the case when you "put yourself in the doctor's hands" in order to have some psychological damage repaired.

It might well be that the field of psychotherapy would be better off without the hovering shadow of "complete responsibility" that is the inheritance from the physicians who got into the business of "healing minds." But the shadow is there. My point is that, *for now*, the professional working in the human-potential movement would help dissolve confusion if he not only said he was offering "growth opportunity" but specified that it was offered in the context of *educational exploration, educational instruction,* or *psychotherapy.* Perhaps one day we shall be free of the medical model of responsibility and the customer will be aware that he is solely responsible for his own growth—whether it is stimulated by exploration, instruction, or psychotherapy—but for now it is confusing, and the responsibility and type of experience must be specified in a clearly drawn contract.

As a nation, a civilization, and a world, we are trying to chart a course into a totally unknown and unknowable future. Educational-exploration techniques found in some encounter groups and in some other human-potential experiences hold out a great promise of understanding ourselves as human beings and developing new human skills. Such techniques—combined with the use of books and computers—can help to develop sufficiently broad and deep understanding that we may conceive and develop the skills, unknowable today, that are needed to provide navigation in that dimly seen future of disaster or delight.

We can no longer afford the antique concept of "teaching" or instructing our young. This has meant a variety of tricky or straightforward techniques applied to youngsters to urge them to "discover" and accept the answers and skills that we older humans already possessed. (A handful of individuals in each generation have taken unorthodox giant steps to find new answers and skills, and we praised them or persecuted them in accordance with how uncomfortable their deviation made us.) Our future concept of education must allow vast opportunity for new answers and new skills or we are as doomed as the dinosaur. The accelerating rate of change in the human world appears unalterable. We can try to harness it for our own use or be trampled by it.

The encounter group and other groups that have an orientation of exploration (not those that mask old-fashioned psychotherapy, teaching, or preaching) do not lead to old answers but to new puzzles, new problems, new modes of experience, and new perspectives; subsequently they provide a possible—though not guaranteed—footing from which one may reach for new answers and new skills.

It is very unlikely that these exploration techniques will filter into the educational establishment in a hurry (though it seems that at least one teacher in every school system has gotten "turned on" and is experimenting). The discovery orientation may reach formal education too late. Teachers are as resistant to change as any other group. No crash course for teachers and no required text will do the job. There is no way to know which technique or experience will reach which student or teacher. Of all my varied experiences during the past year, I was most profoundly touched by experiences in meditative massage. It is an almost totally nonverbal experience that has carried me into an exotic realm of human understanding. I *know* that it has contributed to my growth but am at a loss for verbal understanding or explanation. But other individuals are touched more deeply by verbal encounter games. Most important is that we begin to think of education as exploration into unknown territory. If we develop tolerance for such a concept, the human-potential movement can help us to educate.

Training, Licensing, Ethics, and Organization

Two questions are asked repeatedly. The first is, "How do I find a good group with a leader who knows what he's doing?" The second question is, "Where can I get properly trained to run encounter groups?"

I fumble with the first question in much the same way that I do when a friend wants to find a psychotherapist. I know hundreds of therapists, but there are only four to whom I can send my friends and feel safe. Having traveled around the country, I have had a chance to cross-validate impressions of nationally known group leaders. One, who has achieved wide publicity, I advise friends to avoid as a waste of time at best. There is one whom I consider a brilliant but dangerous virtuoso because of his lack of concern for the outcome of his performance. But there are others, such as Virginia Satir and Marion Saltman, whom I can recommend without hesitation, though I usually point out that Virginia Satir is therapy oriented and Marion Saltman is exploration oriented.

How do you find a good group leader? Find someone who has been in his group and can vouch for him. Better yet, find two people who can vouch for him.

Where do you go for training? There are training programs and training workshops springing up around the country. Esalen has a residency program that does not guarantee to train you as an adequate leader. NTL offers training but is ambivalent about having it used for personal-growth groups rather than organizational-change groups. The Center for Studies of the Person (most staff there used to be at WBSI) offers an exposure to the experience of running groups but avoids saying it offers "training" per se. United States International University in San Diego has some applicable graduate courses. Stiles Hall, the YMCA in Berkeley, offers the best organized and carefully supervised training program, but they do it on a shoestring and you must be invited for training as a result of peer selection from encounter-group participation. One of the poorest group leaders in the country (he has a national reputation for insensitivity and once told me: "Groups are not my thing— I prefer working with one person") now offers a year-around training program for group leaders. Training is available but not in the form of a program leading to certified competence. When I see someone with talent I usually send him to NTL or to C.S.P. in La Jolla, California and then wish him luck.

There is no doubt that comprehensive training programs are needed. We need training that is not based on NTL's desire to build its own organization, that is more willing than C.S.P. to evaluate the candidate's progress, that is more certain in direction than Esalen's residency program, that is more available to applicants than the Stiles Hall program, and that offers more genuine training than most of the supposed training workshops being offered around the country.

Yet it is no accident that workers in the human-potential movement have been wary of certifying competence. Most of us are aware that medicine, clinical psychology, and psychiatric social work have a high score for certifying *incompetence*. A trainee mouths the right words, assumes the proper poses, wades through enough seminars, passes an examination, and is then turned loose on the public as someone who can be considered trustworthy and competent for the remaining years of his professional life (if he continues to pay his license fee).

While training is needed, most of us want to see it offered in a way that will not encourage conformity to some model of "good" group leadership. Ironically, it is concern for "client welfare" or protection of the public that would force a stand *against* certification. The innocent customer must be forewarned that he is taking his life or his growth in his own hands and is responsible for himself when he enters a growth group.

What about ethics and organization? Let me point out again that I am talking about a *variety of techniques* used in the human-potential movement. These techniques can be used, and are used, by teachers, clergymen, psychologists, psychiatrists, social workers, drama directors, management consultants, and countless other professionals and non-professionals. Each profession must take responsibility for policing the ethical utilization of these techniques by its members.

I was recently summoned to a meeting of the American Psychological Association's committee on ethics and professional conduct because they are grappling with the ethical questions involved in the use of "sensitivity training" by psychologists. I said at that meeting that we will do more to protect the public by encouraging psychologists to make a clear contract with the client (the kinds of techniques to be used, who is assuming how much responsibility, and the therapeutic, instructional, or exploratory intent) than can be done by testing and certifying the psychologist's competence in the use of the techniques.

But there is a group or a non-discipline developing. These are workers who *facilitate human exploration for the purpose of promoting human growth.* Their business is growth but it is only tangentially related to psychotherapy, instructional (institutional) education, or any other established profession or discipline. It helps to confuse matters that often the worker is *also* a psychologist, a teacher, or some other kind of professional and lists himself as such from habitual dependence on the respectability of his profession. This "growth explorer" (if I may give him a name) has no professional organization (unless he has an additional professional identity) to offer guidance, security, and respectability.

The growth explorer has been hanging on to one organization that is as yet unsure of its own identity. That organization is the Association for Humanistic Psychology. Its newsletter keeps him in touch with people and events of interest to him and its annual meeting provides a marketplace where he can display his techniques and shop among the techniques of others. It is quite possible that AHP will grow more conservative while the growth explorers grow more adventurous and that they will part company, but for now the two (overlapping) groups are enjoying a productive love affair.

Some growth explorers are interested in forming an organization, but many have been burned too often by the coercive pressures toward conformity and conservatism found in any organization. They are well aware that these pressures seriously diminish the air of creativity and discovery that is the lifeblood of the growth explorer.

I would like to underscore the observation that growth centers are not staffed solely by growth explorers. Some leaders are clearly functioning as psychotherapists, some as instructors, and some as entertainers at best, con men at worst. Some leaders would have a hard time placing themselves in the proper category, so it is small wonder that the purchasing public is confused about the offerings.

My overall impression is that the pre-existing professional organizations will police the ethical utilization of the new growth techniques among their members. I hope that trade union fights for profitable "rights" to use these techniques will be avoided. I also hope that interdisciplinary efforts to deal with ethical standards will leave plenty of elbow room for the growth explorer who is not now a member of any other prestigious professional club.

One last point. Discussions of ethics in the human-potential movement are usually stimulated by rumor of clients being "damaged"; often the rumor involves a psychotic break leading to hospitalization. I found these rumors very difficult to validate. We need hard data but my impression is that psychotic-like episodes of a few minutes to a half hour duration are commonplace happenings in groups while psychotic episodes leading to hospitalization are rare and probably do not exceed the number that would be found in a comparable population not exposed to the group experience. I also have the impression that psychotic episodes (brief and prolonged) occur more frequently in a group led by a clinical psychologist or a psychiatrist than in a group led by a "non-professional." There are plenty of untalented leaders around but the worst damage done by most of them is to spoil what could have been a marvelous growth experience by inept efforts that soured the group process.

Sunsets, Symphonies, and Lasting Value

The question that usually follows the one about dangers is, "What evidence is there that these groups are of any lasting value? You get high on honesty and truth, get to touch some warm bodies, do some laughing or crying, and become sensitive to your body and then you leave the group and go right back into the same hostile world. You can't sustain the high so you end up right back where you started. What's the use? Wouldn't it be better to get involved in social action and try to improve an evil real world?"

Someone at Esalen parried these questions by asking the value of seeing a sunset or hearing a symphony. I would add to his question one on the value of most school learning that does not clearly train some usable skill and another question on the value of travel to different parts of the world.

This question of value is a haunting question deflected from the world of psychotherapy. The psychotherapy enthusiasts have never been able to offer "hard data" answers and have resorted to customer satisfaction as the proof of the pudding. I frankly do not see the need to *prove* changed attitudes, values or ability to function "better" in our marketplace society.

We put an enormous amount of effort into the travel industry (to say nothing of institutional education) and demand no proof that a trip to the Greek Isles is of lasting value to the traveler or that a college degree has more than symbolic value. A summer trip to Italy may cause one to reexamine his values because it helped bring dissatisfactions with life at home into focus. It could subsequently cause major behavioral changes or it could yield only some precious memories to enrich later years. The trip could also turn out to be a tiring bore. The tourist may choose to return to Italy on another trip, see a new part of the world, or stay home and save his money. We congratulate travelers on a good trip and console them after a bad one but we do not demand research to demonstrate the worth of travel.

We may be demanding more of the encounter group or the other experiences offered by the human-potential movement than these experiences are intended to offer at present. Our past experiences with medically oriented psychotherapy may be luring us to look for "cures" where only the experience of exploration is available.

Growth potential experiences *can* be of lasting value to an individual, but I hardly see how such value could be promised in advance. We can only wish the traveler a good trip and try to provide an interesting itinerary. A symphony, a sunset, or a course in nineteenth-century literature can also be of little or great value to a questing, growing human. The movement can only honestly claim to offer more sunsets and symphonies than most of us find in our day-to-day life.

Education and Turning on

Growth exploration techniques are being used in nursery schools, elementary grades, secondary grades, undergraduate and graduate classes, in-service courses for teachers, and various other adult education courses sponsored by employers.

In educational institutions the use of these techniques rarely carries official sanction, though the principal or college president is aware of certain teachers using the techniques. There are at least two new colleges (Johnston College in California and Pima College in Arizona) whose entire programs center around "experiential learning" and "interpersonal encounter." Graduate and undergraduate schools are now offering more courses in "humanistic psychology" and "humanistic education" in addition to the "mental hygiene," "human relations," and other vaguely defined courses that tend to stay with the psychological style of the times. At the college level, I have found growth techniques being most extensively used in education courses and, with much student enthusiasm and faculty caution, in psychology departments. The reaction of academic psychologists is very similar to the reception they offered clinical psychology just after the Second World War. I found these growth techniques at work in courses of drama, speech, nursing, political science, and even in chemistry and engineering. If this is a passing fad, it is impressive in its breadth. The Graduate School of Business Administration at U.C.L.A. may soon be changing its name to more accurately reflect its investment in the use of growth techniques to effect organizational change. The telephone at NTL in Washington is kept warm with inquiries and invitations from official and unofficial student groups looking for "a T-group experience." C.S.P. was recently approached by the Department of the Interior and asked to provide encounter groups for all of the teachers employed by the Bureau of Indian Affairs. The State University of New York at Albany is investing in a large-scale program that is within the university but not articulated in the university's departmental structure.

The human-potential movement has hit institutional education just as it has hit other institutions and professions that profess to serve human growth needs. Techniques are being developed and adapted for use in institutional settings. An example would be the group of teachers organized by George Brown and described in his Esalen Monograph entitled *Now*.

Why has it happened? Probably for the same complex reasons that actors and actresses are taking off their clothes and involving audiences; most of the nation under age thirty are giving marijuana a try (and some are sampling LSD and other "consciousness-altering" drugs); there are "Blacks demanding" rather than "Negroes requesting"; young people are going to jail and to other nations rather than serve the military; sex swingers are advertising their desires in "underground newspapers" rather than seeking treatment and cure for their deviations; ex-drug addicts are setting up model communities where some "squares" are permitted to come and learn; and growth centers are springing up round the nation faster than one can keep count. It is as if people are looking over their needs and see atomic annihilation hanging there, feel at a loss to control it, and have decided that in whatever time is left they want to make a fully honest individual human statement, to be themselves, to "do their thing," and in so doing to confront hypocrisy in others and in themselves. There is not enough time left to lie.

People are "turning-on" or "turning-in" in a vigorous attempt to seek truth and practice honesty in the time that is left. While the movement is making its impression upon institutional education, a far more exciting thing is happening. The movement presents a resurgence of a more genuine but noninstitutional form of education. People are *learning*. A poetic political scientist would probably describe the movement as "the people's educational revolution." It appears to be a white upper-middle-class phenomenon as yet but that may well be because these have been the people most in need of freedom to grow individually and the ones who can easily afford to pay money for such educational help. As yet it is not cheap enough for poor people and most non-whites are otherwise occupied in their own fight for freedom.

The human-potential movement is making a contribution to institutional education and, itself, represents a new (or very old) form of non-institutional education. Professional institutional educators are concerned. More than one has told me, "Those people at Esalen and WBSI are reinventing the wheel. There's nothing new about groups or about people reaching out to touch one another." My reply is that it is about time the wheel was reinvented in a world where most of us have learned to sit in a lonely spot or take tiny, tentative steps over the seemingly vast ground that separates us from our fellow humans. That wheel may help us to get together faster—maybe even in time, before our alienation and unhappiness has caused us to destroy one another.

Another worried comment that I hear from institutional educators, is, "All of this represents a kind of anti-intellectualism. People want to touch and taste and 'trip-out' but they don't want to understand by reading, discussing, and doing experimental research." My impression here is that the intellectual approach as represented by the academic community has been offering its customers dry food for a long time. The growth movement, with its awareness of body and nonverbal searching skills, is providing drink for some *very* thirsty people. My experience in the university setting with students is that once they taste the refreshing drink, many go on a binge and do indeed stop reading and listening to lectures. Eventually (usually a semester to a year and a half) the thirst is quenched and the student becomes aware of his hunger. He then begins to look for readings, conversations and lectures that interest him. He rarely gives up his attempt to satisfy his thirst but he combines it with his attempt to satisfy his hunger. Intellect and emotion have joined forces in the whole person who *demands* satisfaction for both hunger and thirst. This can be understandably unsettling to a university professor who has adjusted to a life in which he prepares dry food and tries to deny or hide his own thirst. Am I worried about the anti-intellectualism of this movement? I am not. I see thirsty people drinking and I know that they will eat when they are hungry.

Growth Centers and Super-Centers

The growth centers springing up around the country have their roots deeper in the past than most people realize. There is a place in Greece called Epidaurus (now on the tourist map for its still-functioning amphitheater) and thousands of years ago mad Greeks were invited to go there and to other "growth centers" because their madness was a sign that some gods looked on them with sufficient favor to inhabit their bodies. There were a variety of growth experiences (including hot baths, massage, meditation, encounter, and drama) made available to these favored citizens. Some of the new contemporary centers approach this ideal. Most are a blend of the thinking and work of three "super-centers" (two of which do not offer accommodations but send leaders out into the world). The three influential super-centers are the National Training Laboratories, the Esalen Institute, and the Center for the Studies of the Person.

Individuals seek training and philosophical footing at the three super-centers for their own individual reasons and the result of the experience is equally individualistic. There is not really any such animal as an Esalen-type group leader any more than there is an NTL-type leader, but the super-centers are distinctly different from one another and each leaves some indelible impression on the leader whom it nourished.

Esalen is the kitchen laboratory for the movement. Mike Murphy, its president and leader, tries hard to accept any approach that promises a better understanding of humans. The institution transcends the tradition of our culture in an attempt to give the search free reign. Esalen-Big Sur (there is also an Esalen in San Francisco) is the prototype that most of the smaller growth centers around the country try to emulate. When I am there I feel that I have stepped into a world that is highly accepting of any behavior that does not intrude on another person's search. You can do just about anything by yourself and you can do just about anything with another person if that person is willing to cooperate. The unspoken rule is to search honestly while telling the truth to yourself and others. From Esalen, ideas and techniques spill forth to a waiting nationwide network of growth explorers and other interested workers.

C.S.P. was formed when many of the professionals at WBSI in La Jolla, California decided they needed the greatest possible individual freedom combined with group support and stimulation to pursue their search for understanding in the human potential movement. C.S.P. is an Esalen that speaks English. The people at C.S.P. are adventurous, innovative, and receptive to new ideas but, as a group, they are more cautious and speak without condescension to the man-on-the-street. Esalen seems more concerned with new discoveries, while C.S.P. is dedicated to sharing what it knows with ordinary fellow humans.

NTL is the elder of the trio and takes its maturity-responsibility seriously. It is determined to profit by the mistakes made in its earliest enthusiastic years. It is already *the* voice most frequently consulted by a public anxious for interpretation and reassurance about the human-potential movement. Of the three super-centers, NTL appears to put the most effort into building and protecting itself as an institution. People trained by NTL become candidates for the network of associates who pay some homage and cash to the mother institution. NTL has done a lot of work in industry and is now concerned with using personal growth experiences as a *means* for fostering organizational change. It is their belief that mankind will profit more in the long run from institutions and organizations that are humanistic in orientation.

One would say that Esalen is discovering what it means to be human, C.S.P. is sharing the discoveries with interested people, and NTL is building the tested discoveries into our culture by seeding organizations. When this movement is finally taken seriously by institutional education, we will have all three super-centers to thank. There is some lack of understanding and considerable lack of communication among the three centers and it is regrettable. It is like watching three generations of a family. Each generation finds it embarrassing to look to the other two for stimulation and guidance, yet it is there to be had for the asking.

I think that the growth centers offer great hope. People who are bored by a sedentary vacation, disenchanted by the abundance of pseudo-discoveries in psychotherapy, angry at the docility demanded in college courses, and uneasy with the unreal inhuman world presented in most churches, find a kind of religious, active, thought-provoking, emotion producing vacation experience available at their local growth center. These growth centers could become the new secular, human institutions of adult learning in the not too distant future.

Personal Growth as Education

We may be at present witnessing the beginning or the preview of a profound change in our cultural definition of education. Formal education was once the domain of the church but this placed a limit on freedom of inquiry that became intolerable and secular education gained in stature because it did a better job of permitting human growth. The religious centers of learning followed the path established by secular education. Times had changed and cultural tolerance for increased individual freedom made an older style of education irrelevant.

There are signs that this is happening again. No one can deny the increased cultural permission for personal freedom. Seemingly established taboos are falling as individuals "do their own thing," make their personal statement, or pursue their own path of inquiry. Our established educational institutions do not seem able to keep up. Many major universities have sprouted unorthodox unofficial appendages that do not offer grades or degrees. They are "experimental colleges," or "free universities," often organized and partly staffed by the university's students. In these new institutions the line between teacher and student blurs or disappears altogether. There is a willingness to break the usual rules, discuss anything, take off clothing, touch one another, and otherwise experiment with experiences in ways considered imprudent or improper in an established educational institution. (There is one West Coast "experimental college" where one can take all the courses needed for teacher certification and have them appear on the record as if taken in the regular college. They are inundated with applicants.)

The growth centers often carry the "free university" trend one step further. Some are now branching out from the experimental workshop and adding offerings of on-going seminars that combine the free experiential inquiry with reading and lecture-discussions. It may be that we are seeing the birth of tomorrow's educational centers. It is not too far fetched to see today's respectable universities diminishing in importance because of the irrelevance of their offerings. It is not too hard to imagine these same universities one day following in the footsteps of prestigious growth centers. What I am saying here about adult education can be as easily stated in parallel for the education of children.

The struggle to make the offerings of the present educational institutions more relevant may be like offering blood transfusions to a moribund patient. We may do better to offer life-giving support to the fledgling new educational centers or growth centers and let the irrelevant institutions find the leaders they will follow into a new age of learning.

Recommendations

The human-potential movement is growing and will undoubtedly continue to grow, with or without the aid of its critics. It is going to influence the conceptual foundations and techniques of a variety of disciplines and professions as noted in the last chapter. My concern in this report is the emergence of a new style of growth and learning as the power and influence of the now irrelevant institutions of education fade.

Though I am not a seer, I believe that I can identify the major areas in which this movement needs help in assuming its responsibility for future education in our society.

1. *Improved Informal Communication.* As I travelled the country probing for information and understanding, I found that the leaders in this movement, *without exception,* were desperate for information about what was being done and thought elsewhere in the country. The *AHP Newsletter, NTL Training News* and *STEP Newsletter* have failed to meet the need for prompt, honest, informal information. More formal journals already exist and more will undoubtedly appear, but they do not begin to meet the need because they report too little too late.

2. *Training.* While some training in "working with groups" is available, there must be a rapid growth of opportunity for training "growth facilitators," "learning coordinators," or whatever the final descriptive title of the people will be who will staff the growth centers. They fill a need comparable to the professors

in the universities and many of the most talented today ride the growth-center circuit.

3. *Demonstration Projects.* The worth of the growth-center concept of education in the contemporary world will most easily be made visible in demonstration projects. A place like Esalen or C.S.P. could set up a center for talented college drop-outs who are searching for relevant education. Esalen's residency program sometimes resembles such a project already.

4. *Philosophy and Legislation.* This movement needs a specified philosophical footing if it is to gain sufficiently wide acceptance to put its full energy in future development rather than fighting the critics snapping at its heels. Such foundation will also provide a framework for constructive internal disagreement. This philosophical footing should help establish legal sanction for the truth-searching that sometimes transcends today's morality. The philosophers and legal advocates have not yet surfaced in number.

5. *Ethics.* A formal or informal code of ethics and "professional" conduct must evolve in order to protect both the workers and their customers. It is likely that the eventual code will bear little resemblance to those in existence today because it will be necessary not only to genuinely protect "far out" experimentation but to encourage it. Most current codes of ethics force the elders of the tribe to judge the morality of behavior of the young revolutionaries whom they do not understand.

6. *Public Explanation.* There will be a lot less time and effort wasted in witch hunts and guerrilla warfare if people within the movement roll up their sleeves and try to describe and explain the human-potential movement to a public that is always curious. This need not be a matter of pleading for permission to "be." Popular magazines, newspapers, television, and radio can be used to tell what "is." With the exception of a few individuals like Terry Borton, most reporting efforts have come from writers who are outside the movement.

7. *Liaison With Schools.* Traditional schooling is probably dying, but it is far from dead. While the new educational growth centers are developing, schools and universities need individuals who will act as liaison "funnels" to bring the new concepts and techniques of education into the established institutions. These schools and universities will one day follow rather than lead the educational growth centers but they will be important in the transition and they will be needed *as* growth centers eventually.

8. *Research.* Social scientific studies of techniques and process will be helpful in understanding the "what and how" of the movement's concepts and techniques. There is little doubt that "concerned" university faculties and governmental agencies will stimulate an increasingly greater volume of studies using the social scientist's tools, though some support for unorthodox longitudinal studies may be needed.

Illustrative Proposals

Private funding agencies can best help this movement to shoulder its responsibilities and help our society through granting financial support in areas where government agencies and universities fear to tread. Two examples are used to illustrate, though many more could be listed.

1. *Foundation Fellows.* A corps of interested volunteers could be selected for one- or two-year fellowships to pursue their personal interests in the educational relevance of the human-potential movement. With salary, travel, and secretarial expenses furnished, this corps of jet-age "Rhodes Scholars" could provide some of the badly needed informal communication or cross-fertilization of concepts and techniques simply by conversing here and there in their travels. They could also provide written information for both the professionals and the curious public. They might act as catalysts in the formulation of ethical standards and philosophical foundations. And they could form a review board for small grant requests in the area of their expertise. The mere presence of such a group of experts would be reassuring to people in and out of the field.

2. *Letters.* An informal newsletter that gossips, prods workers into putting embryonic thoughts into print, and prints an exchange of personal letters among workers in the field would be very helpful. The growth of the STEP Newsletter mailing list (from 12 to 300+) in a year through word of mouth has brought home to me the need for this kind of communication. Private foundation funds might support the publication of such a non-journal until it became financially independent.

Life and Death

These recommendations do not represent life-or-death issues for the movement in my opinion. I believe that the movement will continue to grow unless catastrophic world-wide near-annihilation refocuses attention on primitive animal survival. The movement will grow as long as our society continues to evolve. It may be that the recommendations would speed the production of relevant education, and it may be that such education could save us from world-wide annihilation, but there are more variables involved here than my frail human computer can handle. I have a hunch that our survival does depend on the relevant education that the human-potential movement can produce. That hunch and the trust I see in my children's faces is enough to set the direction of my professional footsteps.

Myself

People are curious about how I have personally experienced this study. It seems appropriate to attempt a few words about "where I'm at," if for no other reason than to furnish the reader with additional data that may help him to evaluate the impressions and recommendations. There have been moments when I thought that I should have requested hazardous-duty pay (such as the time I sat in on Hussein Chung's "psychological karate" in Palo Alto or the time when, in the middle of a nude marathon, I found myself in a dawn motorcade on a superhighway after about two hours sleep and ten hours of uneasy encounter, on my way to unknown happenings in someone's swimming pool). These were the times when a surprised inner voice said, "What's a nice college professor like you doing in a place like this?" There have also been the treasured moments when I was able to transcend all previous experience and enter the vast unexplored area where much of human potential has been hidden (like the times in meditative massage when I experienced a head-spinning range of previously known emotions and then found an "emotion" of reassurance about the as yet unexpressed parts of me). Much of the joy and some of the sadness experienced was nonverbal and is as yet impossible to communicate in words.

Behaviorally, I don't suppose that I look much different. I have a tendency to speak out honestly more often now when fear of disapproval would have previously kept my mouth sealed and my heart pounding. I don't eat meat any more, not because I gave up something I liked but because I gave in to my long-standing distaste for the slaughter of animals. I am not reading as many books because I think I "should" read them but I am reading more books that I want to read. A friend recently told me that I seem "more calm yet somehow more in a hurry" and I suspect that is a reflection of a keen awareness that my human days are numbered and I want to find a lot of my truth before I die, yet I see that I cannot tell other people what they "should" do or not do even when their behavior looks silly or destructive to me. I find a typical "social evening" almost unbearable, because the empty words barely cover the unspoken thoughts and feelings in the room and bodies are held captive in chairs when I can see that one wants to push, another wants to embrace, and almost all want some genuine satisfaction for long-term skin hunger.

The experiences have not helped me "to adjust" or give in to my society but they have enabled me to give in to myself considerably more and to be the person I am in the "here and now." I guess that is a kind of "adjustment" to myself that contains a clause encouraging future change.

But the prize is not some therapeutic change. I have been privileged to preview a dream. My concern about what education *can* do and what it actually *does* do for people has been close to my professional and personal heart for many years. I have thought more than once lately of Martin Luther King, Jr.'s strange happiness when he said he had been to the mountain top and seen that his dream could come true. He was happy because that realization relieved a lot of sorrow and frustration. This study has permitted a peek from my mountain top. I think I see what is coming in education and if it does not get here in the next few decades, I'll wait because I see it is coming. My worry is that it may not get here while the earth is still in one piece. My regret is that it is not here now for my children.

Can I tolerate or even enjoy my previously made professional commitments? Most of them. Some must be winnowed away but I look forward to "teaching" in the university again even though I know that "the university," "courses," and "teaching" are part of a fading scene. I look forward to being with "students" and receptive colleagues who sense that they are in an era of institutional nonsense. It makes the frustrations less important because there is a new world to look to and a lot of exploring work to be done.

In case anyone is worried that I have found a new religion or "flipped out on acid" (like a famous one-time psychologist) let me say that this study did not involve the use of any drugs and that I can still function in the contemporary world. I appear at weddings and funerals in dark suit and tie and I maintain a very healthy skeptical eye when I view new techniques in the human-potential movement. I may be less judgmental now but I am no less evaluative. I do not think I have seen or heard of any panacea for mankind's woes and I think I see many uninspired clods using the movement's new lingo to seek fame and fortune. So be it. I am not converted but I am excited by the promise of a more permissive kind of educational experience on the horizon. It is not permissive in quite the same sense as "progressive education." This is a more pervasive permission. No one is going to "teach" me something. I will be offered a stimulating variety of experiences that put me in touch with my own and other people's thoughts and emotions, past and present. And while being educationally provoked, I will be *encouraged to reach out into the unknown of human potential*—encouraged to give myself permission to grow. It makes me feel good to have seen evidence that this kind of education is coming and to have reasonable hope that I will live to see it made available to everyone.

Bibliography

1. Alschuler, Alfred and Borton, Terry. A bibliography on affective education, psychological education, the eupsychian network, curriculum of concerns, personological education, synoetics, personal learning, etc. Harvard Graduate School of Education, 1968.

2. Alschuler, Alfred S. Psychological education. *Achievement Motivation Development Project Working Paper No. 1*, Harvard University, 1968.

3. Argyris, Chris. *Personality and Organization.* New York: Harper & Row, 1967.

4. A.S.C.D., 1962 Yearbook Committee. *Perceiving, Behaving, Becoming.* Washington, D.C.: Association for Supervision and Curriculum Development, National Education Association, 1962.

5. Bach, G. R. The marathon group: Intensive practice in intimate interaction. *Psychological Reports*, 1967, **18**, 995-1002.

6. Bassin, Alexander. Daytop Village. *Psychology Today,* December 1968, **2** (7), 48-68.

7. Batchelder, Richard L. and Hardy, James M. *Using Sensitivity Training and the Laboratory Method.* New York: Association Press, Y.M.C.A., 1968.

8. Bessell, Harold. The content is the medium: The confidence is the message. *Psychology Today,* January 1968, **1** (8), 32-61.

9. Bindrim, Paul. Nudity as a quick grab for intimacy in group therapy. *Psychology Today,* June 1969, **3** (1), 24-28.

10. Borton, Terry. Reach, touch, teach. *Saturday Review,* January 18, 1969, 56-70.

11. Borton, Terry. What turns kids on. *Saturday Review,* April 15, 1967, 50, 72-74.

12. Brown, George Isaac. *Now: The human dimension.* Esalen Monograph #1, Esalen Institute, Big Sur, California, 1968.

13. Bugental, James F. L. *Challenges of Humanistic Psychology.* New York: McGraw-Hill, 1967.

14. Chesin, G. A. and Selman, H. M. Group dynamics and in-service education. *Peabody Journal of Education,* May 1967, 350-352.

15. de Mille, Richard. *Put Your Mother on the Ceiling.* New York: Walker & Co., 1967.

16. Dunnette, Marvin D. People feeling: Joy, more joy, and the slough of despondency. *Journal of Applied Behavioral Science,* 1969, **5** (1), 25-44.

17. Esalen Institute. *Cosmopolitan,* 1969, 105-108.

18. Fantini, Mario and Weinstein, Gerald. Reducing the behavior gap. *National Education Association Journal,* January 1968.

19. Fantini, Mario D. and Weinstein, Gerald. Taking advantage of the disadvantaged. *The Record*, Teachers College Columbia University, November 1967, **69** (2), 2-12.

20. Fiebert, W. S. Sensitivity training: an analysis of trainer intervention and group process. *Psychological Reports,* 1968, **22**, 829-838.

21. Gibb, Jack R. Joy self attained (a review of *Joy*). *Contemporary Psychology*, 10, 14, No. 4. 199-201.

22. Gideonse, Hendrik D. Projecting alternative futures: Implications for educational goals. *Achievements and Challenges,* The New Forum Papers, Second Series 1968-1969, U.S. Department of Health, Education and Welfare.

23. Green, Maxine. *Existential Encounters for Teachers.* New York: Random House, 1967.

24. Grossman, L. and Clark, D. Sensitivity training for teachers: A small-group approach. *Psychology in the Schools,* 1967, IV, 267-271.

25. Gunther, Bernard. *Sense Relaxation Below Your Mind.* New York: Collier Books, 1968.

26. Gustaitis, Rasa. *Turning On.* Toronto: MacMillan Co., 1969.

27. Hall, Mary Harrington. A conversation with Carl Rogers. *Psychology Today*, December 1967, **1** (7), 19, 69.

28. Harrison, Roger. Problems in the design and interpretation of research. *Human Relations Training News.* Washington, D.C.: National Training Laboratories, 1201 Sixteenth Street, N. W., 1967.

29. Heinlein, Robert. *Stranger in a Strange Land.* New York: Avon Books, 1967.

30. High schools, Pacific paradise. *Time,* February 2, 1968, page 60.

31. Hill, William Fawcett. Review of *The Lemon Eaters. Psychology Today,* August 1967, **1** (4), 13.

32. Holt, John. *How Children Fail.* New York: Pitman, 1965.

33. Holt, John. *How Children Learn.* New York: Pitman, 1967.

34. Howard, Jane. Inhibitions thrown to the gentle winds. *Life,* July 12, 1968, 48-65.

35. Jones, Richard M. *Fantasy and Feeling in Education.* New York: New York University Press, 1968.

36. Jourard, Sidney M. Education for a new society. *The University Report* (U. of Fla.), November 20, 1968, **1**, No. 14, 1-2.

37. Klein, Herbert E. T-Groups: Talk, training, or therapy? *Science and Technology,* June, 1968, 36-48.

38. Kleiner, Donald A. A school for administrators. *National Association of Secondary School Principals Bulletin*, September 1965, 68-79.

39. Laemmel, Klaus. Psychodynamic sensitization for teachers. *Psychology in the Schools*, April 1969, 6 (2), 204-205.

40. Laing, R. D. *The Politics of Experience.* New York: Pantheon Books, 1967.

41. Leonard, George B. *Education and Ecstasy.* New York: Delacorte Press, 1968.

42. Leonard, George B. The future now. *Look,* October 15, 1968, 57-68.

43. Leonard, George B. The man and woman thing. *Look,* December 24, 1968, 55-72.

44. Liturgy: Let us touch. *Time,* August 2, 1968, 54-55.

45. Litwak, Leo E. Joy is the prize: A trip to Esalen Institute. *New York Times Sunday Magazine,* December 31, 1967, 8-31.

46. Malamud, Daniel I. and Machover, Solomon. *Toward Self-Understanding.* Springfield, Ill.: Charles C. Thomas, 1965.

47. Mann, John. *Changing Human Behavior.* New York: Charles Scribners' Sons, 1965.

48. Maslow, Abraham H. *Eupsychian Management.* Homewood, Ill.: Richard D. Irwin, Inc. and Dorsey Press, 1965.

49. Maslow, Abraham H. *Goals of Humanistic Education.* Esalen Institute, Big Sur, California, 1968.

50. McKean, William J. Encounter: How kids turn off drugs. *Look,* April 15, 1969, 40-42.

51. Mial, Dorothy J. and Jacobson, Stanley I. The fishbowl, design for discussion. *Today's Education,* September 1968, 28-30.

52. Miles, Mathew B. *Learning to Work in Groups.* New York: Teachers College Press, Columbia University, 1959.

53. Mill, Cyril R. A theory for the group dynamics laboratory milieu. *Adult Leadership,* November 1962, 133-160.

54. Murphy, Michael. Esalen: Where it's at. *Psychology Today,* December 1967, 1, No. 7, 34-39.

55. Naranjo, Claudio. The unfolding of man. *Research Memorandum* EPRC-6747-3, Stanford Research Institute, Menlo Park, Calif. 90025.

56. O'Hare, Mary Rita D. Sensitivity training in teacher education. *Teacher Education News & Notes,* May-June, 1968, 19 No. 3, 8-15.

57. Otto, Herbert A. *Explorations in Human Potentialities.* Springfield, Ill.: Charles C. Thomas, 1966.

58. Otto, Herbert A. *Group Methods Designed to Actualize Human Potential.* Achievement Motivation Systems, 1439 South Michigan Avenue, Chicago, Ill. 60605, 1968.

59. Otto, Herbert A. *Human Potentialities, The Challenge and the Promise.*

60. Otto, Herbert A. and Mann, John. *Ways of Growth: Approaches to Expanding Awareness*. New York: Grossman Publishers, 1968.

61. Paris, O. L. and Bowers, N. D. Sensitivity training in a teacher education program: An initial attempt. *Peabody Journal of Education,* September 1961, 68-74.

62. Perls, Frederick, Hefferline, Ralph F., and Goodman, Paul. *Gestalt Therapy*. New York: Dell, 1951.

63. Peterson, Severin and Peggy. Psychedelic exercises. *Ladies Home Journal*, February 1968, 112-114.

64. Rogers, Carl R. The increasing involvement of the psychologist in social problems: Some comments, positive and negative. *Journal of Applied Behavioral Science*, 1969, **5** (1), 3-7.

65. Rolf, Ida P. Structural integration. *Systematics*, June 1963, **1** (1), 3-20.

66. Rose, Brian. T-Group? *Times Educational Supplement,* July 23, 1965, 155.

67. Schmuck, Richard A. Helping teachers improve classroom group processes. *Journal of Applied Behavioral Science*, 1968, **4** (4), 401-435.

68. Schutz, William C. Joy. *Redbook*, July, 1968, 53-60.

69. Schutz, William C. *Joy: Expanding Human Awareness*. New York: Grove Press, 1967.

70. Seashore, Charles. What is sensitivity training? *NTL Institute News and Reports*, April, 1968, **2**, No. 2.

71. Shostrom, Everett L. Group therapy: Let the buyer beware. *Psychology Today,* May 1969, **2**, (12), 36-40.

72. Shostrom, Everett L. *Man: The Manipulator*. New York: Bantam Books, 1968.

73. Simon, D. and Sarkotich, D. Sensitivity training in the classroom. *National Education Association Journal*, 1967, **56** (1), 12-13.

74. Sohl, Jerry. *The Lemon Eaters*. New York: Simon & Schuster, 1967.

75. Stoller, Frederick H. The long weekend. *Psychology Today,* December 1967, **1**, No. 7, 18-33.

76. Sutich, Anthony J. and Vitch, Miles A. *Readings in Humanistic Psychology*. New York: Free Press, 1969.

77. Teachers: Sensitivity in Pontiac.*Time*, September 19, 1969, 44-46.

78. Tebbetts, Ilse Opton. T-groups bring out insights, hostilities, and search for love. *The Antiochian,* January 1969, **40**, No. 1, 4.

79. Thomas, Hobart F. Sensitivity training and the educator. *Bulletin of National Association of Secondary School Principals*, November 1967, **51**, 76-88.

80. Watson, Goodwin. *Change in School Systems*. Cooperative Project for

Educational Development. National Training Laboratories, 1201 Sixteenth Street, N.W., Washington, D.C. 1967.

81. Where executives tear off their masks. *Business Week*, September 3, 1968, 76-83.

82. Yourself as others see you. *Business Week*, March 16, 1963, 160-162.

83. *This Magazine is About Schools.* P.O. Box 876, Terminal A, Toronto 1, Ontario.

84. *Journal of Applied Behavioral Science*, National Training Laboratories, National Education Association, 1201 Sixteenth Street, Washington, D.C. 20036.

85. *Journal of Humanistic Psychology*, Association of Humanistic Psychology, 2637 Marshall Drive, Palo Alto, California.

86. *Psychology Today.* 1330 Camino del Mar, Del Mar, California 92014.

Editor's Comment. The human-potential movement is helping to reconstruct an educational system that has placed too much emphasis on cognition and not enough emphasis on feeling. Clark does not see the movement as anti-intellectual. Rather, his view is that one of the goals of these growth groups is to integrate affect, cognition, and action. I would also add that what has been purveyed as intellectualism by a vast number of schools is really nothing more than a caricature or parody of intellectualism. I shudder when I watch college students preparing for examinations. Students are thirsty for richer affective contacts with one another and with the world. Indeed, emotional education has a developmental priority that formal educational systems have overlooked to their detriment. It is possible that the human-potential movement will force formal education to become more pluralistic and therefore more balanced, more human.

Clark raises questions about the training of competent facilitators for groups. Both professionals and laymen are worried about the competence of trainers. Although much of this worry is justified, the fact is that, when a person's competence depends on knowledge and/or on attributes that are difficult to measure, there is simply no *easy* way to certify his qualifications. Many "certified" people are practicing education without competence, and a far greater number of people are practicing parenthood without any competency at all (see Toffler, 1970, pp. 211-230). We have already mentioned the studies indicating that many counselors and therapists act more like patients than professionals in their encounters with clients. *Caveat emptor!* Just as students must shop around for good teachers and clients for good counselors, so prospective encounter-group members must look around for high-level group experiences. Clark suggests a further solution: let there be a clear contract between the "educator" (facilitator) and client. Perhaps this should be a general principle. Teachers should spend some time at the beginning of courses discussing the goals of the course, the means to be used to achieve these goals, and the responsibilities of both teacher and student (most of us teachers say little about *our* responsibilities in class). The therapist should let the client know precisely what he thinks therapy is about, and he should be open about the concrete behavioral demands it places on himself and the client. In *E:GPFIG* I spell out the rationale for a contract approach to encounter-group experiences and offer a sample contract that deals with the behavior of both the regular group member and the facilitator (see pp. 25-67).

After a three-course sequence dealing with encounter-group experience, methodology, and leadership, a number of my students look for some kind of certification. I have always felt uneasy about such requests and have parried them by suggesting that the degree program itself provides the credentials required by society. But I am more struck by Clark's approach; in too many cases our graduate programs merely certify incompetence.

Why We Need a New Sexuality

George B. Leonard

Editor's Introduction. One problem in assessing the quality of emotional living in our society is the lack of controlled empirical data. Emotional realities are not easily manipulated in the laboratory. Thus, while there is evidence indicating that many persons in our society have failed to develop a full emotional life and have failed to integrate their emotions with the demands of life in a technocratic society, the evidence is clinical, anecdotal, and value-oriented. Still, such evidence should not be ignored. Leonard proposes not only a new sexuality but also a new sensuality, a new emotionality. Man's flight from intimacy does not eliminate his need for intimacy. Leonard suggests that if man does not find ways of fostering intimate emotional contact with a variety of people, he will react destructively, the objects of his destruction being himself and/or his society. Leonard's article is not a blueprint of exactly what to do, but its searching spirit corresponds to the spirit of the encounter group. It offers a challenge to those among us who are irrationally inhibited or overly addicted to ego functions in society.

Every few months, another survey taker comes along to prove there's really no sexual revolution among our young people, because the frequency of sexual intercourse hasn't greatly increased. These researchers are missing the point completely. Back in 1967, Marshall McLuhan and I wrote in *Look* that the frequency of intercourse may actually decrease in the future *"because of* a real revolution in attitudes toward, feelings about and uses of sex."

The survey takers' misconception makes a good starting point for any discussion of sexuality, since it shows exactly what's wrong with this whole area in our time and our culture. Most people, especially those of the older generation, still think of "sex" or "sexiness" in terms of nudity, genitals, breasts, number ("how many times?"), pinups and dirty jokes. They see "male" and "female" as entirely separate and opposite. They find the whole matter fraught with excitement and peril, circumscribed by taboos and guilt.

The taboos unquestionably were useful prior to modern contraception and hygiene. The highly specialized, limiting roles of male and female were probably appropriate to those earlier times when human individuals had to serve as specialized components of hard-striving, underpopulated societies. Today, these same attitudes threaten the social order, heighten the chance of violence and war, increase population pressures and needlessly restrict human pleasure and fulfillment.

Sex actually touches far more of our lives than we generally think. Because of this, sex in the narrow sense can and should become less "important" and certainly less fraught. The erotic impulses flow throughout complex circuits involving both brain and glands. These impulses, though concentrated in the familiar sexual zones, can be felt all over the body, and can affect every aspect of sensing and thinking. The same neural-hormonal forces that cause an erection can make the sky look bluer, a song ring clearer. Sex involves not just coitus but birth, child-rearing, family patterns, uses of affection and personal role in the world. Those censorious people who think they are protecting us from sex are just wringing the joys out of living by pressing sexuality into a dark corner—thus making it far more dangerous.

We might start making sex safe and joyful simply by renouncing all censorship. This means just what it says: Sexual intercourse and birth could be shown on network television and in family magazines. Nothing would be hidden. No need for "X" or "R" ratings for films. As it is, the censors have the age limits backwards. We must surely feel compassion sometimes for older people subjected to revelations that in their youth would have seemed to shake the foundations of the soul. Little children, until directed by word or example to think dirty, find nothing more unusual about the way a man and a woman mate than about how a tree grows or an airplane flies. The ending of all sex censorship might set off a period of adjustment, marked by a temporary increase in the sniggering portrayal of sex that currently corrupts art and life. But a totally free marketplace would give good practice a chance to drive out bad. In a very few years, preoccupation with hyped-up, "hot" sex would very likely begin to fade. Such has been the case in Denmark, where pornography for grown-ups has been legalized.

The awful silence surrounding sex in most American families builds tensions and perpetuates dangerous misconceptions. Many American parents are still so ignorant or hung-up about the subject that they want school lecturers to teach their children the facts of life. But school as it is probably won't help very much. If the traditional classroom can make things as exciting as poetry and mathematics dreaded by most students, what might it not do to sex?

We need a new sexuality; we also need a new sensuality. A society that considers most good feelings immoral and bad feelings moral perpetuates the ultimate human heresy: an insult, if you will, to God and His works. A man cut off from bodily pleasures uses sex compulsively, a spasm of release from his prison. He uses work compulsively, a narcotic to dull the pain of deprivation. Compulsive work and compulsive reproduction are exactly what we don't need in the Seventies. We need a world where people can trust their good feelings, where members of the same sex can touch and caress without fear of homosexuality, where members of the opposite sex can touch and caress without fear of seductiveness. Sensory-awareness-pioneer Bernard Gunther proposes that if every person in the world gave and received a loving, half-hour message every day, there would be no war.

Until very recently, sex in our culture has tended to become more and more specialized—by partner (spouse), part of body (genitals), "position" (male dominant), time (night) and place (bedroom). Every specialization is limiting, but the most limiting and dangerous of all is the one that artificially splits man from woman, trapping each in a rigid "role." "Be a man," often means, "turn off your feelings, wreak your will upon others and act always out of impersonal rationality." "Be a woman," on the other hand, means, "Stay soft and emotional, be submissive, not smart; and act always out of intuition." Unfortunately, this sharp specialization doesn't even allow men to become good rationalists or women good emotionalists; each side, lacking the other, is crippled.

Our tragic adventure in Vietnam may be traced to outmoded ideals of "manliness" as well as to considerations of international strategy. (The strategic reasoning never made sense; the military assurances were obviously wrong.) By the very phrases they use ("pride," "cut and run"), the old men who are willing for young men to keep dying on the other side of the world reveal clearly that they see the war as a test of their manliness. Their "manly" upbringing deprived them of emotions, so they are unable to feel the suffering they cause. And they're just "rational" enough to discover ideologies worth more than other people's "mere biological survival."

The world has become too small and explosive for the narrow-gauge male. We need men who can feel deeply. We need women who can show their intelligence. We need full human beings, proud of their biological differences but unwilling to become puppets marked "male" and "female."

Ethnologists have been reminding us lately of our animal natures. (It takes a pretty disembodied culture to need reminding.) Perhaps it's true that our distant past as hunters required fast breeding, with lasting pair-bonding to assure care for our slow-maturing young. Now, these tendencies work against us, creating overpopulation and a tight little vacuum-packed family. Men and women live a long time these days, and they often keep having children just to give themselves an emotional outlet. (Many people in our culture seem able to express strong emotions—whether caresses or curses—only to their children or their dogs.) Now that the survival of the race depends upon most couples having not more than two children, it becomes particularly important that we broaden the bonds of affection to include more than just spouse, children and pets.

We need bigger, less well-defined "families." We need groups of friends and neighbors who are willing and able to share the strongest feelings, to share responsibility for the emotional needs of all the children in the group. Thus no one will be childless, no one will lack affection, and no one will be deprived of a rich and varied emotional and sensual life. The empirical evidence so far indicates that swapping bed partners does not work. But sexual exclusivity shouldn't mean (as it now does) emotional and sensual exclusivity. The new sexuality leads eventually to the creation of a family as wide as all mankind, that can weep together, laugh together and share the common ecstasy.

Editor's Comment. Much of the work done in encounter groups is remedial. Theoretically, the school should play an important role in the emotional development of students; but most schools, if we are to believe the criticisms of educators themselves, fail in this respect. Some schools are introducing courses in psychology and attempting in various ways to oversee emotional development, but most of the programs encourage the subordination of emotion to cognition rather than the development of a rich emotional life. Instead of standing as critics of "the system," schools train people to fit into it. A recent article in a national daily newspaper indicated that some companies were dropping sensitivity-training programs. It was not that such programs were not having any impact; rather, the impact ran counter to the needs of the organization. For instance, some managers, after tasting life a bit differently in the sensitivity group, found life back on the job less than satisfying. So they quit. Obviously, while this might have been good for the individual managers, it was bad for the organization. This points to the need for "organizational development" work aimed at integrating individual and organizational growth into a compatible system.

Schools rely too heavily on what may be called "parallel" learning (A learns sitting next to B) instead of interactional learning (A and B learn by interacting with each other). Schools have to learn to deal with emotional realities actively and positively, even though these realities lack the modular neatness of cognitive input. Organizations, even while they become more and more efficient, must become more and more human. Encounter groups and similar processes can help enrich both schools and organizations only if school administrators and corporate managers see the need for developing and utilizing the emotional resources of students and employees. However, until that need is recognized, much of what occurs in the encounter group will remain remedial.

The Therapeutic Conditions Antecedent to Change: A Theoretical View

Carl R. Rogers
Charles B. Truax

Editor's Introduction. By now it should be evident how important a climate of support is for the functioning of the encounter group. The kinds of behavior expected of such groups—for example, self-disclosure, expression of feeling, self-exploration as a response to confrontation—are impossible without a climate of support. People are rightfully concerned about the question of psychological safety in encounter groups, for they are potentially powerful experiences and power should always be respected. Support is central to establishing a culture of psychological safety; yet, too many participants seem inept at giving meaningful support, even though they might want to.

I would suggest that the three elements discussed by Rogers and Truax—congruence or genuineness, unconditional positive regard or nonpossessive warmth, and accurate empathic understanding—form the basis for a climate of support, not just in psychotherapy, but in encounter groups and in human living in general. Rogers (1957) had discussed these elements before as the necessary and sufficient conditions of therapeutic personality change. The present formulation stems from added experience, research, and refinements gained from interchanges with colleagues. If the encounter group is to go well, there must be a minimal "pool" of these resources. Obviously, the facilitator should possess these qualities to a high degree. But growth in genuineness, acceptance, and understanding should also be one of the goals of the members of the group.

In Part I an overall view of the concepts, the design, and the findings of the investigation has been given in condensed and general form. In Parts II, III, and IV, we will present, in a much more thorough and detailed way, the theories

Carl R. Rogers and C. B. Truax, "The Therapeutic Conditions Antecedent to Change: A Theoretical View," in Carl R. Rogers, ed., *The Therapeutic Relationship and Its Impact* (Madison: The University of Wisconsin Press; © 1967 by the Regents of the University of Wisconsin), pp. 97-108.

The conceptualizations on which this chapter is based were hammered out in staff interactions at the University of Chicago and the University of Wisconsin, and it would be impossible to name all of the individuals who helped in sharpening these interactions. The chapter was written, drawing on this experience, by Carl R. Rogers and Charles B. Truax.

which constitute the underpinning of the research, and the data analyses of findings expressed in much more complete and complex form.

The first theoretical problem has to do with our views as to the elements which underlie change. What do we as therapists do that actually leads to constructive change in our clients or patients? This is a question of paramount importance to all who are engaged in helping relationships, for certainly only a small percentage of the events occurring in the therapeutic relationship make any real contribution to the work of psychotherapy. What, then, are the essential ingredients in effective psychotherapy among all the attempts we make to help the patient resolve his conflicts and anxieties? Which of these efforts actually contribute to the individual's positive personality growth?

Many therapists have felt that the answers to such questions are so subtle as to be impossible of investigation. How can one be scientific about relationships which are completely subjective? When a previously suicidal woman says, "I was kept from destruction by the look in one man's eyes," how can one investigate such a situation with the blunt tools of current research? It seems clear that the therapeutic relationship differs from one therapist to another. With a given therapist it differs from one client to another. Thus a therapist finds himself using sophisticated, polite, and even academic language with one client, and vulgar and coarse terminology with another. He is blunt with one individual, gentle with another. Even with the same client his relationship differs over time, from the first interviews with their tentative testing and uncertainty on both sides of the desk to the later relationship, deeper and more knowing on both sides.

In the light of this it is a very real question as to how this can possibly be a field for research. How can one isolate those therapist behaviors which have any relevance for personal growth, especially since it is almost certainly not his *behaviors* which are relevant to the process of therapy? In spite of all these considerations we have elected to study certain elements in the therapeutic relationship, recognizing that the findings of research can never be as complex or subtle as the total experience, and yet recognizing too that investigation may point to certain generalities or commonalities which are important in furthering both our knowledge and our practice.

The Search for Common Elements

There appears to be general agreement as to at least some of the elements which are important in a helping relationship. Psychoanalytic writers (Ferenczi, 1930; Alexander, 1948; Schafer, 1959; Halpern and Lesser, 1960), eclectic therapists (Strunk, 1957; Raush and Bordin, 1959; Strupp, 1960; Hobbs, 1962; Fox and Goldin, 1963), and client-centered therapists (Dymond, 1949; Rogers, 1951, 1957; Jourard, 1959; Truax, 1961) have all emphasized the importance of the therapist's ability to understand sensitively and accurately the inner experiences of the client or patient. They have also stressed such qualities as the maturity of the therapist and his integration or genuineness within the relationship. Finally, they have stressed his warmth and his acceptance of the individual with whom he is working. Thus these three characteristics of the therapist as he enters the process of psychotherapy have been stressed in a wide variety of therapeutic approaches, even though they have been differently defined by different writers. Cutting across parochial viewpoints, they can be considered as elements common to a wide variety of therapies.

Some years ago, Rogers (1957) attempted an organized theoretical statement in which it was hypothesized that three characteristics of the therapist in the relationship, when adequately communicated to the client, constituted the necessary and sufficient conditions for constructive personality change. These three conditions were that the therapist be a genuine or self-congruent person within the therapeutic hour; that he experience an unconditional positive regard for his client; and that he experience and communicate a sensitively empathic understanding of the client's phenomenological world.

Though it would be difficult if not impossible to establish either the necessity or the sufficiency of these three therapist's "conditions" (Ellis [1959] has pointed out that any specific condition is unlikely to be either necessary or sufficient), this theoretical statement has had considerable heuristic value. It has been the springboard for a number of significant studies. By setting forth a rigorous and reasonably well-defined set of hypotheses, it has made possible a testing of the effectiveness of these three conditions.

Some Initial Assumptions

It was made clear in the reference mentioned above that there are certain initial assumptions which must be fulfilled if the hypotheses are to hold. The first assumption is that the therapist and his client have a psychological contact. This means simply that they have the minimum essentials of a relationship, namely, that each makes a perceived or subceived difference in the experiential field of the other. This difference may be quite minimal and in fact not immediately apparent to an observer. Thus it might be difficult to know whether a catatonic patient perceives the therapist's presence as making a difference to him. But it is almost certain that at some physiological level he does sense or subceive this difference.

The second assumption is that the client has some degree of incongruence between his awareness and his experiencing. What this means is that the percepts, concepts, and constructs regarding self, environment, and others which are present in the person's awareness are not entirely matched by the experiencing going on in him at the physiological level. This is indeed a minimal assumption, since such incongruence is to some degree characteristic of all of us as imperfect human beings. It does not necessarily mean that the individual is severely disturbed. Put in the more technical terms of Rogers' theory (1959), it indicates that he is "vulnerable" to anxiety, meaning that there is an incongruence but that the individual is defensively unaware of it. Or it may mean that he is "anxious," a state in which the incongruence between awareness and experiencing is approaching symbolization. When such a discrepancy enters awareness, a change in the construct system is forced.

When thus defined in technical terms, this assumption may sound elaborate or unusual. Actually it necessarily exists in every person who comes voluntarily for psychotherapy, since some dim awareness of such a discrepancy is the very problem which brings him to us. Even with most individuals who do not come for psychotherapy, such a condition is met. Our clinical experiences with "well-adjusted" industrial executives indicate that even their minimal degree of anxiety, tension, or incongruence between self and experience is quite enough to meet this assumption.

A final assumption which is basic to the theory is that the patient will perceive at least to a minimal degree the therapist-offered conditions of genuineness, warmth, and empathy. In ordinary relationships with normal or mildly disturbed individuals it can be taken for granted that such a perception exists if the conditions are indeed offered. Most individuals have a sufficiently realistic perception of their environment to have a minimal awareness of these conditions when they are present. In dealing with deeply disturbed and psychotic individuals this assumption cannot be taken for granted, and a phenomenologically based measure of the patient's perception is necessary to establish whether there is some degree of realistic appreciation of these therapeutic conditions.

The description of the therapeutic conditions which follows and the predictions related to them will take for granted that the assumptions described above are, in any particular relationship, already met.

Therapist Congruence

The order in which the three therapeutic conditions are described has some significance because they are logically intertwined. Perhaps this can be made clear. It is important that the therapist achieve a high level of accurate empathy. However, to be deeply sensitive to the moment-to-moment "being" of another person requires of us as therapists that we first accept and to some degree prize this other person. Consequently a satisfactory level of empathy can scarcely exist without there being also a considerable degree of unconditional positive regard. But neither of these conditions can possibly be meaningful in the relationship unless they are real. Consequently unless the therapist is, both in these respects and in others, integrated and genuine within the therapeutic encounter, the other conditions could scarcely exist to a satisfactory degree. Therefore it would seem that this element of genuineness, or congruence, is the most basic of the three conditions. The following paragraphs attempt to describe the meaning of this concept.

We readily sense this quality of congruence in everyday life. Each of us could name persons who always seem to be operating from behind a front, who are playing a role, who tend to say things that they do not feel. They are exhibiting incongruence. We tend not to reveal ourselves too deeply to such people. On the other hand, each of us knows individuals whom we somehow trust because we sense that they are being what they *are* in an open and transparent way and that we are dealing with the person himself, not with a polite or professional facade. This is the quality of congruence.

In relation to therapy it means that the therapist is what he *is*, during his encounter with his client. He is without front or facade, openly being the feelings and attitudes which at the moment are flowing in him. It involves the element of self-awareness, meaning that the feelings the therapist is experiencing are available to him, available to his awareness, and also that he is able to live these feelings, to be them in the relationship, and able to communicate them if appropriate. It means that he comes into a direct personal encounter with his client, meeting him on a person-to-person basis. It means that he is *being* himself, not denying himself.

Since this concept is liable to misunderstanding, it may be well to state some of the things that it does not imply. It does not mean that the therapist burdens his client with the overt expression of all of his feelings. It does not mean that he blurts out impulsively anything which comes to mind. It does not mean that the therapist discloses his total self to his client. It does mean, however, that he does not *deny* to himself the feelings that he is experiencing, and that he is willing *transparently to be* any persistent feelings which exist in the relationship and to let these be known to his client if appropriate. It means avoiding the temptation to present a facade or hide behind a mask of professionalism or to adopt a confessional-professional relationship.

It is not a simple thing to achieve such reality. Being real involves the difficult task of being acquainted with the flow of experiencing going on within oneself, a flow marked especially by complexity and continuous change. So if I sense that I am feeling bored by my contacts with this client and this feeling persists, I think I owe it to him and to our relationship to share this feeling with him. The same would hold if my feeling is one of being afraid of this client, or if my attention is so focused on my own problems that I can scarcely listen to him. But as I attempt to share these feelings I also want to be constantly in touch with what is going on in me. If I am, I will recognize that it is *my* feeling of being bored which I am expressing, and not some supposed fact about him as a boring person. If I voice it as my *own* reaction, it has the potentiality of leading to a deep relationship. But this feeling exists in the context of a complex and changing flow, and this needs to be communicated too. I would like to share with him my distress at feeling bored and the discomfort I feel in expressing this aspect of me. As I share these attitudes I find that my feeling of boredom arises from my sense of remoteness from him and that I would like to be more in touch with him, and even as I try to communicate myself to him in this way, and I am far from bored as I wait with eagerness and perhaps a bit of apprehension for his response. I also feel a new sensitivity to him now that I have shared this feeling which has been a barrier between us. I am very much more able to hear the surprise or perhaps the hurt in his voice as he now finds *himself* speaking more genuinely because I have dared to be real with him. I have let myself be a person—real, imperfect—in my relationship with him.

It should be clear from this lengthy description that congruence is helpful even when negative feelings toward the client are involved. Of course it would be most helpful if such feelings did not exist in the therapist, but if they do it is harmful to the patient to hide them. Any therapist has negative attitudes from time to time, but it is preferable for him to express them, thus to be real, than to put up a false posture of interest, concern, and liking which the client is likely to perceive, or subceive, as ungenuine.

It is not an easy thing for the client, or for any human being, to trust his most deeply shrouded feelings to another person. It is even more difficult for a disturbed person to share his deepest and most troubling feelings with a therapist. The genuineness, or congruence, of the therapist is one of the elements in the relationship which makes this risk of sharing easier and less fraught with dangers.

In view of the subtlety of this concept, it is not surprising that behavioral cues which permit us to measure the degree of congruence are also subtle. At a very low level of congruence the therapist may be clearly defensive in the interaction, as evidenced by the contradiction between the content of his message and his voice qualities or the nonverbal cues which he presents. Or the therapist may respond appropriately but in so professional a manner that he gives the impression that his responses are formulated to sound good rather than being what he really feels and means. Thus incongruence may involve a contrived or rehearsed quality or a professional front.

At the upper ranges of therapist genuineness, his openness to all types of feelings and experiences, both pleasant and hurtful, without trace of defensiveness or retreat into professionalism, is usually most evident from the quality of his voice and the manner of his expression. It is no doubt fortunate in trying to rate such a subtle quality that all of us have had a lifetime of experience in judging genuineness or facade in others. Hence we are able to detect extremely subtle cues in this respect.

Unconditional Positive Regard

A second condition which is hypothesized as essential for therapeutic movement and change is the experiencing by the therapist of an unconditional positive regard for the client. This means that the therapist communicates to his client a deep and genuine caring for him as a person with human potentialities, a caring uncontaminated by evaluations of his thoughts, feelings, or behaviors. The therapist experiences a warm acceptance of the client's experience as being a part of the client as a person, and places no conditions on his acceptance and warmth. He prizes the client in a total rather than a conditional way. He does not accept certain feelings in the client and disapprove others. He feels an *unconditional* positive regard or warmth for this person. This is an outgoing, positive feeling without reservations and without evaluations. It means *not* making judgments. It involves as much feeling of acceptance for the client's expression of painful, hostile, defensive, or abnormal feelings as for his expression of good, positive, mature feelings. For us as therapists it may even be that it is easier to accept painful and negative feelings than the positive and self-confident feelings which sometimes come through. These latter we almost automatically regard as defensive. But unconditional positive regard involves a willingness to share equally the patient's confidence and joy, or his depression and failure. It is non-possessive caring for the client as a separate person. The client is thus freely allowed to have his *own* feelings and his *own* experiencing. One client describes the therapist as "fostering my possession of my own experience and that I am actually having it; thinking what I think, feeling what I feel, wanting what I want, fearing what I fear; no 'ifs,' 'buts,' or 'not reallys.' " This is the type of acceptance which is expected to lead to a relationship which facilitates the engagement of the patient in the process of therapy and leads to constructive personality change.

The question is often raised: But what about the therapist's attitude toward his client's asocial or antisocial behavior? Is he to accept this without evaluation? Sometimes this question is answered by saying that the effective therapist prizes the person, but not necessarily his behavior. Yet it is doubtful if this is an adequate or true answer. To be sure, the therapist may feel that a particular behavior is socially unacceptable or socially bad, something he could not approve of in himself, and a way of behaving which is inimical to the welfare of the social group. But the effective therapist may feel acceptant of this behavior in his client, not as desirable behavior, but as a *natural consequence* of the circumstances, experiences, and feelings of this client. Thus the therapist's acceptance may be based upon this kind of feeling: "If I had had the same background, the same circumstances, the same experiences, it would be inevitable in me, as it is in this client, that I would act in this fashion." In this respect he is like the good parent whose child, in a moment of fear and panic, has defecated in his clothing. The reaction of the loving parent includes both a caring for the child, and acceptance of the behavior as an entirely natural event under the circumstances. This does not mean that the parent approves such behavior in general.

Thus when the therapist prizes his client, and is searching for the meaning or value of his client's thoughts or behaviors within the client, he does not tend to feel a response of approval or disapproval. He feels an acceptance of what *is*.

Unconditional positive regard, when communicated by the therapist, functions to provide the non-threatening context in which it is possible for the client to explore and experience the most deeply shrouded elements of his inner self. The therapist is not paternalistic, or sentimental, or superficially social and agreeable. But his deep caring is a necessary ingredient in providing a "safe" context in which the client can come to explore himself and share deeply with another human being.

Accurate Empathic Understanding

The ability of the therapist accurately and sensitively to understand experiences and feelings *and their meaning to the client* during the moment-to-moment encounter of psychotherapy constitutes what can perhaps be described as the "work" of the therapist after he has first provided the contextual base for the relationship by his self-congruence or genuineness and his unconditional positive regard.

Accurate empathic understanding means that the therapist is completely at home in the universe of the patient. It is a moment-to-moment sensitivity that is in the "here and now," the immediate present. It is a sensing of the client's inner world of private personal meanings "as if" it were the therapist's own, but without ever losing the "as if" quality. Accurate sensitivity to the client's "being" is of primary value in the moment-to-moment encounter of therapy; it is of limited use to the individual if the therapist only arrives at this insightful and empathic understanding of the patient's experience as he drives home at night. Such a delayed empathy or insight may be of value if the therapist has a later chance to respond to the same theme, but its value would lie in formulating his empathic response to the patient's *immediate* living of the relationship.

The ability and sensitivity required to communicate these inner meanings back to the client in a way that allows these experiences to be "his" is the other major part of accurate empathic understanding. To sense the patient's confusion, his fear, his anger or his rage as if it were a feeling you might have (but which you are not currently having) is the essence of the perceptive aspect of accurate empathy. To communicate this perception in a language attuned to the patient that allows him more clearly to sense and formulate his confusion, his fear, his rage or anger is the essence of the communicative aspect of accurate empathy.

At a high level of accurate empathy the message "I am with you" is unmistakably clear so that the therapist's remarks fit with the client's mood and content. The therapist at a high level will indicate not only a sensitive understanding of the apparent feelings but will *by his communication* clarify and expand the patient's awareness of these feelings or experiences. The communication is not only by the use of words that the patient might well have used, but also by the sensitive play of voice qualities which reflect the seriousness, the intentness, and the depth of feeling.

An accurate empathic grasp of the patient's conflicts and problems is perhaps most sharply contrasted with the more usual diagnostic formulation of the patient's experiences. This diagnostic understanding which is so different but so common involves the "I understand what is wrong with you" or "I understand the dynamics which make you act that way" approach. These evaluative understandings are external and sometimes even impersonal. While they may at times be very useful in developing external understanding, they are in sharp contrast to an accurate and sensitive grasp of events or experiences and their *personal meaning to the client.* The external and evaluative understanding tends to focus the client's being on externals or upon intellectualizations which remove him from an ongoing contact with the deeper elements of his self. The empathic understanding when it is accurately and sensitively communicated seems crucially important in making it possible for a person to get close to himself, to experience his most inward feelings, to maintain contact with his inner self-experiences, thus allowing for the recognition and resolution of incongruences. It is this self-exploration and consequent recognition and resolution of incongruities that we believe allows the client to change and to develop his potentialities.

Though the accuracy of understanding is central, the communication of intent to understand can in itself be of value. Even the confused, inarticulate, or bizarre individual, if he perceives that the therapist is *trying* to understand his meanings, will be helped because he will be encouraged to communicate more of his self. The very effort to understand communicates to the patient the value placed on him as an individual, thus conveying an element of unconditional positive regard. It gets across the fact that the therapist perceives his feelings and meanings as being *worth* understanding. It is in this sense that the intent to be empathic is of value. If the intent should continue without actualization, however, there is the possibility that it could become harmful. That is, if as a therapist I am consistently unable to understand the inarticulate or bizarre individual, he may become even more hopeless about the possibility of ever communicating himself.

There are many ways in which the therapist can communicate a low level of accurate empathic understanding. The therapist may be off on a tangent of his own, or may have misinterpreted what the patient is feeling, or may be so preoccupied and interested in his own intellectual interpretations of the client's behavior that he is scarcely aware of the client's "being." He may have his focus of attention on the intellectual content of what the client says rather than what the client "is" during the moment, and so ignores, misunderstands, or does not attempt to sense the client's current feelings and experiences.

The common element in a low level of empathy involves the therapist's doing something other than "listening" or "understanding"; he may be evaluating the client, giving advice, offering intellectual interpretations, or reflecting upon his own feelings or experiences. Indeed, a therapist may be accurately describing psychodynamics to the patient, but in a language not that of the client, or at a time when these dynamics are far removed from the current feelings of the client, so that there is a flavor of teacher-pupil interaction.

At a relatively low level of empathic sensitivity the therapist responds with clarity only to the patient's most obvious feelings. At an intermediate level, the therapist usually responds accurately to the client's more obvious feelings and occasionally recognizes some that are less apparent, but in the process of tentative probing, he may anticipate feelings which are not current or may misinterpret the present feelings. At a higher level the therapist is aware of many feelings and experiences which are not so evident but his lack of complete understanding is shown by the slightly inaccurate nature of his deeper responses. At this level he is simply "pointing" to some of the more hidden feelings. He is aware of their existence and so points to them but he is not yet able to grasp their meaning. At a very high level of empathic understanding the therapist's responses move, with sensitivity and accuracy, into feelings and experiences that are only hinted at by the client. At this level, underlying feelings or experiences are not only pointed to but they are specifically identified so that the content that comes to light may be new but it is not alien. At this high level the therapist is sensitive to his own tentative errors and quickly alters or changes his responses in midstream, indicating a clear but fluid responsiveness to what is being sought after in the patient's own explorations. The therapist's words reflect a togetherness with the patient and a tentative trial-and-error exploration while his voice tone reflects the seriousness and depth of his empathic grasp.

It is this sensitive and accurate grasp and communication of the patient's inner world that facilitates the patient's self-exploration and consequent personality growth.

The Theoretical Predictions

The three constructs defined in the preceding pages—empathic understanding, unconditional positive regard, and therapist congruence or genuineness—are central to the research. It is part of the theoretical background of the study that if these three conditions exist, then a process of therapy will occur in which the client deeply explores himself and comes to know and experience the full range of his being. As a consequence of the patient's engagement in this process of psychotherapy, personality growth and constructive personality change are theoretically predicted to occur.

Since these conditions—as offered by the therapist—vary in degree, and since the variables of process movement and therapeutic outcome also exist in varying degrees, the theoretical predictions are cast in the following form:

1. The greater the degree to which the therapist is congruent in the relationship, the greater will be the evidences of process movement in the client, and the greater will be the degree of constructive personality change in the client over therapy.

2. The greater the degree to which the therapist evidences unconditional positive regard for the client in the therapeutic relationship, the greater will be the evidences of the client's engagement in the process of therapy and his consequent personality change.

3. Finally, the greater the degree of accurately empathic understanding exhibited by the therapist toward the client, the greater will be the evidences of the client's engagement in the process of therapy and his consequent personality change.

These theoretic predictions are made with the understanding that three assumptions may be made about the therapeutic relationships in which these elements are studied. These are that the client and therapist are in psychological contact—that each makes a perceived or subceived difference in the experiential field of the other; that the patient is, at least to a minimal degree, incongruent and hence anxious or vulnerable to anxiety; and that the therapist's behavior communicates these attitudinal conditions so that they are to some degree perceived or subceived by the client.

Although the conditions are listed in the order of their theoretical importance, no specific predictions are made as to whether the conditions might be separately effective, or whether they are effective only when they exist together. The theory favors the view that each must be minimally present for effective therapy.

References

Alexander, F. *Fundamentals of Psychoanalysis.* New York: W. W. Norton, 1948.

Dymond, Rosalind. A scale for the measurement of empathic ability. *J. consult. Psychol. 13:*127-233, 1949.

Ellis, A. Requisite conditions for basic personality change. *J. consult Psychol. 23:*538-540, 1959.

Ferenczi, S. The principle of relaxation and neocatharsis. *Int. J. Psycho-Anal. 11:*428-443, 1930.

Fox, R. E., and Goldin, P. C. The empathic process in psychotherapy: A survey of theory and research. Unpublished manuscript, 1963.

Halpern, H., and Lesser, Leona. Empathy in infants, adults, and psychothera-pists. *Psychoanal. Rev. 47:*32-42, 1960.

Hobbs, N. Sources of gain in psychotherapy. *Amer. Psychologist 17:*741-747, 1962.

Jourard, S. I-thou relationship versus manipulation in counseling and psycho-therapy. *J. indiv. Psychol. 15:*174-179, 1959.

Raush, H. L., and Bordin, E. S. Warmth in personality development and in psychotherapy. *J. study Interpers. Processes 20:* No. 4, 1957.

Rogers, C. R. *Client-Centered Therapy.* Boston: Houghton Mifflin, 1951.

Rogers, C. R. The necessary and sufficient conditions of therapeutic personality change. *J. consult. Psychol. 21:*95-103, 1957.

Rogers, C. R. A theory of therapy, personality, and interpersonal relationships as developed in the client-centered framework. In S. Koch (ed.), *Psychology: A Study of a Science.* Vol. III, *Formulations of the Person in the Social Context.* New York: McGraw Hill, 1959, pp. 184-256.

Schafer, R. Generative empathy in the treatment situation. *Psychoanal. Quart. 28:*342-373, 1959.

Strunk, O., Jr. Empathy: A review of theory and research. *Psychological Newsletter 9:*47-57, 1957.

Strupp, H. H. Nature of psychotherapist's contribution to the treatment process. *Arch. gen. Psychiat. 3:*219-231, 1960.

Truax, C. B. Therapeutic conditions. *Discussion papers,* University of Wisconsin Psychiatric Institute, 1961, No. 13.

Editor's Comment. Members of encounter groups are generally willing to give one another support, but often they do not seem to know how. They either say nothing in response to another's openness or mutter cliches such as "I know how you feel." In order to give support effectively, one must both be open to the emotions of the other and be capable of communicating one's own. In many cases of failed support, this is precisely the rub: the participant who is not at home with his own emotions, much less those of others, cannot bring himself to be very supportive.

The three elements described in the article constitute perhaps the core of what I would call *social intelligence,* the ability to involve oneself growthfully and nonmanipulatively with others. The socially intelligent person is one who is in contact with himself. He is not without problems, but he understands and is realistic about his strengths and deficits. He does not have to put up a facade, because his defenses, though adequate, are not rigid. Even when he sees open contact with others as potentially painful, he does not see it as destructive. For him such contact is life itself and is avoided only at the cost of avoiding life. He is basically "for" others simply because they "are." This translates itself into acceptance, nonpossessive warmth, and tolerance. While he does not abdicate his own values in any way, he does not demand that others be like him. He may question another's behavior, especially when he sees that this behavior is self-destructive or destructive of others, but he confronts because he cares, because he wants to be involved, not because the other disturbs his world and fails to conform to his standards. When he is with others he is really present to them even though he does not impose himself on them. He not only has a feeling for what is happening in the world of the other, but he has the willingness or the agency or the guts to enter the other's world, to communicate his understanding, but without making himself an intruder. He may not be able to predict the behavior of the other, but he makes sufficient contact to understand the sources of the other's behavior, even when these sources are irrational. Even when he loses control of himself and does what he really does not want to do in interpersonal situations, he knows how to recover—not just to save face, but to reestablish contact. He can admit his shame and guilt without being overwhelmed by the experience. Social intelligence as it is described here is obviously an ideal, but it is the kind of behavior that makes encounter groups effective.

Low-level encounter groups caricature much of the behavior described by Rogers and Truax. In such groups, being "nice" or adopting a "you-be-careful-with-me-and-I'll-be-careful-with-you" style takes the place of more authentic and contacting nonpossessive warmth. Tacit rules are made allowing facades, forbidding the discussion of them, and permitting them to pass as reality. Empathy takes the form of discussions of one another's psychodynamics, the hypothetical foundations of behavior. Cliché-talk and cliché-behavior abound. In its own way this kind of group culture is just as destructive as a culture of hostile, punitive confrontation. It is certainly more phony.

The behavior in any particular encounter group need not fulfill either the irresponsible-confrontation or the effete-support caricature. The participants can have the kind of group they want, and they probably get the kind of group they deserve. In a sense, the participants must fight for a good group. There are many factors that tend to make the group entropic—lack of support is just one of them.

Psychotherapy: Reverence
for Experience

E. Mark Stern

Editor's Introduction. Stern's article presents a somewhat unique approach to the variables of genuineness, unconditional positive regard, and empathy. In a sense, the article constitutes an extended definition of what it means to *respect* another. Stern makes a distinction between an instrumental and a sacramental approach to human experience. The instrumental view stresses a past to be overcome and a present to be mastered, while the sacramental view stresses the appreciation of experience, even though it must be transcended. Since the present may need to be transformed through concerned and appreciative confrontation, the sacramental approach does not view confrontation as antithetical to appreciation, acceptance, and nonpossessive warmth. Although Stern speaks of the therapist-client relationship, what he says applies to the relationship of member to member in the encounter group.

In his practice the psychotherapist knowingly or unwittingly gives allegiance to some general approach to experience. For convenience I shall divide such approaches into two types: the instrumental and the sacramental. The first is concerned with mastery; the second, at bottom, is concerned with appreciation. The instrumental approach considers the patient's past as something to be overcome through emotional insight and regards his present as a problem to be resolved through learning how to adjust to reality. The sacramental approach considers the patient's past as worth respect, even though it may need to be transcended, and his present as an experience which can be transformed through concerned and appreciative confrontation. The therapist who uses the instrumental approach must necessarily treat the therapeutic situation as something apart from the patient's life, however significant it may be for that life. He stands aloof although he may be genuinely concerned. The therapist who uses the sacramental approach seeks to integrate the treatment experience into the patient's life. He enters into therapy as a self confronting and interacting with

From the *Journal of Existentialism*, 1966, 6, pp. 279-287. Reprinted by permission of Libra Publishers, Inc.

another self rather than as a mirror in whose clear surface the patient can finally come to appreciate how he is distorting his experience.

The therapist who takes the instrumental approach may define cure as achieving mastery over the environment. Here the therapeutic experience seeks to have the patient pluck out uncertainties, discover and then eliminate dormant fears. Classical psychoanalysis with its emphasis on reaching below the ego defenses into the unconscious illustrates the instrumental approach to experience. Analytic neutrality actually becomes a maneuver in working with recalcitrant individuals who are filled with shame and foreboding over their inadequacies. In other words, the therapist induces the patient to pull out of the past those elements which have contributed to the present day's so-called neurotic needs. Patients who feel alienated from other human beings and from the objects of their daily lives are introduced to a momentous curiosity about reliving early infantile and prepubertal encounters with defeat. They are asked to look into the past and into their fantasy lives in order to blot out the neurotic remnants which are supposedly imprisoning them. It may be useful to analyze past experience in this way, but over-emphasis on this material tends to flatten the patient's affective life. A classical analyst may thus trap patient and himself into focusing on Oedipal obstacle courses and the crises of the formative years. If one sees a patient as weighed down by early traumata, he cannot help but reach the conclusion that the patient has lost command of his fate because of specific infantile and childhood hurts. Never once can they be seen as healthful experiences. The individual who comes to treatment is seen as short-changed by his past; he can no longer achieve self-determination in his daily life. Traditional analytic therapy accordingly looks toward the goal of helping the patient master his intrapsychic conflicts and cope with his environment—and especially with his human relationships in it.

This approach to therapy and to existence has certain limitations which become apparent as soon as one looks at the world not as something to be reckoned with, an object of mastery, but rather as something to be appreciated, a context in which all experience has imminent value. In this frame of reference, the past is more than a fetter. As Andras Angyal[1] has it ". . . causation works back and forth, and the present can change the past; the future is influenced by the past as the past is *now*." A therapist who sees experience as something to be appreciated tends to stress mastery less and reverence more. Accordingly, the patient's task becomes that of learning how to recognize himself as a unique and total being. Nothing that the patient does, no way in which he behaves, is merely a limitation upon his freedom. The therapist must see every act in a patient's life as a vital incarnation of the vast variety which existence offers.

Seeing experience as something to be reverenced, the therapist is concerned less with defense than with renewal. To be sure, the patient like all other human beings must protect himself against a great number of risks. Yet even the most apparently restrictive forms of defense can themselves be modalities of singularly individual kinds of experience. For example, a patient may refuse to leave his home; he shuns going out into the open. The classical analyst would see this as deprivation only and probe for the trauma or threat which makes this patient willing to give up contact with the real world for the neurotic satisfaction of life indoors. A therapist who takes the broader view described earlier will acknowledge that a man who shuts himself into his house may familiarize himself with an unsuspected range of the varieties of life within doors. Experience will not end for him; happenings will continue to exist, and their direction may be no less deep or shallow than the way of life characterized by going out into streets and fields.

Conversely, the therapist may encounter a man who chooses to rove the country and refuses to take on the customary role of stable paterfamilias. A classically oriented analyst might regard such a person as a man in need of treatment that would help him accept the realities represented by the responsibilities of middle-class life. A therapist whose focus was on respect for experience might be more aware that a life which seemed to evade responsibility may be marked by the depth of pilgrimage. I am reminded, at this point, of G.K. Chesterton's remark:[2] "A clergyman may be apparently as useless as a cat, but he is also as fascinating, for there must be some strange reason for his existence."

To approach the world as experience to be regarded for itself rather than as raw material to be manipulated, to look upon reality as opportunity for experience rather than as that which exacts adjustment to it, we must understand that each being and thing is a furtherance of its own cause. It is possible to look upon objects themselves as responding to their environment with the potentiality of future action. When we scale a stone over water, the stone reveals its dimensions as the water shows its breadth; thus the stone itself informs the person who throws it where it may best be held. The artist knows how he interacts with his material. The sculptor feels the stone guide him through its response to the chisel; the striations literally lead the artist. The dancer, too, responds to his own body, to the self in that body. Indeed, dancing requires responsiveness to the self, to the relationship between self and other, between the two and the music, between the music and the ground, and between this dynamic composite and time. Dancers thus actualize what each moment presents to them. All movement develops as a significant complex of melody, harmony, dissonance, and dynamic relationship. Modern music, too, represents the appreciation of experiences in sound which cannot be fitted into traditional patterns. Literature, both in prose and verse, seeks out the concrete uniqueness of this our singular and fearsome present.

The modern artist encounters his material; he sees it as experience, not simply as malleable stuff. In relationships between persons the same sensitivity to experience allows one to be sufficiently open and responsive to "read" the other. Response to appropriate response tends toward refinement and artistry in personal encounter rather than toward a dead exploitiveness.

The personal encounter which leads to a real relationship between persons is of peculiar significance in the therapeutic situation. Classically, the therapist is present in a fashion somewhat divorced from what is generally known as human presence. His unperturbed surface allows the patient to create and live out other relationships in great variety; the therapist may be anybody to the patient, anybody except the self he is outside the therapeutic hour. The therapist who reveres experience does not thus stand apart. He *accompanies* his patient to fulfillment. He will not arbitrarily define any mode of being as dysfunction only, for such a definition prevents acknowledgment of its possible contribution to the patient's existence. Only when both patient and therapist can stand back from, while participating in existence, can or will they begin to recognize direction. The patient, looking at the products of his life, can usually learn where he is going by means of the skilled encouragement which reveals the character of individual experience through basic respect for it as partaking in the sacredness of all experience. The therapist, in other words, takes it for granted that the patient's venture into therapy is a movement toward a statement and a development of the self.

In therapy, action and fantasy both must be seen to function within an integral process where even memories of the traumatic past emerge into words through desire to transmit the flavor of a personality. Here, too, Angyal[3] helps delineate our concepts: "... the meaning of an early primitive expression of a trend," he says, "is clarified by our knowledge of its later mature expression: To understand an embryo, we must know the structure of the later mature organism." The therapeutic situation is one in which patient and therapist can act to perfect, not merely to correct experience. In dealing with children, for example, one encounters the mal-contents, those who are ill at ease in outgoing social situations. It is more than questionable whether, in these instances, the therapist should concentrate on helping such young people to accept the social mold gracefully. Might their "problem in adjustment" not be more fruitfully dealt with if it were seen as an early indication of capacity to function in such spheres of work as are concerned with religion, psychology, philosophy, and pure mathematics? Similarly, would those who give early evidence of capacity to deal with outgoing social situations not find maximum self-expression in fields ranging from commerce to engineering?

Here again the therapist can assume a respectful rather than a somewhat manipulative attitude toward treatment. He can encourage and guide toward an enrichment of expression by *witnessing* a person's direction. People cry out for witnesses just as a woman ready to give birth looks to a midwife or obstetrician to help her in her labor. The therapist has an analogous role. He must witness the birth pangs of experience which are trying to find form and expression in the patient. This resembles the work of the good teacher who offers constructive encouragement to the student who is trying to comprehend and express an idea new to him.

Witnesses of this sort help to create a climate favorable for self-belief. This they do best not by intervening in a "show-and-tell" manner (to use current pedagogical parlance), but by standing by, encouraging the other, be he patient, woman struggling to become mother, or pupil, to accept what is trying to come into being. This act of accompaniment in therapy helps the patient know his personal strengths.

The therapist stands witness to renewed emerging experience. In this, he can be likened to the primitive religious leader who, by ceremonially witnessing the movement of the seasons gives existence itself a sacramental character. In a more sophisticated context, the priest consecrating the bread and wine of the Eucharist points toward the sacred character of all life. In the sacrifice of the mass, he speaks the prayer: ". . . through him O Lord/you always make/you make holy/you make alive/you make blessed/and you give to us/these and all good things." Thus, like the primitive worshippers who preceded him, the priest demonstrates that the material world is on the point of divine transformation.

The therapist, too, tries to bring human experience into focus as purposeful, having a function and a potential. Thus each act has a quality of sacredness; each experience becomes the "presence of things hoped for and the evidence of things not yet seen." Campbell[4] cites an ancient Indian saying: "No one who is not himself divine can successfully worship a divinity."

Contemplative religious practice is aware of the special nature of "things" as subject. The Reverend Arthur Vogel[5] states: "When we consciously recognize in our very living, our relation to the whole of creation, we then live in the direct presence of God." In his *Rule for Monasteries*, St. Benedict[6] declares: "We believe that the Divine presence is everywhere." With this witness to encourage them, monks are urged so to conduct themselves that their "mind may be in harmony with [their] voice." Each gesture, every occupation in a Benedictine monastery ought to reflect Divine presence. The manner in which meals are served, the mode of manual labor, the use of speech, the teaching of the young, the reception of guests: all is seen as worthy of sacramental reverence. When the world is thus reverenced, balance and temperance are equivalent to tenderness and appreciation. "Above all things," says St. Benedict, ". . . over-indulgence must be avoided . . . for there is nothing so opposed to the Christian character as over-indulgence."

Food, in this context, like all other objects and activities, takes on the special significance of God's purpose. In trying to relate this regard for the sacredness of common life to my own psychotherapeutic practice, I have found some useful applications of this principle. One woman patient felt great anxiety related to strong fear that the love she felt needed in her life would never be truly provided for. This anguish and sense of lack expressed itself through over-eating: she could not be satisfied with moderate portions of food. I recognized that she was so fearful that her needs would not be met that she would rather stuff herself rapidly than pause to learn what she really might be wanting or getting from her food. She would push in as much as her mouth would hold and then swallow the mass whole. This meant swallowing air too, and frequent gastric distress as well as hampering overweight.

By helping this patient to learn to know there could be real satisfaction in chewing food and tasting it, she was able to enjoy smaller quantities of food. As she began to appreciate tastes and textures, mastication became enjoyable in itself. For the first time in her life, she learned how to appreciate the full significance of aromas. This helped her to get more out of her meals and to need less food at them. She was introduced to her own role in providing something important for herself.

In order to understand what this new awareness meant to her, one need think only of such stylized food rituals as the classic Japanese tea ceremony. In such ceremonial behavior, we see how taste can become heightened and in a sense sanctified when encouraged by significant gestures. Such gestures transmute the consumption of food and drink into an adoration of the beautiful in the everyday routine of living.

Patients who sense that they are estranged from relationships have frequently never learned to appreciate the many things that are presently happening. This disjunction from feeling what is happening can often be remedied through heightening the interplay which takes place in the process of therapy. I have said elsewhere that the psychotherapist must above all be a guide who constantly introduces the patient to the experiences which he sees are happening between them. His task thus becomes one of training sensitivity by becoming alert to the many sensations and tendencies he feels take place in his relationship to his patient.

For example, a person I was seeing in therapy became fearful of the questions which she felt were coming. In particular, she related this worry to her feeling that she never could get things through to her dearest friend without the thought that she was "messing up the works" and potentially destroying their closeness. She most feared her friend's rebukes, which took the form of protesting that she was not interested in someone else making up her mind for her. Her intense fear of being asked any questions at this point seemed tied to her fear of being considered destructive.

I asked her whether she wouldn't like to see how "give and take questions" fitted into our relationship. I encouraged her to ask me those questions she most feared would hamper what had come to be a growing friendship. She agreed, and began to inquire into areas of curiosity she had about my life. Eventually, this resulted in my being confronted by all the fears which she had described as part of her. The questions related to areas of my personal life which I customarily found it uncomfortable to expose. In her presence, I could certainly understand something of what she meant, but this time from *my* vantage point. I slowly and hesitantly answered her honestly. I began to know what she meant by the "eyes which stared and darted at her." My first reaction was discomfort felt in my stomach. As I continued to answer her inquiries, however, I understood why the idea of the questions was possibly so intriguing to both of us.

The questions acted as an opening force making us both care about each other's feelings. Her fears that she would be destructive or destroyed were related to the painful feeling that people should stay in their respective places. As a result of my revelations, however, I found that I could no longer play detached expert. The experience itself was filled with great warmth and a sense of communion. The "bugging" quality of the questions which I had provoked could be seen in greater significance and depth. The reason for their being so frightening was precisely that they could only bring me closer and therefore might threaten the traditional boundaries which have become part of the ground rules of professional psychotherapy. However, feelings of being "done in" by her questions were only preliminary. In my own terms, I recognized the sacramental aspect of her cross-examination. If she were to point to weaknesses in my conduct of my life and inadequacies in my working with her, she might also be of some help to me. Far from being disillusioned, she came to realize that she, too, was frightened of remarks which were not praise.

The communication which grew from simply *hearing* what we each had to say to the other allowed her to realize that we could be concerned for each other. Sharing what each was most interested in, rather than having each maintaining boundaries, allowed for the full flowering of friendship. Beyond the simple need to confess, to reveal oneself, there is also a need to become part of a living community. Each action, each experience is necessarily the truth of the self, offered to the self and, concurrently, to all the community. Michael Polanyi[7] develops the point further as he states: ". . . authentic feeling and authentic experience jointly guide all intellectual achievement. . . . as we pass thus from verification to validation and rely increasingly on internal rather than external evidence, the structure of commitment remains unchanged, but its depth becomes greater." Thus we see that the therapist can do no greater service than to help the individual learn how to *need* what he is trying to express. Religious and mythological accounts point to a realm of basic human expression which incorporates experience, even long past experience, into the radical present. This realm is akin to what a philosopher like Josiah Royce has described as "the beloved community" and what religious persons sometimes label the body of the church.

On another level we have Jung's[8] concept of a *collective unconscious,* a common heritage in which all experience becomes everyone's experience. The "existence of" such a psychological entity, Jung acknowledges "can be inferred only from individual phenomenology." Every phenomenon, physical and environmental, can be seen to be the equivalent of some individual human experience. As individual birds, insects, or fish carry through cyclical and ritual activities characteristic of the species to which they belong, so on another plane, it is possible that the human individual may need to express his wholeness by partaking of common human experience. Joseph Campbell[4] observes: ". . . it therefore has to be asked whether man, like those other members of the kingdom does not possess any innate tendencies to respond, in strictly patterned racial ways, to certain signals flashed by his environment and his own kind."

The therapist may profit by recalling such speculations about uniquely human experiences which can be shared by all, for it is through approaching such sharable experience that the individual can participate in what we have called community—the sense of the vital continuity of experience. Within the therapeutic situation there exists the possibility for the patient's reawakening to himself as a member not of the human community alone, but of the universal continuity of life and being.

Rebirth and regeneration which come through understanding are essential elements in a psychotherapeutic encounter. The disquieting factors of early childhood cannot be easily tossed aside. They must be enlisted as forces for growth. A classical analytic approach regards childhood traumata and experiences as simply etiological and so confines them to a merely diagnostic frame of reference. The sacramental approach to therapy does not "think positively"; it does not dismiss the pain of early experiences. Nevertheless, the therapist who uses this frame of reference can see painful experiences as contributions to the rich social fabric of life even while he recognizes their painful character. As the patient gains insight into his early wounds, he may increase his understanding of his own potential worth. For all his helplessness he has kept alive and that has required some knowledge, albeit it may be unconscious, of personal and vital meaning in his life.

My own observation has made me feel that the little child's first struggle with separation and helplessness can be focused by this approach, and help him awaken to knowledge that being alone is inherent in the human condition, not an experience with no possible content but fear. The experience of being alone allows the child to begin finding his own creative potential in solitude when he is, for some moments, not constantly nurtured by outside parental forces. As he grows, he learns to recognize his uniqueness through being separate from his parents. He can thus learn that their letting him go apart for a while allows him to fill his life with meaning. He becomes progressively sensitive to his own need for a life of his own and thus learns to respect the rights of others. Through being alone, however painful the experience may be, even in retrospect, the child is enabled to move toward his broader life task: participation in existence as an autonomous member of mankind.

The child is a visibly growing being so that it is comparatively easy to see his unhappiness as part of a process of significant becoming. But the adult involved in an unhappy life is not excluded from such a process. The unhappy life is stagnant only when the person feels faced with dread that his actions and destiny are insignificant. As a patient comes to note that within even the most difficult relationship or encounter, the life one lives is made manifest through relationships to people, he becomes aware of a new force in experience. This creative force makes for life's vitality. The therapeutic process can proceed to *guide* individuals to a fuller idea of what a personal life really is. The patient can begin to appreciate that, according to his own situation, either the antagonist or the friend becomes a healer since he makes for fresh possibilities of interpersonal response. This, by the way, is the significance of the Christian Incarnation in that God had to become man in order fully to relate to man. Recognition of interpersonal possibilities is also the lifeblood of any restorative social force or action, for such recognition accepts the truth that meaningful potentials for an expanding life can exist only through the admission that one belongs in the community, not in the sense of conforming but in the sense of fuller awareness that, as an individual, one lives in a context of possible relationships. When a person loses his footing, he becomes unable to appreciate his own vital meaning; then he must search for himself and for an approach to community.

If he pursues his search in therapy, he has a companion in the therapist. The therapist, in order to grasp the insights provided by personality study and theory, must have command of studies of individual differences in sensation and body chemistry, in cognition, and motivation. But the therapist is to use these insights to increase his own openness to the directions in which the patient may be going. The therapist does not point out the "right" direction; he guides and encourages the patient to see that there are many directions in which movement is possible for him. Only when no sense of adventure is present does the patient reach the stage of resigned attitudes and fearful poses. His trials and tribulations are his passion, the suffering by which he may come to be. Therefore, trial and tribulation must be engaged in rather than merely submitted to. As the patient begins to sense the sacredness of all aspects of his life, he learns to look toward his own potentials and toward the potentialities in his encounters with other people. If he is to be thus sensitive to his life, he must be responsive to it; otherwise he will act in stilted and inappropriate ways. As the person begins to communicate, he achieves a more sacramental attitude toward his existence. Life is a challenge which must be replied to in spite of the confusing circumstances which are always present. For there is some guiding point of which each person must become aware. Within human relationships, it is necessary to find the live man beneath the hard shell of appearance.

In *Peanuts*, Charles Schulz[9] shows older sister Sally's feeling of utter hopelessness as she mutters, in her little brother's presence: "Why life is a drag ... I'm completely fed up." Her brother tries to reassure her, but his generalities do not help; she continues to bawl that she has no blessings to count. Just then, Linus apparently sees light and says: "Well, for one thing, you have a little brother that loves you." She stares at him in utter amazement, and then begins to cry. He looks at her and says: "Every now and then I say the right thing."

Finding the appropriate word or the fitting gesture leads to heightened moments of responsiveness to life. They point to individual meaning and sanctification. Approaching an undeveloped piece of land which needs to be cultivated is not too different from trying to find what is important in the transaction between human beings; in both instances, one must become a friend to the potentially responsive other.

The psychotherapist must involve himself in his patient's cry to be discovered. For each person represents all of mankind. Therefore, there is a journey in which both patient and therapist must find the basis of what is responsive in their venture. The patient can endure through this journey as his authenticity is constantly acknowledged. This is done not through mere reassurance but through the therapist's "bearing with" all that comes to be in the therapeutic situation. Emerson[10] spoke of this as love: "Into the most pitiful and abject it will infuse a heart and courage to defy the world, so only it have a countenance of the beloved object. In giving him to another it still more gives him to himself. He is a new man, with new perceptions, new and keener purposes, and a religious solemnity of character and aims. He does not longer appertain to his family or society: he is somewhat: *he* is a person: *he* is a soul."

This then is the essence of the therapeutic experience: that the therapist provide the patient with the means by which he may learn to know and to respect his unique way of meeting the world. For each man must discover his own "genius" by knowing that he is. The psychotherapeutic encounter can therefore be seen as a relationship dedicated to heightening sensitivity to existence by regarding all personal experience, even the traumatic, as sacred.

References

1. A. Angyal, *Neurosis and Treatment: A Holistic Theory* (New York: John Wiley & Sons, 1965).

2. G. K. Chesterton, *Orthodoxy* (Garden City, N.Y.: Image Books, 1959).

3. Angyal, *op. cit.*

4. J. Campbell, *The Masks of God: Primitive Mythology* (New York: The Viking Press, 1959).

5. A. Vogel, *The Christian Person* (New York. Seabury, 1963).

6. St. Benedict, *Rule for Monasteries,* Trans. by L. J. Doyle (Collegeville, Minn.: The Liturgical Press, 1948).

7. M. Polanyi, *Personal Knowledge: Towards a Post-Critical Philosophy* (New York: Harper & Row, 1964).

8. C. Jung, *Psychological Types,* Trans. by B. H. Goodwin (New York: Harcourt, 1923).

9. C. Schulz, in *The Gospel According to Peanuts* by R. L. Short (Richmond, Virginia: John Knox Press, 1965).

10. R. W. Emerson, *Selected Writings,* B. Atkinson (ed.) (New York: The Modern Library, 1940).

Editor's Comment. Not unlike therapist and client, the members of an encounter group interact to perfect, and not merely to correct, experience. Participants are, or at least can be, psychological midwives for one another. Confrontation is too often seen merely as a demand on the part of one that another stop engaging in irresponsible forms of behavior. But it is also possible to confront the strengths—the underdeveloped or underused potential—of the other. This means that the confronter is both open to the other and has some initial appreciation of him and his possibilities. Such confrontation is at root supportive precisely because it is an act of appreciation of the other.

In order to appreciate another it is necessary to listen to him— "listen" in the broadest sense, not just to words, sentences, and paragraphs, but to the person himself. Real interpersonal listening means becoming aware of all the cues the other emits, and this implies an openness to the totality of the communication of the other. Total listening means that the participant listens not just with his ears, but with his eyes, his sense of touch. He listens by becoming aware of the feelings and emotions that arise within himself because of his contact with others (that is, his emotional resonance is another "ear"); he listens with his mind, his heart, his imagination. He listens to the words of others, but he also listens to the messages that are buried in the words or encoded in all the cues that surround the words. Listening, then, if it is to provide one of the bases for intelligent support, is an active process. A good listener is an active listener, one who goes out of himself in search of significant cues emitted by others; but he is also one who does not manufacture cues because he projects his own needs into the messages of others.

As Stern suggests, being with one another in a caring, concerned way is a sacred act in some sense of the term. If the group becomes a loving (even though a temporary) community, a community that provides the kind of mutual support absolutely necessary for intimacy, then much can be expected from the interaction of the group. The creation of such a supportive community is obviously an ideal toward which the participants must work. Giving support is perhaps the most demanding work of the group.

In Search of an Honest
Experience: Confrontation
in Counseling and Life[1]

R. R. Carkhuff
B. G. Berenson

Editor's Introduction. A great deal of confrontation is taking place publicly in our society. Some of it is violent, but even when it is peaceful (or rather nonviolent) there is often great tension and hostility involved, for the assumption is that the confrontee (whether this means the president, the congress, a university administration or some other person or institution) does not want to listen and, even if he does want to listen, does not want to change. The situation in the encounter group is different, at least theoretically. The assumption is that the individual participant enters the group freely precisely because he does want to examine his interpersonal life-style and entertain possibilities for growth and change.

Confrontation, if carried out maturely, can be one of the most growthful kinds of interaction in the encounter group. But sometimes that is a big "if." Sensitivity training in general is caricatured as a situation in which people sit around "telling one another off." Unfortunately, at times there are groups in which hostile confrontation is the central dimension of the group (and I am speaking now of regular encounter groups and not the hostile and often highly abusive "encounter" sessions associated with drug-addict rehabilitation centers such as Synanon or Daytop Village). Hostility is for most people a relatively "cheap" emotion in the sense that it is readily available and is often used, substitutively and noncreatively, when perhaps other more difficult and taxing interactions would be more fruitful. It is not that hostility does not have a kind of beneficial shock value. For instance, I recall a group in which one of the members had been baiting the facilitator for more than a week (in a two-week residential lab). His snide remarks, his innuendos, and his subtly obstructionistic behavior were always accompanied by a smiling face so that his behavior never seemed to merit a broadside from the facilitator. But one day, the facilitator burst into a hostile confrontation of his antagonist. Perhaps it would have been better if the facilitator had not saved up his anger, if

From *Beyond Counseling and Therapy* by Robert R. Carkhuff and Bernard G. Berenson. Copyright ©1967 by Holt, Rinehart and Winston, Inc. Reprinted by permission of Holt, Rinehart and Winston, Inc.

[1] Chapter 11 is a collaborative effort under the direction of John Douds in conjunction with the authors and with assistance from Richard Pierce.

he had said earlier: "I keep hearing antagonistic remarks from you, and I find them almost impossible to handle. Let's talk about how you and I relate or do not relate." Fortunately, however, the facilitator's outburst proved to be somewhat redemptive for the game-player. For the first time, this participant saw his behavior in a total way and he saw its irresponsibility.

In the following article, Carkhuff and Berenson and their associates decry the failure of theorists to discuss the growth possibilities of confrontation in counseling and therapy as well as the failure of practitioners to use confrontation effectively. As the title of the article suggests, confrontation, like any other "therapeutic" variable, belongs in life first; and because it belongs in life, it also belongs to that intensification of living which we call therapy. Plato, more than two millennia ago, proposed that the unexamined, the unchallenged life is not worth living. In the encounter group the participants must learn both how to challenge and how to reply creatively when challenged.

Confrontation, as life, continues independently of all therapeutic models. With the possible exception of the existentialist, none of the major systems leaves room for the concept of confrontation: the existentialists alone approach confrontation by their concept of "encounter."

The case for direct confrontation has been restricted to special instances of therapeutic practice; namely, character-disordered clients and families, short-term crisis situations, aggressive delinquents, and preventative therapy. In general, *the therapist can only confront in the face of client aggressiveness*. Thus, we may have a situation where the client, rather than the therapist, is reaching out with his "being" to evoke the therapist's "being." The learning for the person designated as "less knowing" is that confrontation, rather than being a valued act, is a defensive reaction.

The marked avoidance and resistance to direct confrontation on the part of therapists and theoretical systems alike may have a cultural base. Unconsciously, it is tied to middle-class conditioning which equates challenging directness and honesty in communication with an aggressive, hostile, and destructive attack. Even the dictionary defines confrontation in these terms: facing another, especially in a challenge. Instead, "middle-class therapy" hopes to seduce the illness away; perhaps seduction as opposed to confrontation is the manner of attack.

The Nature, Quality, and Function of Confrontation

Direct confrontation is an act, not a reaction. It is initiated by the therapist, based on his core understanding of the client. It brings the client into more direct contact with himself, his strengths and resources, as well as his self-destructive behavior. The purpose of confrontation is to reduce the ambiguity and incongruities in the client's experiencing and communication. In effect, it is a challenge to the client to become integrated; that is, at one with his own experience. It is directed at discrepancies within the client (his ideal versus real self); between what the client says and does (insight and action); and between illusion and reality (the therapist's experience of the client versus the client's expression of his experience of himself and the therapist). The therapeutic goal is nondestructive and emerging unity within the client. It implies a constructive attack upon an unhealthy confederation of miscellaneous illusions, fantasies, and life avoidance techniques in order to create a reintegration at a higher level of health. The strength and intensity of a confrontation may correspond with how dominant and central the emotional pattern is to the client's life style. The therapeutic risk will also depend upon the amount of disorganization both the therapist and client can handle.

The quality of a confrontation, then, corresponds to the experiential skill, emotional integration, and intent of the therapist. It is a risk which the therapist takes out of deep commitment to the client in the recognition that the client's defenses are his enemy and do not allow him direct contact with himself: they interfere with nourishing contact with other men. In this sense, the therapist pits his health against the client's sickness while at the same time being a formidable ally of the client's health. The therapist is the enemy of the client's self-destructive tendencies.

Confrontation and Impotence

Confrontations may range from a light challenge to a direct collision between therapist and client. It constitutes a challenge to the client to mobilize his resources to take another step toward deeper self-recognition or constructive action on his own behalf. Frequently, it will precipitate a crisis that disturbs, at least temporarily, the client's personal and social equilibrium. Again, crises are viewed as the very fabric of growth, invoking new responses and charting new developments. Growth is viewed as a series of endless self-confrontations. Confrontation is the vehicle that ultimately translates awareness and insight into action, directionality, wholeness, and meaning in the client's life. A life without confrontation is directionless, passive, and impotent.

Confrontation is a useful therapeutic ingredient in combatting the pervasive, passive-reactive stance which the alienated person assumes toward life in general, and his present difficulties in particular. The vicious cycle in which he is engaged leaves him with a feeling, at his deepest level, that he is trapped and helpless to *act* constructively on his own behalf. He can only experience himself *in reaction to* others, and, at best, he believes he knows "pieces" of himself in contrast to experiencing himself with a sense of wholeness. Having transferred the locus of evaluation and sense of direction to forces outside himself, he finds himself ruled by fate, society, rituals, obsessions, and "luck." His desperate struggle is a passive one; he feels paralyzed to *act*. He desperately and magically hopes for life to come to him to fill the void created by his repetitive cycle. The secondary gains which he struggles to maintain are tenuous, hollow, and unfulfilling: like gelatin, they temporarily relieve his hunger. To fill the void created by a passive existence and in order to sustain himself between secondary gains, he lives in illusions of false hope. In his moments of despair and intense anxiety he hopes for a magic solution to his problems: either the realization of his illusions or some solution from an *external* source. Reality cannot compete with his fantasies, and he is afraid to sacrifice his fantasies to reality. He fears that the void will grow bigger if he gives up the temporary nourishment from his fantasies, although it was the initial void which created the fantasies. He desperately needs to break the vicious cycle, to confront himself in order to feel himself as an active force in his own life; that is, to function out of his own experience.

In his helplessness and confusion he seeks therapy. More often than not, he receives insight in the form of a conceptual integration of himself. He may choose insight as a way of life, a culturally higher, secondary gain. Insight may, seemingly, reduce confusion by subsuming the conceptualizations he has about himself in a neater package, allowing him the illusory belief of being "on top of his problems"—he can now explain his anxiousness in high level terms. Victimized by a wishful need for a magic solution, he accumulates insights based upon his *reactions* to different people and situations, hoping for *THE ULTIMATE INSIGHT* which will be an answer to everything. Still paralyzed to act, he remains dependent and passive, noticeably lacking action and directionality in his existence.

The following illustration points up how the therapist uses direct confrontation as a vehicle to translate insight into action for a male client in his thirties who is functioning around level 2:

Client: I now understand what my father has done to me. It's all very clear to me. I think I've got the situation licked.
Therapist: But you're still getting up at 5 o'clock in the morning for him when he could get rides from a lot of other men.
Client: Well, uh, he is still my father.
Therapist: Yeah, and you're still scared to death of him . . . scared that he'll beat you up or disapprove of you and you're thirty-five years old now. You still fear him like you were a kid.
Client: No, you're wrong, because I don't feel scared of him right now.
Therapist: You're scared right now—*here—with me—he's here.* . . .
Client (pause): I guess I understand him better for what he is, but when I'm around him, I'm still scared, and always think of standing up to him after I leave him. Then I talk myself out of doing what I really want to do.

The client believes, in this instance, that understanding and insight is enough; having the illusion that an organized picture of his situation leaves him in control. In fact, however, he continues to behave in his stereotyped manner. The therapist confronts him with the insight/action discrepancy in the hope of facilitating client movment out of an authority/dependency relationship.

In this regard, the alienated person often has a cognitive filter between himself and his real experience. Although insight may serve to organize him cognitively, it also helps him to rationalize a passive orientation to life. This is precisely why he needs an experience of his "self." The therapist, in confronting the client in order to facilitate the client's self confrontation, may have to knock out the intricate cognitive system to bring the client back in touch with his *real* experience, his substantive core. It is from this base that the client can best build upon his real potential.

Confrontation and Risk

The closer the decision affects the inner core of the person, the greater the fear of the life and death choice. A constructive therapeutic confrontation frequently does result in death of a sort; the death of an illusion, hence, an illusory death. *In return for the loss of an illusion, one receives an experience of who he really is, in all of his humanity, strengths, and weakness.*

The illusions may be of strength or weakness, depending upon the client's defensive and situational needs. In every case, however, they are calculated to prevent the client from coming into contact with his own experience. Thus, the next illustration provides an example of a therapist's confrontation of a high-level functioning young woman's discrepancy between her ego ideal and real self:

Client: I like to see myself as different from all the others.
Therapist: Your uniqueness, that's not real for you though.
Client: I don't know. I don't want to be a nobody, just part of the crowd so I try to do things that are different from everyone else.
Therapist: You try to *act* unique.
Client: I guess that's true because I always come back to doing what everyone else does anyway. I've always been a nobody and no one ever really noticed me like a few of the girls who are natural about things and seem to know what they want. I envy them!
Therapist: But what about *you?*
Client: I don't know who *I* am.

In this instance, the client in her ego ideal wants to see herself as being "unique," and in order to realize her illusion she self-consciously looks for ways to act uniquely. In reality, she is afraid of the group's disapproval, and more consistently conforms to the prevailing norms. In therapy, she becomes involved, for the first time, in a process of searching for herself.

The following segment, in turn, is an illustration of therapy with a forty-five-year-old female client functioning at about level 2. The therapist confronts the client's discrepancy between illusion and reality, that is, between the client's verbal expression of her experience of herself as being weak as opposed to the therapist's experience of the client:

Client: I know I sound weak and mousy. My question is—am I?
Therapist: I get your question, but you don't really come across as being this upset over it, and I don't experience you as a weak person.
Client: I don't really *feel* weak, but somehow. . . .
Therapist: You don't like being seen as a weak person.
Client: I know people like me better when I act weak.
Therapist: Maybe you're afraid people won't like you if you come on strong.

The client confronts herself but cannot answer for herself. The therapist responds with his experience of the client. There is no loss for the client here, but rather a confirmation of the kind of strength which will allow the client to make a full investment in therapy. Constructive therapeutic process movement ensues.

Thus, the death of an illusion can lead to a rebirth of strength. After an initial experience of death to the illusory self, the void which is temporarily created has a chance to fill up with the person's real being. *While building upon the shadow, there is little energy to expand the substance.*

The therapist, then, uses confrontation as a vehicle to initiate a crisis and facilitate a choice point (life or death) by bringing the client in touch with himself, and confronting him with implications and alternatives. The therapist, in a very real sense, clears away the "crud" for the client at the choice point. The therapist takes responsibility for precipitating the crisis—but *the client takes responsibility for his choice.*

Intervention and Attack

The therapist frequently becomes a target of a passive-reactive attack from the client. The client may verbally attack the therapist in and out of therapy and, in rare instances, even physically attack the therapist. Usually, however, the client takes a more subtle mode which serves to both attack the therapist and defend his emotional patterns. The client may assume the defensive posture which has been most rewarding for him; he perpetuates the ways in which he was able to intimidate people in his world. As a result of prior destructive attacks from significant others in his past, he is unable to differentiate between attacks upon his defensive structure and attacks upon his person. There are a variety of modes of expression of his passive intimidation: playing the helpless victim who has been "needlessly" attacked, threatening a psychotic break, threatening termination, threatening to tarnish the therapist's reputation with suicide, and other destructive and self-destructive acts. Most modes attempt to subtly intimidate the therapist to feel responsible *for* the client's own self-destructive acts. The therapist, by active confrontation, precipitates an awareness of crisis; *he did not create the crisis.*

A piece of the responsibility for temporary disorganization does belong to the therapist, but the client implicitly transfers *total* responsibility to the therapist. The message is clear in one form or another—"you are responsible for destroying me." If the therapist out of his own fears and illusions of omnipotence accepts this intimidation, he is neutralized by the client.

Precipitating the crisis, however, is only a small part of the struggle. The therapist needs to be able to intervene actively in the crisis; *active intervention is the real therapeutic task.* Frequently, the crisis will bring the client's self-destructive trends into clear relief. If the therapist is able to "deliver the goods," he has the opportunity to break the vicious destructive cycle and allow the client's growth potential to emerge. For the client, this experientially translates into having a glimpse of "daylight" (real hope) for the first time. Again, what the client thought would destroy him—loss of an illusion—he finds was not destructive. This is *a key growth experience.*

Indeed, there are a myriad of rationalizations that both therapists and clients use to avoid direct confrontation in therapy. (The therapist's rationalizations, of course, are more sophisticated.) Ultimately, the rationalizations take the therapist "off the hook"; the client is too fragile, in short, "It is because of the client's weaknesses that I cannot confront him." Analytically oriented theorists reason that a frontal attack on an anxious client will make him more anxious if he sees the "evil" in him. Implicitly, this assumes that confrontation does *not* bring a client to a feeling knowledge of his resources. Client-centered theorists rationalize that confrontation would be an unnecessary imposition on the client's being and, therefore, "shaping" his behavior. In short, they are willing to leave him *alone* to die.

Certainly, *it is true that confrontation from a destructive therapist is destructive to a client.* Ultimately however, these rationalizations allow the therapist to avoid a recognition of his own inadequacies and the necessity to concentrate upon them, as well as his responsibility to the client. Actually, *confrontation is the ultimate in taking therapeutic responsibility, since it implies that the therapist makes himself a target for the client's self-destructive impulses, as well as leaving himself open to being confronted by the client.* Much of the time it is the fear of exposure that is at the base of the therapist's avoidance.

Therapeutic confrontation is a risk. There is the all too familiar fear of suicide! Yet, the implication of not confronting the client is taking more of a risk, for without confrontation, understanding is not communicated, and a psychotic break or even suicide may occur. The risk of not confronting means no further growth for the client. At best, the client's alternative is gradual decay, and, at worst, psychological or physical death. Many join the groups of the living dead who have "tried everything," or remain in the interminable limbo of lifeless therapy.

The following is an illustration of a woman in her fifties, functioning around level 2, confronting herself and the therapist with a discrepancy in saying/doing behavior:

Therapist: I think it is very important to be completely open and honest with each other.

Client: Well, how do I seem to you, how do I come across when you listen to me?

Therapist: Well, er, umm . . . I like you. You're a nice woman.

Client: Don't equivocate!

Therapist: Maybe we need to get to know each other better.

Client: Maybe.

Clearly, in this instance, the client openly confronts the therapist by challenging his "open, honest" statement. The therapist avoids the issue and offers therapy cliches. There is no prospect for growth of either party so long as the client cedes the therapist the power as the agent of her change.

Confrontation offers *growth.* The advantage of the nonconfronting mode is that society will not blame the therapist for the client's failure, and he is left with an "untarnished" reputation. The therapist who is willing to take the responsibility of confrontation needs to know, at his deepest level, that he is a constructive human being *who wants life for the client because he has chosen life for himself.*

Confrontation and Insight

The alienated person learns to develop a conceptual integration of himself. In effect, his affects become more intellectually organized. He develops the secret, superior feeling that he knows himself better and better. He becomes able to explain himself in high level terms which seem to render him invulnerable. Culturally he is rewarded for his self-knowledge, and he can feel himself "a step above" the rest. He collects more and more insights about parts of himself and becomes an accurate observer for himself and others. Any affect is suspect, a signal, not for action but for ponderous introspection with the potential for further insights. In exchange for analyzing his affect, he is rewarded with an intellect as a weapon and the passive-defensive belief that he can explain himself at every turn. He is engaged in looking for the one insight which will provide a solution to life. *There is no one solution, only a series of confrontations.* At best, insight inundates affect with ideas and drowns it in a whirlpool of words. At worst, the person is left with the feeling of being splintered into a thousand pieces, in contact with the fact that he has no identity of his own, only fitting in relation to specific people and situations.

Feeling alone, without action, leads to no change. Thus, the alienated person who seeks *only* insights slowly decays while having the illusion of making progress. For the alienated person, confrontation as a way of life is diametrically opposed to insight. It is action-oriented. Life is experienced as effecting the self rather than some third person. Because action is a way of life, the person becomes willing to experience in full the implications of the situation. He becomes aware that the situation is a life and death crisis. He becomes one with what he wants to be, stemming from listening to his own inner silence.

Confrontation: A Systematic Evaluation

Research into the nature, process, and effects of confrontation is sparse. However, the research accomplished has produced extremely interesting results (Anderson, Douds, and Carkhuff, 1967; Berenson, Mitchell, and Laney, 1967; Berenson, Mitchell, and Moravec, 1967). In studies of both hospitalized schizophrenics and counseling center clients, they have established that high-level functioning therapists confront significantly more often than low-level functioning therapists; that is, therapists functioning above minimally facilitative levels present both clients and patients with honest confrontations significantly more frequently than therapists functioning at less than minimally facilitative levels. It would appear, then, that the offering of high levels of conditions, such as empathy and positive regard, is not mutually exclusive of therapeutic confrontations directed at discrepancies in the client's activities. The field has lived too long with the artificial dichotomy between the offering of (1) warmth and understanding and like conditions and (2) honesty of communication in the therapeutic process. Perhaps the client comes to therapy not only seeking the safety of a therapeutic relationship in which he can explore himself and his difficulties, but also trusting that relationship, the honesty in communication which he does not experience in his everyday activities.

It is interesting to note in the research that high-level functioning therapists confront both clients and patients with their assets and resources more often than they confront them with their limitations. On the other hand, low-level functioning therapists confront their clients and patients more often with their limitations than they do with their resources.

The issue of how these confrontations can be translated into client benefits was also addressed. It was found that both client and patient depth of self-exploration tend over time to move toward higher or deeper levels, however we wish to consider it, following confrontations with high-level functioning therapists, while the depth of self-exploration tends to go down over time following confrontations with low-level functioning therapists. Thus, with the kind of confrontation which typifies the activities of the high-level therapist, the client becomes more deeply involved in constructive therapeutic process movement with all of the intensity, extensiveness, and immediacy that this implies.

There is some controversy concerning whether different populations have a differential effect upon the type of confrontation offered by both high and low-level therapists. However, the strongest evidence suggests that honest confrontation by high-level functioning therapists of both clients and patients with discrepancies in their expressed behavior elicits constructive therapeutic process movement and, ultimately, constructive gain or change.

Summary

Facilitative conditions, techniques, and insight per se are *not enough* for effective therapy. Ultimately, the client needs not only to understand but to resolve the discrepancies between his ideal and real self, insight and action, and illusion and reality, if he is to achieve emotional integration. Confrontation is an act initiated by the therapist which serves as a vehicle to bring the client in direct touch with his own experience so that he can move from a passive-reactive stance toward an existence rooted in action, direction, and meaningful confrontation. It may be constructive or destructive depending upon the experiential skill, emotional integration, and intent of the therapist. It is done with the recognition that there is no magic solution to life in illusions or external sources, and that, ultimately, we need to be in touch with our substantive core if we are to function out of our own experience. *Confrontation precipitates crisis;* but crises are viewed as the fabric of growth in that they challenge us to mobilize our resources and invoke new responses. Growth is a series of endless self-confrontations. The therapist who serves as an authentic model of confrontation offers the client a meaningful example of effective living.

References

Anderson, Susan, J. Douds, and R. R. Carkhuff. The effects of confrontation by high and low functioning therapists. Unpublished research, Univer. of Mass., 1967.

Berenson, B. G., K. M. Mitchell, and R. Laney. Level of therapist functioning, types of confrontation and type of patient. *J. clin. Psychol.*, in press, 1967.

Berenson, B. G., K. Mitchell, and J. A. Moravec. Level of therapist functioning, patient depth of self-exploration and type of confrontation. *J. counsel. Psychol.*, in press, 1967.

Editor's Comment. An encounter group that is devoid of confrontation is an anemic, low-level group. Members rationalize their failure to confront one another in a variety of ways—for instance, "I really had nothing to say," "I did not want to hurt anyone." Underneath many of these rationalizations, however, lies a basic fear: "If I challenge another, then I open myself up to be challenged."

The authors rightfully challenge the constant pursuit of insight in growth experiences. The encounter group that develops an "insight culture" is usually boring and in flight from more substantial issues. The participants should challenge one another's behavior and attitudes, and not merely discuss the hypothetical foundations of such behavior.

Confrontation usually leads to some kind of temporary disorganization in the confrontee. Such disorganization can be beneficial if it takes place in a climate of support. Client-centered emphasis on nonpossessive warmth, congruence, and empathy—though absolutely essential—need not prevent participants from confronting one another responsibly. It is true that there are those who confront in order to exercise control over the life of the other, but there are also kinds of confrontation that stem from care and concern.

Though there are many areas of confrontation, perhaps one should be singled out here. Any group with a significant number of noncontributing members is in trouble, for it is difficult for a climate of trust to develop in such a group; moreover, too much energy is usually spent in trying to get the delinquent members to participate. The group experience itself is a challenge to its members to be agents rather than patients. The whole atmosphere, then, should encourage confrontation in the sense that everyone should be encouraged to take interpersonal initiative in the group.

Part Five.
Cautions, Research

Sensitivity-training experiences have generally not been presented very favorably in the popular press. So many articles have appeared decrying the excesses of these experiences that even people who are ordinarily quite open to new ideas wince when sensitivity training is mentioned. Some of these articles admit that encounter groups can offer participants certain benefits, but even in these articles the negative aspects of such groups are the focus of attention. Almost everyone has knowledge of some horror story: "I know a person who . . ."—and the rest is an account of how someone was destroyed by participating in some kind of group. However, few of those who criticize sensitivity training take pains to present any kind of adequate account of the phenomenon under attack. Therefore, it is easy for the man in the street to come away from his reading with such a confusing caricature of sensitivity training that he wonders why anyone would want to expose himself to it.

Sensitivity training, like any enterprise that claims to be influential in the formation of human personality, is open to various abuses. The encounter-group movement has certainly attracted its share of entrepreneurs, faddists, healers, magic-seekers, and passive-dependent participants. Despite a twenty-five year history, the movement is still in many ways in its infancy or adolescence.

Well-trained and socially intelligent facilitators are needed to lead groups. Good research is needed, but it is difficult to do because it is not easy to introduce controls into group situations.

Many things can go wrong in an encounter group. The facilitator might be ignorant or inexperienced, or he might be using the group to satisfy his own needs. A group may fail to develop a climate of trust and support so that the participants refuse to engage one another at any deep level. The members might confront one another in such irresponsible ways that the group becomes in fact what it is often described to be in caricature. A flight culture might be established so that no one really accomplishes anything. If the encounter experience is carried out poorly, then it can prove to be harmful. But the same is true of friendship, marriage, psychotherapy, religion, and education. Indeed, all these institutions exist because of the benefits they afford both individuals and society. If the participants are immature and make a caricature out of any particular enterprise or institution, the fault lies in their immaturity and not in the nature of the institution. The following articles are not meant to provide an exhaustive critique of encounter groups; they merely point out certain areas in which caution must be exercised in evaluating the encounter-group process.

Some Ethical Issues in
Sensitivity Training[1]

Martin Lakin[2]

Editor's Introduction. Lakin states that one of the ethical crises presently facing laboratory training stems from the change that has taken place in laboratory populations. In past years laboratories were composed of rather highly sophisticated professionals (the first lab I attended included NASA officials, psychiatrists, psychologists, directors of nursing in large hospitals, doctors, school supervisors, college teachers and administrators, advanced graduate students in the helping professions, etc.). With the proliferation of laboratory opportunities, the participants are less educated and less sophisticated; and, although most reputable laboratories discourage the emotionally disturbed from participating, there is evidence that more and more people are seeking therapy in encounter groups and other forms of sensitivity training. New populations mean new problems; or at least problems that have always existed now seem more acute. But, while the whole sensitivity-training movement should be subjected to the most critical evaluation, it should also be kept in mind that the movement shares many of its problems and challenges with other growth or training endeavors such as education. It is not that we should not be alarmed by excesses that take place in training groups. Rather, irrational criticism and witch-hunting should yield to constructive programs of reformation and change in all institutions that affect society deeply. It is interesting to substitute the word "teacher" for "trainer" in the following article—not to minimize the problems encountered in training groups, but to place critical evaluation of such groups in a wider social context.

Sensitivity training, in its various forms, has evolved over the past two decades. It is a powerful form of experiential learning that includes self, interactional, and organizational understanding. It has its origins in the study of change and conflict resolution through attention to underlying as well as overt

Reprinted from *American Psychologist,* 1969, 24, pp. 923-928. Used with the permission of the publisher and the author.

[1] This paper was presented at the meeting of the Southeastern Psychological Association, New Orleans, February 1969.

[2] Requests for reprints should be sent to Martin Lakin, Department of Psychology, Duke University, Durham, North Carolina 27706.

interactional processes. It has been widely used to reexamine managerial, pedagogic, and "helping relationships" from the factory to the classroom, from the community to the home. Typically, small groups of participants under the guidance of a "trainer" use the data of their own spontaneous interactions, and reactions to one another. The trainer functions to facilitate communication, to indicate underlying problems of relating, and to model constructive feedback. He keeps the group moving and productively learning about processes and persons and helps to avoid counterproductive conflict or unnecessary damage to participants. With the evolution of mutant forms of training, particularly over the past few years, and their growing popularity, examination of latent ethical questions has become urgent. This article is presented not to censure an obviously significant and often helpful growth in American psychology, but rather to open for discussion and scrutiny elements of it that affect public welfare and reflect on professional standards.

The number of persons who have experienced some form of training is rapidly growing. However named (training, encounter, human relations), the experience invariably involves emotional confrontations and even an implicit injunction to reconsider if not actually to change personal behavior patterns. Since participants are not self-avowed psychotherapy patients but "normal" persons, and because the trainers are presumably not concerned with reparative but with learning or personal enhancement, it is difficult to draw a firm line between it and other psychotherapeutic forms. Indeed, comparison inevitably forces itself upon us and suggests strongly what many of us realize so well, that a distinction between "normal" and "pathological" behavior is hazy at best. However, the comparison also compels one to consider ethical implications of the differences between the contractual relationships between participant and trainer, on the one hand, and those between patient and therapist, on the other. Concerns about the contractual implications have been only partially met by statements of differences in the goals of training from those of therapy and by the difference in self-definition of a participant from that of a patient, as well as by the avowed educational objectives of trainers. Also, formerly it could be argued that the trainer had little therapeutic responsibility because he initiated little; that interactions of the group were the resultant of collective interchange and give-and-take, and did not occur at his instance; that is, a participant "discloses" intimate details of his life or "changes" behavior patterns as a result of a personal commitment or a collective experience rather than because a trainer directs him to do so. Training groups evolved from a tradition of concern with *democratic* processes and *democratic* change. The generally accepted hypothesis was that the best psychological protection against unwarranted influence was individual and collective awareness that could forestall insidious manipulation by dominant leaders or conformist tyranny by a group.

Many people currently involved in the various forms of training are not as psychologically sophisticated or able to evaluate its processes as were the mainly professional participants of some years ago. The motivation of many present participants is cathartic rather than intellectual (e.g., seeking an emotional experience rather than an understanding). Particularly because training is increasingly used as a vehicle for achieving social change, it is necessary to explore its ethical implications—notwithstanding our as yet incomplete understanding of its special processes. There are ethically relevant problems in setting up a group experience, in conducting the group, and following its termination.

Pregroup Concerns

A psychotherapeutic intention is clear by contrast with the training intention. Sophisticated therapists know that this clarity is not absolute; complex issues of values and commitment to specific procedures cannot really be shared with patients, despite the best intentions of a therapist to be candid. Nevertheless, the therapist's mandate is relatively clear—to provide a corrective experience for someone who presents himself as psychologically impaired. By contrast, participant expectancies and fantasies about training vary much more widely. By comparison with the therapist, the trainer's mandate is relatively ambiguous. For example, some trainers view the group experience primarily as a vehicle to produce increased awareness of interactional processes to be employed in social or organizational settings. However, currently, some others dismiss this goal as trivial in favor of an expressive or "existential" experience. Both approaches are similar in that they require a participant-observer role for the trainee. Yet, the emphasis upon rational and emotional elements differs in these approaches, and this difference makes for divergent experiences. The problem is that there is no way for a participant to know in advance, much less to appraise, intentions of trainers, processes of groups, or their consequences for him. It is not feasible to explain these because training, like psychotherapy, depends upon events that counter the participant's accustomed expectations in order to have maximum impacts. Since it is inimical to training to preprogram participant or process, the nature of the training experience depends more than anything upon the particular translations, intentions, and interventions the trainer makes. This makes it imperative for the trainer to be first of all clear about his own intentions and goals.

Training has begun to attract the participation of more psychologically disturbed persons in recent years—a higher proportion of more frustrated individuals seeking personal release or solutions. Correspondingly, there is a larger supply of inadequately prepared persons who do training. To my knowledge, only the National Training Laboratories—Institute of Applied Behavioral Science has given systematic consideration to the training of leaders, but even its accredited trainers are not all prepared to deal with the range of expectations and pathologies currently exhibited by some participants. Some people who are inadequately prepared are suggesting to other people what they feel, how to express their feelings, and interpreting how others respond to them. Some, equally poorly prepared persons, are engaged in applying training to social action and to institutions. Recently, it has come to my attention that there are inadequately prepared trainers who lead student groups on college campuses without supervision. Several eye-witness accounts of these groups suggest that highest value is placed upon intensity of emotionality and on dramatic confrontations. Screening of participants is virtually unknown and follow-up investigation of the effects of these groups is unheard of. Their leaders are usually individuals who have participated in only one or two experiences themselves. Most disturbing of all, there is no sign that these leaders are aware of or concerned about their professional limitations. I think it must be recognized that it will be difficult to restrain poorly prepared individuals from practicing training in the absence of a clear statement of standards of training, trainer preparation, and the publication of a code of training ethics. (An antiprofessional bias is very popular just now, as we all know, and training fits nicely the image of "participative decision making.") Unfortunately, accredited and competent trainers have done little to deter the belief that training requires little preparation and is universally applicable. I do not exempt the National Training Laboratories from responsibility in this regard.

"Adequate preparation" should be spelled out. One would wish to avoid jurisdictional protectionism, although a degree in a recognized educative or therapeutic discipline is certainly one index of responsible preparation. For work with the public, trainers should have had, in addition to a recognized advanced degree in one of the "helping professions," background preparation in personality dynamics, a knowledge of psychopathology as well as preparation in group dynamics, social psychology, and sociology. They should also have had an internship and extensive supervised experience.

It should be recognized that it is difficult, if not impossible, to do effective screening in order to prevent the participation of persons for whom training is inappropriate. One reason is that it is almost impossible to prevent false assertions about one's mental status on application forms. It is also true that it is difficult to assess the precise effects of training upon a particular individual. It could be argued that short-range discomfort might be followed by long-range benefits. Probably the most important step that could be taken immediately would be the elimination of promotional literature that suggests by implication that training is, indeed, "psychotherapy," and that it can promise immediate results. Why has such a step not been taken until now? I suggest that one reason is that currently many trainers do indeed view training as a form of therapy even though they do not explicitly invite psychologically troubled applicants. They do not wish to screen out those who do seek psychotherapy. But this reluctance to exclude such persons makes it almost certain that psychologically impaired individuals will be attracted in large numbers to training as a therapy.

More serious is the fact that there is little evidence on which to base a therapeutic effectiveness claim. To me it seems indefensible that advertising for training should be as seductive as it is in offering hope for in-depth changes of personality or solutions to marital problems in the light of present inadequate evidence that such changes or solutions do occur. Greater candor is necessary about the needs that are being addressed by the newer training forms. A legitimate case could perhaps be made for the temporary alleviation of loneliness that is unfortunately so widespread in contemporary urban and industrial life, but the training experience as a palliative is neither learning about group processes nor is it profound personal change. Such candor is obviously a first requisite in face of the fact that some training brochures used in promotion literally trumpet claims of various enduring benefits. I suggest that immediate steps need to be taken to investigate these claims, to reconsider the implementation of screening procedures, set up and publicize accreditation standards, and monitor promotional methods in order to safeguard the public's interest and professional integrity.

Ethical Questions Related to the Process of Training Groups

Being a trainer is an exciting role and function. Being looked to for leadership of one kind or another and being depended upon for guidance is a very "heady" thing as every psychotherapist knows. On the other hand, training, in its beginnings, was based on the idea that participation and involvement on the part of all the members of the group would lead to the development of a democratic society in which personal autonomy and group responsibility were important goals. The trainer had only to facilitate this evolution. Personal exertion of power and influence, overt or covert, was naturally a significant issue for study and learning in group after group. Evaluation of the trainer's influence attempts was crucial for learning about one's responses to authority. The trainer was indeed an influence, but the generally accepted commitment to objectification of his function made his behavior accessible to inquiry and even to modification. Correspondingly, experienced trainers have almost always been aware that the degree of influence they wield is disproportionately large; therefore they, themselves, tried to help the group understand the need for continual assessment of this factor. Awareness of this "transference" element has stimulated trainers in the past to emphasize group processes that would reveal its operations and effects.

However, with the advent of a more active and directing training function that includes trainer-based pressures upon participants to behave in specific ways, but without provision for monitoring of trainer practices, the "democratic" nature of the group interaction is subverted. More important is the fact that there is less possibility for participants to overtly evaluate the influences exerted upon them by the trainer. In some groups that emphasize emotional expressiveness, some trainers purposefully elicit aggressive and/or affectionate behaviors by modeling them and then by inviting imitation. Some even insist that members engage one another in physically aggressive or affectionate acts. Still others provide music to create an emotional experience. Such leadership intends to create certain emotional effects. It does so, however, without sufficient opportunity to work them through. Moreover, analytic or critical evaluation of such experiences would almost certainly be viewed as subversive of their aims.

It will be argued that participants willingly agree to these practices. The fact that the consumer seeks or agrees to these experiences does not justify them as ethically defensible or psychologically sound. It should be remembered that "the contract" is not between persons who have an equal understanding of the processes involved. It cannot be assumed that the participant really knows what he is letting himself in for. At the request of the trainer, and under pressure of group approval, some aggressive displays (e.g., slappings) or affectional displays (e.g., hugging) have occurred that some participants later came to view as indignities.

The question of group acquiescence involves a related point. A crucial element in the history of training was its stress upon genuine consensus. This emphasis was a deterrent to the domination of any single power figure or to the establishment of arbitrary group norms. Action and "decision" were painstakingly arrived at out of group interaction, consisting of increasingly candid exchanges. Influence could be exerted only under continuing group scrutiny and evaluation. Some trainers who are impelled to elicit expressiveness as a primary goal are also committed to democratic values; however, owing to their primary commitment to the significance of emotional expressiveness, they may employ their sensitivities and skills to achieving it in ways that are relatively subtle or even covert. When the participant is encouraged to experience and express strong emotions, the trainer's function in promoting these is often obscured. What is often *his* decision or initiative is presented as *group* initiative. In his recent book, Kelman (1968) has suggested that a group leader has the responsibility of making group members aware of his own operations and values. I find no fault with that suggestion; however, it is very difficult to accomplish this. It is made even more difficult, if I am correct, because some trainers may even have an interest in the group remaining *unaware* of their particular manipulations because they wish to sustain the illusion that it is the group's rather than their own personal decision that results in a particular emotional process. The intention may not be to deceive consciously. It is difficult for trainers to practice complete candor with their participants and yet to facilitate the processes of training for reasons I suggested above. Nevertheless, in the light of these questions, trainers should reexamine their own activities. It might be that aroused concern will lead established trainers to take the necessary steps to educate aspirants for professional status to a new sensitivity to these issues.

Learning and Experiential
Focuses

There are genuine differences in point of view and in emphasis between trainers. Some regard the emotional-experiential as the primary value in training. Others uphold a more cognitive emphasis, while recognizing that a high degree of emotional engagement is a vital part of training. For their part, participants are, more often than not, so emotionally involved as to be confused about just what it is that they are doing, feeling, or thinking at a given point in time. We know that participants slide back and forth between cognitive and affective experiencing of training. The participant must partially depend upon external sources for confirmation or disconfirmation. He looks to other members, but most of all to the trainer himself, for clarification. Surely, dependency plays a huge role, but it will not be destroyed by fiat. It is the responsibility of the trainer to make as clear as he can his own activities, his own view of what is significant, and to encourage exchanges of views among participants so that all can have the possibility of differential self-definition and orientation during the training process. This would help prevent a situation where inchoate and inarticulated pressures push individual participants beyond their comprehension.

In training, as in any other society, there are pressures of majority upon minority, of the many upon the one. Scapegoating, where recognized, would be objected to as demeaning whether it occurs as a means of inducing conformity or to build self-esteem. When the focus is upon group processes, it is often brought into the open, discussed, and countered. Where, however, the emphasis is purely on personal expressiveness, the same phenomenon may be used as a pressure rather than exposed. The implicit demand for emotionality and emphasis upon nonverbal communication even makes it more difficult to identify scapegoating when it occurs in such groups.

Ethical Issues and Evaluations

Participants sometimes come to training under "threat" of evaluation. The implications of a refusal to participate by an employee, a subordinate, or a student have not been sufficiently studied. I recall one instance where an employee of a highly sensitive security agency was sent for training. His anxious, conflicted, and disturbed response to training norms of "trust" and "openness" were not only understandable but, in retrospect, predictable. True, the commitment to maintain confidentiality was honored; nevertheless, should his participation have been solicited or even permitted? Evaluation as a participant concern is unavoidable, despite protestations and reassurances to the contrary. Training of trainers should emphasize the professional's ethical responsibility in these matters, but it will not obviate these concerns. The increase in unaccredited and marginally prepared trainers must increase them. It is difficult for most people to monitor their own tendencies to gossip or inform. Especially if the trainer is also an evaluator of participants, he cannot really compartmentalize the impressions he gets of behavior in training, from other data that he has about the participants. Perhaps it would help to make everyone aware of this fact. At least the "risk" then becomes explicit from everyone's point of view.

A diminution of risk was thought to be one of the major advantages of "stranger" groups where time-limited contact was thought to encourage a degree of candor and interpersonal experiment that was nominally proscribed. Obviously, this cannot be the case in groups where participants are related, classmates, or involved in the same company or agency. It should be recognized that it is almost impossible to assure confidentiality under such circumstances or to prevent "out of school" reports. Trainers need to be especially sensitive to this in preparing other trainers. For example, where graduate students are involved in training groups and have social or other connections with one another, or with those they observe, numerous possibilities for teaching the importance of professional detachment present themselves. Trainees should learn how important it is to avoid irresponsible behavior in order to maintain the confidence of participants, how vital it is to inhibit a desire for personal contact when they have a professional role to play. Essentially, they have the same problem that faces the fledgling psychotherapist in inhibiting his own curiosity and social impulse in order to fulfill a professional function. The necessary detachment emphasized here is yet another significant and ethically relevant area that emotional expressiveness as an end in itself does not articulate. Responsibility is taught and modeled. It should be as consciously done in training as in any other helping relationship.

Post-Training Ethical Issues

A strongly positive reaction to training more frequently than not impels the gratified participant to seek further training experiences. Unfortunately, almost as frequently he seeks to do training himself. After all, it appears relatively easy. The apparent power and emotional gratifications of the trainer seem very attractive. If steps in professional preparation in becoming a trainer are not better articulated, and closely wedded to the traditional helping professions, we shall soon have vast numbers of inadequate trainers who practice their newly discovered insights on others, in the naive conviction that they have all but mastered the skills involved in group processes and application to personal and social problems.

A final issue to which I wish to call your attention is that of posttraining contact with the participant. Participants are often dramatically affected by training. In some cases, trainer and group are mutually reluctant to end the group. In a recent case that came to my attention, my view is that the trainer was seduced, as it were, by the group's responsiveness to him. In turn, the participants were delighted by the trainer's continuing interest. Trainers must be aware of the powerful desire to sustain a relationship with them. Therefore, they must be clear at the outset what limits they propose for training. It is as important to be determinate about the termination point of training as about any other aspect of its conduct. Under the conditions of ambiguity and ambivalence of an "indeterminate" relationship, participants appear to be caught, as it were, midstream, uncertain as to the definition or possibilities of a relationship with this presumed expert upon whom they naturally depend for guidance and limit setting.

The questions that I have raised do not admit of a quick solution. They are ethical dilemmas. Steps to eliminate or ameliorate the grossest of them can be taken through awareness and self-monitoring. One practical step that I propose is the immediate creation of a commission by our professional organization to investigate training practices, standards of training preparation, and to recommend a code of ethics for accredited trainers. Research may help, but I doubt that it can come quickly enough to affect the increasing danger of the current and potentially still greater excesses in this area.

Sensitivity training is one of the most compelling and significant psychological experiences and vehicles for learning as well as a promising laboratory for the study of human relationships, dyadic, and group. It may be a superior device for personal and social change, even for amelioration or resolution of social conflict. However, it may also be abused or subverted into an instrument of unwarranted influence and ill-considered, even harmful, practices. The immediate attention of the profession is necessary to maintain its positive potential and correspondingly respectable standards of practice.

Reference

Kelman, H. C. *A time to speak—On human values and social research.* San Francisco: Jossey-Bass, 1968.

Editor's Comment. Lakin says that it is "inimical to training to preprogram participant or process" in sensitivity groups; yet he realizes that under such conditions it is quite easy for a trainer to manipulate the laboratory participants in order to gratify his own needs for power and influence. I would challenge Lakin's statement or at least make a distinction between participant preparation or instruction and preprogramming. If today's laboratory populations are less educated and sophisticated than yesterday's, then perhaps we have a responsibility to instruct prospective participants in what to expect in a laboratory—in terms of the growthful possibilities as well as the dangers. In my experience, the general nature of the laboratory experience—goals, nature of leadership, general kinds of interactions expected of members, cautions—can be revealed without lessening the impact of the experience. I see no reason why high visibility cannot be a dimension of the training experience, especially if it is seen as a means of lessening manipulation and other dangers. For instance, it has already been suggested that one way of lessening the danger of overcontrol on the part of the trainer or facilitator is to state from the beginning that one of the goals of the laboratory is the diffusion of leadership. A good trainer can effectively "teach" his skills in a variety of ways. He should receive a good deal of his gratification from seeing the individual participants come to share in the leadership function of the group. The good trainer is one who is aware of all the issues discussed by Lakin and who is willing to discuss them with the group as the need arises. The good trainer oversees the group, not in order to control the participants, but to protect their dignity and freedom. If the group is not a "stranger" group, then perhaps the trainer should broach the issue of confidentiality. Some nonstranger groups have no problem with confidentiality. Others do. The good facilitator can spot problems and encourage the group to deal with them just as he can challenge the group to move away from pseudo-problems and get down to the work of the group.

The problem of training effective trainers is a most critical one. Many people criticize the lack of good trainers, but few people seem to be willing to set up good trainer programs. Unlike Lakin, I do not think that a trainer need have an advanced degree in the behavioral sciences. Indeed, there are those with advanced degrees whom I would not let near groups under my responsibility. If we are serious about using nonprofessionals as therapists and as trainers, then we have to establish well-supervised programs for them. If we do not, they will become self-educated trainers and it will do little good for us to sit on the sidelines and lament.

Sensitivity Training as a Medium for Personal Growth and Improved Interpersonal Relationships

Jack R. Gibb

Editor's Introduction. Of the several reviews of the research on sensitivity training, the following report by Gibb is, for our purposes, the most comprehensive. It has a more direct focus on interpersonal-growth issues than the other reviews; it deals positively with the phenomenon of "growth through group interaction"; and, particularly important in view of the startling proliferation of group techniques, it is the most recent review available. Gibb's article is both sobering and stimulating. It should temper the ardor of those who believe that salvation lies in laboratory training, but it should also stimulate more interesting and more relevant investigation of training groups.

Abstract: The growth of sensitivity training as a method for effecting personal and interpersonal change is noted and the principal varieties of sensitivity training are described and distinguished. These types include methods oriented toward creativity-growth, marathons, emergent groups, authenticity groups, T groups, programmed groups, micro-experiences, inquiry groups, embedded groups, discussion groups and instructional groups. Studies on the effectiveness of sensitivity training are reviewed, and judged in terms of attainment of training goals such as increase in sensitivity to self and others, management of feelings, management of motivations, development of functional attitudes toward self and others, and development of interdependent behavior. Implications for practitioners are discussed.

The growth of sensitivity training throughout the world in the past two decades has become a notable cultural phenomenon. The method has become a basic element in programs of teacher training, therapy, executive development, personal growth, group counselling, sex education, community mental health, treatment of drug addicts and alcoholics, family counseling, organizational

Reprinted from *Interpersonal Development,* 1970, 1(1), pp. 6-31. Used with the permission of the publisher and author.

change, recreation, social work, vocational rehabilitation, and formal education. Highly controversial, it has been praised as a panacea for all social ills and damned as a dangerous form of brainwashing. The dramatic applicability of the method to these varied fields has stimulated many innovations in methodology and considerable research on its effectiveness in producing personal growth, improvement of interpersonal relationships, and organizational change. Since the method was used by the National Training Laboratories in 1947, something like three-quarters of a million participants have had an intensive experience in some kind of sensitivity training group. Indicative of the potential impact of such training upon contemporary life is the fact that the large proportion of these participants have been people in responsible roles in industry, government, the churches, the schools, and volunteer organizations.

It is the purpose of this article to describe and classify the wide range of methods used in sensitivity training, to survey and evaluate the research on the effectiveness of these methods, and to suggest some generalizations that hopefully might lead to further research and innovation in this critical field.

Varieties of Sensitivity Training

Stemming from the original 'T group' (*Bradford, Gibb and Benne,* 1964), a cross-pollination among a variety of professional disciplines has produced diversity and richness of method. Table 1 presents a tentative classification of current methods, ranging from those at the top of the table which most nearly approximate therapy to those at the bottom which most nearly approximate formal education.

Table 1.
Varieties of Sensitivity Training Groups

Method	Primary Aim	Definitive Activities or Characteristics	Reference
1. Creativity-growth	Awareness Creativity Release of potential	Induced experiences designed to expand human awareness and create personal growth	Otto and Mann (1968)
2. Marathon	Greater intimacy	Uninterrupted interpersonal intimacy and depth relationships	Stoller (1968)
3. Emergent	Personal growth Group growth	Absence of leader; non-programmed, unpredictable, emergent activities	Gibb and Gibb (1968b)

Table 1.
Varieties of Sensitivity Training Groups (Continued)

Method	Primary Aim	Definitive Activities or Characteristics	Reference
4. Authenticity	Openness Authentic encounter	Interventions and experiences focussed upon openness and human encounter	*Bugental* (1965)
5. T groups	Personal competence Group effectiveness Organizational effectiveness	Focus on here and now experiences, and on group processes	*Bradford, Gibb and Benne* (1964)
6. Programmed	Personal growth, and/or competence Group effectiveness Organizational effectiveness	Experiences initiated and/or directed by absent leaders and planners with various kinds of instrumentation	*Berzon and Solomon* (1966)
7. Micro-experience	Interpersonal skills Group effectiveness Organizational effectiveness	Limited time (2 to 20 hours; 1 to 2-1/2 days); restricted depth or range; increased pre-structuring	*Bradford, Gibb and Lippitt* (1956)
8. Inquiry	Skills of inquiry Group effectiveness System effectiveness	Data-gathering, quasi-structured experiences Focus on explicit and predictable individual and group learnings, skills, attitudes	*Miles* (1965)
9. Embedded	Team effectiveness Organizational effectiveness	Training experience embedded in sequential and continuous organization-based program of inputs, data-gathering, and experiences	*Argyris* (1962) *Friedlander* (1968)
10. Discussion	Knowledge, insight Improved interpersonal relations	Some blending of group discussion, case method, demonstrations, exercises, simulations, and theory inputs	*Hacon* (1961)

Table 1.
Varieties of Sensitivity Training Groups (Continued)

Method	Primary Aim	Definitive Activities or Characteristics	Reference
11. Instructional	Knowledge, insight inter-personal relations	Instructions by lectures, demonstrations, discus-sions, and readings; focus on instructing and theory input	*Hacon* (1961)

Although there is great overlap among activities in 'therapy groups' and 'training groups', most practitioners make distinctions between the two (e.g. *Bradford, Gibb and Benne*, 1964; *Schein and Bennis*, 1965). Training is usually characterized by the following conditions:

1. Focus more upon analysis of here-and-now data perceptually available in the group rather than upon historical data or upon external organizational or family life.

2. Focus more upon personal growth and increased human potential than upon remedial or corrective treatment.

3. Focus more upon the available interpersonal data than upon analysis of unconscious or motivational material.

4. Focus more upon group processes, the functioning of the group, and the inter-member interactions than upon leader-patient relationships.

5. Focus more upon trying out new behavior in the training group than upon achieving new insight or new motivation.

6. The immediate and primary intent of the leader is to improve effectiveness or change behavior of normal people in the organizational or natural-group setting, rather than to relieve distress or to change personality or character structure.

7. Participants usually see themselves as normal people attempting to function more effectively at the interpersonal level as group or organization members rather than as sick people seeking treatment to relieve suffering.

Although great changes are taking place in the classroom as well as in the training group, it is possible to distinguish sensitivity training from education. Three distinctions are usually made in the literature:

a) Training has an explicit focus upon behavior change, whereas education usually emphasizes changes in knowledge and insight.

b) Training places a focus upon 'process' rather than upon the 'content' of group interaction. The central activity of training groups is the analysis of persons *qua* persons and of process *qua* process. That is, groups focus upon the available interactions, leadership, feelings, structural patterns, perceptions and other dynamics of the 'here and now'. When group methods are used in the classroom the focus is usually upon content and the use of such participatory 'activities' as field trips, case methods, group discussions, seminars, simulations, and visual aids. The methods classified as 'discussion' and 'instructional' in the table are in the borderland between education and sensitivity training.

c) In sensitivity training there is usually a greater concern with affective and conative processes than with ideational processes. While in each case leaders may speak of working with the 'whole person', for instance, the trainer is more likely to concentrate upon feelings and interactions among group members and the educator upon ideas and cognitive problems.

Complicating the attempt to classify variations of sensitivity training is the fact that trainers continually experiment with training designs, intervention styles and new techniques. Trainers adapt to the purposes and plans of the persons and organizations sponsoring the training. Trainers learn from each other and from participants, who are usually encouraged to innovate. In the following pages an attempt is made to distinguish among eleven more or less distinct patterns of sensitivity training.

Creativity-Growth Groups

Particularly during the past decade, stimulated by humanistic trends in psychology and religion, a dramatic surge of activities has been directed at increasing human potential and releasing creativity. This 'growth potential movement' has been sparked by the phenomenal rise of 'growth centers' such as the Esalen Institute at Big Sur, California; Aureon Institute at Tarrytown, New York; Shalal at Vancouver, B.C.; Oasis and Ontos in Chicago, Illinois; and Kopavi in Minneapolis, Minnesota. There are 106 other such centers at current count. The quality of their professional leadership varies greatly, ranging from clinical psychologists and philosophers to interested laymen and dilettanti with no professional training. The methodology is an innovative and fermentative blending of such sources as somatopsychic medicine, interpretative dance, psychodrama, clinical psychology, yoga, and psychiatry. The activities include some kind of integration or exploratory mixing of bio-energetic analysis, meditation, calligraphy, kinetic-theatre, nude marathons, finger painting, breathing therapy, psychedelic experiences, hypnotism, sensory awakening, transcendent philosophy and whatever creative impulses might occur to the trainers or participants.

The excitement generated among many competent professionals in clinical psychology and psychiatry suggests that new frontiers are being explored in a micro-environment that permits experimentation, innovation, and freedom from the usual restraints of university, clinic, or private office. Many growth center activities are more controversial than the more 'respectable' forms of sensitivity training and create some concern among professional societies responsible for maintaining the standards of therapeutic and quasi-therapeutic practice. There is as yet no published research available on the effects of these activities.

Marathon Groups

The marathon format was devised to intensify the effects of the training group experience. The original method, devised by George Bach and Frederick Stoller as a method of therapy and applied by Bach and Jack Gibb to a variety of organizational-development programs, uses uninterrupted and deeply personal contact for periods of from 24 to 26 hours (*Stoller*, 1968a). The usual professional impression is that sustained marathon experience is far more powerful as a change-inductive agent than is a comparable experience spread over longer time in periodic training sessions.

Although the method has generated modifications in many sensitivity training programs, as yet no evaluation research is available in the published literature.

Several theories have been advanced to account for the apparent power of the method. It has been hypothesized that fatigue generates intensity of interaction and reduction of inhibition to disclosure; that persons who spend continuing energy in facade maintenance are physiologically incapable of maintaining the energy over marathon distance and that sustained interpersonal depth contact creates intrinsic pressures toward self-disclosure.

Emergent Groups

As *Mowrer* (1964) and others have pointed out, there is a current rapid rise in the number of quasi-therapeutic and training groups that meet without appointed leaders or that meet with lay volunteers who have no special professional training as therapists or as trainers. As *Gibb* (1964, *Gibb and Gibb*, 1968a, b) and others have demonstrated, essentially the same processes occur in these 'emergent' groups as occur in groups with skilled professional leaders (*Berzon and Solomon*, 1966; *Hanson, Rothaus, Johnson and Lyle*, 1966). Groups sponsored by Alcoholics Anonymous, the Laymen's Movement, and Synanon, for example, are thought by some professionals who consult with the programs to have similar effects to those that accrue from sensitivity training groups led by professionals. Unfortunately, the evidence is clinical and impressionistic and there have been no studies of the effectiveness of these programs. There is, however, good evidence that sensitivity training in groups without leaders produce changes in behavior of group members (*Gibb and Gibb*, 1952; *Johnson, Hanson, Rothaus, Morton, Lyle and Moyer*, 1965). Leaderless groups

Cautions, Research

have become part of the standard methodology of team training in industry, religious organizations, and youth organizations (*Gibb and Gibb,* 1968a; *Davis,* 1967).

Authenticity Groups

Particularly during the past decade there has been a growing emphasis in therapy, management, philosophy, and religion upon authenticity, openness, transparency, encounter, and confrontation. In response, there has been a rise of quasi-therapeutic sensitivity training groups that focus on openness of communication of the person with himself and with others. Sometimes called 'growth groups' or 'encounter groups', these experiences are an extension of methods found to be effective in dyadic therapy and are, in a sense, 'therapy for normals'. Leaders, often coming to training groups from experience or training in individual or group therapy, rely upon time-tested methods of feeling expression, personal feedback, mirroring, role playing, confrontation, and fantasy analysis. There is no available published research on training in these groups.

T Groups

The classic form of sensitivity training is the 'T group' (*Bradford, Gibb and Benne,* 1964). In the first decade after their invention by the National Training Laboratories in 1947, these groups followed a fairly clear and consistent model. The group trainer was a process observer and reporter. He was a relatively inactive leader who attempted to keep attention on process rather than content and to keep interaction in the 'here and now', continually dealing with perceptions and feelings that members generated about each other within the group setting. Progressively the model has been broadened to include a wide variety of 'intervention styles', theories of leadership and behavior change, and most of the other methods discussed in this chapter.

From the beginning, the practitioners of T-group training have been strongly research oriented. Eighty-nine of the 106 studies reviewed here have been performed on T-groups, 43 of which have gathered data on the standard heterogeneous groups in the relatively isolated 'cultural islands' sponsored by the National Training Laboratories at Bethel, Maine, or at one of the regional centers.

Programmed Groups

Modelled after programmed learning and machine teaching concepts, several experimenters have shown that tapes, training booklets, phonograph records, and data-gathering instruments can serve in part as functional leader surrogates.

Professional trainers, through the use of such training tools, can guide the goal-formation, discussion content, and directional focus of the groups along lines suggested by their training theories.

The effectiveness of programmed sensitivity training has been well demonstrated. Research at the Human Development Institute (*Berlin*, 1964), at the Western Behavioral Sciences Institute (*Berzon and Solomon*, 1966; *Berzon, Pious and Farson*, 1963), with the Management Grid model (*Blake, Mouton, Barnes and Greiner*, 1964; *Greiner*, 1965), and with hospitalized patients (*Johnson, Hanson, Rothaus, Morton, Lyle and Moyer*, 1965; *Rothaus, Johnson, Hanson and Lyle*, 1966) has clearly indicated the feasibility of doing programmed group training.

There is no clear evidence as yet to indicate differential effects of programmed and non-programmed groups. The indication is very strong that they are as effective as groups led by professionals. Criticisms of these methods center around the potential dangers and effects of manipulation of the group by trainers. In favor of the use of such methods are considerations such as the following: the potential economy of the designs if they prove to be as effective as groups with professionals, the inventiveness and adequacy of the theories underlying the designs, and the relative ease with which evaluative research can be related to training objectives.

Micro-Experience Groups

In order to bring sensitivity training to a larger group of participants, many attempts have been made to abbreviate the experience in some way, while still maintaining some degree of effectiveness. The classic week-end laboratory (*Bradford, Gibb and Lippitt*, 1956) was devised to bring the Bethel-type experience to members of organizations who were unwilling to devote work time to the training. Due to the appreciable attrition of effects, particularly when the training time is brief, a critical question confronting training designers is whether such truncated training is of sufficient strength to warrant doing at all. Sometimes such training simply is given for orientation and information.

Practitioners have devised a number of 'micro-lab' methods which present critical elements of a total group experience in a series of three- to twelve-minute segments, in periods of from one to five hours. While favorable reactions are reported by participants, we have no clear evidence of the effectiveness of these abbreviated experiences.

Inquiry Groups

One group of T-group practitioners has moved in the direction of training for personal growth and other quasi-therapeutic outcomes. This has led to the invention and enrichment of the methods mentioned above. Another group of practitioners has moved toward providing more structure, focussing upon the direct practice of specified interpersonal skills, the integration of personality theory into the experience, and the use of training *designs* such as simulation, role playing, data collection, structured practice sessions, and demonstrations. In what we may call 'inquiry groups', emphasis is upon attaining skills of inquiry, problem solving, data-gathering, diagnosing group forces, receiving help, and giving and receiving influence. The effectiveness of such designs has been greatly improved by recent advances in machine processing of data, in integration of research instruments into training designs, in the use of video-tapes as feedback tools (*Stoller*, 1968b), and in the use of expressive behavior and non-verbal communication.

Embedded Groups

The inquiry group methods have been particularly useful in introducing sensitivity training into organizational settings. The face validity of such training is high. The explicit goal is expressed in terms familiar to executives and administrators: improvement of human relations and management skills.

Experiences in the past decade have led practitioners to embed training in the organization, to integrate training aims with personnel and line practices, and to make sensitivity training one of several events in a program of planned organizational change. Thus, change programs might include testing, consulting, personal therapy, changed personnel practices, architectural design, reorganization of the socio-technical system, and changed production technology. The program is usually system-oriented and clearly focussed on organizational change rather than directly on personal growth or therapeutic changes, which, if they occur, would be by-products of the design. *Friedlander* (1967) describes the thinking behind one variety of embedded design.

Several studies (*Bowers and Soar*, 1961; *Clark and Miles*, 1954; *Khanna*, 1968; *Schmuck*, 1968) have reported on work directed toward modification of an educational system. Some studies have evaluated efforts to change personnel practices and increase production in an industrial system (e.g. *Argyris*, 1962; *Greiner*, 1965; *Nath*, 1964).

Discussion Groups

Sensitivity training has been blended with content-oriented programs that make use of simulations, structured exercises, case method, and other teaching techniques aimed at improved interpersonal relations. In the purist sense, these activities are not 'sensitivity training', but many practitioners are fusing process and content in such a way that the concept of process-focus that was definitive of sensitivity training a decade ago is greatly expanded in current practice. Some blending of demonstration with action research on human-relations issues is being enriched by quick data processing methods.

Instructional Groups

'Instructional groups' focus on cognitive learnings or aim for integration of existing personality and group theory with experiential learning. In the classic T group, learnings emerged as personal and collective inductions from relatively unpredictable experiences that were illuminated by process orientation. In an instructional group the learning situation is constructed to predispose the emergence of phenomena that will illustrate the leader's theory. As theory becomes more precise and more elegant it is likely that some emergence of models of learning groups will occur that will blend classic T groups with more structured experiential settings.

Effectiveness of Sensitivity Training

In spite of the frequent mention in the general psychological literature of the relative lack of research on sensitivity training, the quantity and quality of available research is surprisingly high. In preparing this evaluation of sensitivity training we found 219 formal and informal research reports. Included in the bibliography at the end of the article is a listing of 106 studies that contain quantitative data relevant to an appraisal of the effects of sensitivity training upon interpersonal effectiveness. Reports were omitted if the primary emphasis was on organizational outcomes, if the report was not yet available in a standard publication, or if the data were largely clinical or impressionistic.[1] Twenty-four doctoral dissertations from 13 different graduate schools

---

[1] The evaluation of research in this section of the article is a condensation and reorganization of a more comprehensive review by the author of the literature, to appear in a forthcoming *Handbook of Psychotherapy*, edited by A. Bergin and S. Garfield, to be published by Wiley in 1970.

and a wide variety of disciplines are included. The great range of disciplines illustrates graphically the interdisciplinary nature of the impact of sensitivity training. The bibliography includes seven earlier reviews of the work on sensitivity training, each of which has a special emphasis and none of which attempts a comprehensive or complete survey of the effects of sensitivity training (*Bradford*, 1953; *Buchanan*, 1965; *Bunker*, 1965; *Campbell and Dunnette*, 1968; *Hampden-Turner*, 1966; *House*, 1967; *Stock*, 1964), and two annotated bibliographies (*Durham and Gibb*, 1960; *Knowles*, 1967).

Sensitivity

Sensitivity training is aimed at inducing greater sensitivity to self, to the feelings and perceptions of other people, and to the general interpersonal environment. Sensitivity is seen as an input process involving greater awareness of the feelings and perceptions of others. It also has an output component, aspects of which are described variously as availability of self, transparency, openness, authenticity, or spontaneity. Most trainers have placed primary emphasis upon observation and feedback of data on group processes, and accuracy in perceiving 'social reality'. The first doctoral dissertation on sensitivity-training groups (*Kelley*, 1948), for instance, found that changes in perceptions of trainers were a function of the self-assertiveness of the trainer and of his ability to fulfill the needs of individual participants.

An early goal of trainers was to help participants to understand and predict the feelings and reactions of others. Research has demonstrated that the accuracy of such predictions can be improved through developing more valid subcultural stereotypes, greater sensitivity to assumed similarities, or more consistent response sets (*Smith*, 1966).

Seventeen studies report data on the influence of training on sensitivity to people and processes. *Bass* (1962a) found, on the basis of an incomplete-sentence questionnaire, that participants became more sensitive to interpersonal relationships seen in the film 'Twelve Angry Men'. Using a Problem Analysis questionnaire, *Oshry and Harrison* (1966) found that after training, participants saw 'clearer connections between how well interpersonal needs are met and how well the work gets done'. *Miles, Cohen and Whidman* (1959) found a consistent improvement in 'sensitivity to feelings', but not in sensitivity to other aspects of the social situation. Studies report increases, after training, in sensitivity to rankings of problem solving technologies (*Dietterich*, 1961), in seeing other members in more interpersonal terms (*Harrison*, 1962), in more frequent use of interpersonal concepts to describe associates (*Harrison*, 1966), in sensitivity toward social factors in the interpersonal situation (*Kelley and Pepitone*, 1952), in sensitivity toward affective states in comparison to thought processes (*Ford*, 1964), and in sensitivity toward social factors in the work situation (*Blansfield*, 1962).

Wedel (1957), *Gage and Exline* (1953), and *Bennis, Burke, Cutter, Harrington and Hoffman* (1957) all found no change in the ability of participants to predict responses of other participants. *Lohman, Zenger and Weschler* (1959) found that participants were better able after training to predict the leader's answers on a Gordon Personal Profile. However, participants took the same test twice and there was no control group. *Sikes* (1964) found that participants were more accurate in predicting the responses of other members of a test discussion group than were members of a control group that had no training. They predicted how members ranked others in the discussion group. The results, however, were not confirmed in a second study of a different training group.

The most promising data on the question are provided in a study by *Bunker* (1965). He confirms other findings that when changes do occur as a result of sensitivity training they are likely to occur first in changes in sensitivity. In analyzing data from a sample of 341 participants in two-week training programs, he found the greatest differences in the sensitivity-input variables: increased openness, greater 'tolerance for new information', and a greater acceptance of difference.

Several theorists have suggested that any permanent changes in new behavior must be preceded by greater sensitivity to self. While clinical evidence for change in self-perception is frequent, hard data are difficult to come by. *Wedel* (1957) and *Dietterich* (1961) each report no significant change in ability of participants to predict how they are seen by others. Three studies (*Gibb*, 1953; *Burke and Bennis*, 1961; *Carson and Lakin*, 1963) report a statistically significant increase, after training, in the ability of participants to predict how they are seen by other participants in a ranking or in a semantic differential measure. In somewhat less precise measures, others report greater insight into own role (*Valiquet*, 1964), increase in awareness of reactions of others to self (*Blansfield*, 1962), awareness of own role in his own interpersonal problems (*Culbert*, 1966; 1968) and increased self-awareness using a Problem Expression Scale (*Clark and Culbert*, 1965).

Sensitivity has been measured by means of attitude scales. *Haiman* (1963) found that experimental subjects were more 'open-minded'. *D. R. Bunker* (1965) and *Oshry and Harrison* (1966), among others, have found that those who are most open to ideas and to expression of feelings learn most from sensitivity training.

In spite of the high interest in the output side of sensitivity among theorists in a variety of fields, there is surprisingly little evidence of increases in spontaneity, authenticity, and transparency. *Massarik and Carlson* (1960) found no statistically significant differences in scores on a California Psychological Inventory. The small differences they did find are in the predicted direction of increased spontaneity and less use of control. In the following section it will be seen that there is some evidence that training leads to greater ease in expressing feelings, and this may be the basis for greater spontaneity. *Gold* (1967) found no statistically significant changes, comparing experimental with control groups, in reactions to the Jourard self-disclosure questionnaires given three months after training. In the *Bunker* (1965) studies mentioned above it is notable that there is no significant improvement in the 'sending' side of communication, but that there were significant improvements in the 'receiving' component.

Managing Feelings

The management of feelings has been a central aim of trainers, particularly those of the personal-growth wing. Trainers speak of such outcomes as awareness of own feelings; acceptance by self of the feeling component in one's own actions and speech ('owning' one's feelings), consonance between feelings and behavior, clarity of expression of feelings, and integration of emotionality into various life processes. There seems little doubt that training arouses intense emotions. This fact has contributed to the growing controversy surrounding the field.

The University of Chicago researchers working with Herbert Thelen have made the most significant contributions to our understanding of the development of emotionality in the T group. *Ben-Zeev* (1958b) found, for instance, that members of T-groups who participated with those they liked showed a tendency on a Bionic projective test to express warmth and friendliness and to inhibit expressions of hostility and anger. *Ben-Zeev* (1958a) was able to predict conditions under which work will be least suppressed and emotionality most suppressed. *Lieberman* (1958d) studied the emotional predispositions to fight, withdraw, pair, or be dependent, and composed groups on the basis of these Bionic patterns. He found that members whose emotional habits were closely attuned to the prevailing group atmosphere seemingly had little pressure or opportunity to change. When behavior changes did occur in participants they tended to occur in areas where an individual's affect was aroused, and where a person's predispositions were counter to the prevailing group atmosphere.

Bass (1962b) had group members check adjectives designating different moods at each of five different times during a ten-day training period. He found statistically significant trends in the development of four of the nine moods studied. Several studies indicate that feelings thus aroused are the most salient stimuli in the group situation, and that changes in sensitivity, if they occur, take place in reference to feelings (*Bunker and Knowles,* 1967; *Harrison,* 1966). *Gibb, Smith and Roberts* (1955) provide data that indicate that defensive feelings that were inadequately 'managed' are associated with reduction of task efficiency in an interdependent work situation. *Gibb and Gibb* (1952) found that training subjects, when placed as unknowns in test work groups, were rated by experienced observers as having higher 'general emotional adjustment'. *Foster* (1958) was able to make predictions from observed data on how participants managed affect in role playing. *Argyris* (1965b) found evidence that participants, after training, received higher ratings on the tendency to 'own' one's feelings.

Managing Motivations

Some theorists hypothesize that the key to permanent behavior change lies in basic changes in the motivational structure. The training literature refers to such hoped-for motivational outcomes as self-actualization, awareness of own motives, clear communication of one's own motives to others, self determination, commitment, greater energy level, inner-directedness, and becoming. Changes in motivations can be inferred from other changes reported in the studies. Direct measures have been few.

Kassarjian (1965) used a forced choice questionnaire to measure changes in inner-directedness and outer-directedness and found no significant differences following training. *Boyd and Elliss* (1962) used a scale assessing the degree to which a person assumed responsibility for his own work situations. They found that both an increase and a decrease in motivation to take personal responsibility were associated with on-the-job changes. *Livingston* (1951) found that motivation in training groups was influenced by perceived structure, and that one's perceived power and influence was dependent upon the emergent structure in the group.

Greiner (1965) reports a 24% increase in number of supervisors who described their work groups as more highly motivated toward greater effort following a Management Grid laboratory using instrumented groups. Supervisors initiated more activities and took greater risks. In a design particularly focussed upon encouraging participants to 'take charge of their own lives', *Byrd* (1967) found changes in greater risk taking, greater variability in actions, and emergent feelings of responsibility.

In view of the centrality of self-generating impulses in many theories of personal growth, it is likely that research in this area will be fostered particularly by the creativity-growth trainers.

Functional Attitudes Toward Self

Practitioners mention acceptance of self, self-esteem, congruity of actual self and ideal self, and feelings of confidence as potential positive outcomes of training. The research evidence is fairly clear that such changes do occur in sensitivity training.

Inasmuch as investigators show that increase of congruence is a function of increase in positive view of the self rather than of a change in view of the ideal self, change in degree of congruence can be interpreted as a change in self-esteem. Several studies indicate, that, following training, such congruence is increased due to changes in the perceived actual self (*G. L. Bunker*, 1961; *Burke and Bennis*, 1961; *Gassner, Gold and Snadowsky*, 1964; *Grater*, 1959; *Peters*, 1966). *Gassner, Gold and Snadowsky* (1964), however, found similar differences in the control group. *Burke and Bennis* (1961) found significant differences, but did not use a control group. An earlier study by *Bennis, Burke, Cutter, Harrington and Hoffman* (1957) showed no change following training. *Lohman, Zenger and Weschler* (1959) predicted that students would see themselves as 'more adequate' after training, and found no significant differences in the experimental group.

G. L. Bunker (1961) used a Hilden Q-sort to measure changes in self and ideal concepts. He found a significant change in self-concept following group training in two-hour sessions twice a week over a period of sixteen weeks. *Peters* (1966) reports a significant convergence in semantic differential tests of self-concept and ideal concept, with no such convergence in control groups not taking training. *Zimet and Fine* (1955) found an increase in positive attitudes toward the self. Administrators reported self-concept changes in the positive direction in the study by *Clark and Miles* (1954). Particularly important is the *Bunker and Knowles* (1967) finding that significant changes in observer ratings of self-confidence were produced by two weeks of training and reached even greater levels of significance after three weeks of training. Perhaps the surprising finding is that the relative short periods of training studied by other investigators produced any changes at all in presumably enduring concepts of self.

Sherwood (1962, 1965) sheds some light on the dynamics of such changes. He found evidence that self-concept is dependent upon a participant's subjectively held version of the peer group's actual rating of him, a rating which is in turn a function of objective public identity. These data became more important as peers became seen as more important, as the data became communicated to the participant in feedback, and as the participants became involved in the group. *G. L. Bunker* (1961) discovered that these perceptions play an important part in the potential of the group as a learning milieu. He reports that individuals ranked in the upper third of the group in perceived esteem will receive significantly more net positive feedback than will individuals ranked in the lower third in group-perceived esteem.

These self-perception changes may serve as a powerful mediator of other potential changes during group training. Making a detailed analysis of individuals undergoing group experiences, *Stock* (1952) found that the persons who made few changes in perceptions of self tended to make few changes in observable behavior. Those who did show more unstable perceptions of the self tended to make greater changes in behavior in the groups and following the group experience. These and similar data corroborate Lewin's hypotheses about the leverage effect of 'unfreezing'. It is likely that one's feelings about one's self must undergo some disruption in order for major growth to take place. *Johnson's* (1966) finding that no changes occurred in his groups other than in self-percept might indicate that he was dealing with significant 'early change' that must precede other effects.

The training group can serve as a powerful reference group for perceptual changes. *Lieberman* (1958b), for instance, found that stereotyped impressions of a 'good group member' were developed during group interaction, that these stereotypes influenced the ways that members saw themselves, and presumably influenced their attitudes toward items in the tests and their ratings of actual selves. These studies of phenomenological data indicate the great importance of such data in illuminating the conditions that must prevail in groups if they are to be optimally powerful as media for change.

Functional Attitudes Toward Others

Training is thought to produce such changes in attitudes as: decreased authoritarianism, reduced prejudice, greater acceptance of others, reduced regard for structure and control, and attitudes commensurate with interdependence theories of management, such as 'Theory Y' (*McGregor,* 1960), and 'participative management' (*Likert,* 1967). Significant trends, following training, toward less authoritarian, and more democratic and participatory attitudes are reported in many studies (*Argyris,* 1962; *Blake and Mouton,* 1966; *Bowers and Soar,* 1961; *Dietterich,* 1961; *Gassner, Gold and Snadowsky,* 1964; *Seashore,* 1955; *Spector,* 1958; *Taylor,* 1967; *Wedel,* 1957; *Zimet and Fine,* 1955). It is not surprising that participants would move in the direction of the values of the group leaders. Many pressures work in the same direction: identification with important and relevant authority figures, group forces toward conformity, desires to please the staff, knowledge of the 'correct' test answer, and basic shifts in underlying values. Of greater importance than test-score changes would be data on whether these changes in expressed attitudes were embedded in deeper attitudes of trust toward others and whether they were accompanied by behaviors consistent with the attitudes. There is some evidence that this is the case.

Rubin (1967a, b) showed that high acceptance of self was related to high acceptance of others in the laboratory setting. *Carron* (1964) found that group participants came to place a lower value on 'structure' and a higher value on 'consideration'. *Haiman* (1963) found a significant increase in more positive attitudes toward openmindedness. Most training groups provide a climate where data on feelings are given high visibility, and, in light of trainer attitudes and emphasis it is not surprising that *Ford* (1964) found that, after training, participants come to value feelings more than thoughts. This finding is consistent with a number of other studies.

Cautions, Research

Baumgartel and Goldstein (1967), using FIRO-B tests, showed that training lowered religious values, increased wanted control, and decreased wanted affection. *Smith* (1964) found that the disparity between own behavioral tendencies and those desired in others decreased after training. *Schutz and Allen* (1966) found significant changes in attitudes as measured by FIRO-B.

Several studies show no significant changes in measured attitudes. *Kernan* (1963) found no significant changes on the Ohio State Leadership Opinion Questionnaire. *Beer and Kleisath* (1967) found significant changes using this instrument, but used no control group. *Kassarjian* (1965) found no changes in inner-directedness and outer-directedness. *Zand, Steele and Zalkind* (1967) discovered no changes in attitudes toward 'Theory Y' (*McGregor,* 1960).

Interdependent Behavior

In one sense, no changes are of consequence that do not manifest themselves in changes in overt behavior on the job and in the home. Effective behavior is described variously, by experimenters and by practitioners, as interpersonal competence, task effectiveness, teamwork, being a 'good group member', democratic leadership, problem-solving effectiveness, or inter-dependence.

Several studies show that participants, after training, are rated by observers as performing more effectively. *Bunker and Knowles* (1967) report observer ratings of participants as having 'increased interdependence' and greater 'functional flexibility'. *Gibb* (1953) used a 'role flexibility' test, and discovered that people, after training, were rated as better able to take assigned roles and were rated as 'more sincere' than members of control groups. In the *Friedlander* (1967) study, members of work groups reported themselves on questionnaires given six months following training to have changed in higher participation, effectiveness in problem solving, and greater mutual influence.

Geitgey (1966) reported that trained nurses were significantly superior to a control group in four measures: patient evaluation of nursing care: instructor evaluation of nursing care; interpersonal relations with peers (peer rating), and interpersonal relations with instructors (ratings by instructors). The patient ratings of nursing care are especially crucial data, inasmuch as they are less likely to be influenced by knowledge that the nurses have participated in training groups. Two other studies (*Gibb and Gibb,* 1952; *Sikes,* 1964) report that experimental subjects did significantly better than control subjects in ratings of performance made several months after training. One limitation of the rating studies is that raters use all kinds of relatively superficial cues (e.g. higher participation rates, 'sophisticated' words, etc.) in judging effectiveness of performance.

Argyris (1962) reports that ratings of interpersonal competence of a trained management team were significantly better after training than before but that the new values and attitudes tended to 'wear off' after six to nine months. Many experimenters have noted this phenomenon. The 'wearing off' seems to occur less often when training is embedded in the organization (*Argyris,* 1962; 1965a; 1965b; *Gibb and Gibb,* 1952) and when follow-up training is given at periodic intervals. However, the optimal length of the latter has not yet been determined.

Boyd and Elliss (1962) report that experimental groups of managers, when compared with control groups, showed a significantly greater number of positive changes on the job (ratings by job associates), but also a greater number of negative changes. Many of the 'negative' changes might be coded as increased spontaneity (e.g. an increase in irritability), and may be part of the 'unfreezing' effect. A similar interpretation can be made of the *Underwood* (1965) discovery that trained managers made a significantly higher percentage of observed positive changes on the job, but also a significantly greater number of observed unfavorable changes.

Many investigators give evidence of greater job effectiveness following training. Thus, *Clark and Miles* (1954) show positive changes in school administrators in long range planning skills, skills in seeking and obtaining help, and ability in relating agenda formation to group work. *Miles* (1960; 1965) found that elementary school principals showed observed changes in interdependent behavior communication and leadership skills, and group problem solving skills. *Nath* (1964) gave team training to managers, who showed observed changes, in the predicted direction, toward goal clarity, interpersonal skills, and greater two-way communication.

Implications for Practitioners

An examination of the growing body of literature on sensitivity training seems to warrant several generalizations that may be of interest to therapists, trainers, teachers, parents, managers and other practitioners who use groups as a medium for learning and potential change.

1. Sensitivity training is having a significant impact upon many institutions. Although methodological impurities in the studies reported herein contribute ambiguity to a statement on the specific effects of training, there is little doubt that sensitivity training does produce significant change in people when it is conducted under optimal conditions. The evidence is sufficiently conclusive to cause responsible management in a wide variety of social institutions to increasingly institute programs of organizational change, using sensitivity training as an essential ingredient. The demands for training have far outstripped the supply of professional trainers.

2. Due to the diversity of leadership and procedure, the great increase in the amount of training, wide rumors about risks and damage, the lack of availability of evaluation data, the method's apparent power, the accelerating publicity by

national news media and the frequent use of the method by 'progressive' and 'liberal' educators, sensitivity training has become highly controversial. The increased virulence of attacks by right wing groups is some measure of the method's societal influence.

Responsible efforts have shown no evidence of appreciable negative effects of the training. For instance, a recent study by the national *YMCA (Batchelder and Hardy,* 1968) made a systematic effort to track down all instances of alleged negative effects in the 1200 *YMCA* executives who had participated in training groups. In contrast to the widespread rumors, the investigators found only four 'negative experience cases' out of 1200 participants. After interviewing clinicians, supervisors, and peers of the four executives involved, they found that in three of the four cases the experience had turned out to be a helpful one, and that it was now appraised by the participants themselves as being a 'valuable learning experience which had enhanced their effectiveness as individuals and as *YMCA* directors'. In the case of the fourth individual, he still evaluated his experience as not positive, though his superior reported that he still continues to do 'an effective job' as a director. These results are typical of several studies that have examined assertedly disruptive effects of training. Such findings, however, have had little effect upon the spread of rumor by right wing publications (*Allen,* 1968).

3. Sensitivity training provides a provocative and interdisciplinary arena for necessary cross-fertilization among academic fields, and between scholars and practitioners. Theory, engineering and art blend in training in a way that is forcing necessary changes in both theory and practice. Suggestive attempts to integrate theory and practice have been made by *Whitaker and Lieberman* (1964) in showing implications for group therapy of studies of group training; *Kurkin* (1964) in relating the work on group growth to analytic therapy; *Lakin and Carson* (1964), *Reisel* (1959), *Steele* (1965; 1968), and *Watson* (1953) in relating personality theory to group process training, and by a wide variety of people who are relating training theory to theories of organization and society.

4. Recent advances in research methodology have made it possible and highly desirable to integrate training and research programs. Research designs can easily be embedded into the training design in a way that can improve the training without detracting from its face validity and without adding appreciably to training expense. *Morton* (1965) and *Morton and Bass* (1964), for instance, show how data can be gathered in an organizational laboratory. Some instruments have been devised directly in the training situation and are particularly well suited to gathering training-relevant data. The Chicago methods of working with emotionality have been applied in many studies (*Hill,* 1955; *Lieberman,* 1958a, 1958c; *Mathis,* 1955; and *Stock and Ben-Zeev,* 1958). Some coding categories (*Hill,* 1965; *Glad,* 1959; *Simon and Agazarian,* 1967) emerge directly from group experiences in such a way as to be training-relevant to members as they learn to learn. Modern methods of data processing (*Wagner,*

1965) make possible computer analysis of data as the group engages in feedback sessions. Both researchers and trainers are interested in immediate evaluation of effectiveness of behavior in the group, actions of the trainer, and elements of the training design.

5. The evidence is mounting that the group *qua* group can be a powerful setting for growth. Both training and managing are done most effectively by focussing on actions that increase growth. Group training is considerably more than training individuals in a group setting. Healthy groups take over growth-producing functions and make trainers and managers less necessary. The material on group growth is largely clinical, but there is a growing body of theory and some empirical data relating group growth to training effectiveness.

Lakin and Carson (1964) experienced the same difficulty in establishing discernible trends that other experimenters have found, but did show some trends in 'competitiveness' and 'cooperation'. *Bass* (1962b) showed some consistent trends in such feelings as 'depression' and 'skepticism'. Far more promising are the explorations of greater depth in the studies of *Stock and Ben-Zeev* (1958) and *Reisel* (1959), though consistent empirical results relating to current theory are not as yet available.

6. The effects of training seem to be more enduring when integrated in long range programs of institutional change and growth. The most promising programs use sensitivity training as an organic part of continuing programs of management team training, organizational consulting, family life training, data collection, theory building, and various phases of organization management. Training, to be effective, must link closely, support, or change the management practices (*Argyris,* 1962; *Gibb,* 1965; *Likert,* 1967), parental and family life patterns, and organizational procedures of the sub-cultures in which training takes place.

7. Most sensitivity training, as now practiced, is too short in duration to be of optimal enduring effects. There is a wide variation in the amount of time spent in groups in the studies reported here, ranging from 12 to 150 hours in total training time. Because uninterrupted training time is so important, the effect of this time difference is made even greater when the short-time groups involve considerable gaps between sessions, e.g. as in weekly two-hour meetings. Five studies contain data that strongly suggest that continuous time in group may produce some kind of accelerating effect within the learner such that learning actually increases over time rather than showing the usual decay or fallout effect after the termination of training. The studies suggest that short term experiences may not bring changes to a critical point of insight or of integration into the behavioral systems of the learner. When attitudes and new behavior are congruent, the changes may, to a point, continue to accelerate. Thus, *Bunker and Knowles* (1967) showed that three weeks of training was superior to two weeks of training, particularly in overt behavior changes. *Khanna* (1968) found that the significant changes produced in scores on the Personal Orientation

Inventory increased after a three-month interval. *Gibb and Gibb* (1968a) report that many of the changes induced in training groups increase over time, especially when the initial training has been of long duration. *Harrison* (1966) found that a significant effect on feeling-orientation appeared after three months but not after three weeks. *Schutz and Allen* (1966) show that changes that occurred in attitudes measured by FIRO-B, administered immediately following a two-week session, were increased when scales were administered six months following the training. Research in several quarters is now focussing on the factors that produce acceleration rather than decay.

8. The conditions under which feedback to individuals occurs is one of the most critical variables determining learning effects. *French, Sherwood and Bradford* (1966) have performed a series of studies showing the primary importance of feedback. Several promising studies illuminate these conditions. *Harrison* (1965) and *Harrison and Lubin* (1965) indicate the conditions under which composition of groups can facilitate feedback. *Lippitt* (1959), *Powers* (1965), *Rosenthal* (1952); and *Rothaus, Morton, Johnson, Cleveland and Lyle* (1963) give empirical data on the optimal conditions of feedback. *Psathas and Hardert* (1966) suggest that norms for feedback are related to trainer behavior.

9. The professional competence of the people who staff sensitivity training programs is greatly increasing. It is probable that a new profession is emerging that will attract persons trained in psychotherapy, group work, psychology, political science, sociology, speech, the arts, theology, and a wide variety of fields that are concerned with the growth of the person and with the development of organizational life. Doctoral programs in a wide variety of fields are oriented toward group behaviors as a major substantive area, and toward group training as a major professional practice.

10. Along with the growth of professional competence, there is an almost startling increase in the use of leaderless groups and groups led by laymen. Industry, churches, voluntary organizations, and educational institutions are either using leaderless groups or training volunteers to conduct or convene training groups. Preliminary evidence suggests that (a) the effects of such training are comparable to the effects of training in groups led by professionals, and that (b) the occasional counter-therapeutic effects found in groups led by inexperienced or under-competent professionals do not necessarily occur in leaderless groups. Obviously, from the standpoint of mental hygiene and cultural change, it would be very important to obtain adequate research data examining the effects of such training.

Massive and fundamental changes are taking place in various institutions as a result of the widespread use of deeply intensive and personal experiences in sensitivity training groups. This accelerated use of the method is consonant with other humanistic developments in the social institutions of the 1970's—in the USA, and elsewhere in the world.

References

Allen, G.: Hate therapy. Amer. Opinion *January:* 73-86 (1968).

Argyris, C.: Interpersonal competence and organizational effectiveness (Irwin-Dorsey, Chicago 1962).

Arygris, C.: Explorations in interpersonal competence I. J. appl. Behav. Sci. *1:* 58-83 (1965a). – Explorations in interpersonal competence II. J. appl. Behav. Sci. *1:* 255-269 (1965b).

Bass, B. M.: Reactions to '12 Angry Men' as a measure of sensitivity training. J. appl. Psychol. *46:* 120-124 (1962a). – Mood changes during a management training laboratory. J. appl. Psychol. *46:* 361-364 (1962b).

Batchelder, R. L. and Hardy, J. M.: Using sensitivity training and the laboratory method (Association Press, New York 1968).

Baumgartel, H. and Goldstein, J. W.: Need and value shifts in college training groups. J. appl. Behav. Sci. *3:* 87-101 (1967).

Beer, M. and Kleisath, S. W.: The effects of the Managerial Grid Lab on organizational and leadership dimensions; in *Zalkind* (Chm.) Research on the impact of using different laboratory methods for interpersonal and organizational change. Symposium: meeting of the Amer. Psychol. Assn., Washington, D.C., September 1967.

Bennis, W.; Burke, R.; Cutter, H.; Harrington, H., and Hoffman, J.: A note on some problems of measurement and prediction in a training group. Group Psychother. *10:* 328-341 (1957).

Ben-Zeev, S.: Comparison of diagnosed behavioral tendencies with actual behavior; in *Stock and Thelen* Emotional dynamics and group culture, pp. 26-34 (National Training Laboratories, Washington, D.C. 1958a). Sociometric choice and patterns of member participation; in *Stock and Thelen* Emotional dynamics and group culture, pp. 84-91 (National Training Laboratories, Washington, D.C. 1958b).

Berlin, J. I.: Program learning for personal and interpersonal improvement. Acta psychol. *13:* 321-335 (1964).

Berzon, B.; Pious, C., and Farson, R. E.: The therapeutic event in group psychotherapy: A study of subjective reports by group members. J. Individual Psychol. *19:* 204-212 (1963).

Berzon, B. and Solomon, L. E.: Research frontier: The self-directed therapeutic group – three studies. J. Counseling Psychol. *13:* 491-497 (1966).

Blake, R. R. and Mouton, J. S.: Some effects of managerial grid seminar training on union and management attitudes toward supervision. J. appl. Behav. Sci. *2:* 387-400 (1966).

Blake, R. R.; Mouton, J. S.; Barnes, L. B., and Greiner, L. E.: Breakthrough in organization development. Harvard Bus. Rev. *42:* 133-155 (1964).

Blansfield, M. G.: Depth analysis of organizational life. Calif. Mgmt. Rev. *5:* 29-42 (1962).

Bowers, N. D. and Soar, R. S.: Evaluation of laboratory human relations training for classroom teachers. Studies of human relations in the teaching-learning process: V. Final report. US Office of Educ. Contract No. 8143 (University of South Carolina, Columbia 1961).

Boyd, J. B. and Elliss, J. D.: Findings of research into senior management seminars (Pers. Res. Dept., Hydro-Electric Power Commission of Ontario, Toronto 1962).

Bradford, L. P.: Explorations in human relations training (National Training Laboratories, Washington, D.C. 1953).

Bradford, L. P.; Gibb, J. R., and Benne, K. D.: T group theory and laboratory method (Wiley, New York 1964).

Bradford, L. P.; Gibb, J. R., and Lippitt, G. L.: Human relations training in three days. Adult Leadership 4: 11-26 (1956).

Buchanan, P. C.: Evaluating the effectiveness of laboratory training in industry; in Explorations in human relations training and research, Number 1 (National Training Laboratories, Washington, D.C. 1965).

Bugental, J. F. T.: The search for authenticity (Holt, Rinehart and Winston, New York 1965).

Bunker, D. R.: Individual applications of laboratory training. J. appl. Behav. Sci. 1: 131-149 (1965).

Bunker, D. R. and Knowles, E. S.: Comparison of behavioral changes resulting from human relations training laboratories of different lengths. J. appl. Behav. Sci. 3: 505-523 (1967).

Bunker, G. L.: The effect of group perceived esteem on self and ideal concepts in an emergent group. Master's thesis, Brigham Young Univ. (1961).

Burke, R. L. and Bennis, W. G.: Changes in perception of self and others during human relations training. Human Relations 14: 165-182 (1961).

Byrd, R. E.: Training in a non-group. J. Humanistic Psychol. 7: 18-27 (1967).

Campbell, J. P. and Dunnette, M. D.: Effectiveness of T group experiences in managerial training and development. Psychol. Bull. 70: 73-104 (1968).

Carron, T. J.: Human relations training and attitude change: A vector analysis. Personnel Psychol. 17: 403-424 (1964).

Carson, R. C. and Lakin, M.: Some effects of group sensitivity experience. Paper presented at meeting: Southeastern Psychol. Ass., Miami Beach, Fla. (1963).

Clark, J. V. and Culbert, S. A.: Mutually therapeutic perception and self-awareness in a T group. J. appl. Behav. Sci. 1: 180-194 (1965).

Clark, T. C. and Miles, M. B.: Human relations training for school administrators. J. Soc. Issues 10 (2): 25-39 (1954).

Culbert, S. A.: Trainer self-disclosure and member growth in a T group. Doctor. Diss., UCLA (1966).

Culbert, S. A.: Trainer self-disclosure and member growth in two T groups. J. appl. Behav. Sci. *4:* 47-73 (1968).

Dietterich, P. M.: An evaluation of a group development laboratory approach to training church leaders. Doctor. Diss., Boston Univ. (1961).

Durham, L. E. and Gibb, J. R.: An annotated bibliography of research, 1947-1960. Research Reprint Series, Number 2 (National Training Laboratories, Washington, D.C. 1960).

Durkin, H. E.: The group in depth (International Universities Press, New York 1964).

Ford, J. D., Jr.: Computer analysis of test for the measurement of social perception during human relations training. Doc. No. SP-1373/001/00. System Development Corporation, Santa Monica, Calif. (1964).

Foster, B. R.: Some interrelationships between religious values, leadership concepts, and perception of group process of professional church workers. Doctor. Diss., Univ. of Michigan (1958).

French, J. R. P., Jr.; Sherwood, J. J., and Bradford, D. L.: Change in self-identity in a management training conference. J. appl. Behav. Sci. *2:* 210-218 (1966).

Friedlander, F.: The impact of organizational training laboratories upon the effectiveness and interaction of ongoing work groups. Personnel Psychol. *20:* 289-308 (1967).

Friedlander, F.: A comparative study of consulting processes and group development. J. appl. Behav. Sci. *4:* 377-399 (1968).

Gage, N. L. and Exline, R. V.: Social perception and effectiveness in discussion groups. Human Relations *6:* 381-396 (1953).

Gassner, S. M.; Gold, J., and Snadowsky, A. M.: Changes in the phenomenal field as a result of human relations training. J. Psychol. *58:* 33-41 (1964).

Geitgey, D. A.: A study of some effects of sensitivity training on the performance of students in associate degree programs of nursing education. Doctor. Diss., UCLA (1966).

Gibb, J. R.: Effects of role playing upon (a) role-flexibility and upon (b) ability to conceptualize a new role. Paper presented at meeting: Amer. Psychol. Ass., Cleveland, Ohio (1953).

Gibb, J. R.: Climate for trust formation; in *Bradford, Gibb and Benne* T group theory and laboratory method, pp. 279-309 (Wiley, New York 1964).

Gibb, J. R.: Fear and facade: defensive management; in *Farson* Science and human affairs, pp. 197-214 (Science and Behavior Books, Palo Alto 1965).

Gibb, J. R. and Gibb, L. M.: Leaderless groups: growth-centered values and potentials; in *Otto and Mann*, Ways of growth, pp. 101-114 (Grossman, New York 1968a). – Emergence therapy: The TORI process in an emergent group; in *Gazda* Innovations to group psychotherapy, pp. 96-129 (Thomas, Springfield, Ill. 1968b).

Gibb, J. R.; Smith, E. E., and Roberts, A. H.: Effects of positive and negative feedback upon defensive behavior in small problem-solving groups. Paper presented at meeting: Amer. Psychol. Ass., San Francisco, Calif. (1955).

Gibb, L. M. and Gibb, J. R.: Effects of the use of 'participative action' groups in a course in general psychology. Paper presented at meeting: Amer. Psychol. Ass., Washington, D.C. (1952).

Glad, D. D.: Operational values in psychotherapy (Oxford University Press, New York 1959).

Gold, J. S.: An evaluation of a laboratory human relations training program for college undergraduates. Doctor. Diss., Columbia Univ. (1967).

Grater, H.: Changes in self and other attitudes in a leadership training group. Personnel and Guidance J. *37:* 493-496 (1959).

Greiner, L. E.: Organizational change and development. Doctor. Diss., Harvard Univ. (1965).

Hacon, R. J.: Management training: aims and methods (English Universities Press, London 1961).

Haiman, F. S.: Effects of training in group processes on open-mindedness. J. Communication *13:* 236-245 (1963).

Hampden-Turner, C. H.: An existential 'learning theory' and the integration of T group research, J. appl. Behav. Sci. *2:* 367-386 (1966).

Hanson, P. G.; Rothaus, P.; Johnson, D. L., and Lyle, F. A.: Autonomous groups in human relations training for psychiatric patients. J. appl. Behav. Sci. *2:* 305-324 (1966).

Harrison, R.: Impact of the laboratory on perceptions of others by the experimental group; in *Argyris* Interpersonal competence and organizational effectiveness, pp. 261-271 (Irwin, Homewood, Ill. 1962).

Harrison, R.: Group composition models for laboratory design. J. appl. Behav. Sci. *1:* 408-432 (1965).

Harrison, R.: Cognitive change and participation in a sensitivity training laboratory. J. Consult. Psychol. *30:* 517-520 (1966).

Harrison, R. and Lubin, B.: Personal style, group composition, and learning. J. appl. Behav. Sci. *1:* 286-301 (1965).

Hill, W. F.: The influence of sub-groups on participation in human relations training groups. Doctor. Diss., Univ. of Chicago (1955).

Hill, W. F.: HIM: Hill Interaction Matrix. Youth Study Center, Univ. of Southern Calif., Los Angeles (1965).

House, R. J.: T group education and leadership effectiveness: A review of the empirical literature and a critical evaluation. Personnel Psychol. *20:* 1-32 (1967).

Johnson, D. L.; Hanson, P. G.; Rothaus, P.; Morton, R. B.; Lyle, F. A., and Moyer, R.: Follow-up evaluation of human relations training for psychiatric patients; in *Schein and Bennis* Personal and organizational change through group methods, pp. 152-168 (Wiley, New York 1965).

Johnson, L. K.: The effect of trainer interventions on change in personal functioning through T group training. Doctor. Diss., Univ. of Minnesota (1966).

Kassarjian, H. H.: Social character and sensitivity training. J. appl. Behav. Sci. *1:* 433-440 (1965).

Kelley, H. H.: First impressions in interpersonal relations. Doctor. Diss., Massachusetts Institute of Technology (1948).

Kelley, H. and Pepitone, A.: An evaluation of a college course in human relations. J. Educ. Psychol. *43:* 193-209 (1952).

Kernan, J. P.: Laboratory human relations training: Its effect on the 'Personality' of supervisory engineers. Doctor. Diss., New York Univ. (1963).

Khanna, J. L.: A discovery learning approach to inservice training. Paper presented at meeting: Amer. Psychol. Ass., San Francisco (1968).

Knowles, E. S.: A bibliography of research on human relations training since 1960. Explorations in human relations training research (National Training Laboratories, Washington, D.C. 1967).

Kuriloff, A. H. and Atkins, S: T group for a work team. J. appl. Behav. Sci. *2:* 63-94 (1966).

Lakin, M. and Carson, R. C.: Participant perception of group process in group sensitivity training. Int. J. Group Psychother. *14:* 116-122 (1964).

Lieberman, M. A.: The relationship between the emotional cultures of groups and individual change. Doctor. Diss., Univ. of Chicago (1958a). – The relation of diagnosed behavioral tendencies to member-perceptions of self and of the group; in *Stock and Thelen* Emotional dynamics and group culture, pp. 35-49 (National Training Laboratories, Washington, D.C. 1958b). – Sociometric choice related to affective approach; in *Stock and Thelen* Emotional dynamics and group culture, pp. 71-83 (National Training Laboratories, Washington, D.C. 1958c). – The influence of group composition on change in affective approach; in *Stock and Thelen* Emotional dynamics and group cultures, pp. 131-139 (National Training Laboratories, Washington, D.C. 1958d).

Likert, R.: The human organization (McGraw-Hill, New York 1967).

Lippitt, G. L.: Effects of information about group desire for change on members of a group. Doctor. Diss., American Univ. (1959).

Livingston, D. G.: The effects of varying group organization upon perception of power and benefit. Doctor. Diss., Univ. of Kansas (1951).

Lohman, K.; Zenger, J. H., and Weschler, I. R.: Some perceptual changes during sensitivity training. J. Educ. Res. *53:* 28-31 (1959).

Massarik, F. and Carlson, G.: The California Psychological Inventory as an indicator of personality change in sensitivity training. Working paper. Inst. of Indust. Rel., UCLA (1960).

Mathis, A. G.: Development and validation of a trainability index for laboratory training groups. Doctor. Diss., Univ. of Chicago (1955).

McGregor, D.: The human side of enterprise (McGraw-Hill, New York 1960).

Miles, M. B.: Human relations training: processes and outcomes. J. Counseling Psychol. 7: 301-306 (1960).

Miles, M. B.: Changes during and following laboratory training: a clinical-experimental study. J. appl. Behav. Sci. 1: 215-242 (1965).

Miles, M. B.; Cohen, S. K., and Whidman, F. L.: Changes in performance test scores after human relations training. Horace Mann-Lincoln Institute of School Experimentation, New York (1959).

Morton, R. B.: The organization training laboratory: some individual and organizational effects. J. Advanc. Mgmt. 30: 58-67 (1965).

Morton, R. B. and Bass, B. M.: The organizational training lab. J. Amer. Soc. Tr. Dir. 18 (10): 2-15 (1964).

Mowrer, O. H.: The new group therapy (Van Nostrand, Princeton 1964).

Nath, R.: Dynamics of organizational change: some determinants of managerial problem solving and decision making competences. Doctor. Diss., Massachusetts Institute of Technology (1964).

Oshry, B. I. and Harrison, R.: Transfer from here-and-now to there-and-then: Changes in organizational problem diagnosis stemming from T group training. J. appl. Behav. Sci. 2: 185-198 (1966).

Otto, H. A. and Mann, J.: Ways of growth (Grossman, New York 1968).

Peters, D. R. Identification and personal change in laboratory training groups. Doctor. Diss., Massachusetts Institute of Technology (1966).

Powers, J. R.: Trainer orientation and group composition in laboratory training. Doctor. Diss., Case Institute of Technology (1965).

Psathas, G. and Hardert, R.: Trainer interventions and normative patterns in the T group. J. appl. Behav. Sci. 2: 149-169 (1966).

Reisel, J.: A search for behavior patterns in sensitivity training groups. Doctor. Diss., UCLA (1959).

Rosenthal, D.: Perceptions of some personality characteristics in members of a small group. Doctor. Diss., Univ. of Chicago (1952).

Rothaus, P.; Johnson, D. L.; Hanson, P. G., and Lyle, F. A.: Participation and sociometry in autonomous and trainer-led patient groups. J. Counseling Psychol. 13: 68-76 (1966).

Rohaus, P.; Morton, R. B.; Johnson, D. L.; Cleveland, S. E., and Lyle, F. A.: Human relations training for psychiatric patients. Arch. gen. Psychiat. 8: 572-581 (1963).

Rubin, I.: The reduction of prejudice through laboratory training. J. appl. Behav. Sci. 3: 29-50 (1967a).

Rubin, I.: Increased self-acceptance: A means of reducing prejudice. J. Personality and Soc. Psychol. *5:* 233-238 (1967b).

Schein, E. H. and Bennis, W. G.: Personal and organizational change through group methods (Wiley, New York 1965).

Schmuck, R.A.: Helping teachers improve classroom group processes. J. appl. Behav. Sci. *4:* 401-435 (1968).

Schutz, W. C. and Allen, V. L.: The effects of a T group laboratory and interpersonal behavior. J. appl. Behav. Sci. *2:* 265-286 (1966).

Seashore, C. N.: Attitude and skill changes in participative action training groups. Master's thesis, Univ. of Colorado (1955).

Sherwood, J. J.: Self-identity and self-actualization: A theory and research. Doctor. Diss., Univ. of Michigan (1962).

Sherwood, J. J.: Self-identity and referent others. Sociometry *28:* 66-81 (1965).

Sikes, W. W.: A study of some effects of a human relations training laboratory. Doctor. Diss., Purdue Univ. (1964).

Simon, A. and Agazarian, Y.: Sequential analysis of verbal interaction (Research for Better Schools, Inc., Philadelphia 1967).

Smith, H. C.: Sensitivity to people (McGraw-Hill, New York 1966).

Smith, P. B.: Attitude changes associated with training in human relations. Brit. J. Soc. Clin. Psychol. *3:* 104-112 (1964).

Spector, A. J.: Changes in human relations attitudes. J. appl. Psychol. *42:* 154-157 (1958).

Steele, F. I.: The relationship of personality to changes in interpersonal values effected by laboratory training. Doctor. Diss., Massachusetts Institute of Technology (1965).

Steele, F. I.: Personality and the 'laboratory style'. J. appl. Behav. Sci. *4:* 25-45 (1968).

Stock, D.: The relation between the sociometric structure of the group and certain personality characteristics of the individual. Doctor. Diss., Univ. of Chicago (1952).

Stock, D.: A survey of research on T groups; in *Bradford, Gibb and Benne* T group theory and laboratory method, pp. 395-441 (Wiley, New York 1964).

Stock, D. and Ben-Zeev, S.: Changes in work and emotionality during group growth; in *Stock and Thelen* Emotional dynamics and group culture, pp. 192-206 (National Training Laboratories, Washington, D.C. 1958).

Stoller, F. H.: Marathon group therapy; in *Gazda* Innovations to group psychotherapy, pp. 42-95 (Thomas, Springfield, Ill. 1968a). — Focussed feedback with video tape: Extending the group's functions; in *Gazda* Innovations to group psychotherapy, pp. 207-255 (Thomas, Springfield, Ill. 1968b).

Taylor, F. C.: Effects of laboratory training upon persons and their work groups; in Zalkind (Chm.) Research on the impact of using different laboratory methods for interpersonal and organizational change. Symposium presented at meeting: Amer. Psychol. Ass., Washington, D.C. (1967).

Underwood, W. J.: Evaluation of laboratory-method training. Trg. Dir. J. *19:* 34-40 (1965).

Valiquet, I. M.: Contribution to the evaluation of a management development program. Master's thesis, Massachusetts Institute of Technology (1964).

Wagner, A. B.: The use of process analysis in business decision games. J. appl. Behav. Sci. *1:* 387-408 (1965).

Watson, J.: Some social psychological correlates of personality: A study of usefulness of psychoanalytic theory in predicting to social behavior. Doctor. Diss., Univ. of Michigan (1953).

Wedel, C. C.: A study of measurement in group dynamics laboratories. Doctor. Diss., George Washington Univ. (1957).

Whitaker, D. S. and Lieberman, M. A.: Psychotherapy through the group process (Atherton, New York 1964).

Zand, D. E.; Steele, F. I., and Zalkind, S. S.: The impact of an organizational development program on perceptions of interpersonal, group and organizational functioning; in Zalkind (Chm.) Research on the impact of using different laboratory methods for interpersonal and organizational change. Symposium presented at meeting: Amer. Psychol. Ass., Washington, D.C. (1967).

Zimet, C. N. and Fine, H. J.: Personality changes with a group therapeutic experience in a human relations seminar. J. Abnorm. Soc. Psychol. *51:* 68-73 (1955).

Editor's Comment. As Clark has noted in an earlier article, there is such a great proliferation of group processes for releasing human potential that it is impossible for any one person to keep abreast of all new developments in group work. By making distinctions among certain classes of groups, Gibb helps to bring some order to this confusing field; but, in practice, there is overlapping even among the categories he delineates.

As necessary as research is for the evaluation and development of responsible and effective encounter-group programs, such research is very difficult to do with any kind of precision and creativity. This should be evident from even a casual reading of the research reported by Gibb. Unlike Campbell and Dunnette (1968), Gibb is optimistic with respect to the research that has been done. He believes that both the quantity and quality of research is "surprisingly high." In the context of the remarks made by many indicating that there has been little or no research done in this area, I would certainly agree with Gibb. Still, the available research is so scattered that it is difficult to determine the groups to which such research applies. Research on group work is made particularly difficult by the fact that even groups included under the same rubric—for example, encounter groups—can differ radically from one another. In the same residential laboratory, for instance, one group can differ radically from another because of different leadership styles. Therefore, if research is to be effective, something has to be done to establish a unitary phenomenon for study. The "contracts" I suggest in *E: GPFIG* give some assurance that there is some basic similarity in groups being studied. The minimum requirement for decent research is that the researcher adequately describe the kind of group being studied—its goals, its style of leadership, the means used to achieve the goals, the kind of population, the size of the group, the number of sessions, the length of each session, etc.

I am also bothered by studies that discuss "group averages." In therapy some people get better because they are engaged in a high-level experience with a high-level therapist, while others get worse because they are in a low-level experience with a low-level therapist. There are high-level and low-level encounter-group experiences also. In groups it is also true that participants give themselves differently to the group experience; thus, there seems to be little value in those studies (called "outcome" or "benefit" studies) that lump together active and passive participants. I am more interested in seeing what happens to the person who gives himself to the experience than to the person who is merely exposed to it. Few, if any, studies rate the participants' degree of participation before rating outcome.

Epilogue

The encounter-group process is seductive. It seems to offer much to the person who gives himself to the experience, but many participants mistakenly think that they will be carried along on some growthful path if they merely submit themselves passively to the dynamics of the group. Such participants are destined for an uncomfortable group experience and ultimate failure, for it is the relatively active participant who benefits most from the training experience. The group has no miraculous powers: it cannot serve to enrich the life of the participant who remains a spectator of the interaction, much less the life of the one who actively resists the experience. It is impossible to "do nothing" in a group, even by remaining silent. A refusal to accept the challenge of agency in a group is a refusal to face one's potential.

The encounter-group movement is young. Even though it is beset by serious problems, it still offers great promise. Good research is desperately needed, but it takes time. In the field of psychology, needs are usually so great that application has always tended to run ahead of definitive research. Such a procedure would probably spell disaster in the drug industry, and it poses serious problems for those who practice psychology—for example, psychotherapists and facilitators. But we are also in desperate need of a broader understanding of research. It is easy to stand at the sidelines and criticize the lack of tightly controlled experimental programs. But when socially intelligent men with high ethical standards and a deep concern for their fellow men put themselves in contact with others in order to create and develop types of community in which human potential can be discovered and fostered, then they become searchers. Without these searchers there would be no research.

At a recent meeting of the American Psychological Association it was predicted that within ten years many people would belong to ongoing encounter groups. Whether this prediction is realized or not, the notion of ongoing groups is intriguing. Membership in a continuing experience in which the participants would be constantly striving to achieve the goals outlined in these readings would, in my estimation, be extremely growthful. Some have criticized the encounter-group movement, claiming that participants become so overconcerned about intrapersonal and interpersonal issues that they neglect involvement in the wider social issues that face the community, the country, and the world. Again, only research could substantiate such a claim. However, there is nothing intrinsic to an ongoing encounter-group experience that would justify such an apprehension. In any given week there is ample time for involvement in intrapersonal, interpersonal, and social concerns. In fact, a person's sense and style of social involvement should ultimately become one of the principal concerns of the ongoing encounter group. Moreover, the encounter group is designed to make a person freer and more productive in his intrapersonal and interpersonal life so that he might more fruitfully involve himself with others in wider social concerns. Perhaps all of us have experienced the person who immerses himself in social issues because he seemingly cannot handle intrapersonal and interpersonal concerns. Even if such a person does much good, one wonders how much more effective he might be if he were to face the issues he flees.

Author Index

Subject Index

Subject Index